ELEVEN

THE HEROIC LEGEND OF
ARSLAN

STORY BY
YOSHIKI TANAKA

MANGA BY
HIROMU ARAKAWA

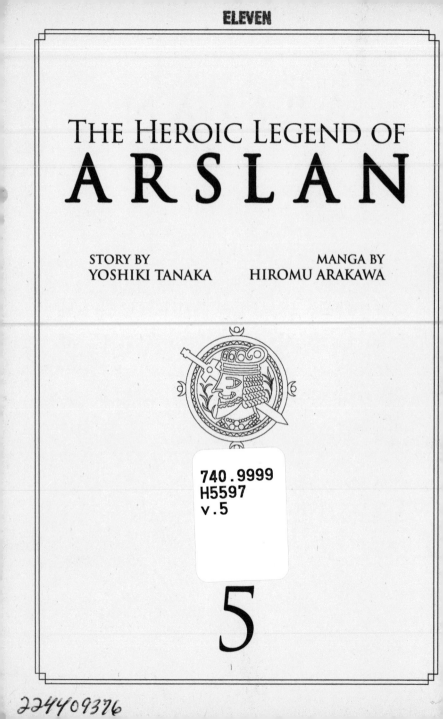

5

THE HEROIC LEGEND OF
ARSLAN

TABLE OF CONTENTS

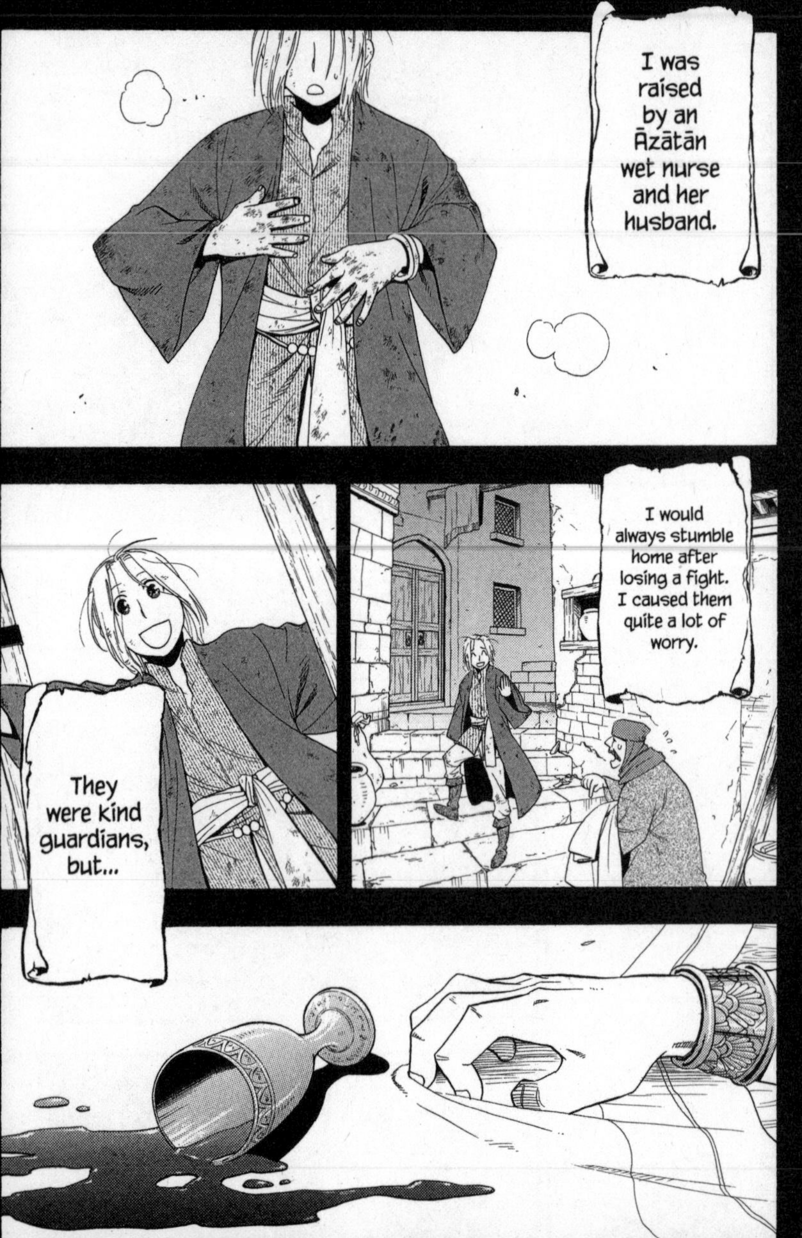
I was raised by an Āzātān wet nurse and her husband.
I would always stumble home after losing a fight. I caused them quite a lot of worry.
They were kind guardians, but...

Chapter 28: Daughter of the Zot Clan

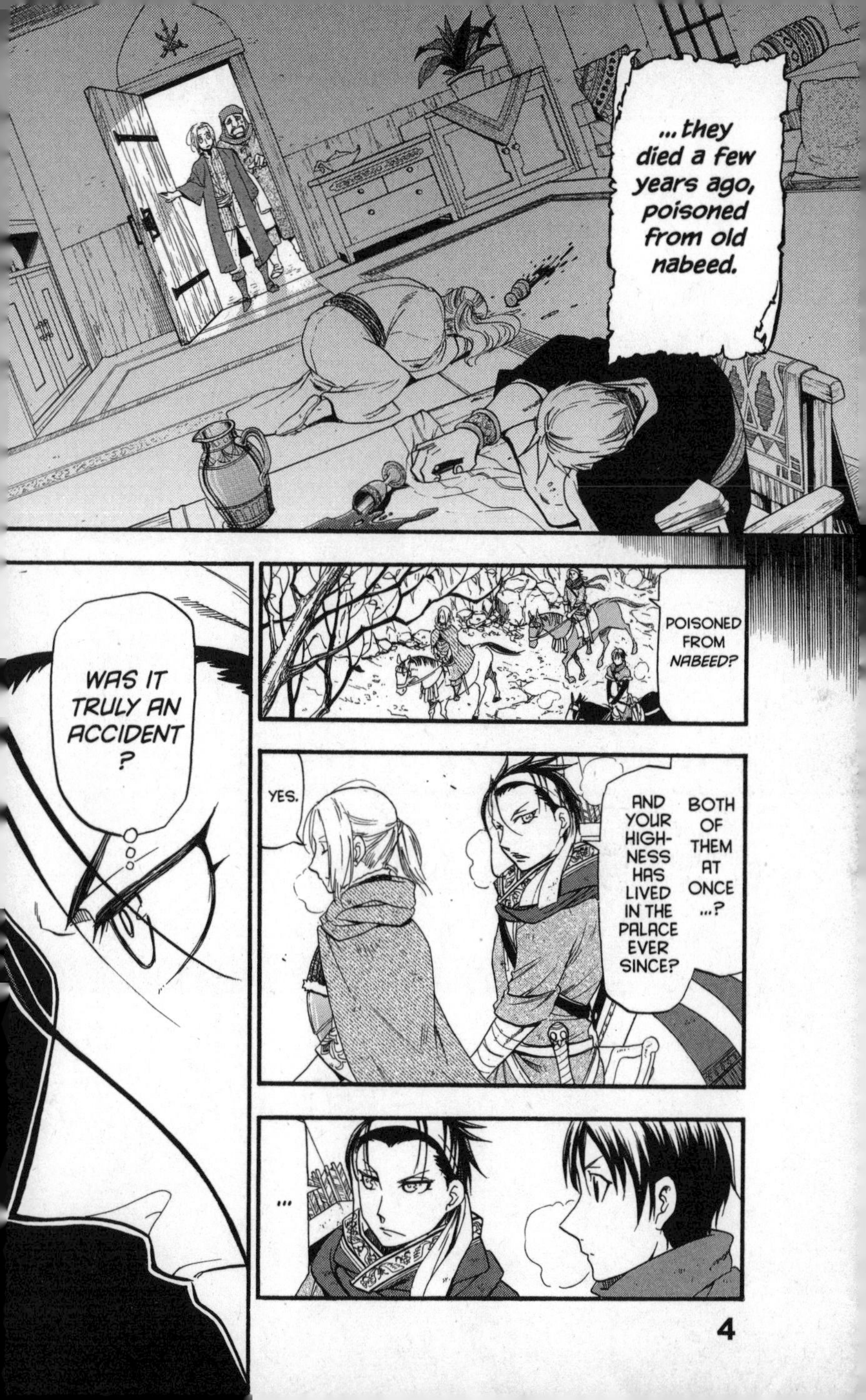
...they died a few years ago, poisoned from old nabeed.
POISONED FROM NABEED?
BOTH OF THEM AT ONCE ...?
AND YOUR HIGHNESS HAS LIVED IN THE PALACE EVER SINCE?
YES.
...
WAS IT TRULY AN ACCIDENT ?

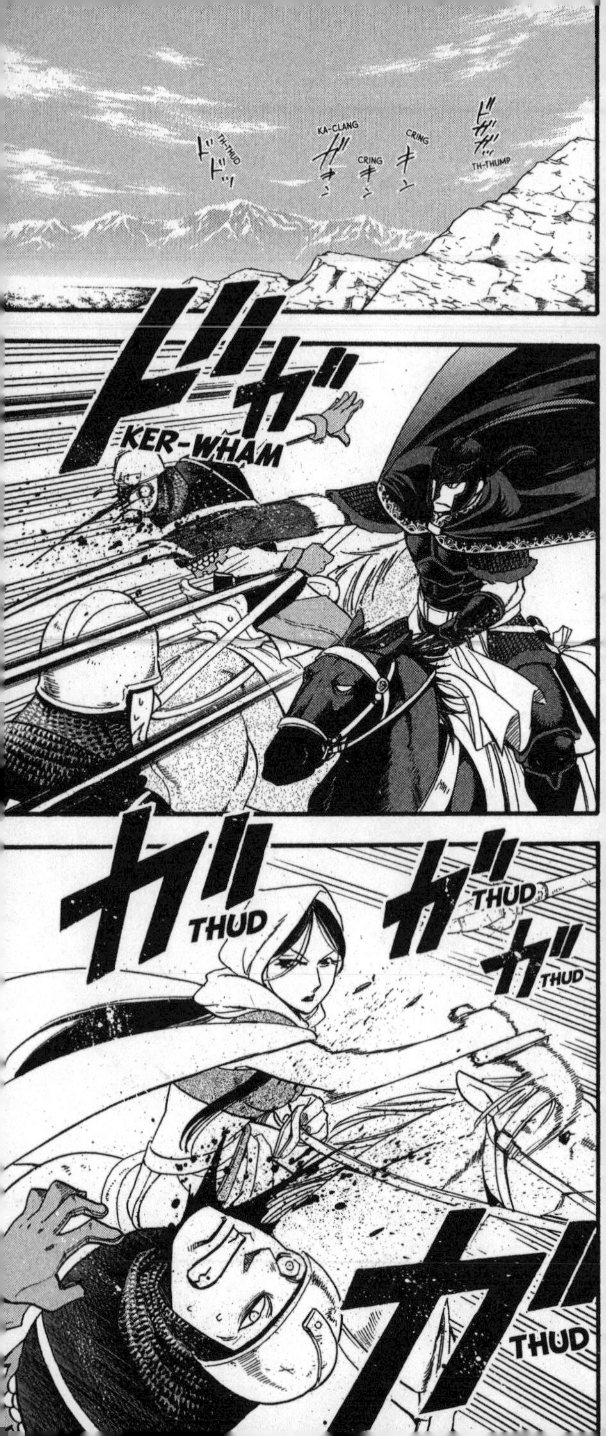

TH-THUMP
CRING
CRING
KA-CLANG
TH-THUD
KER-WHAM
THUD
THUD
THUD
THUD

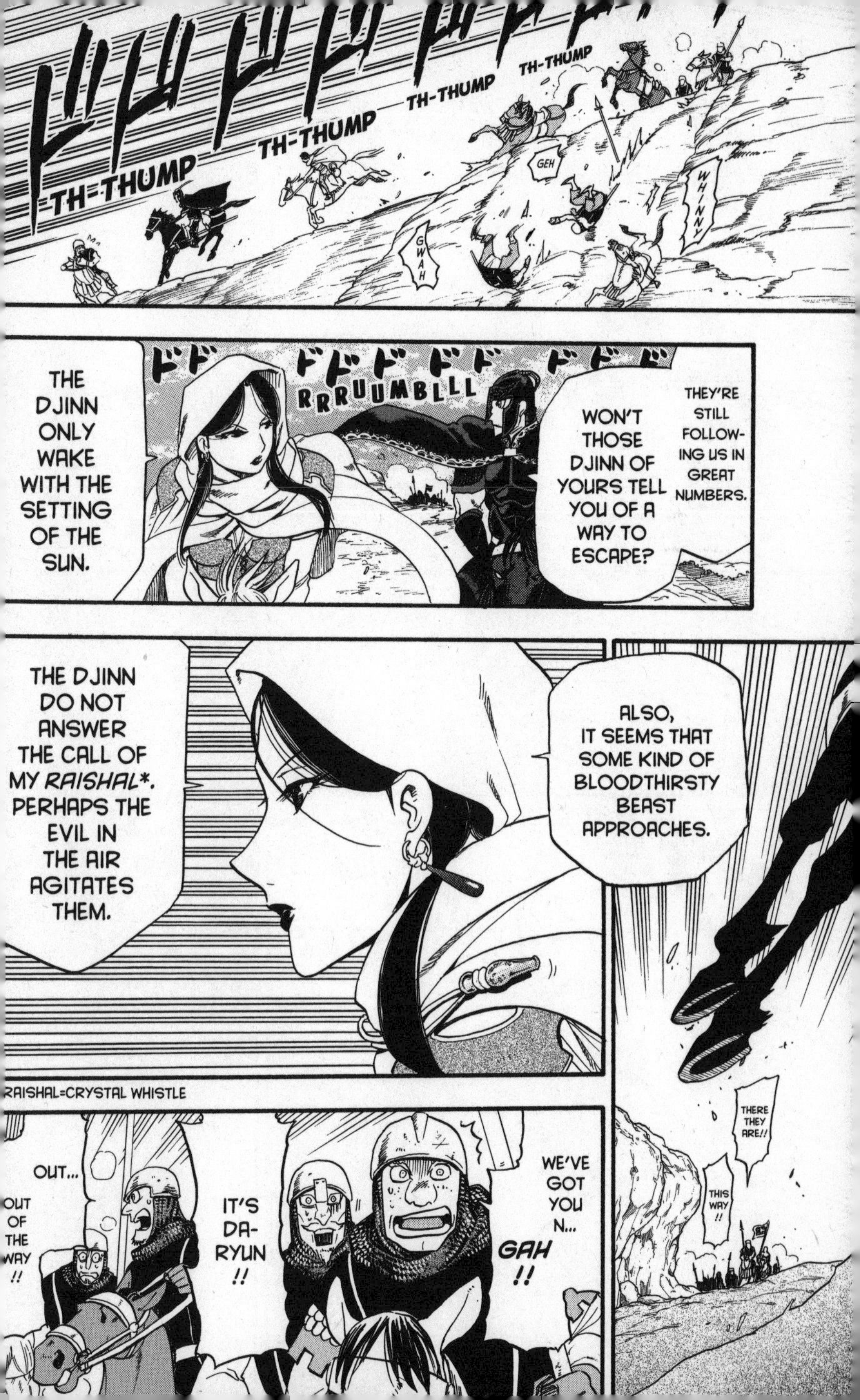
TH-THUMP
TH-THUMP
TH-THUMP
TH-THUMP
WHINNY
GEH
GWAH
THEY'RE STILL FOLLOWING US IN GREAT NUMBERS.
WON'T THOSE DJINN OF YOURS TELL YOU OF A WAY TO ESCAPE?
RRRUUMBLLL
THE DJINN ONLY WAKE WITH THE SETTING OF THE SUN.
ALSO, IT SEEMS THAT SOME KIND OF BLOODTHIRSTY BEAST APPROACHES.
THE DJINN DO NOT ANSWER THE CALL OF MY *RAISHAL**. PERHAPS THE EVIL IN THE AIR AGITATES THEM.
RAISHAL=CRYSTAL WHISTLE
THERE THEY ARE!!
THIS WAY!!
WE'VE GOT YOU N...
GAH!!
IT'S DA-RYUN!!
OUT...
OUT OF THE WAY!!

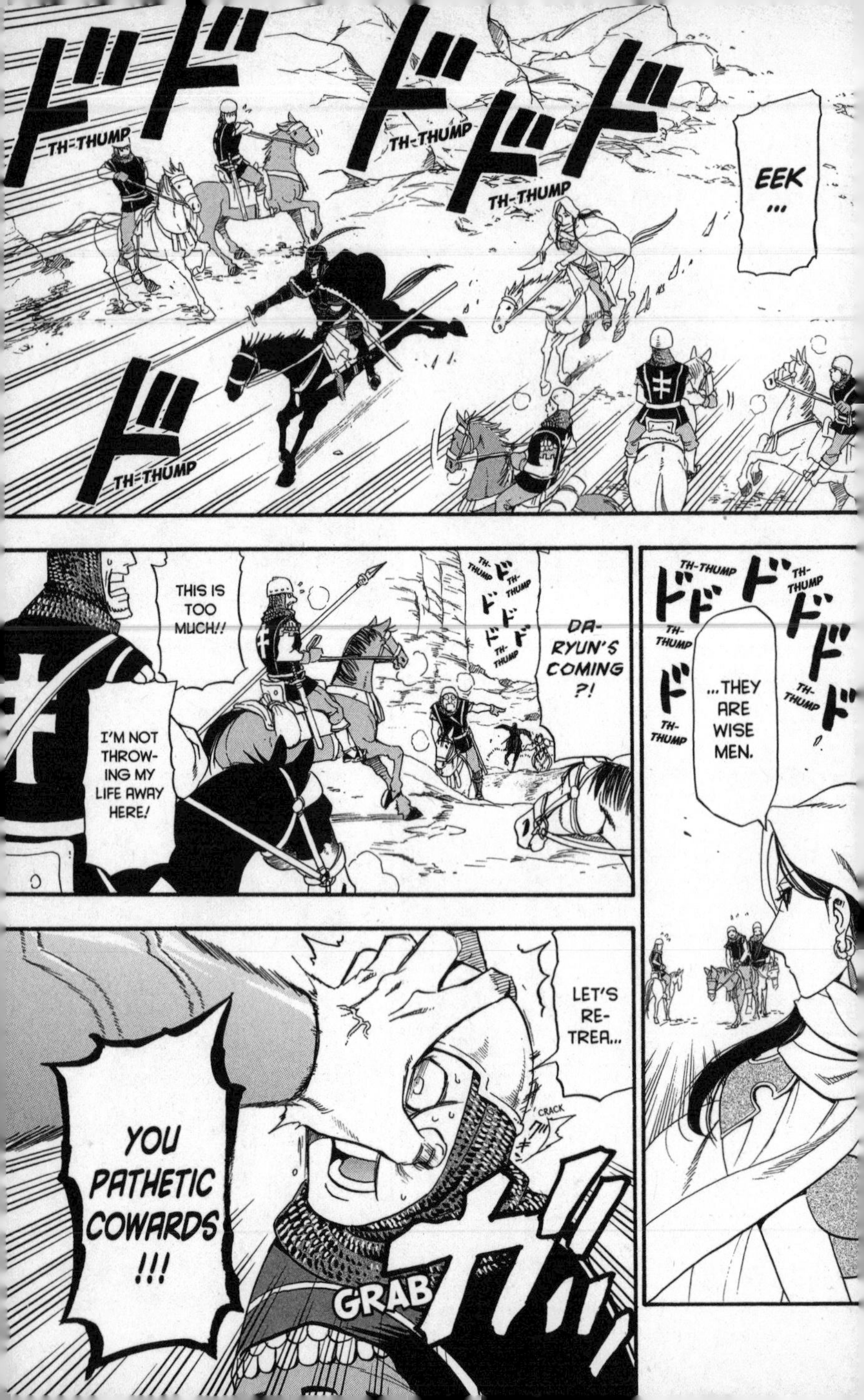
EEK ...
ドド
TH-THUMP
ドドド
TH-THUMP
TH-THUMP
ド
TH-THUMP
ドド TH-THUMP
ド TH-THUMP
ドド TH-THUMP
ド TH-THUMP
ド TH-THUMP
...THEY ARE WISE MEN.
ド TH-THUMP
ドドドド TH-THUMP
DA-RYUN'S COMING ?!
THIS IS TOO MUCH!!
I'M NOT THROWING MY LIFE AWAY HERE!
LET'S RETREA...
CRACK
GRAB
YOU PATHETIC COWARDS !!!

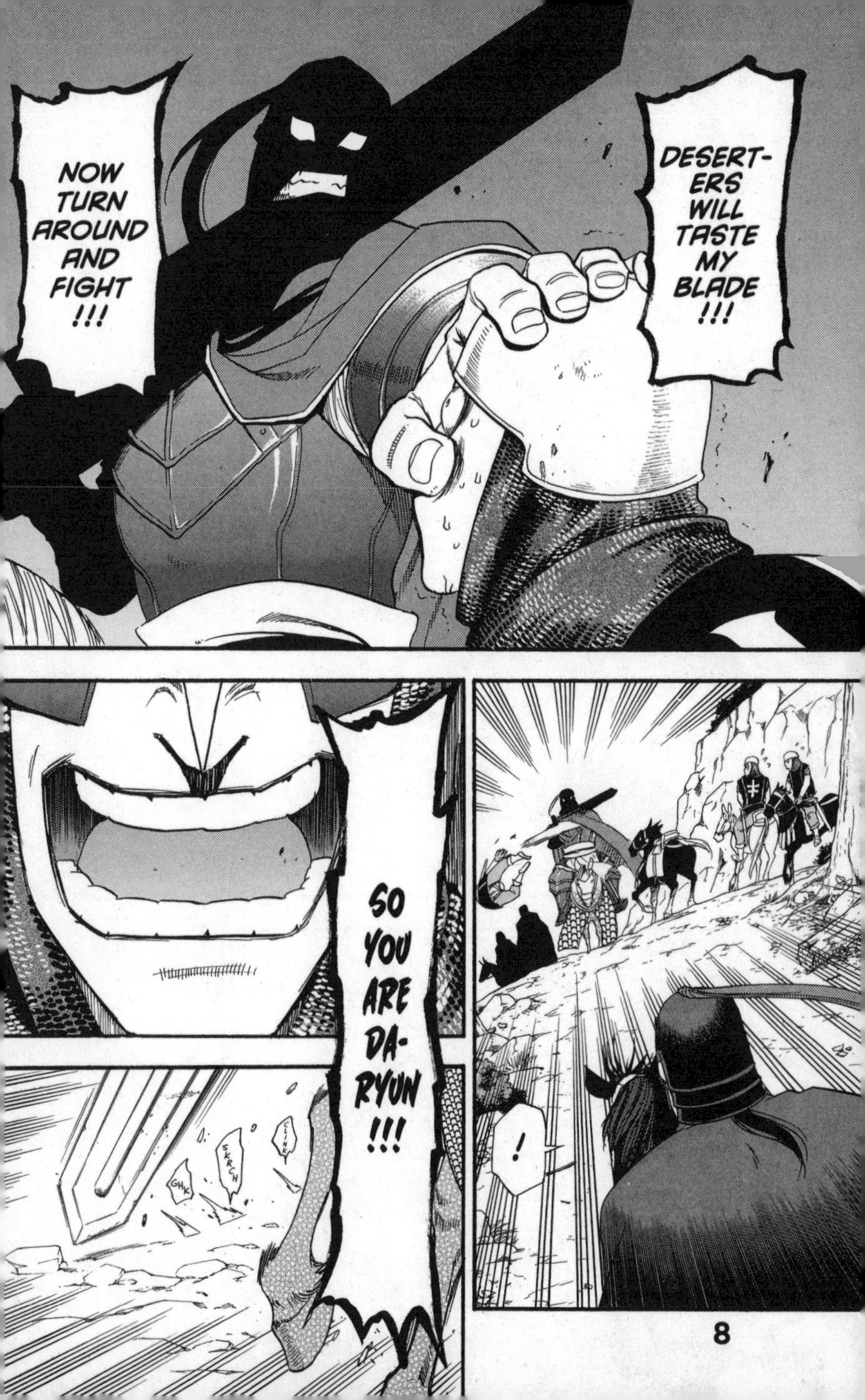
DESERT-ERS WILL TASTE MY BLADE!!!
NOW TURN AROUND AND FIGHT!!!
!
SO YOU ARE DA-RYUN!!!
CLINK
SKRCH
GHK

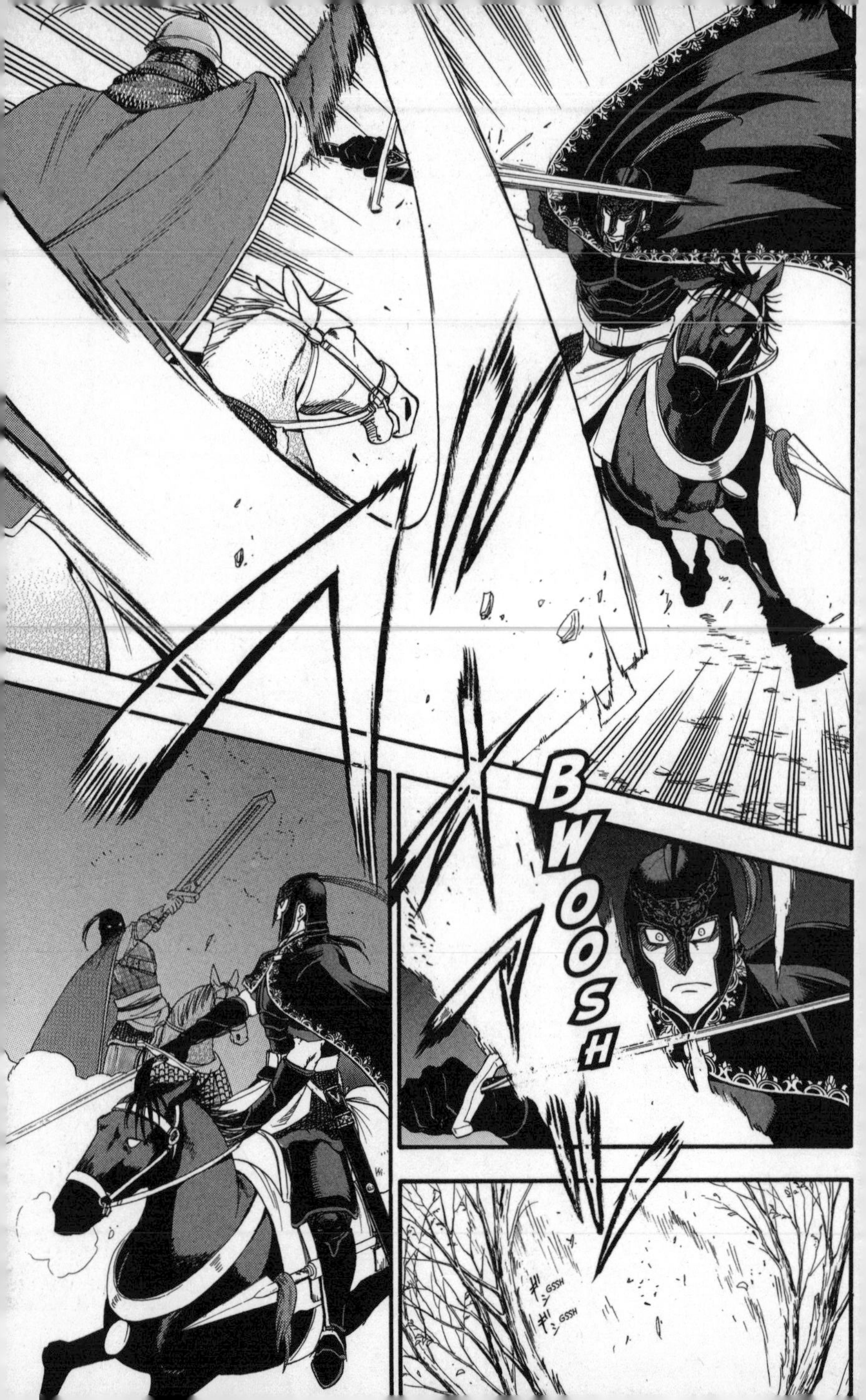
BWOOSH
ギシ GSSH
ギシ GSSH

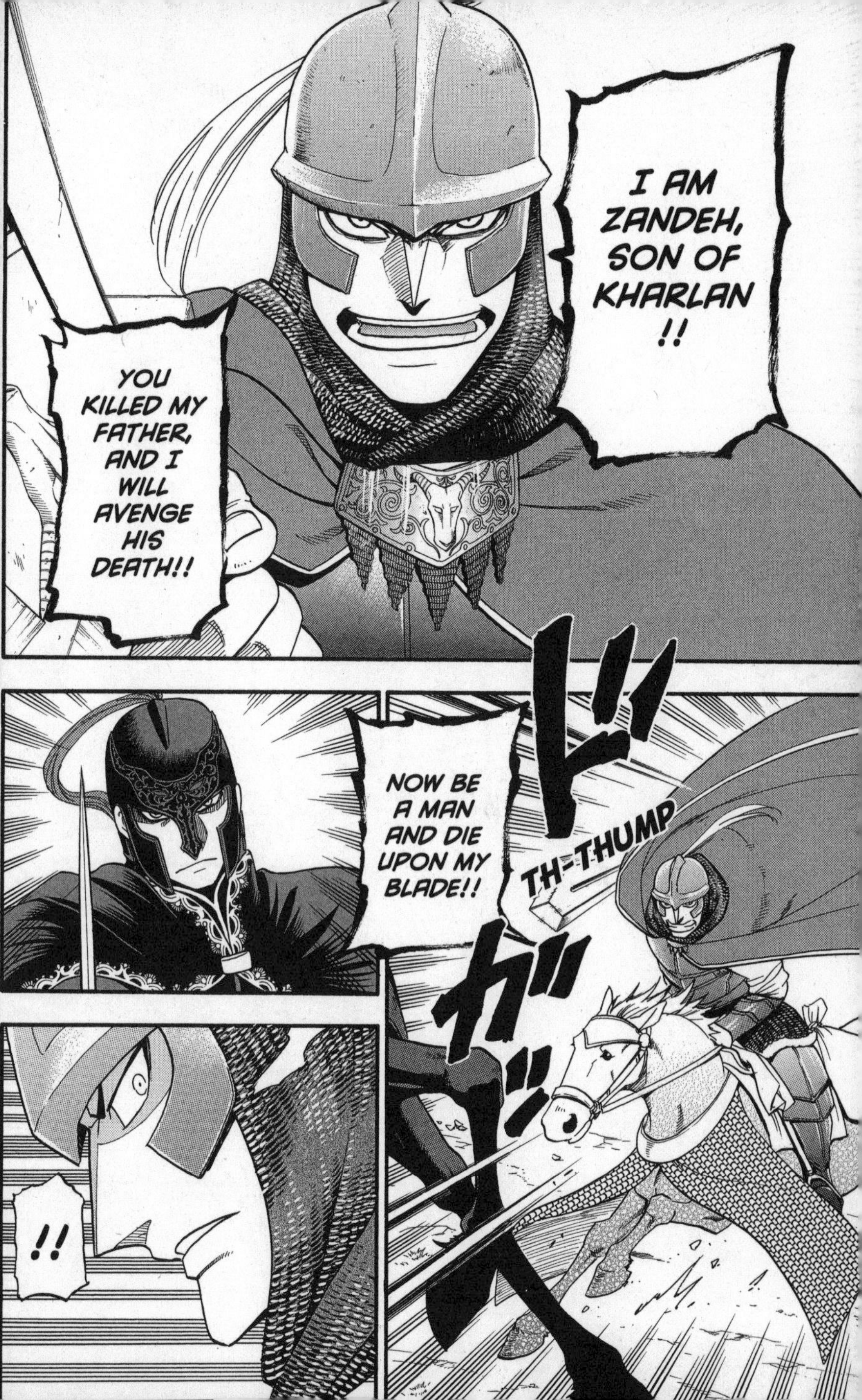
I AM ZANDEH, SON OF KHARLAN!!
YOU KILLED MY FATHER, AND I WILL AVENGE HIS DEATH!!
NOW BE A MAN AND DIE UPON MY BLADE!!
TH-THUMP
!!

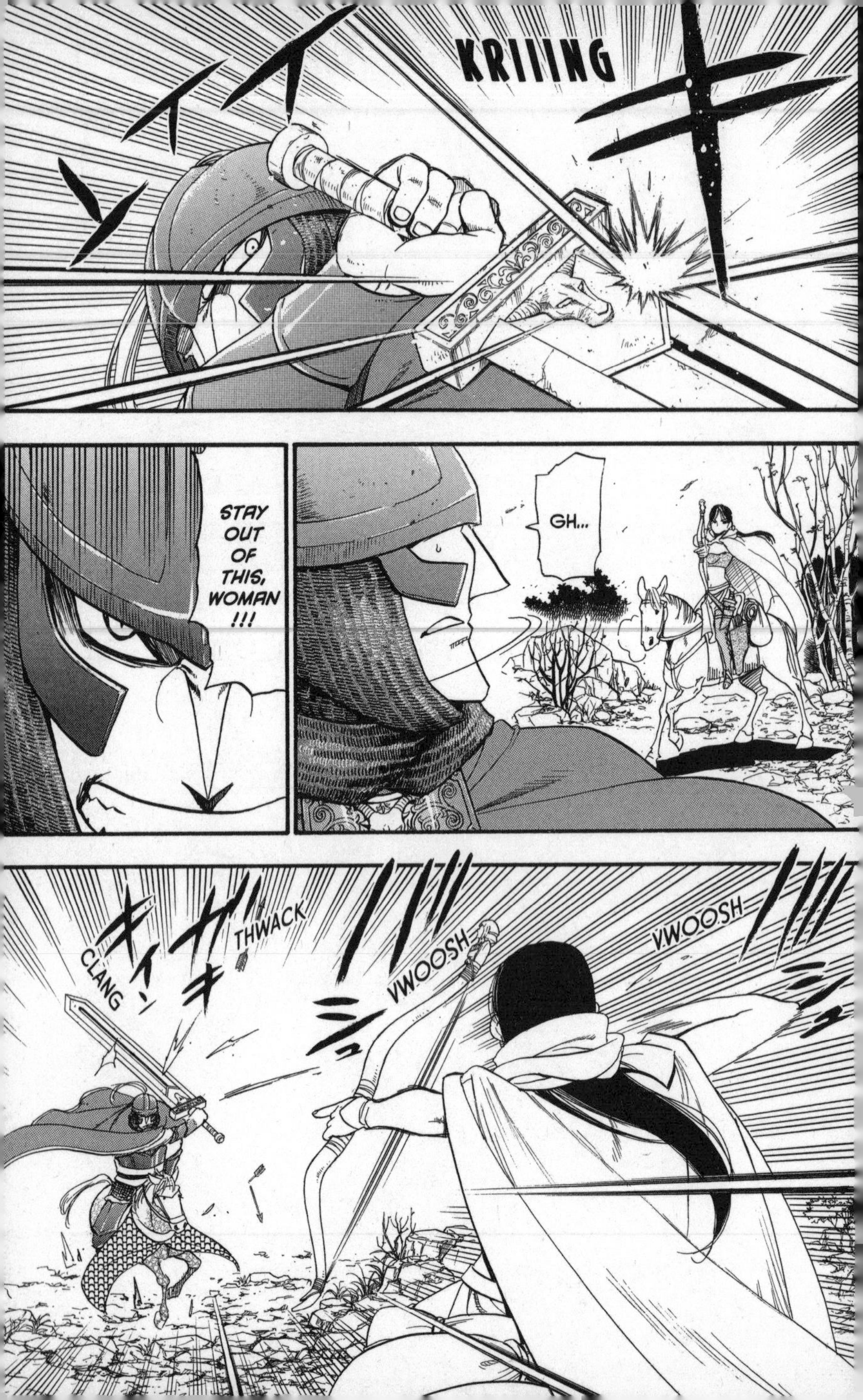
KRIIING
GH...
STAY OUT OF THIS, WOMAN!!!
VWOOSH
VWOOSH
THWACK
CLANG

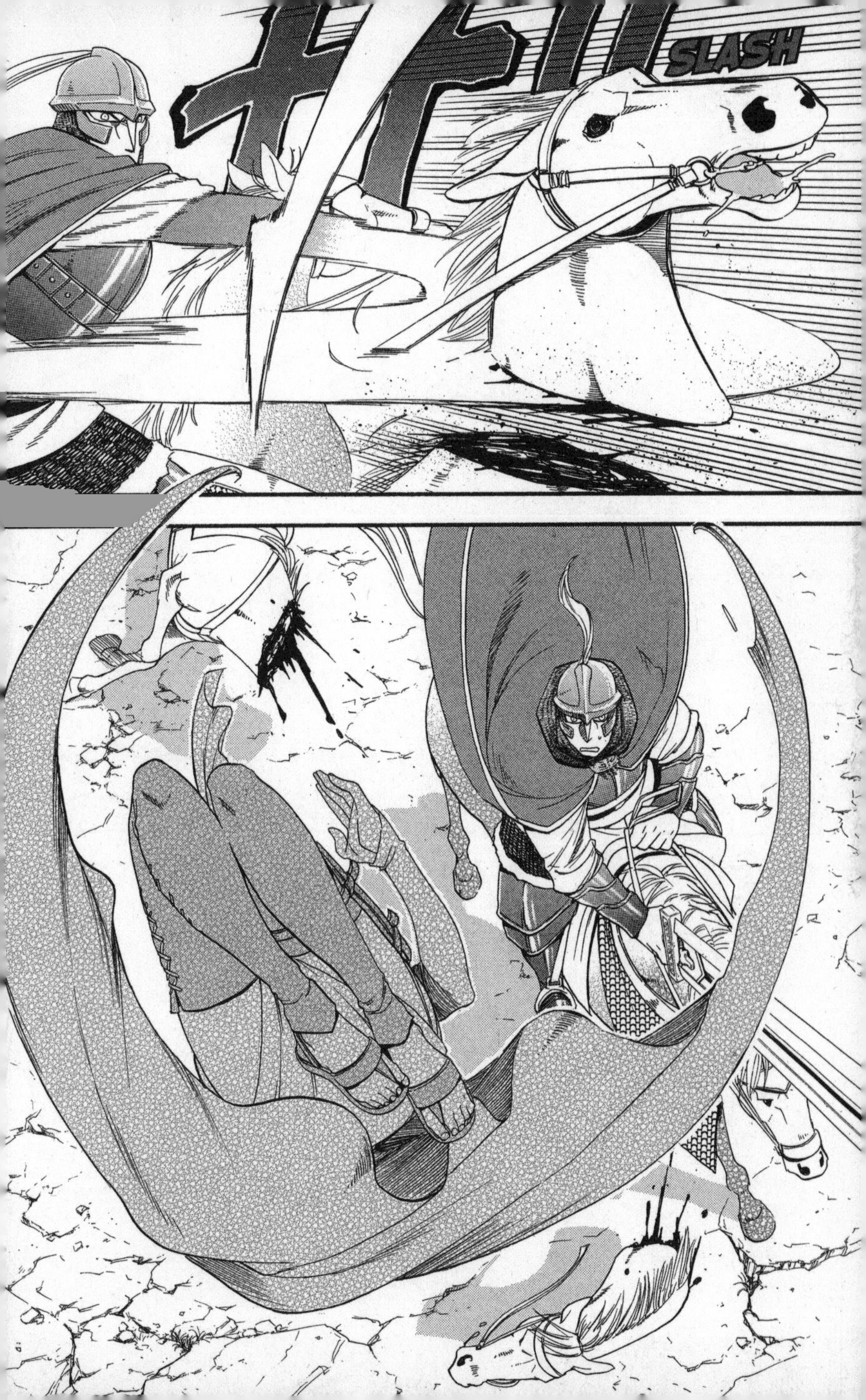
SLASH

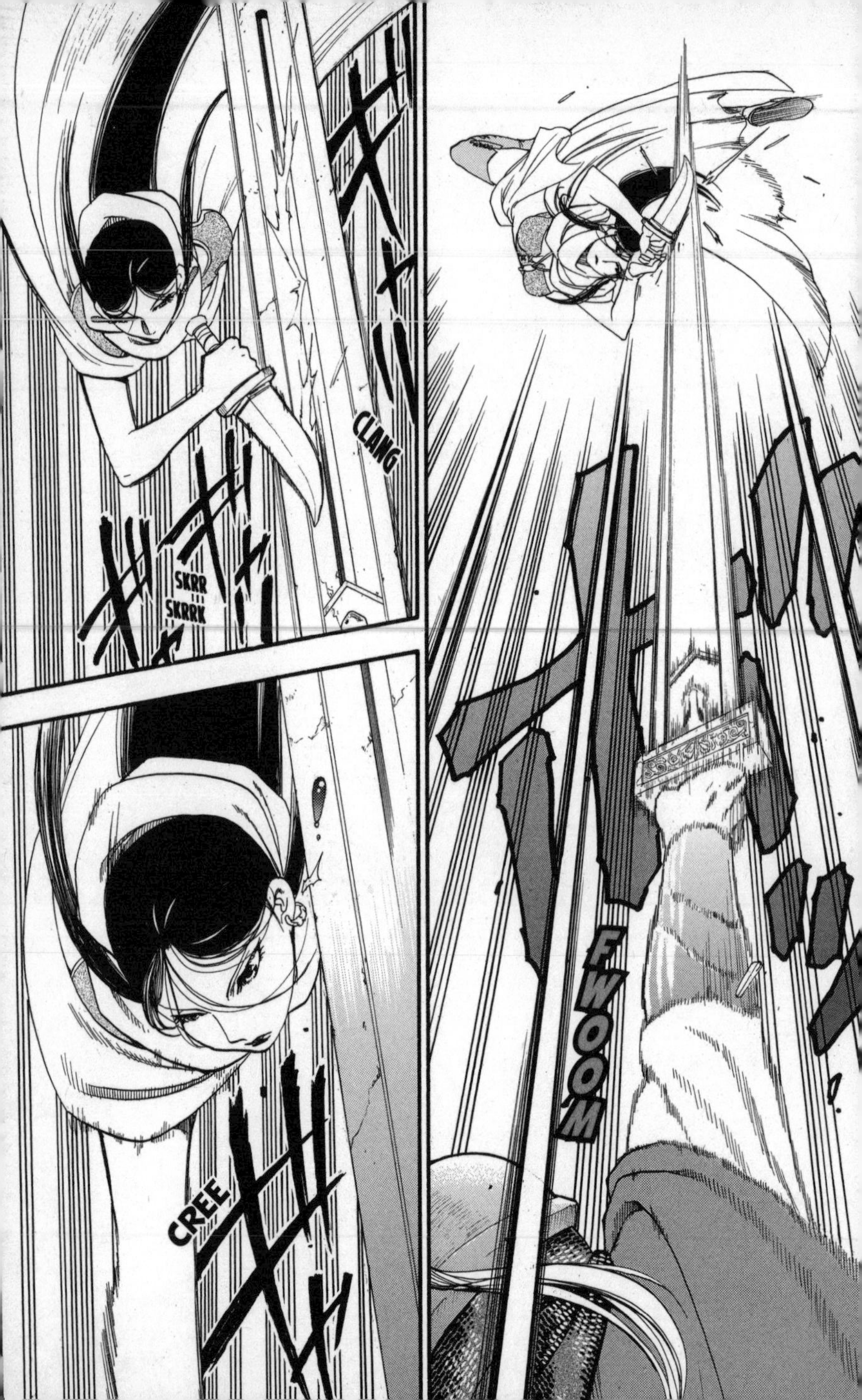
FWOOM
CLANG
SKRR
SKRRK
CREE

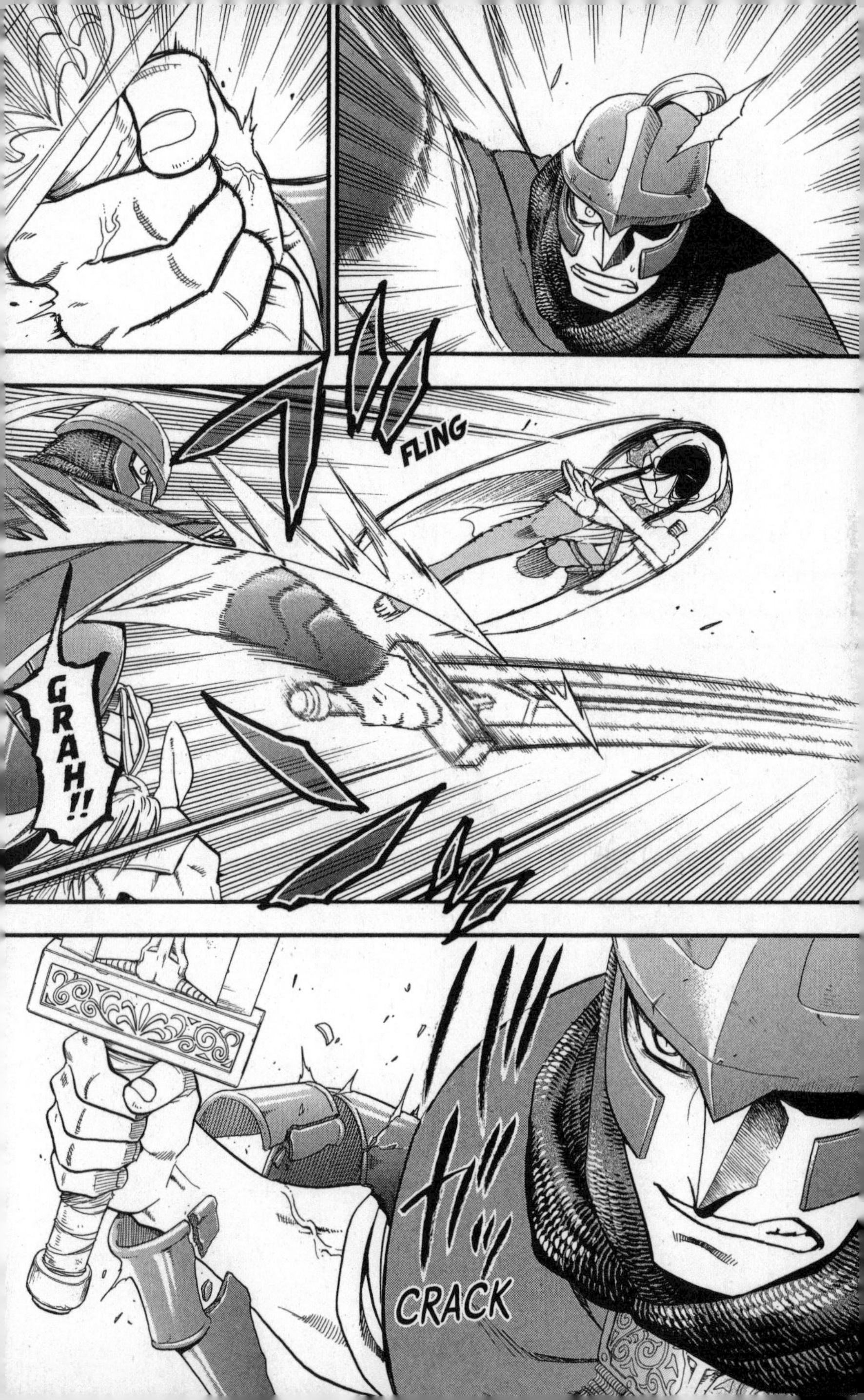
FLING
GRAH!!
CRACK

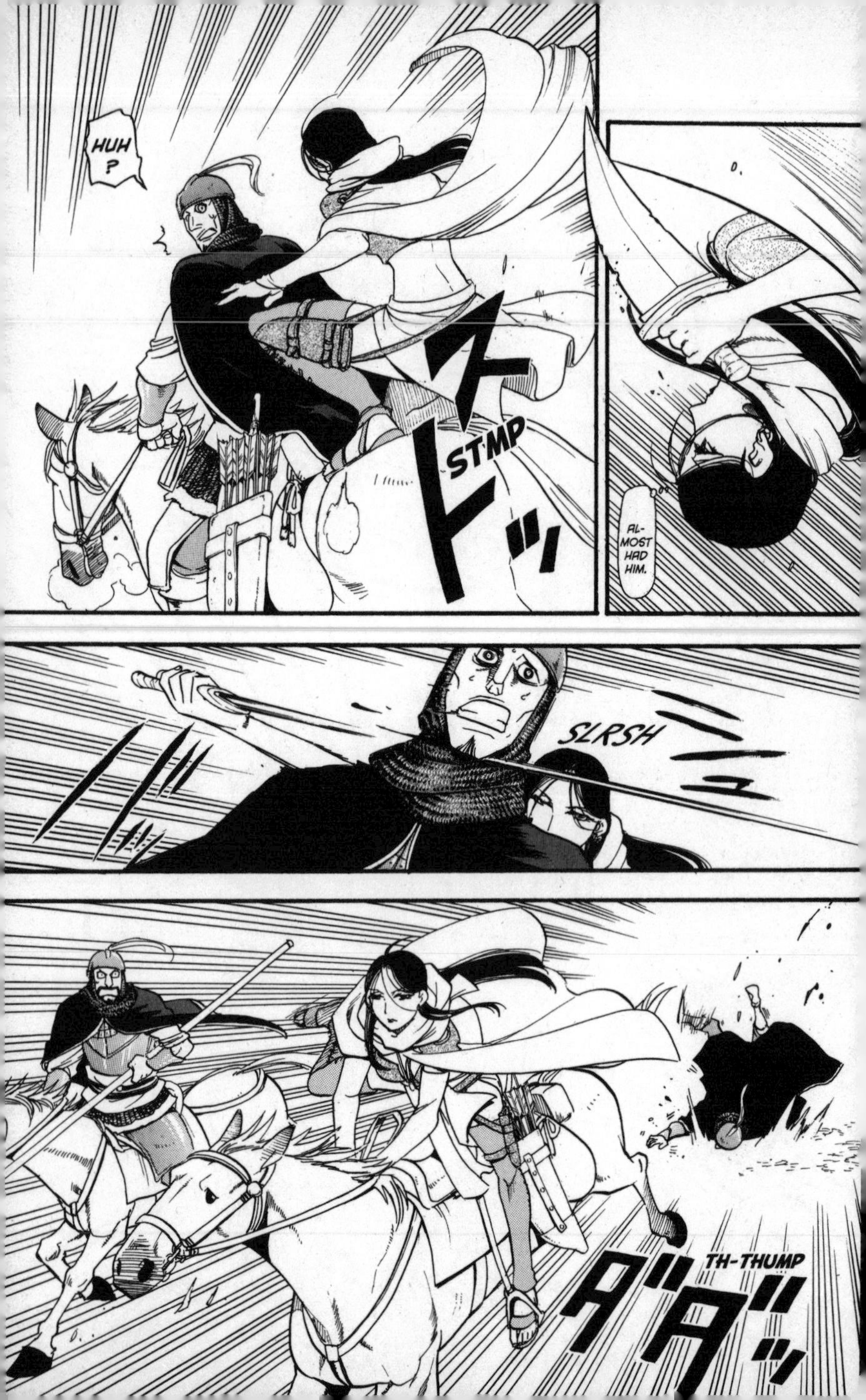
AL-MOST HAD HIM.
HUH ?
STMP
SLRSH
TH-THUMP

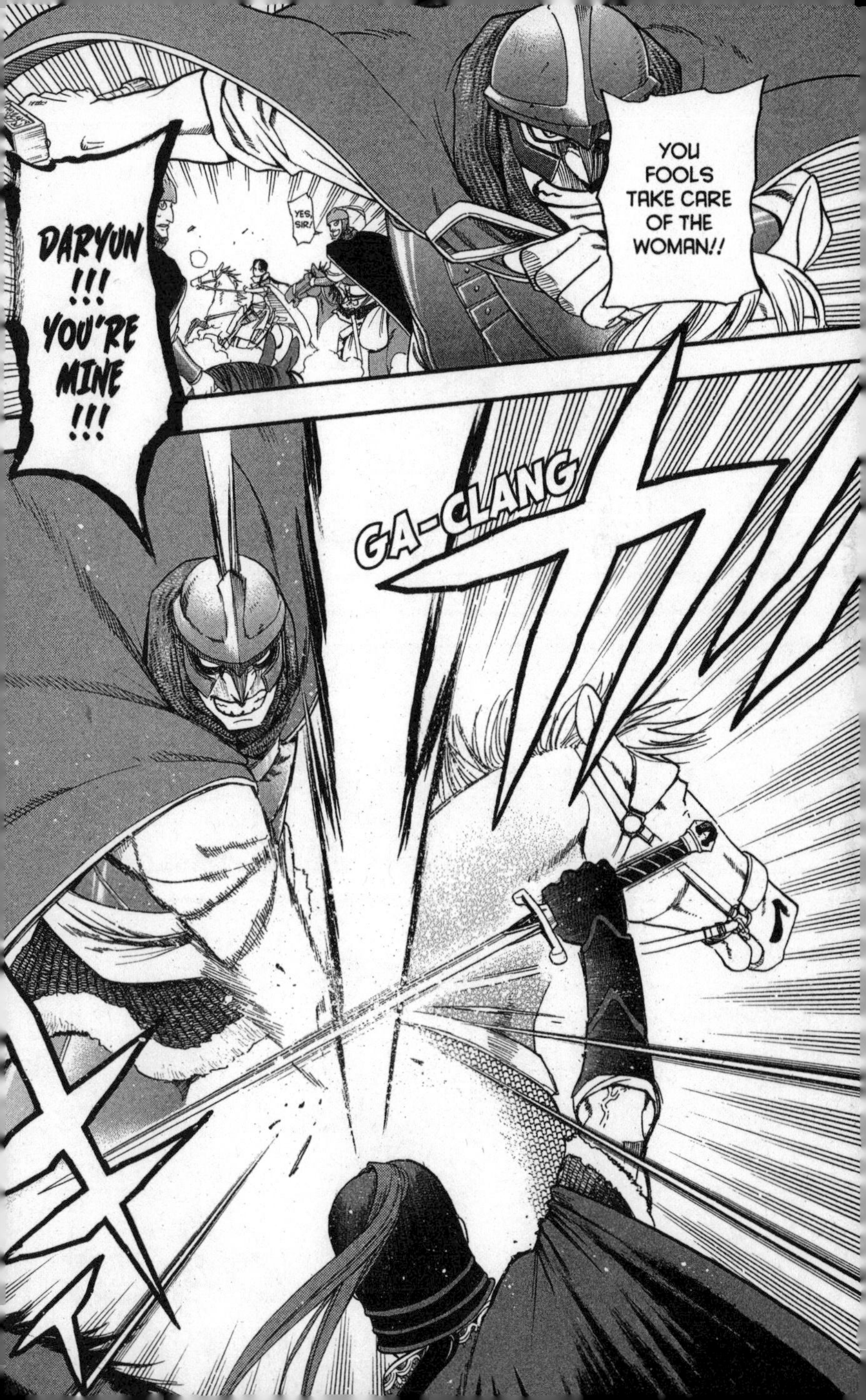
YOU FOOLS TAKE CARE OF THE WOMAN!!
YES, SIR!
DARYUN!!! YOU'RE MINE!!!
GA-CLANG

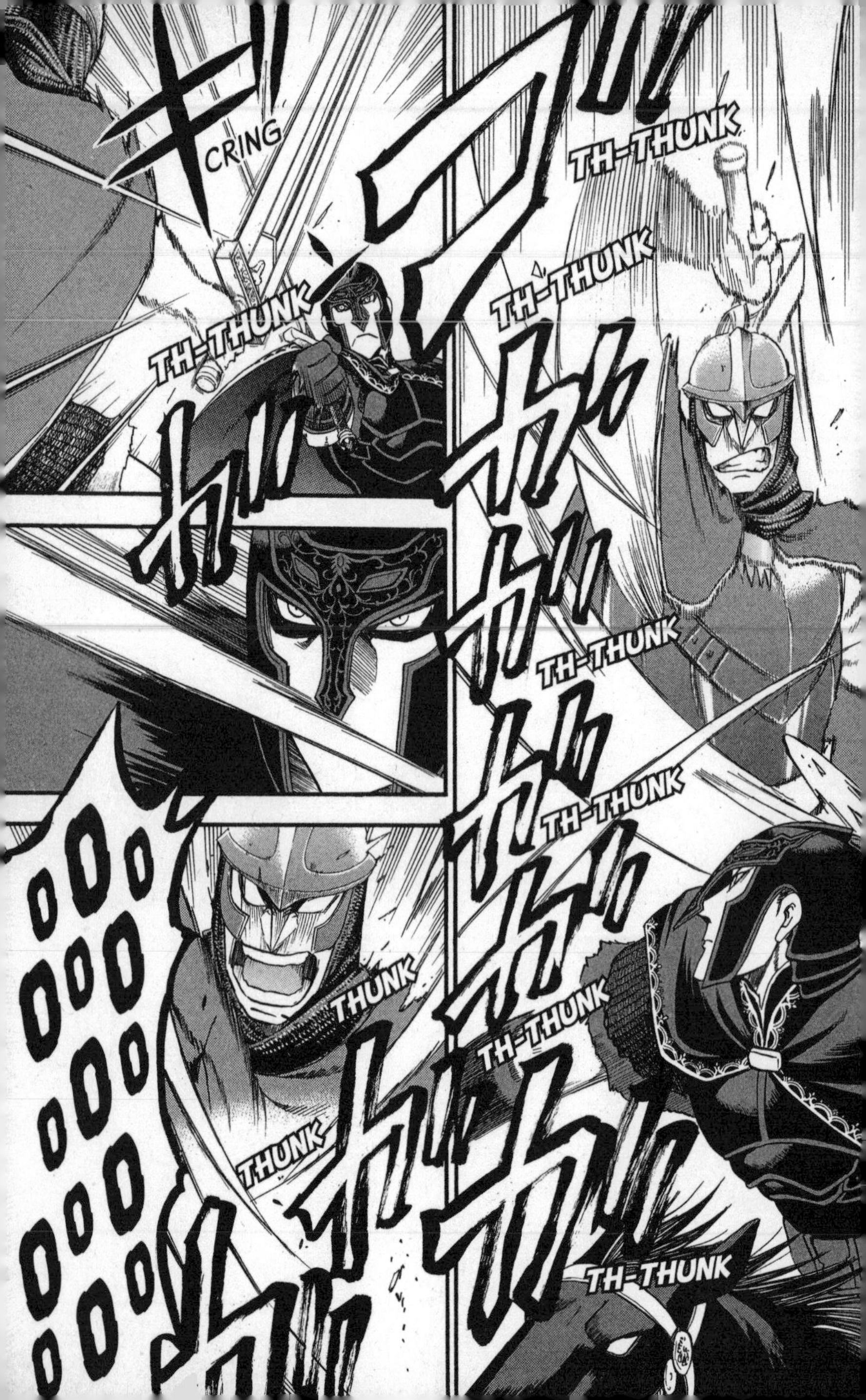
TH-THUNK
TH-THUNK
TH-THUNK
TH-THUNK
TH-THUNK
TH-THUNK
CRING
TH-THUNK
THUNK
THUNK

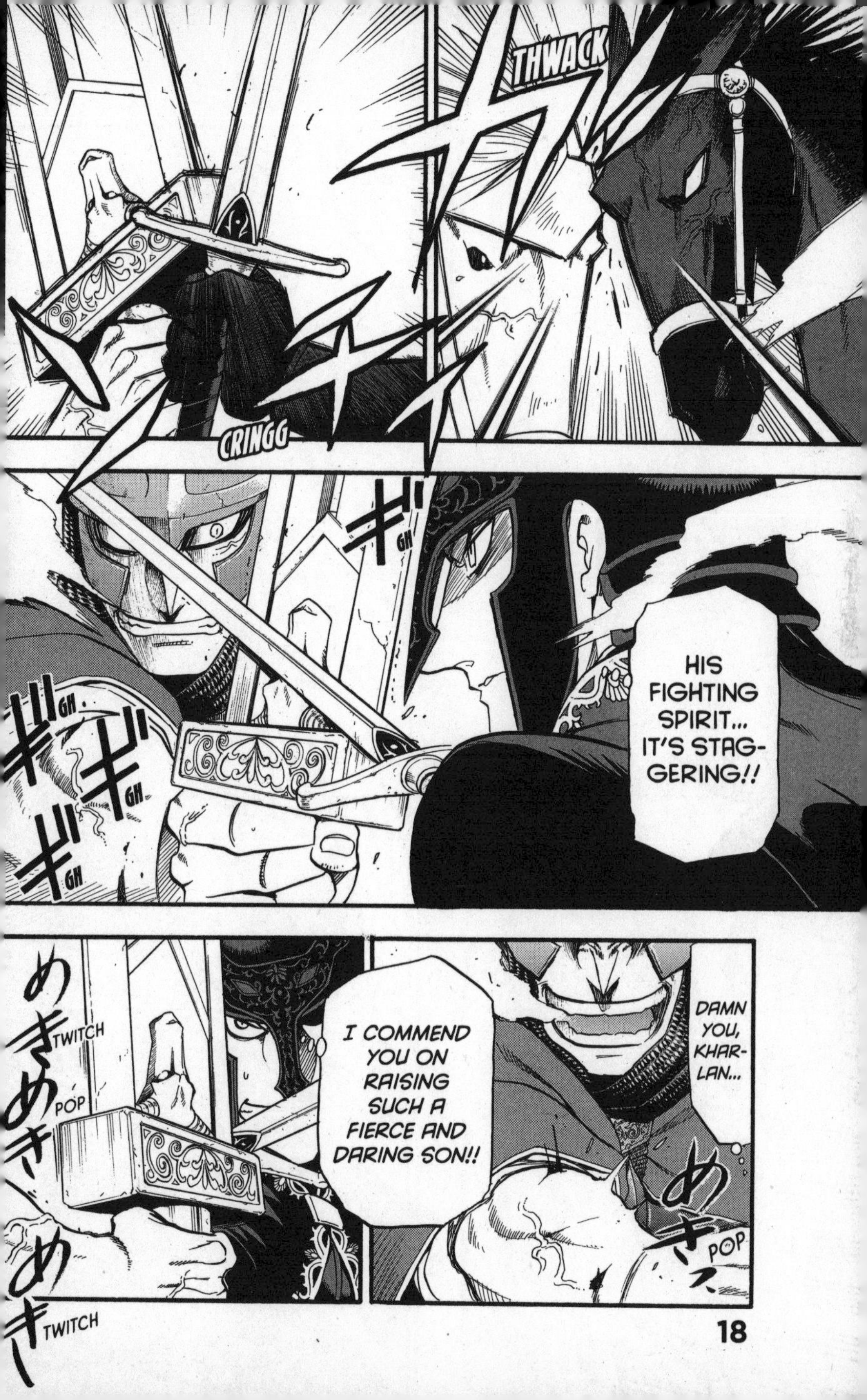
THWACK
CRINGG
GH
HIS FIGHTING SPIRIT... IT'S STAG-GERING!!
GH
GH
GH
DAMN YOU, KHAR-LAN...
めき
POP
I COMMEND YOU ON RAISING SUCH A FIERCE AND DARING SON!!
めきめきめき
TWITCH
POP
TWITCH

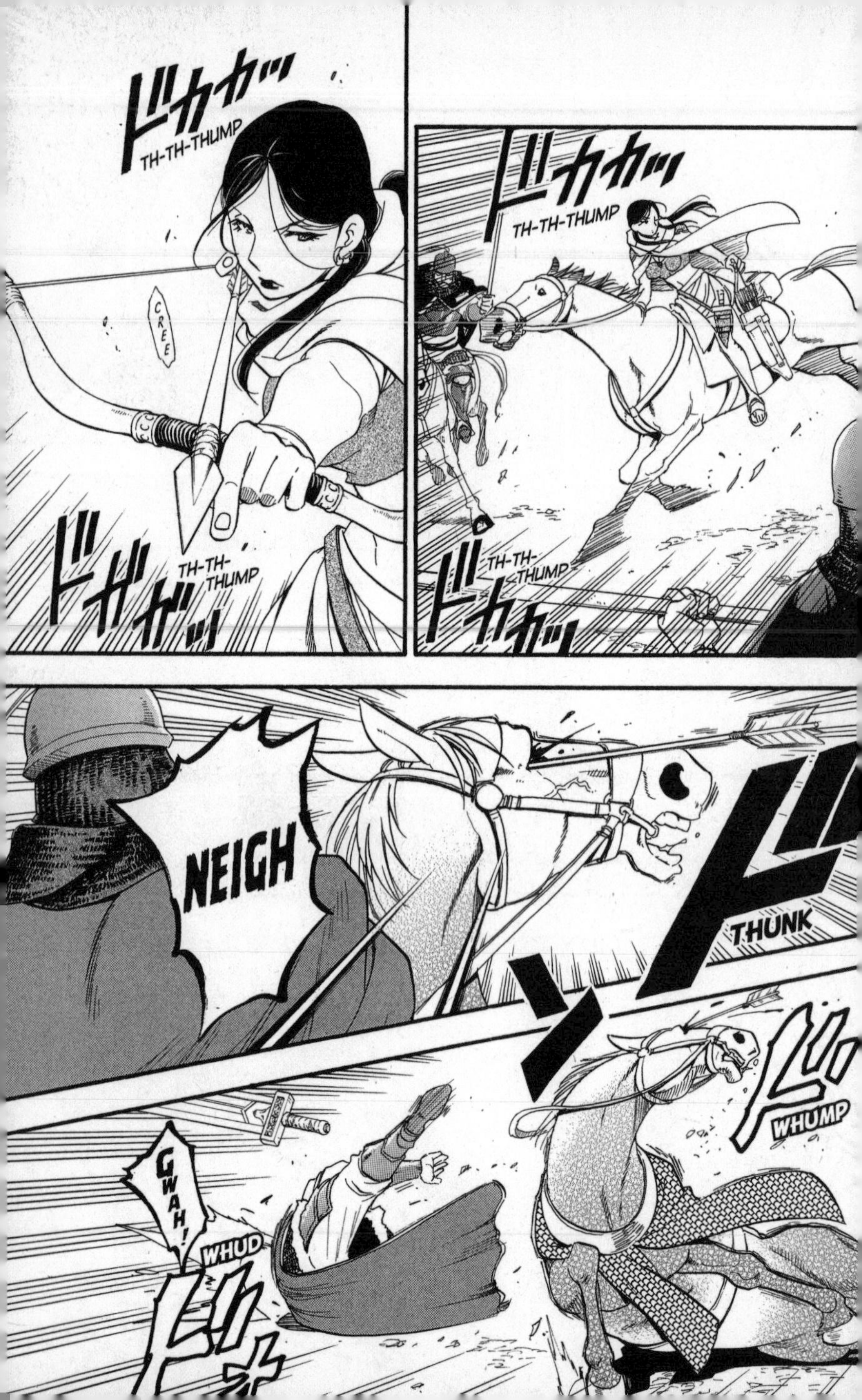

ドカカッ
TH-TH-THUMP
ドカカッ
TH-TH-THUMP
ドカカッ
TH-TH-THUMP
CREEE
ドガガッ
TH-TH-THUMP
NEIGH
THUNK
WHUMP
GWAH!
WHUD

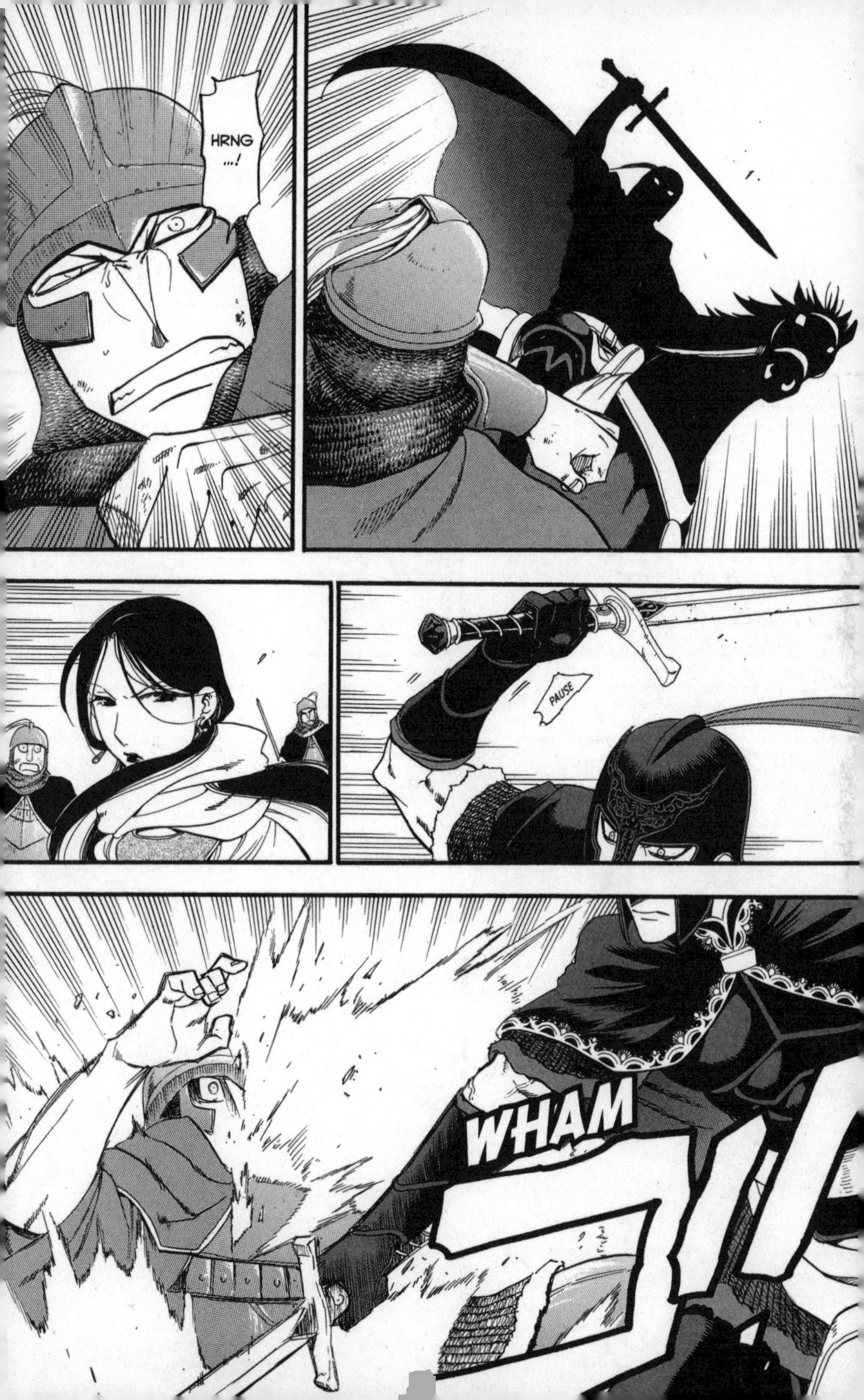
HRNG ...!
PAUSE
WHAM

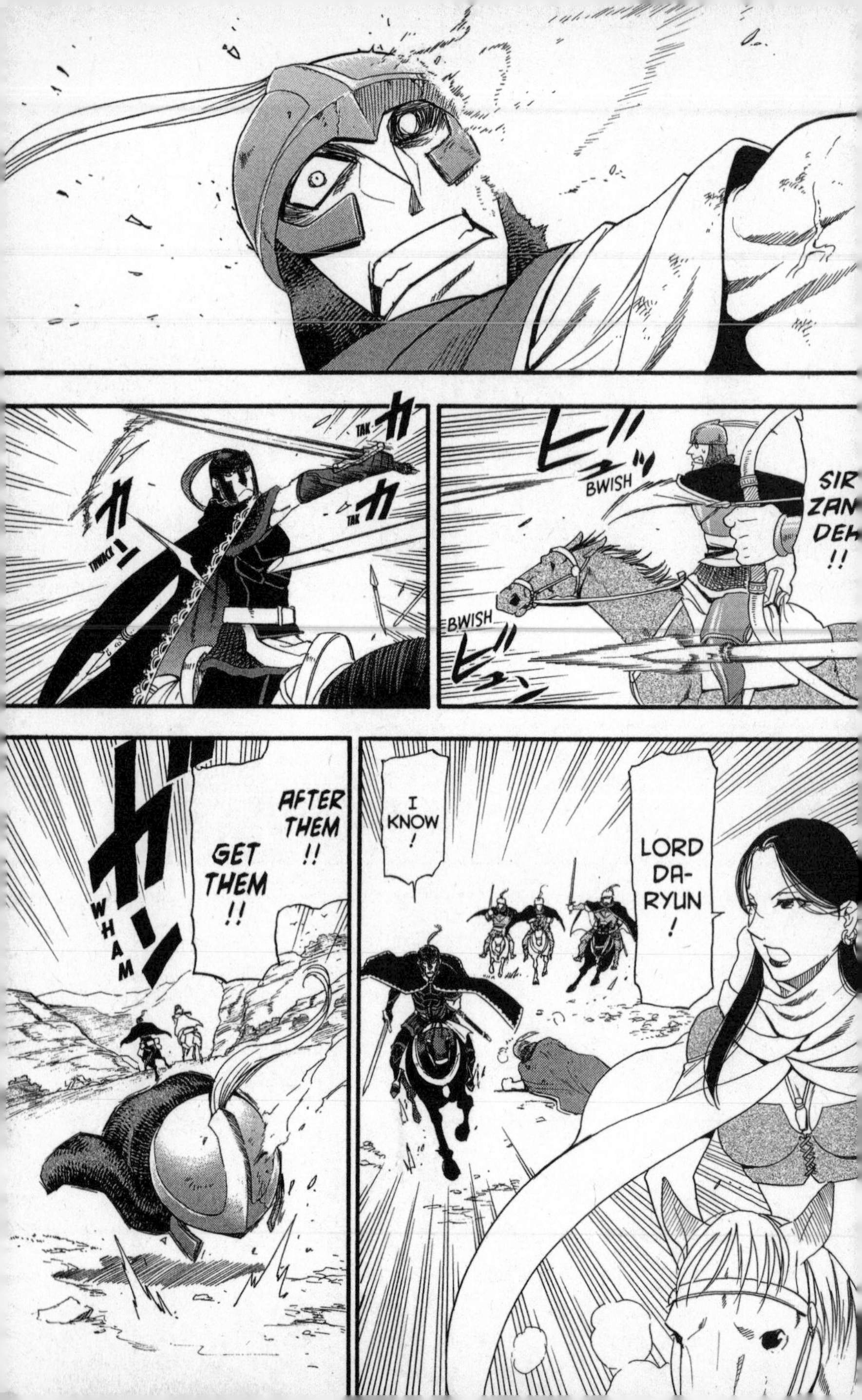
BWISH
SIR ZANDEH!!
BWISH
TAK
TAK
TWACK
LORD DA-RYUN!
I KNOW!
AFTER THEM!!
GET THEM!!
WHAM

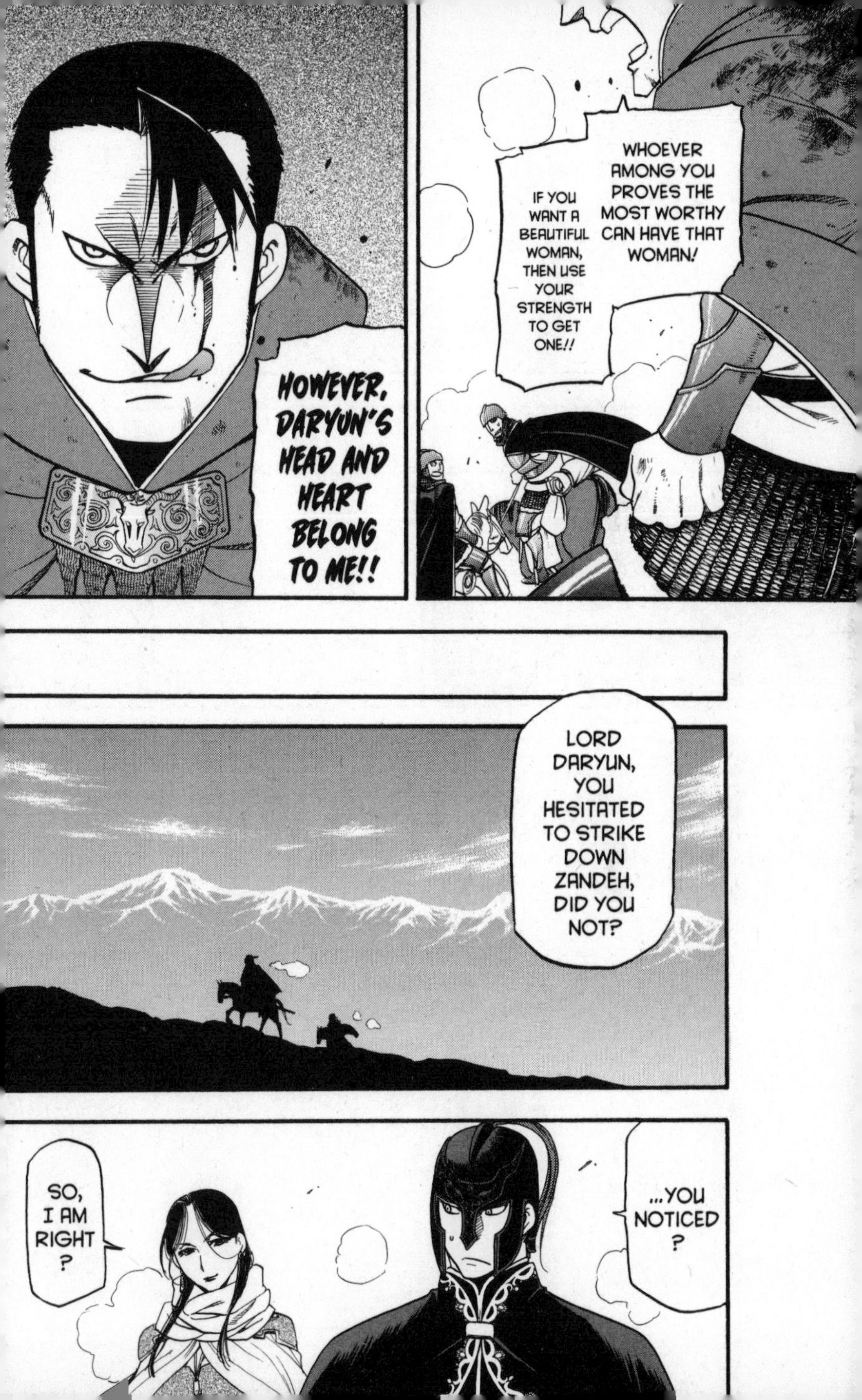
WHOEVER AMONG YOU PROVES THE MOST WORTHY CAN HAVE THAT WOMAN!
IF YOU WANT A BEAUTIFUL WOMAN, THEN USE YOUR STRENGTH TO GET ONE!!
HOWEVER, DARYUN'S HEAD AND HEART BELONG TO ME!!
LORD DARYUN, YOU HESITATED TO STRIKE DOWN ZANDEH, DID YOU NOT?
...YOU NOTICED?
SO, I AM RIGHT?

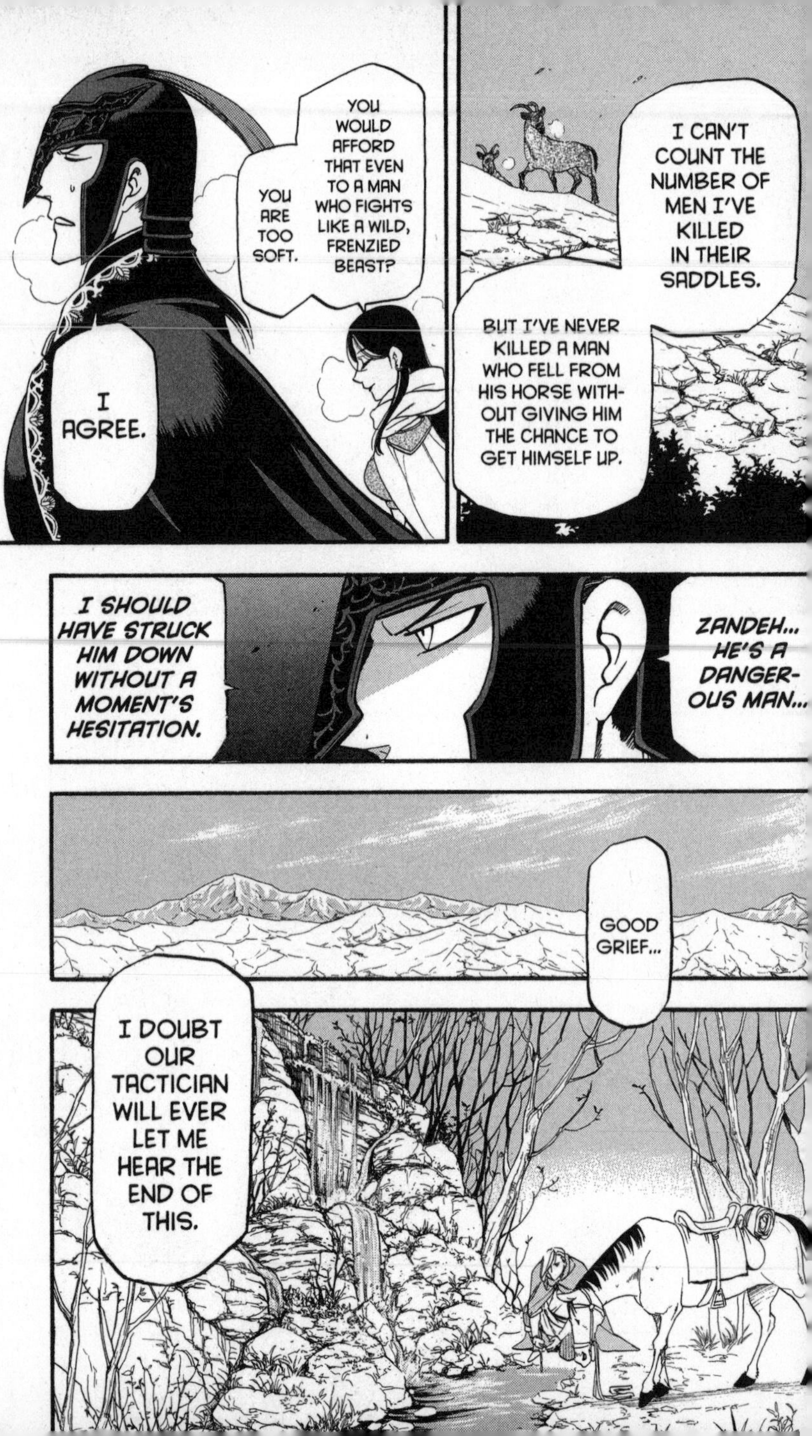
I CAN'T COUNT THE NUMBER OF MEN I'VE KILLED IN THEIR SADDLES.
BUT I'VE NEVER KILLED A MAN WHO FELL FROM HIS HORSE WITHOUT GIVING HIM THE CHANCE TO GET HIMSELF UP.
YOU WOULD AFFORD THAT EVEN TO A MAN WHO FIGHTS LIKE A WILD, FRENZIED BEAST?
YOU ARE TOO SOFT.
I AGREE.
ZANDEH... HE'S A DANGEROUS MAN...
I SHOULD HAVE STRUCK HIM DOWN WITHOUT A MOMENT'S HESITATION.
GOOD GRIEF...
I DOUBT OUR TACTICIAN WILL EVER LET ME HEAR THE END OF THIS.

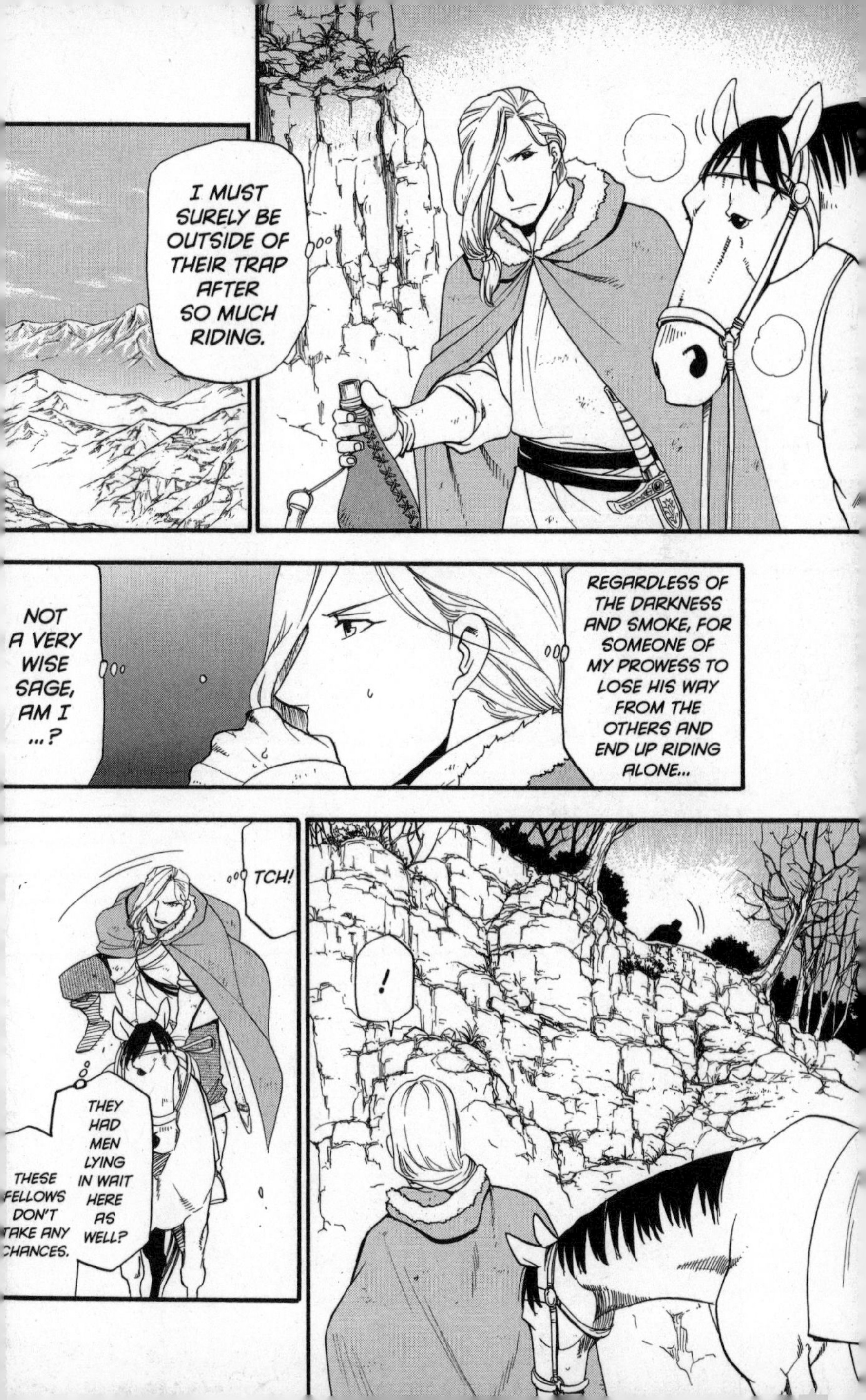
I MUST SURELY BE OUTSIDE OF THEIR TRAP AFTER SO MUCH RIDING.
REGARDLESS OF THE DARKNESS AND SMOKE, FOR SOMEONE OF MY PROWESS TO LOSE HIS WAY FROM THE OTHERS AND END UP RIDING ALONE...
NOT A VERY WISE SAGE, AM I ...?
!
TCH!
THEY HAD MEN LYING IN WAIT HERE AS WELL?
THESE FELLOWS DON'T TAKE ANY CHANCES.

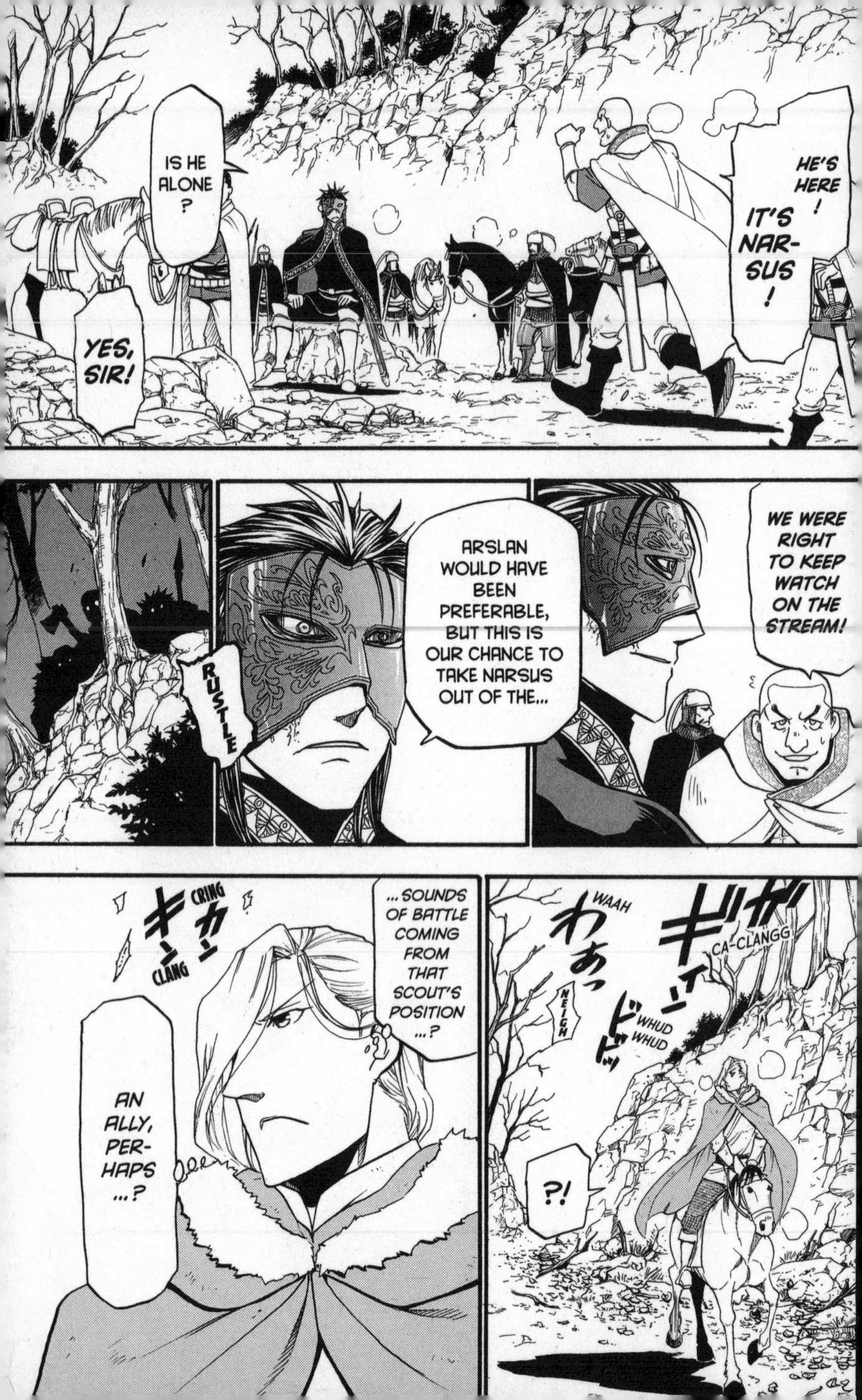
HE'S HERE! IT'S NARSUS!
IS HE ALONE?
YES, SIR!
WE WERE RIGHT TO KEEP WATCH ON THE STREAM!
ARSLAN WOULD HAVE BEEN PREFERABLE, BUT THIS IS OUR CHANCE TO TAKE NARSUS OUT OF THE...
RUSTLE
WAAH
CA-CLANGG
NEIGH
WHUD WHUD
?!
CRING
CLANG
...SOUNDS OF BATTLE COMING FROM THAT SCOUT'S POSITION...?
AN ALLY, PERHAPS...?

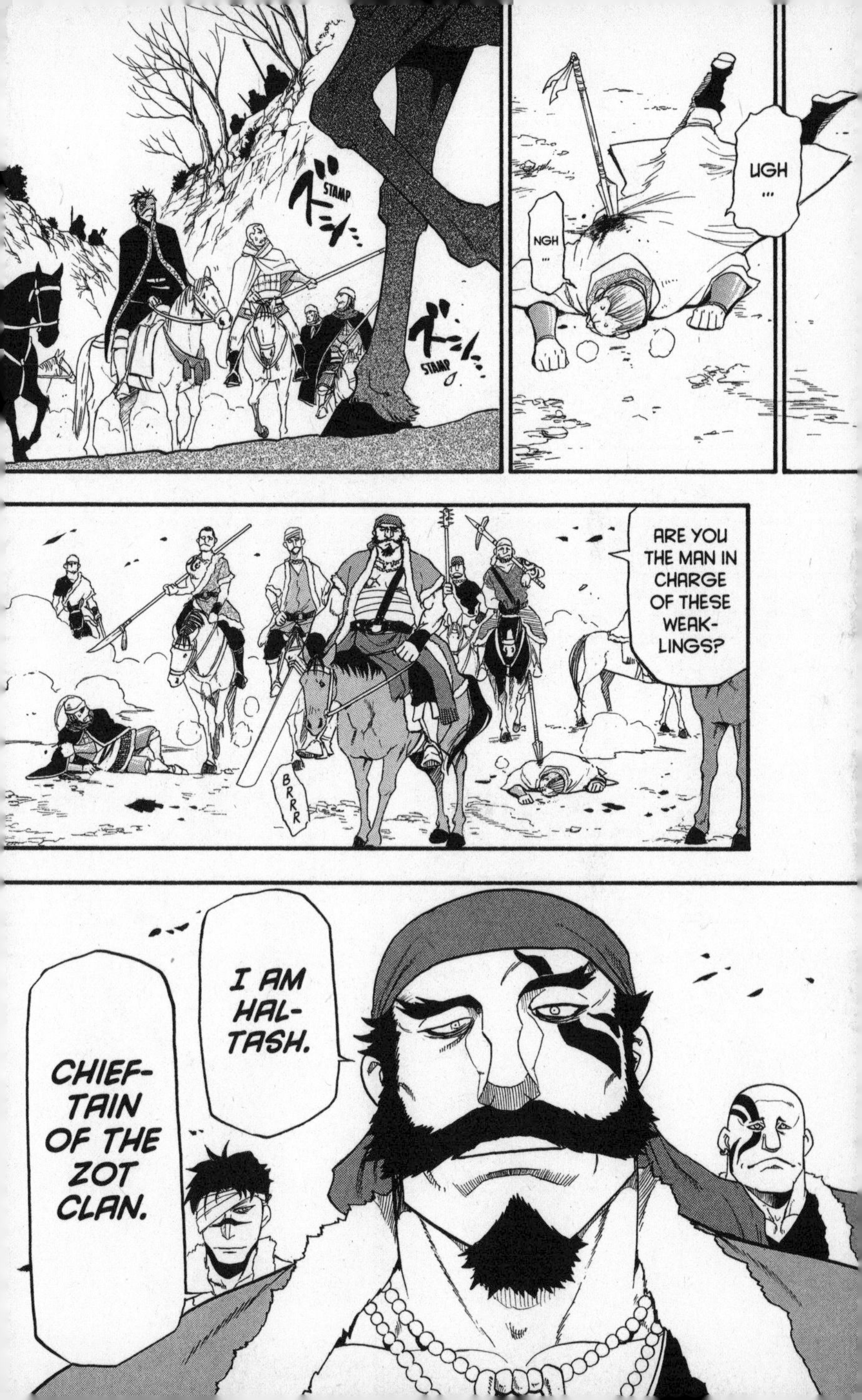
UGH ...
NGH ...
STAMP
STAMP
ARE YOU THE MAN IN CHARGE OF THESE WEAK-LINGS?
BRRR
I AM HAL-TASH.
CHIEF-TAIN OF THE ZOT CLAN.

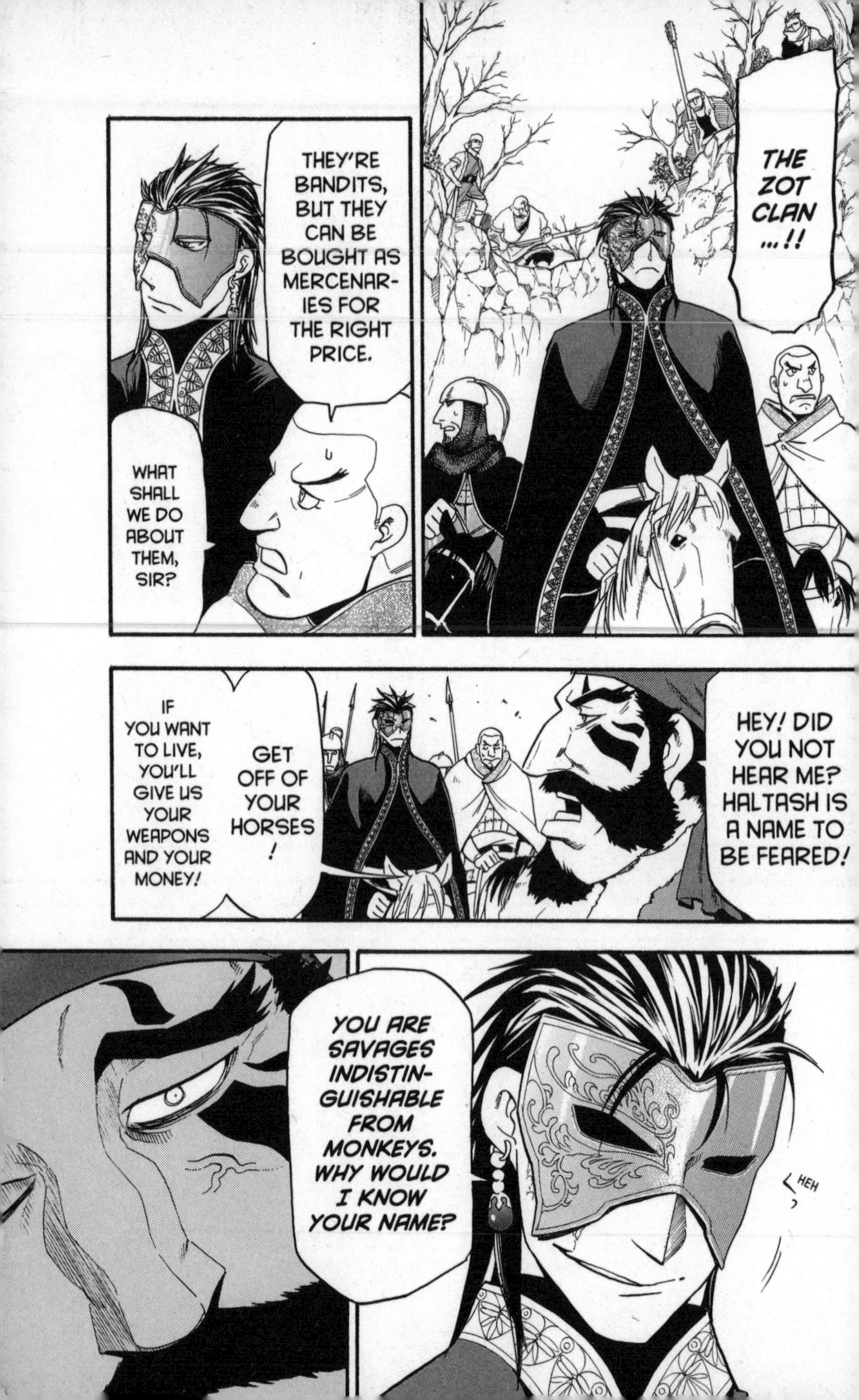
THE ZOT CLAN ...!!
THEY'RE BANDITS, BUT THEY CAN BE BOUGHT AS MERCENARIES FOR THE RIGHT PRICE.
WHAT SHALL WE DO ABOUT THEM, SIR?
HEY! DID YOU NOT HEAR ME? HALTASH IS A NAME TO BE FEARED!
GET OFF OF YOUR HORSES!
IF YOU WANT TO LIVE, YOU'LL GIVE US YOUR WEAPONS AND YOUR MONEY!
YOU ARE SAVAGES INDISTINGUISHABLE FROM MONKEYS. WHY WOULD I KNOW YOUR NAME?
HEH

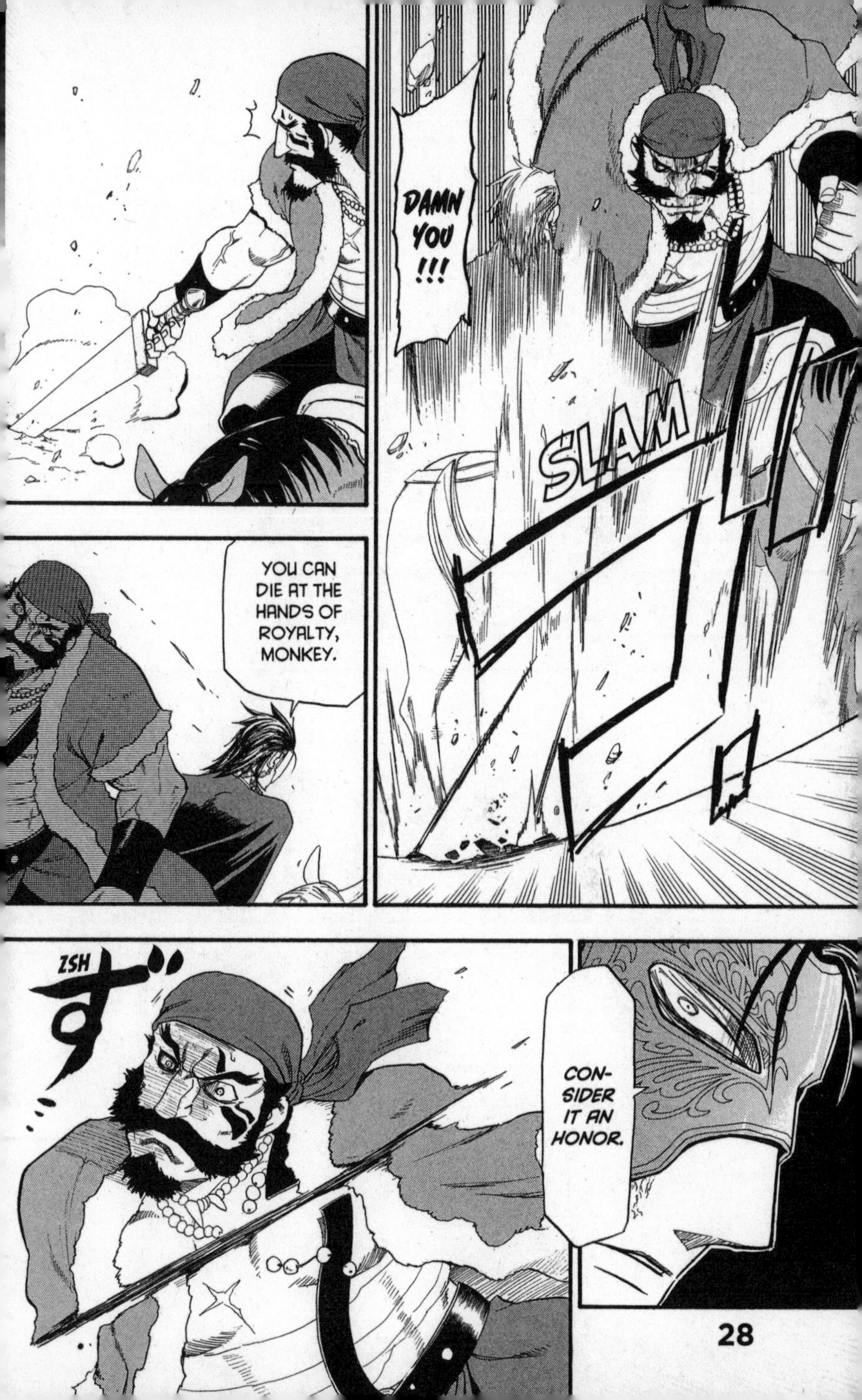
DAMN YOU !!!
SLAM
YOU CAN DIE AT THE HANDS OF ROYALTY, MONKEY.
CON-SIDER IT AN HONOR.
ZSH
すず

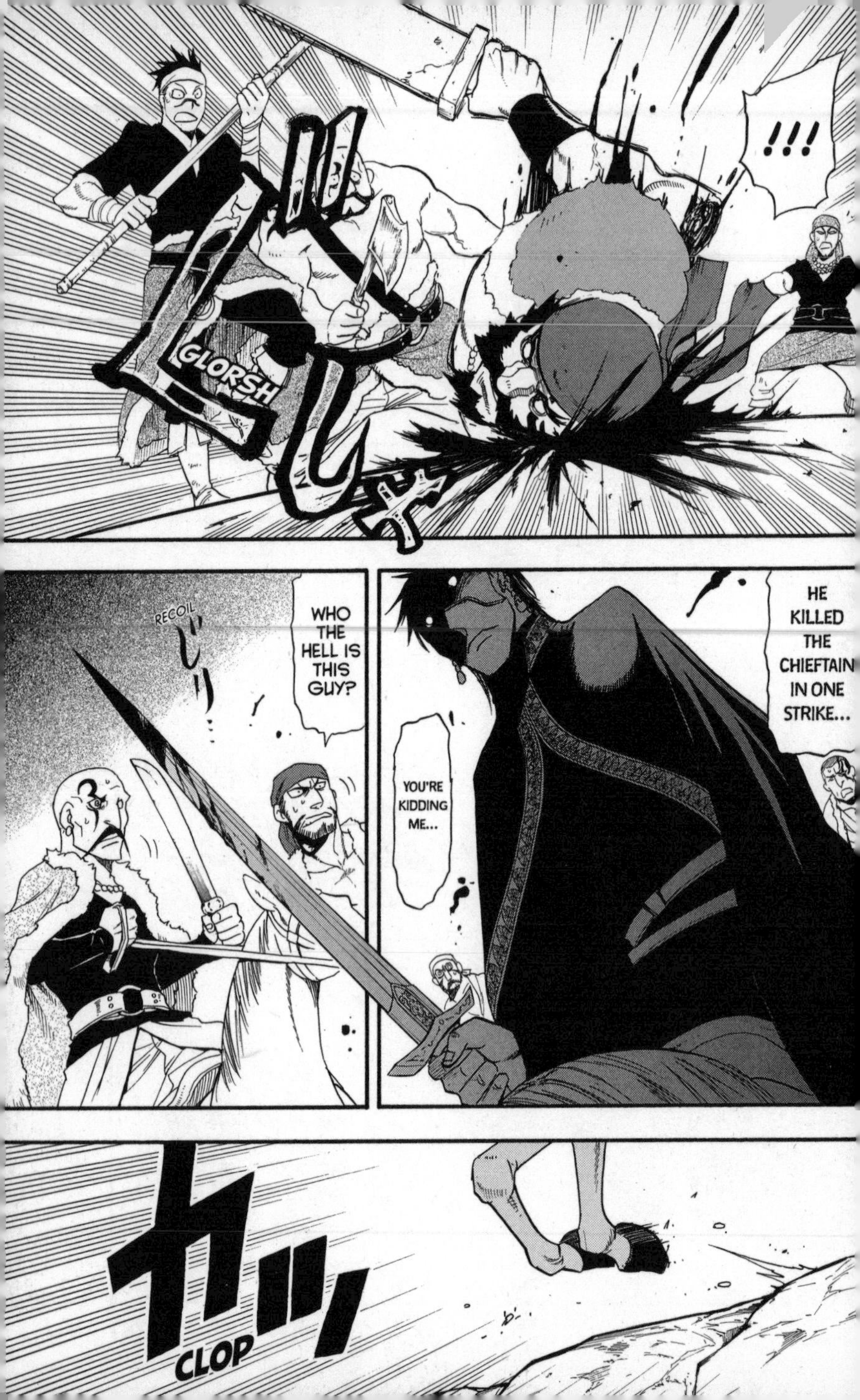
!!!
GLORSH
HE KILLED THE CHIEFTAIN IN ONE STRIKE...
YOU'RE KIDDING ME...
WHO THE HELL IS THIS GUY?
RECOIL
CLOP

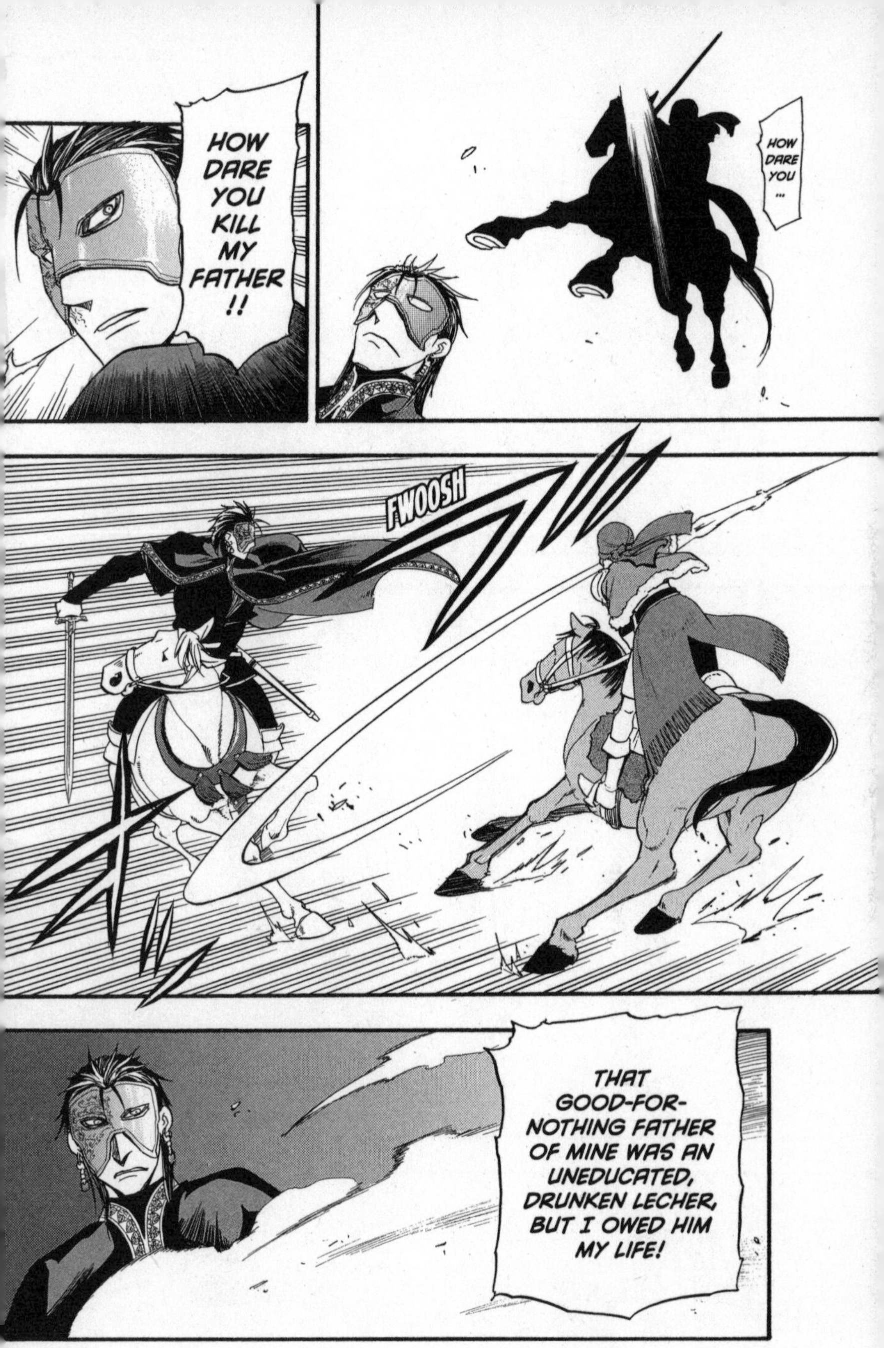
HOW DARE YOU ...
HOW DARE YOU KILL MY FATHER !!
FWOOSH
THAT GOOD-FOR-NOTHING FATHER OF MINE WAS AN UNEDUCATED, DRUNKEN LECHER, BUT I OWED HIM MY LIFE!

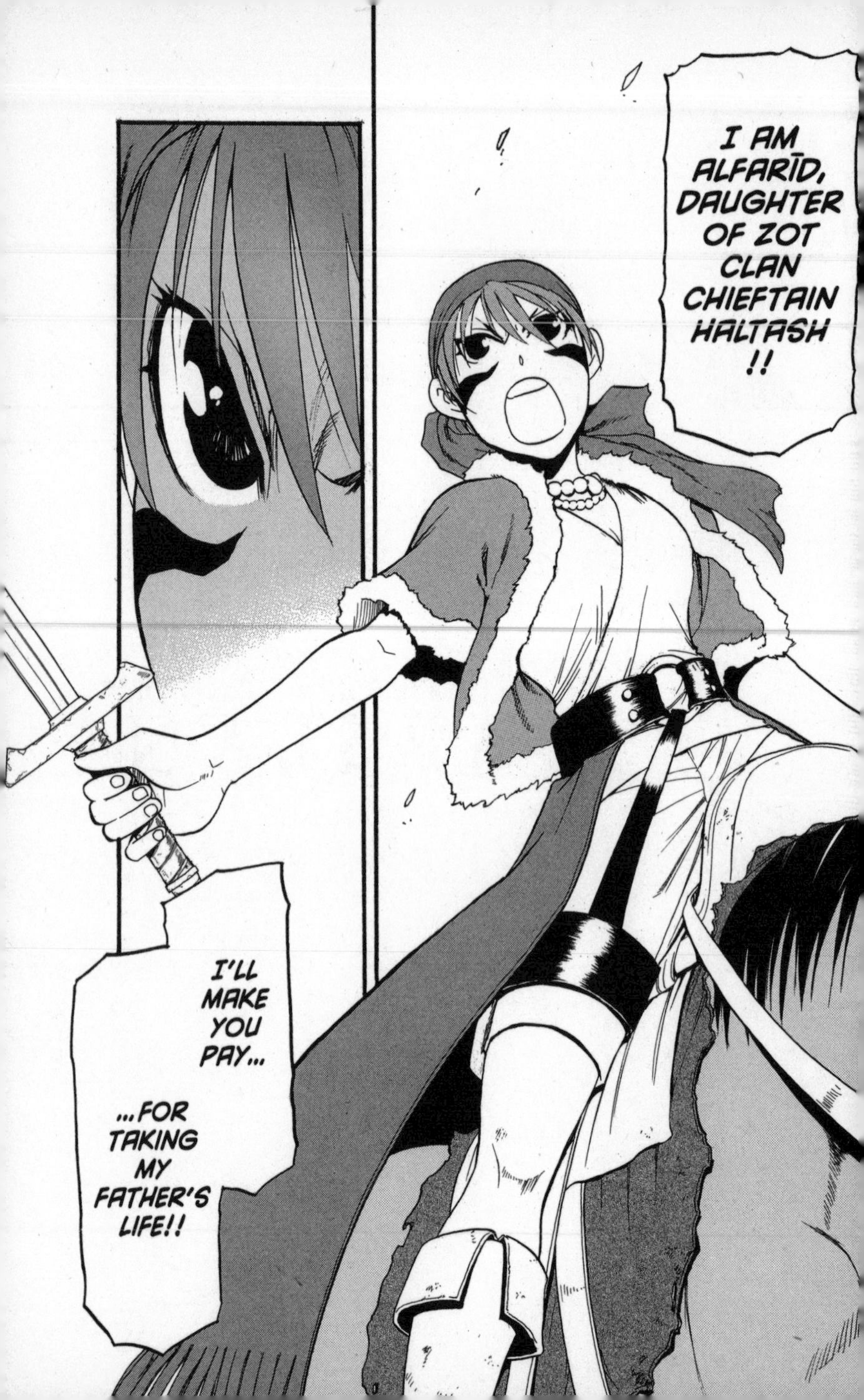
I AM ALFARĪD, DAUGHTER OF ZOT CLAN CHIEFTAIN HALTASH!!
I'LL MAKE YOU PAY...
...FOR TAKING MY FATHER'S LIFE!!

THE HEROIC LEGEND OF
ARSLAN

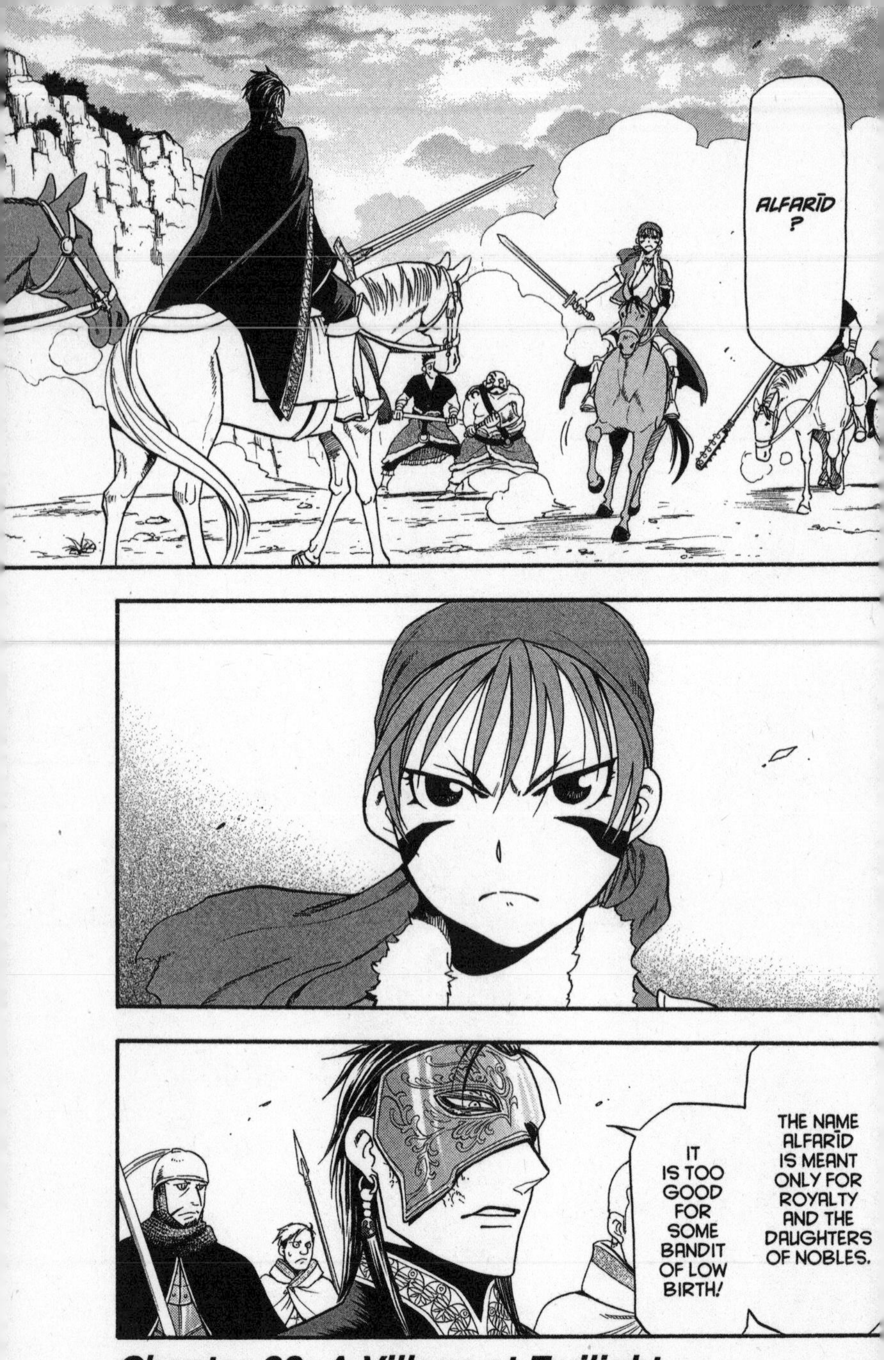
ALFARĪD ?
THE NAME ALFARĪD IS MEANT ONLY FOR ROYALTY AND THE DAUGHTERS OF NOBLES.
IT IS TOO GOOD FOR SOME BANDIT OF LOW BIRTH!

Chapter 29: A Village at Twilight

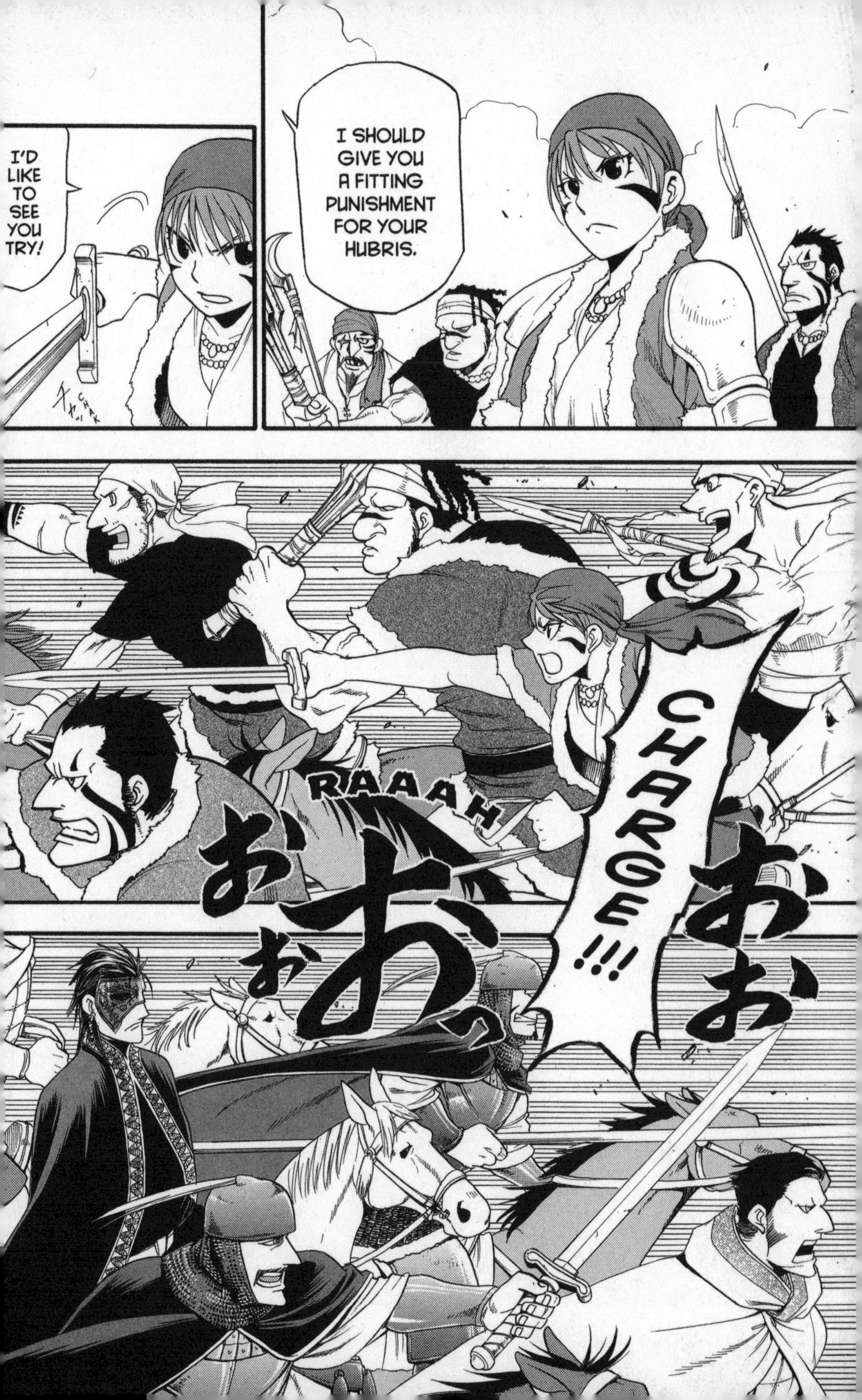
I SHOULD GIVE YOU A FITTING PUNISHMENT FOR YOUR HUBRIS.
I'D LIKE TO SEE YOU TRY!
CHAK
CHARGE!!!
おお
RAAAH
おおお

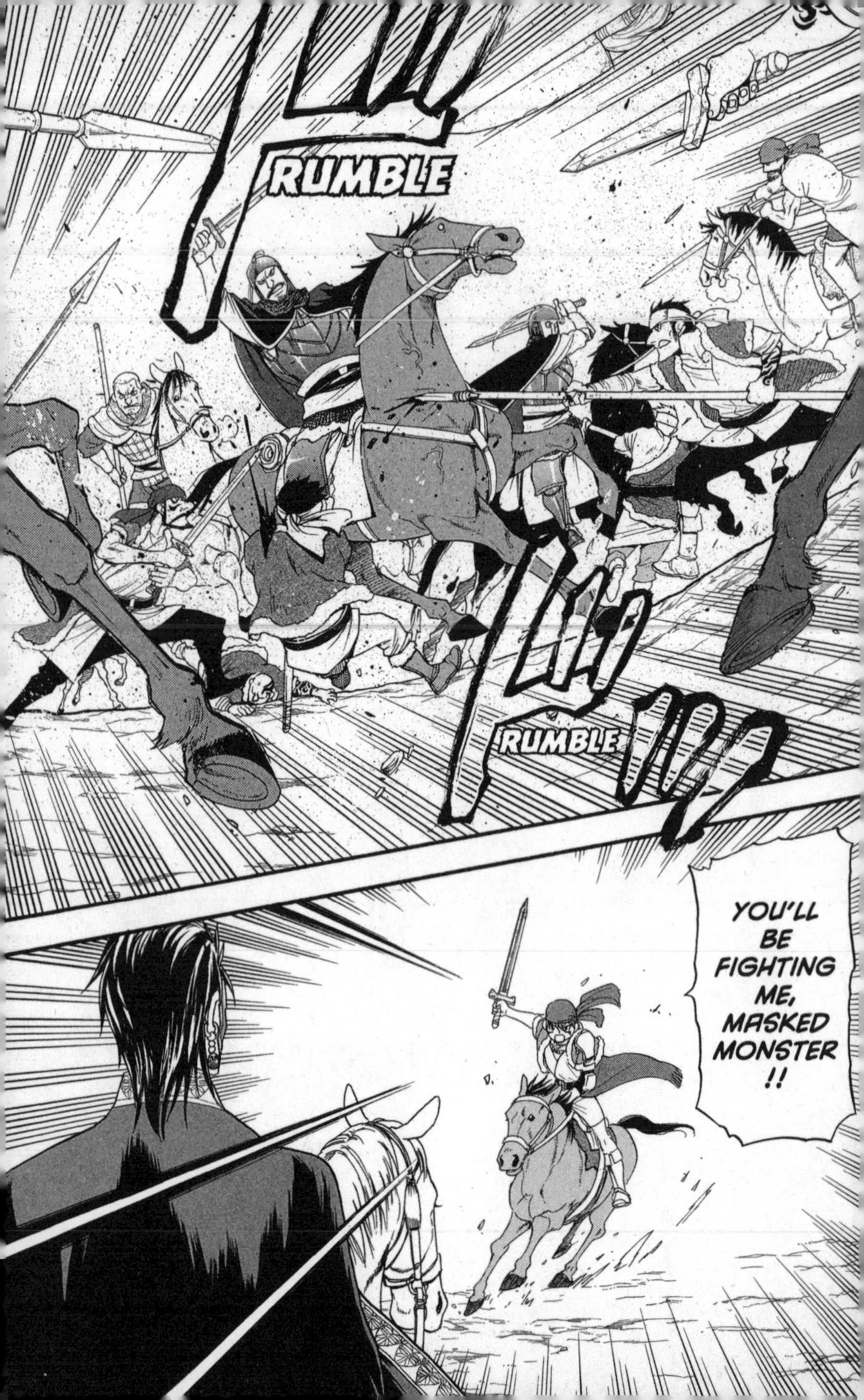
RUMBLE
RUMBLE
YOU'LL BE FIGHTING ME, MASKED MONSTER!!

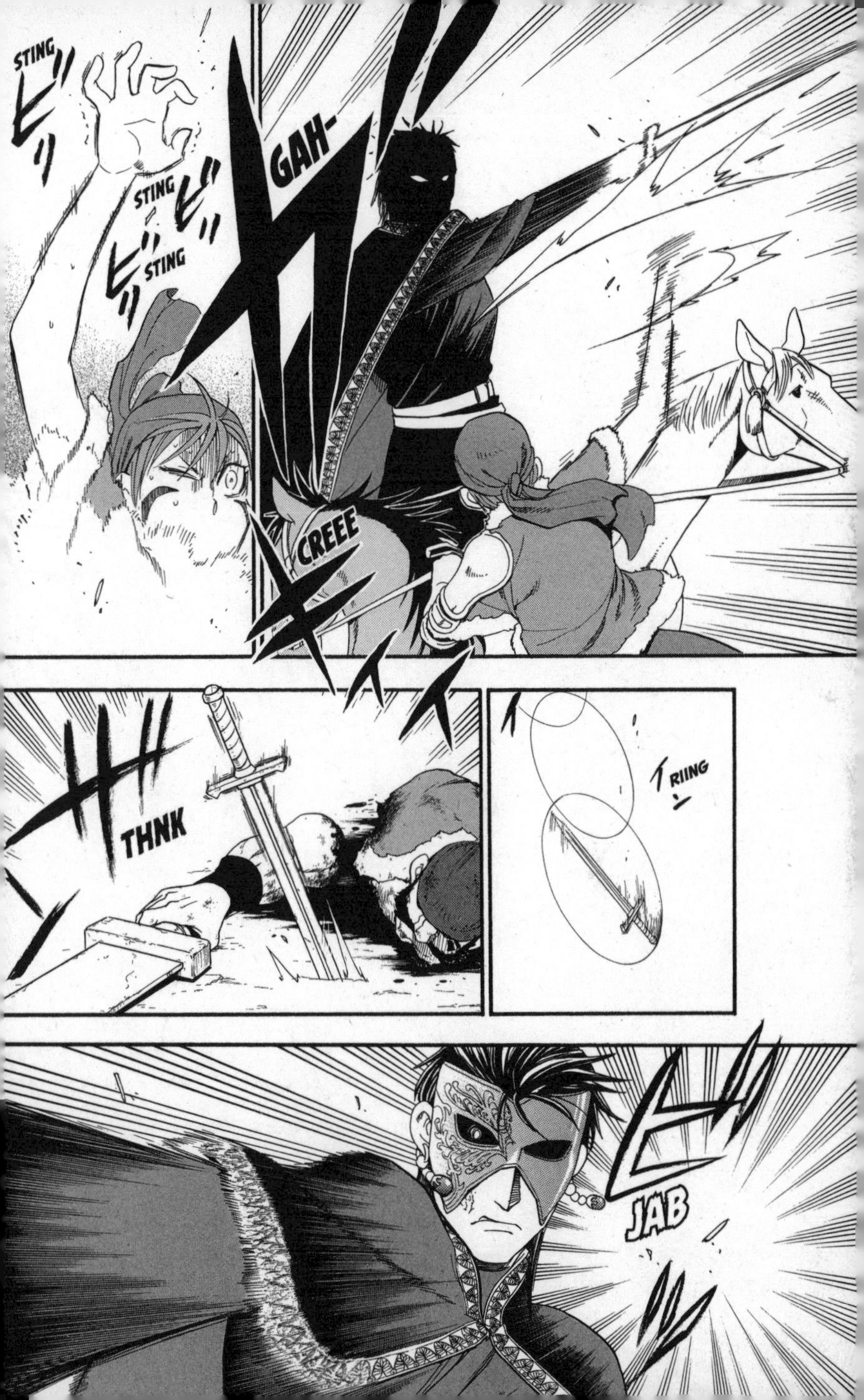
GAH-
STING
STING
STING
CREEE
RIING
THNK
JAB

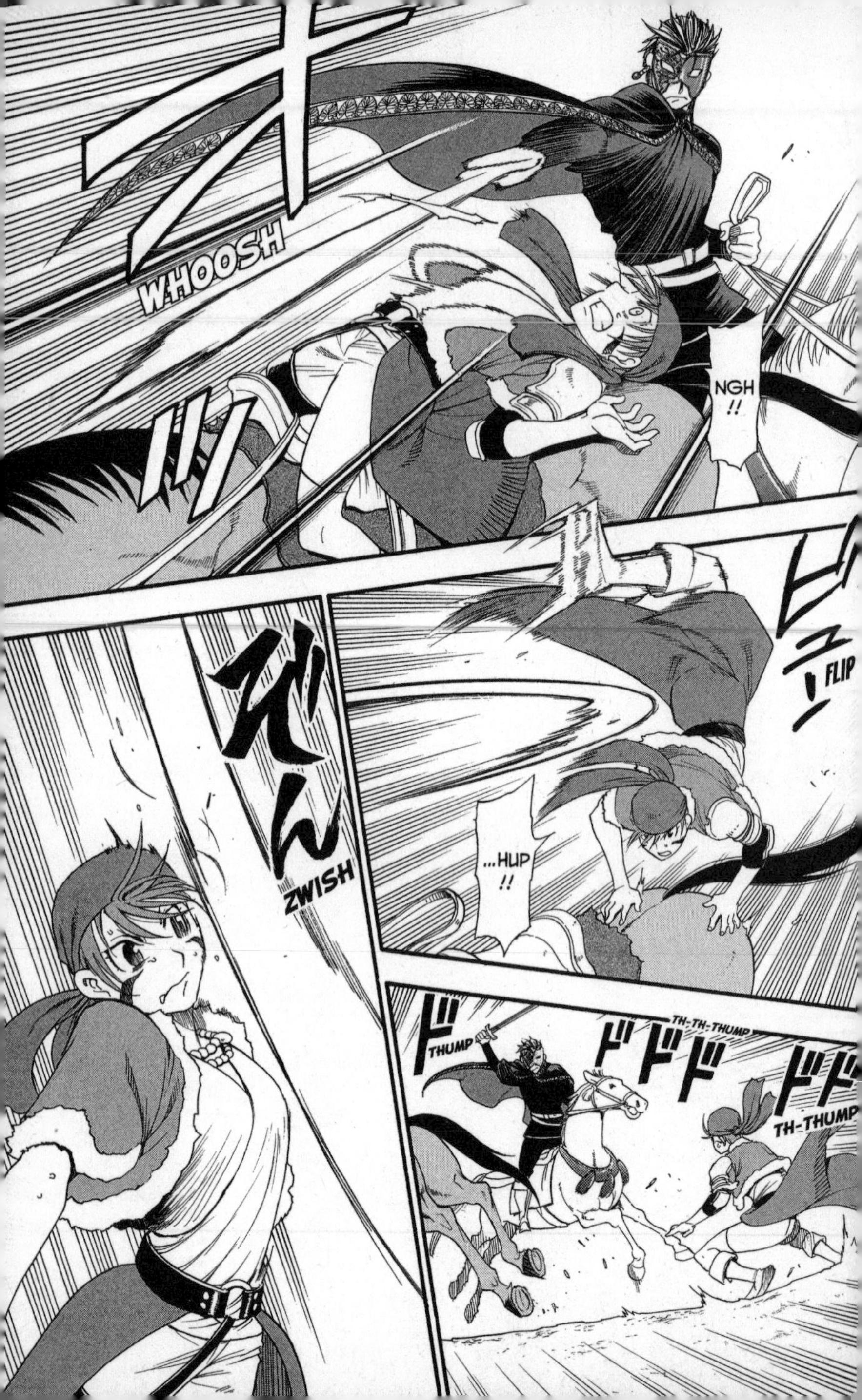
WHOOSH
NGH !!
FLIP
...HUP !!
ZWISH
THUMP
TH-TH-THUMP
TH-THUMP

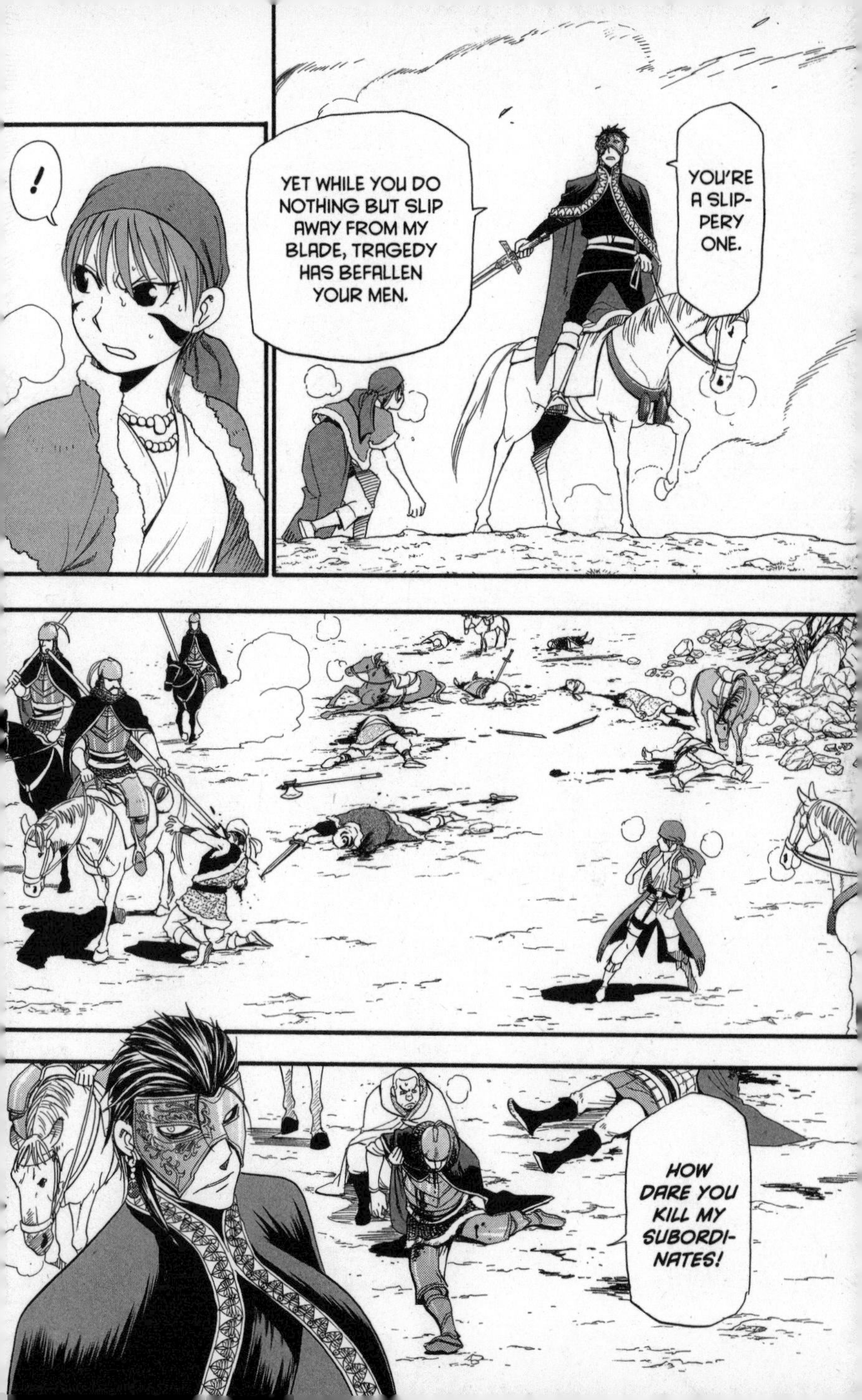
YOU'RE A SLIPPERY ONE.
YET WHILE YOU DO NOTHING BUT SLIP AWAY FROM MY BLADE, TRAGEDY HAS BEFALLEN YOUR MEN.
!
HOW DARE YOU KILL MY SUBORDINATES!

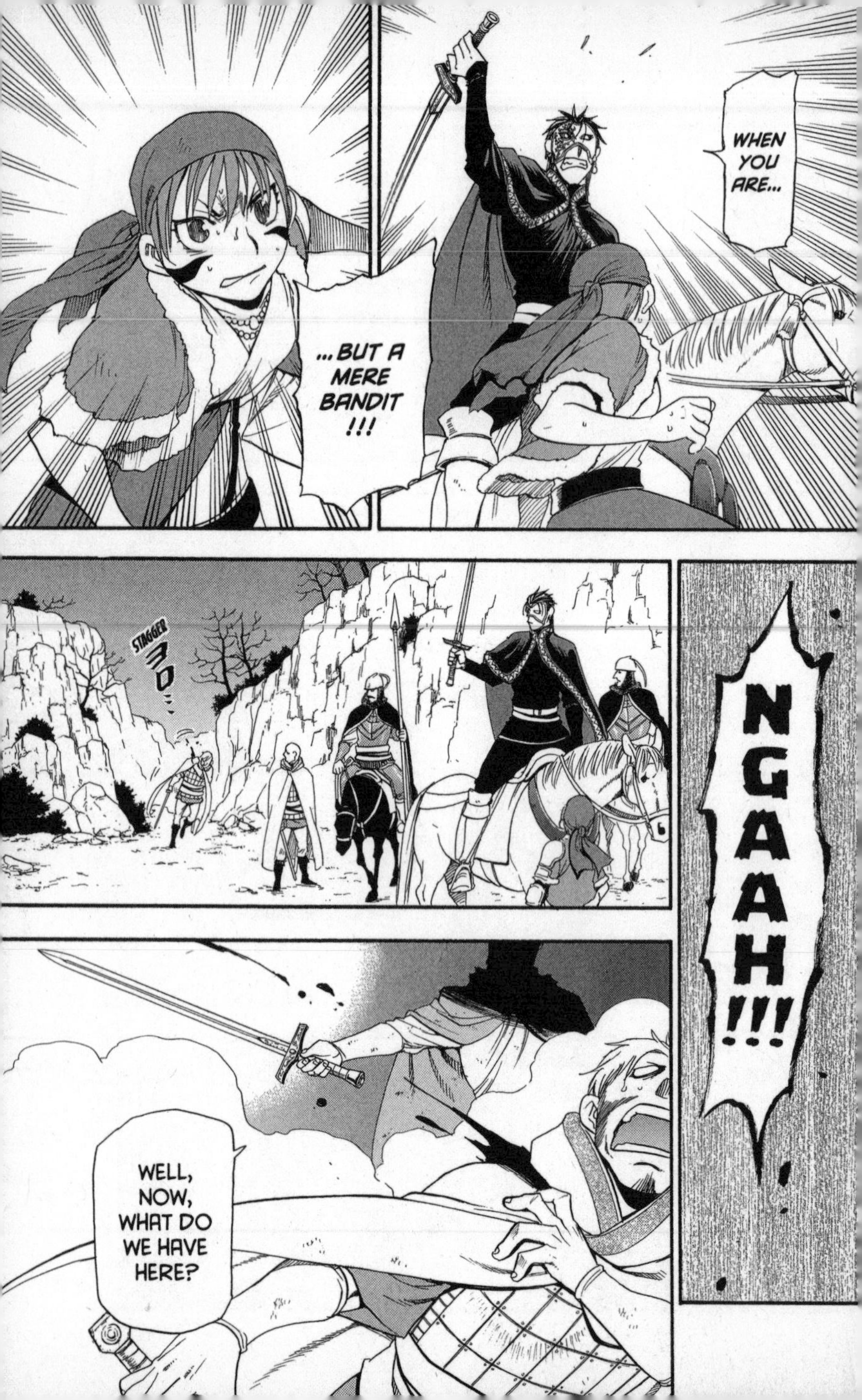
WHEN YOU ARE...
...BUT A MERE BANDIT!!!
NGAAH!!!
STAGGER
ヨロ
WELL, NOW, WHAT DO WE HAVE HERE?

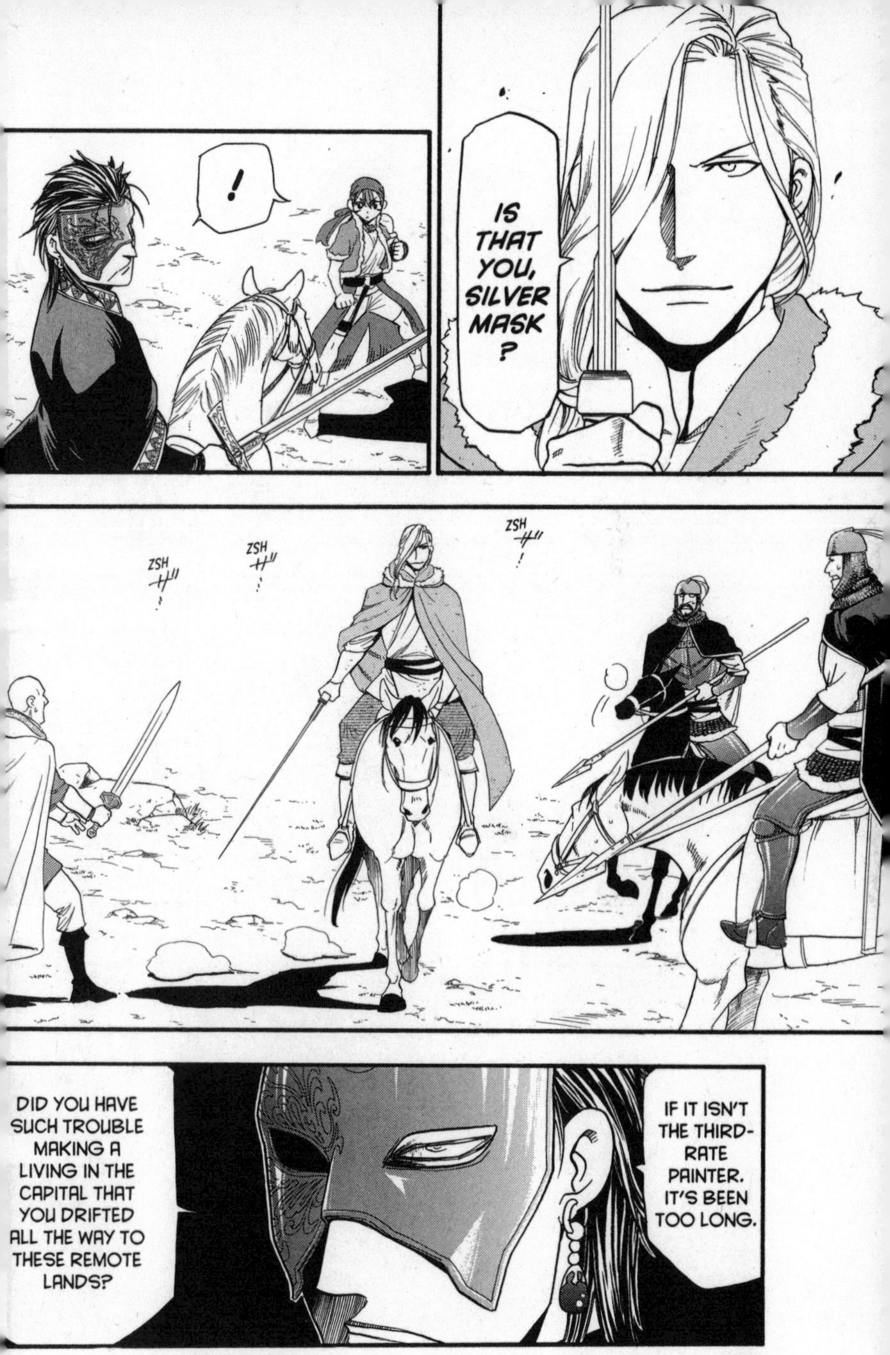
IS THAT YOU, SILVER MASK?
!
ZSH
ZSH
ZSH
IF IT ISN'T THE THIRD-RATE PAINTER. IT'S BEEN TOO LONG.
DID YOU HAVE SUCH TROUBLE MAKING A LIVING IN THE CAPITAL THAT YOU DRIFTED ALL THE WAY TO THESE REMOTE LANDS?

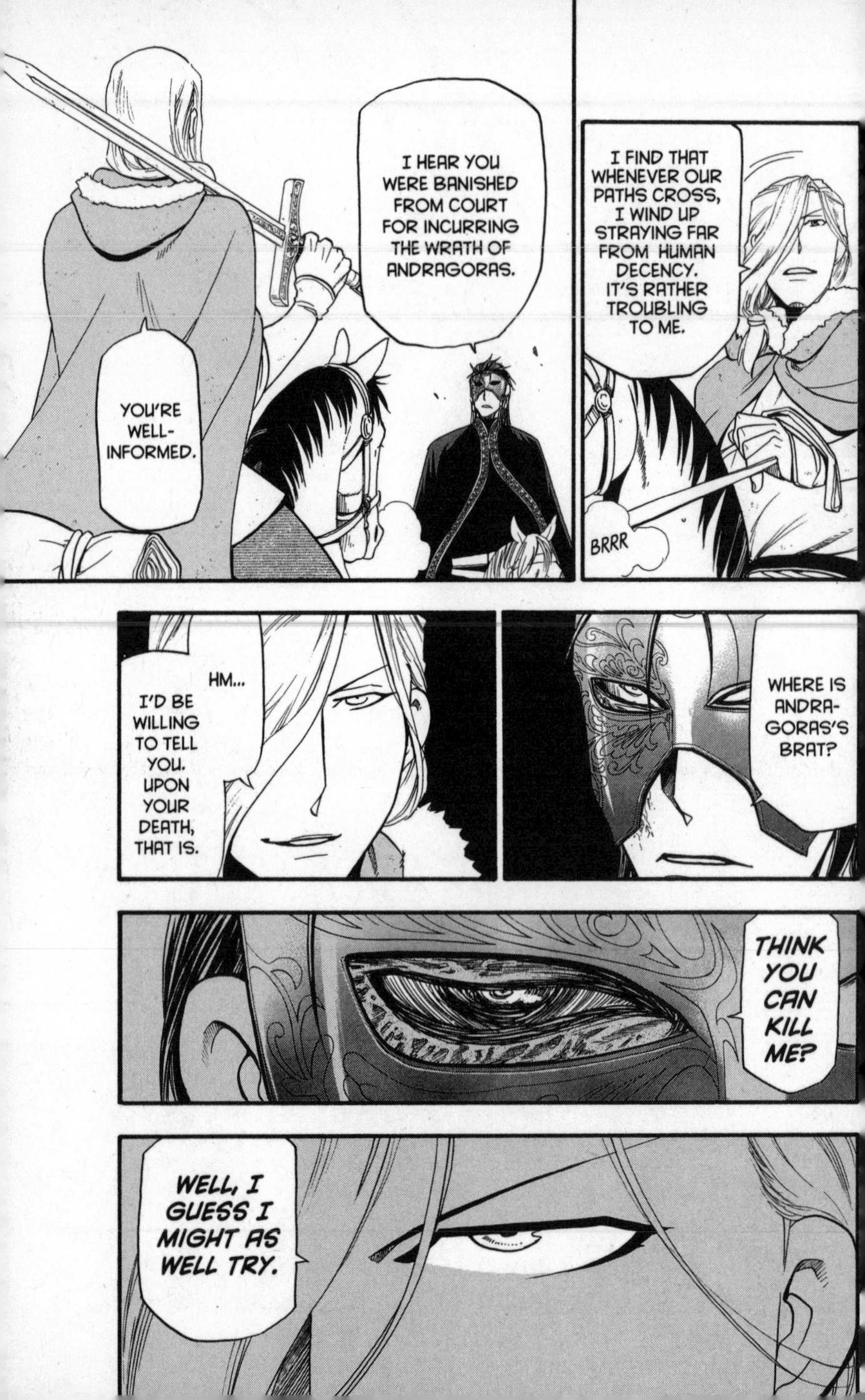
I FIND THAT WHENEVER OUR PATHS CROSS, I WIND UP STRAYING FAR FROM HUMAN DECENCY. IT'S RATHER TROUBLING TO ME.
BRRR
I HEAR YOU WERE BANISHED FROM COURT FOR INCURRING THE WRATH OF ANDRAGORAS.
YOU'RE WELL-INFORMED.
WHERE IS ANDRA-GORAS'S BRAT?
HM...
I'D BE WILLING TO TELL YOU. UPON YOUR DEATH, THAT IS.
THINK YOU CAN KILL ME?
WELL, I GUESS I MIGHT AS WELL TRY.

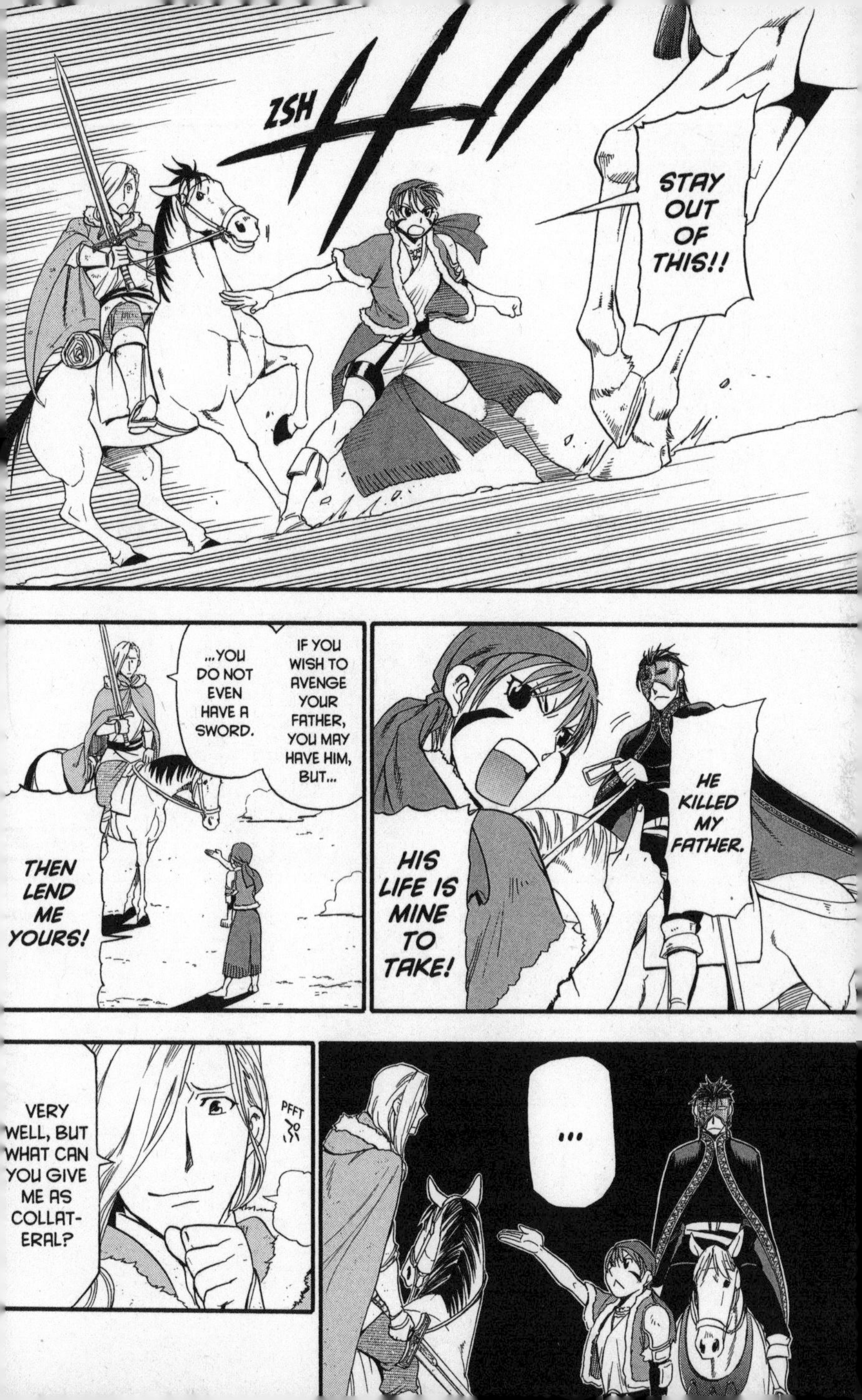
STAY OUT OF THIS!!
ZSH
HE KILLED MY FATHER.
HIS LIFE IS MINE TO TAKE!
IF YOU WISH TO AVENGE YOUR FATHER, YOU MAY HAVE HIM, BUT...
...YOU DO NOT EVEN HAVE A SWORD.
THEN LEND ME YOURS!
...
PFFT
VERY WELL, BUT WHAT CAN YOU GIVE ME AS COLLATERAL?

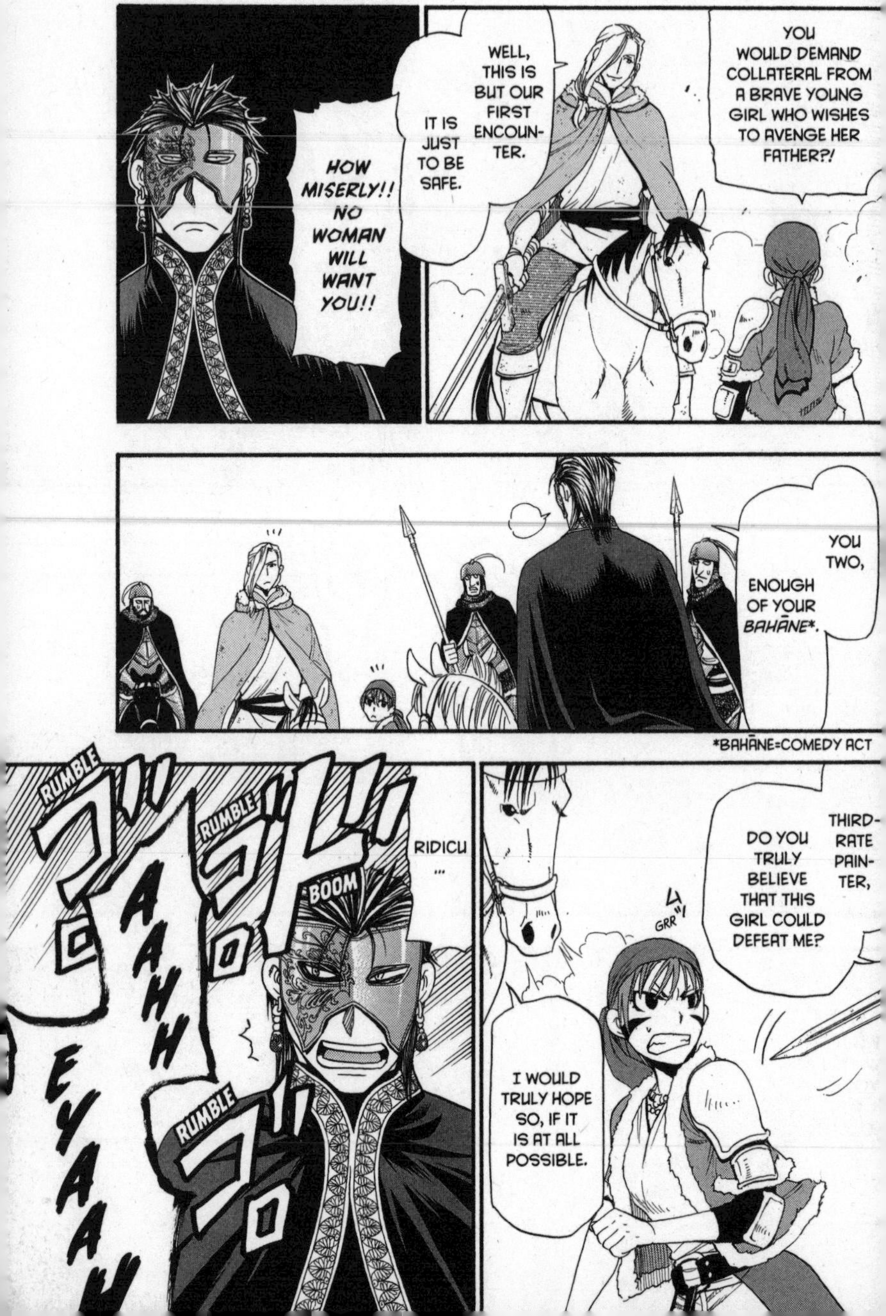
YOU WOULD DEMAND COLLATERAL FROM A BRAVE YOUNG GIRL WHO WISHES TO AVENGE HER FATHER?!
WELL, THIS IS BUT OUR FIRST ENCOUNTER.
IT IS JUST TO BE SAFE.
HOW MISERLY!! NO WOMAN WILL WANT YOU!!
YOU TWO, ENOUGH OF YOUR *BAHANE**.
THIRD-RATE PAINTER,
DO YOU TRULY BELIEVE THAT THIS GIRL COULD DEFEAT ME?
GRR
I WOULD TRULY HOPE SO, IF IT IS AT ALL POSSIBLE.
RIDICU ...
RUMBLE
RUMBLE
BOOM
RUMBLE

*BAHĀNE=COMEDY ACT

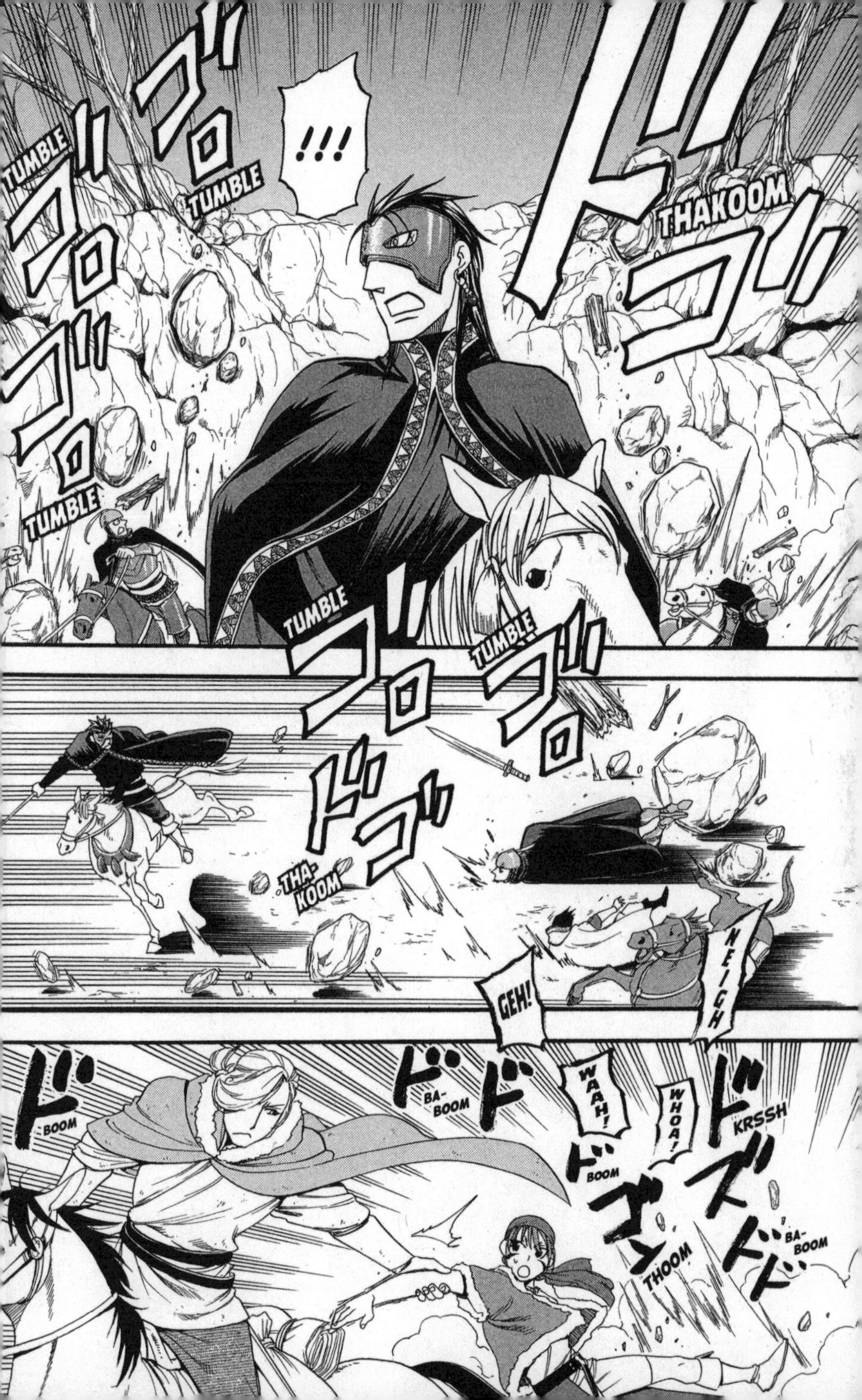

THAKOOM
!!!
TUMBLE
TUMBLE
TUMBLE
TUMBLE
TUMBLE
NEIGH
GEH!
THA-KOOM
KRSSH
BA-BOOM
THOOM
WHOA!
WAAH!
BOOM
BA-BOOM
BOOM

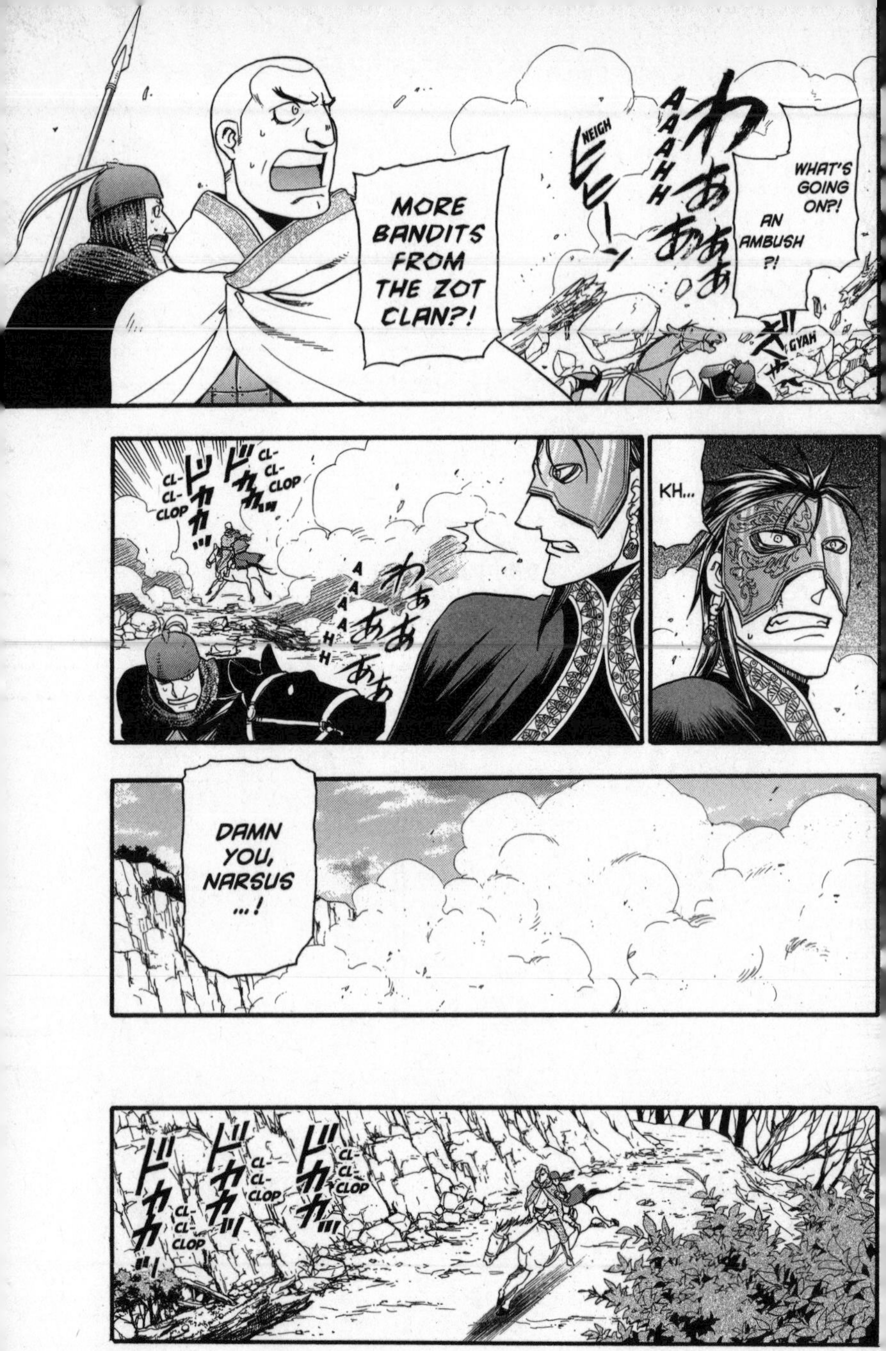
WHAT'S GOING ON?!
AN AMBUSH?!
AAAAHH
NEIGH
GYAH
MORE BANDITS FROM THE ZOT CLAN?!
KH...
AAAAHH
CL-CL-CLOP
CL-CL-CLOP
DAMN YOU, NARSUS ...!
CL-CL-CLOP
CL-CL-CLOP
CL-CL-CLOP

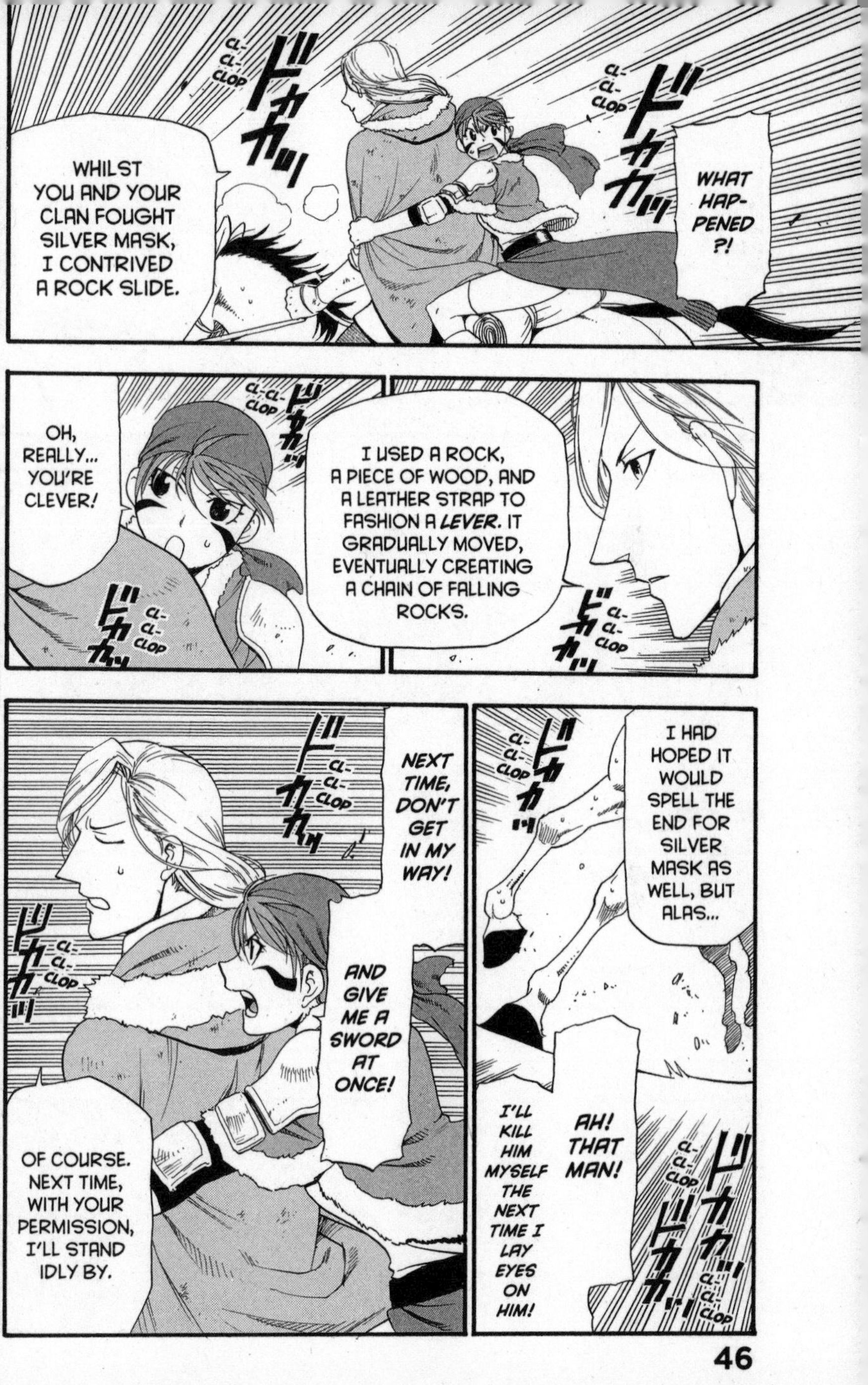
CL-CL-CLOP
WHAT HAPPENED?!
CL-CL-CLOP
WHILST YOU AND YOUR CLAN FOUGHT SILVER MASK, I CONTRIVED A ROCK SLIDE.
I USED A ROCK, A PIECE OF WOOD, AND A LEATHER STRAP TO FASHION A *LEVER*. IT GRADUALLY MOVED, EVENTUALLY CREATING A CHAIN OF FALLING ROCKS.
CL-CL-CLOP
CL-CL-CLOP
OH, REALLY... YOU'RE CLEVER!
CL-CL-CLOP
I HAD HOPED IT WOULD SPELL THE END FOR SILVER MASK AS WELL, BUT ALAS...
CL-CL-CLOP
AH! THAT MAN!
I'LL KILL HIM MYSELF THE NEXT TIME I LAY EYES ON HIM!
CL-CL-CLOP
CL-CL-CLOP
NEXT TIME, DON'T GET IN MY WAY!
CL-CL-CLOP
AND GIVE ME A SWORD AT ONCE!
CL-CL-CLOP
OF COURSE. NEXT TIME, WITH YOUR PERMISSION, I'LL STAND IDLY BY.

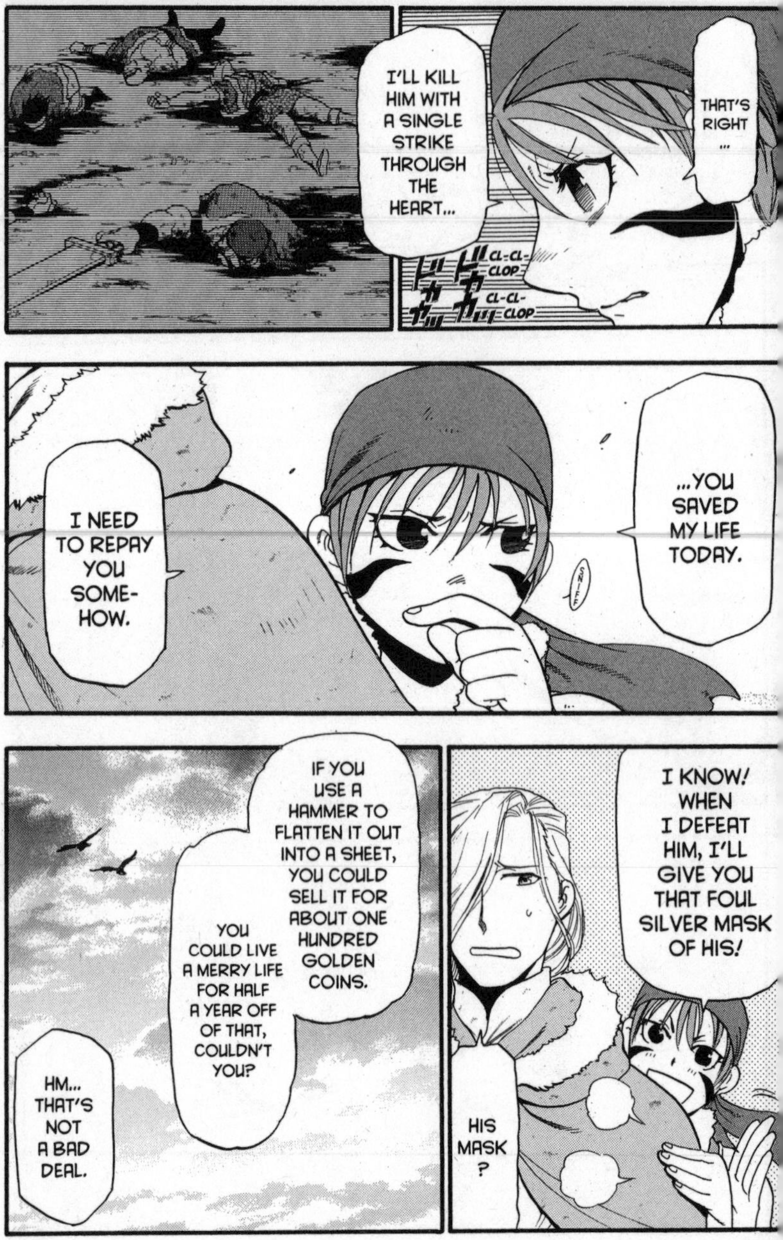
THAT'S RIGHT ...
I'LL KILL HIM WITH A SINGLE STRIKE THROUGH THE HEART...
CL-CL-CLOP
CL-CL-CLOP
...YOU SAVED MY LIFE TODAY.
SNIFF
I NEED TO REPAY YOU SOMEHOW.
I KNOW! WHEN I DEFEAT HIM, I'LL GIVE YOU THAT FOUL SILVER MASK OF HIS!
HIS MASK?
IF YOU USE A HAMMER TO FLATTEN IT OUT INTO A SHEET, YOU COULD SELL IT FOR ABOUT ONE HUNDRED GOLDEN COINS.
YOU COULD LIVE A MERRY LIFE FOR HALF A YEAR OFF OF THAT, COULDN'T YOU?
HM... THAT'S NOT A BAD DEAL.

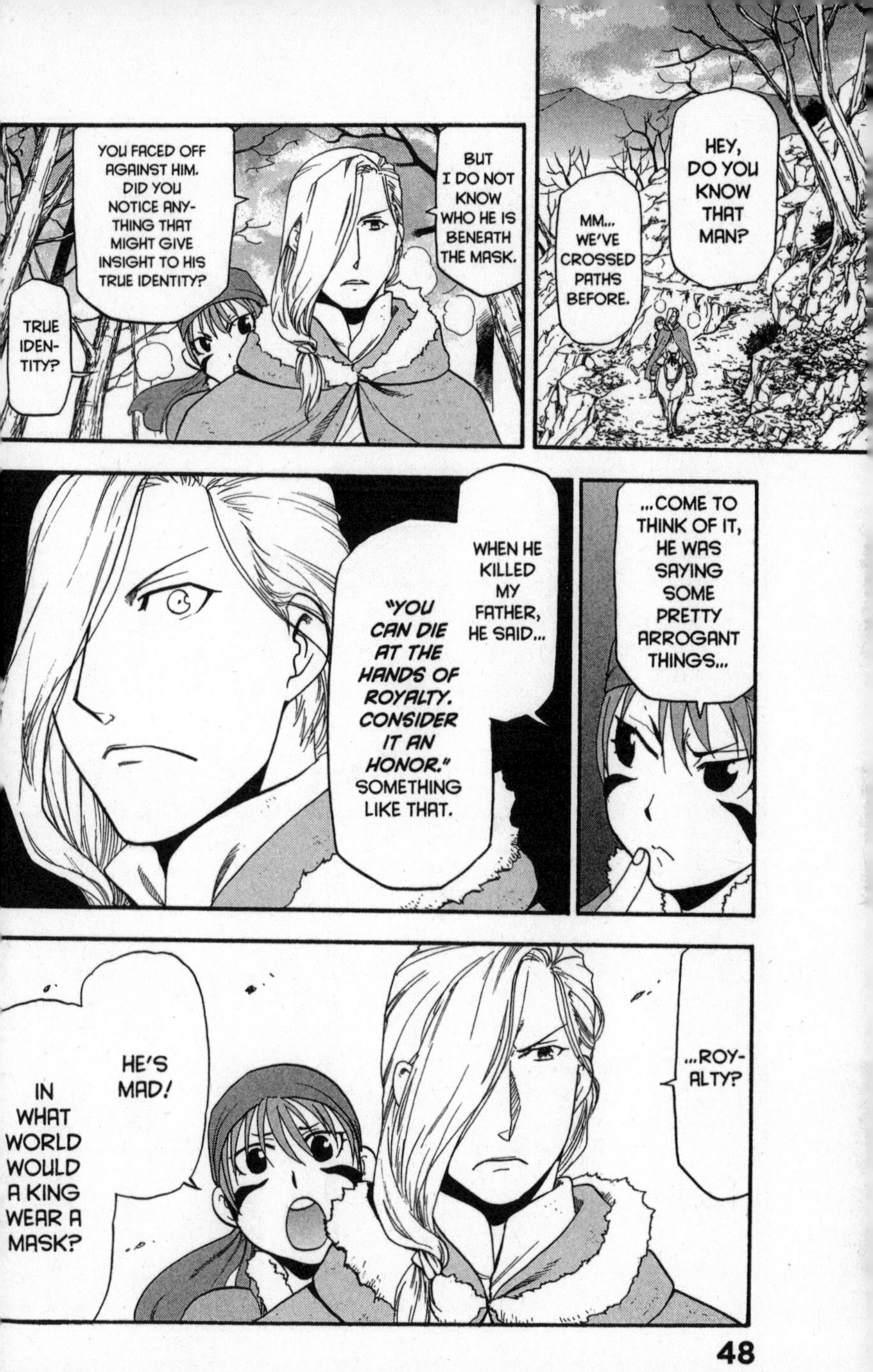
HEY, DO YOU KNOW THAT MAN?
MM... WE'VE CROSSED PATHS BEFORE.
BUT I DO NOT KNOW WHO HE IS BENEATH THE MASK.
YOU FACED OFF AGAINST HIM. DID YOU NOTICE ANY-THING THAT MIGHT GIVE INSIGHT TO HIS TRUE IDENTITY?
TRUE IDEN-TITY?
...COME TO THINK OF IT, HE WAS SAYING SOME PRETTY ARROGANT THINGS...
WHEN HE KILLED MY FATHER, HE SAID...
"YOU CAN DIE AT THE HANDS OF ROYALTY. CONSIDER IT AN HONOR." SOMETHING LIKE THAT.
...ROY-ALTY?
HE'S MAD!
IN WHAT WORLD WOULD A KING WEAR A MASK?

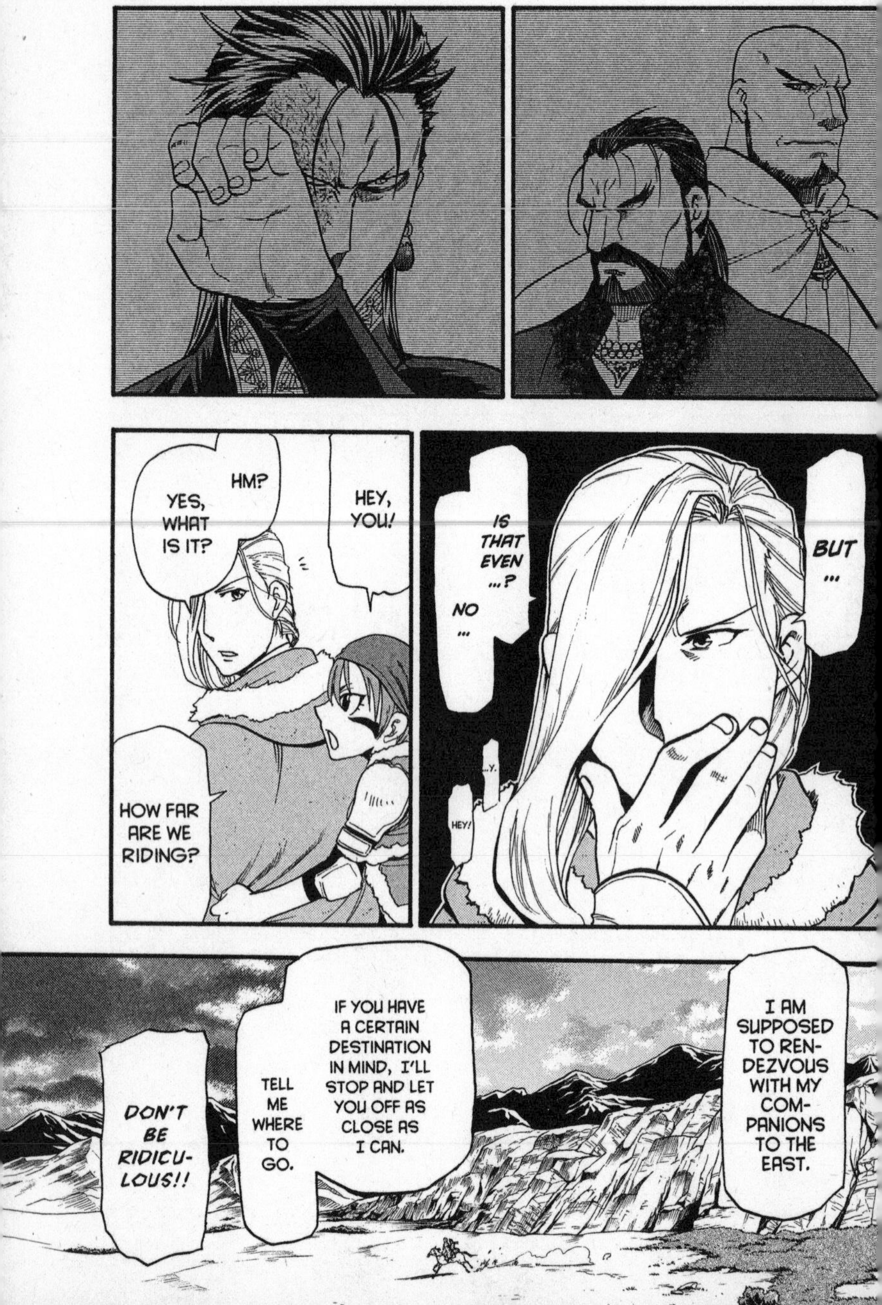
BUT ...
IS THAT EVEN ...?
NO ...
...Y.
HEY!
HEY, YOU!
HM? YES, WHAT IS IT?
HOW FAR ARE WE RIDING?
I AM SUPPOSED TO REN-DEZVOUS WITH MY COM-PANIONS TO THE EAST.
IF YOU HAVE A CERTAIN DESTINATION IN MIND, I'LL STOP AND LET YOU OFF AS CLOSE AS I CAN.
TELL ME WHERE TO GO.
DON'T BE RIDICU-LOUS!!

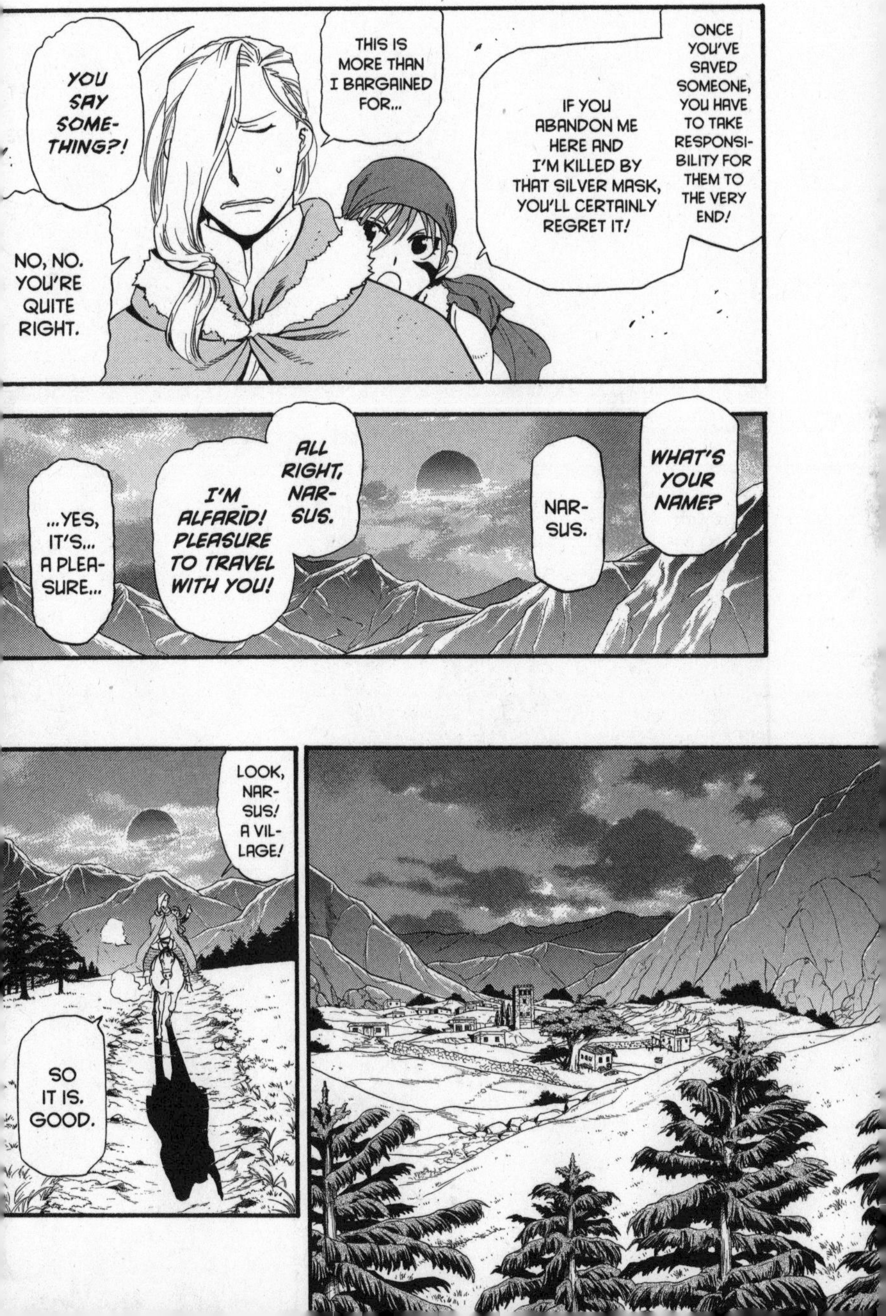
ONCE YOU'VE SAVED SOMEONE, YOU HAVE TO TAKE RESPONSI-BILITY FOR THEM TO THE VERY END!
IF YOU ABANDON ME HERE AND I'M KILLED BY THAT SILVER MASK, YOU'LL CERTAINLY REGRET IT!
THIS IS MORE THAN I BARGAINED FOR...
YOU SAY SOME-THING?!
NO, NO. YOU'RE QUITE RIGHT.
WHAT'S YOUR NAME?
NAR-SUS.
ALL RIGHT, NAR-SUS.
I'M ALFARĪD! PLEASURE TO TRAVEL WITH YOU!
...YES, IT'S... A PLEA-SURE...
LOOK, NAR-SUS! A VIL-LAGE!
SO IT IS. GOOD.

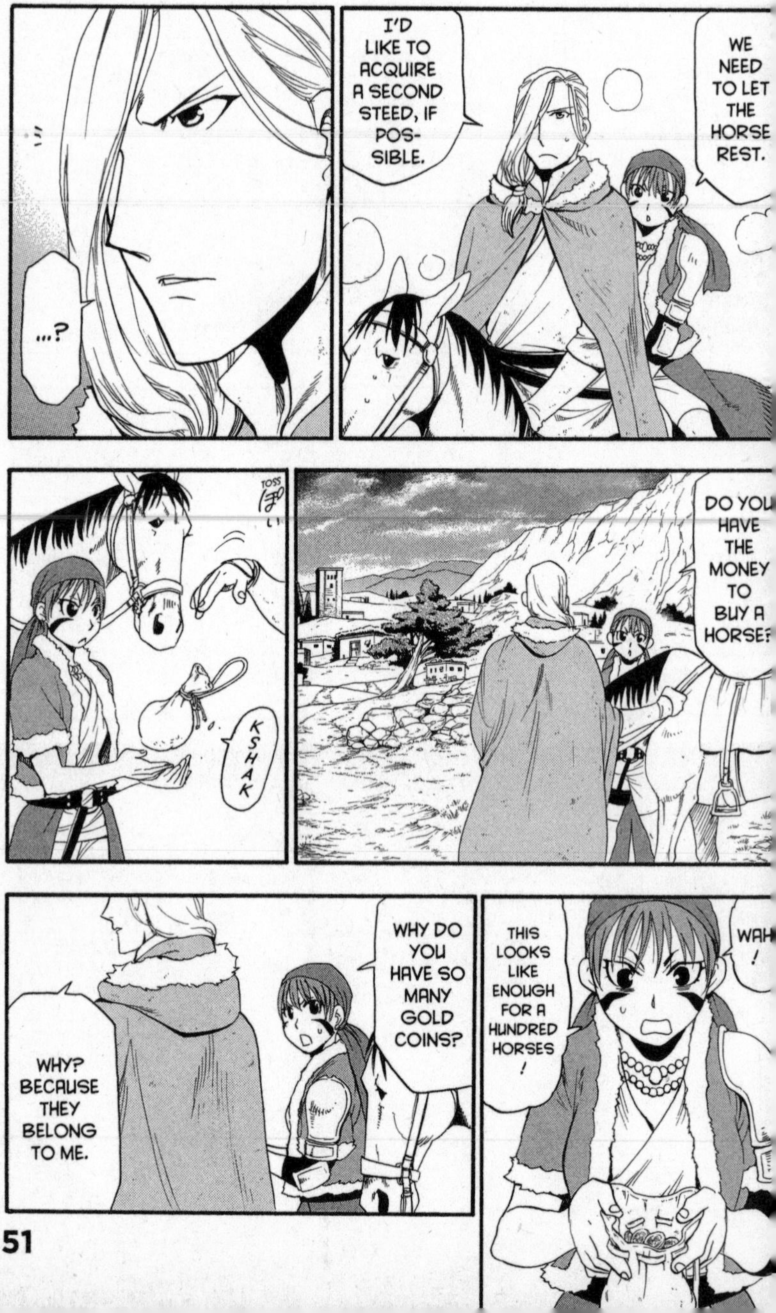
WE NEED TO LET THE HORSE REST.
I'D LIKE TO ACQUIRE A SECOND STEED, IF POS-SIBLE.
...?
DO YOU HAVE THE MONEY TO BUY A HORSE?
TOSS
KSHAK
WAH!
THIS LOOKS LIKE ENOUGH FOR A HUNDRED HORSES!
WHY DO YOU HAVE SO MANY GOLD COINS?
WHY? BECAUSE THEY BELONG TO ME.

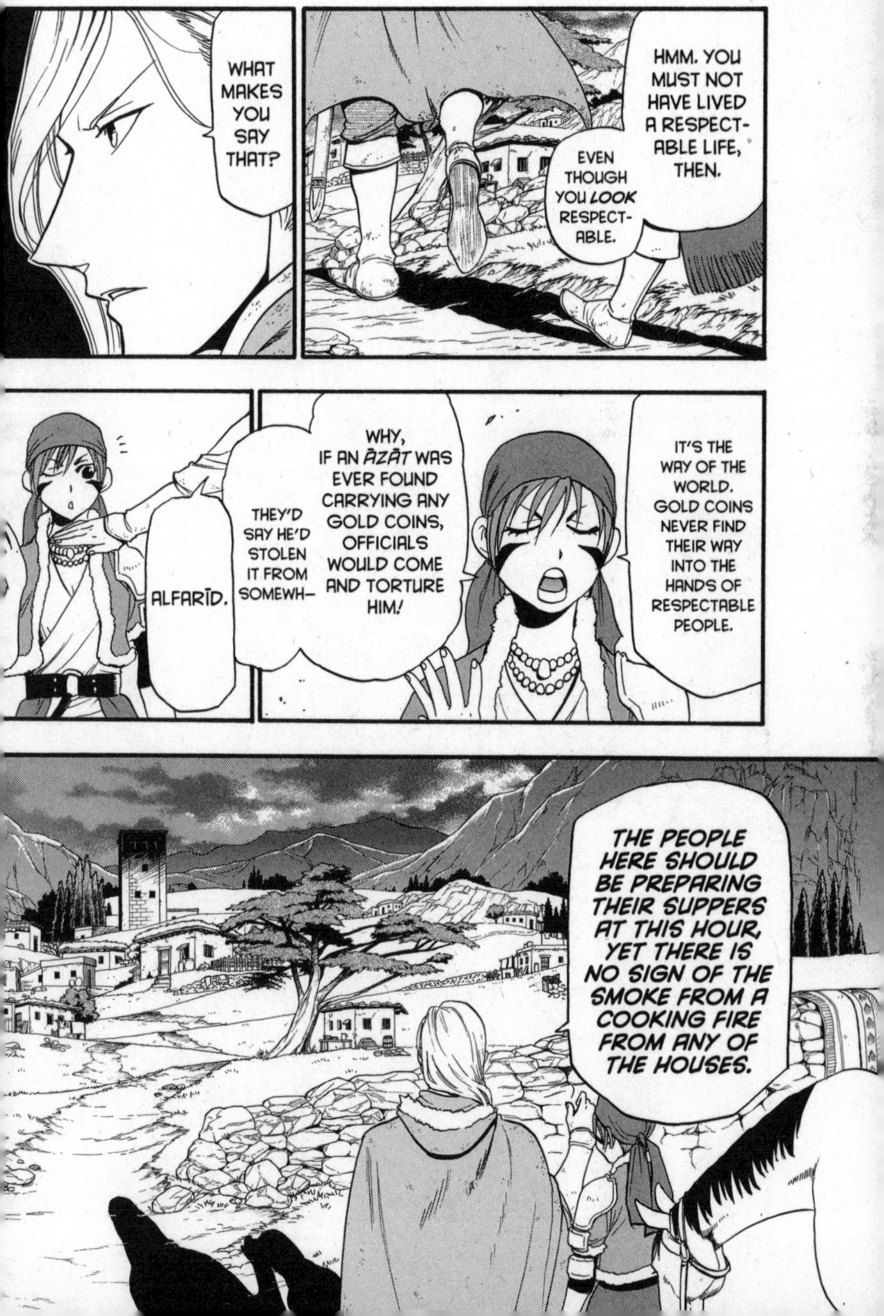
HMM. YOU MUST NOT HAVE LIVED A RESPECTABLE LIFE, THEN.
EVEN THOUGH YOU *LOOK* RESPECTABLE.
WHAT MAKES YOU SAY THAT?
IT'S THE WAY OF THE WORLD. GOLD COINS NEVER FIND THEIR WAY INTO THE HANDS OF RESPECTABLE PEOPLE.
WHY, IF AN *ĀZĀT* WAS EVER FOUND CARRYING ANY GOLD COINS, OFFICIALS WOULD COME AND TORTURE HIM!
THEY'D SAY HE'D STOLEN IT FROM SOMEWH–
ALFARĪD.
THE PEOPLE HERE SHOULD BE PREPARING THEIR SUPPERS AT THIS HOUR, YET THERE IS NO SIGN OF THE SMOKE FROM A COOKING FIRE FROM ANY OF THE HOUSES.

MORE THAN A LACK OF SMOKE, THERE'S NOT A SINGLE LIGHT TO BE SEEN...

...

BRRR

TUG

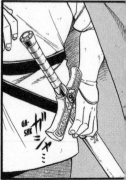

GA-SHK

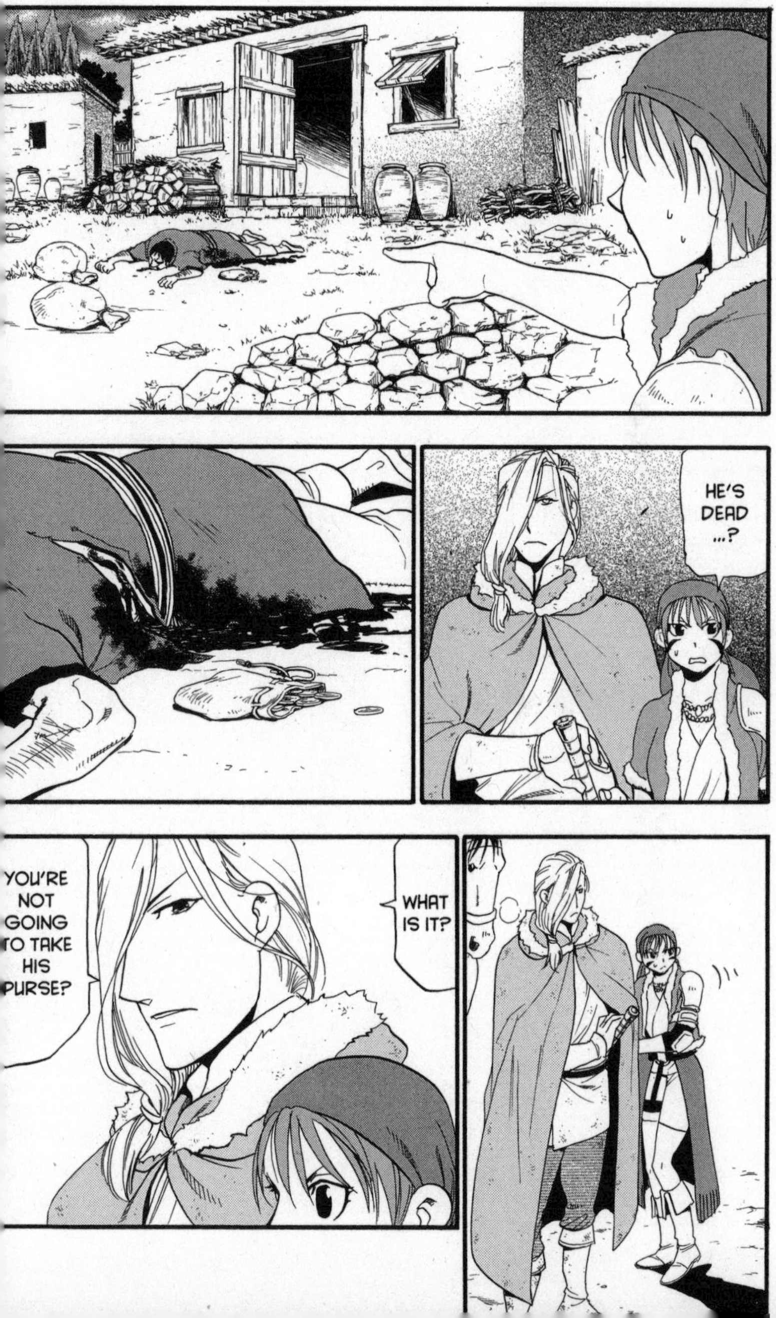
HE'S DEAD ...?
WHAT IS IT?
YOU'RE NOT GOING TO TAKE HIS PURSE?

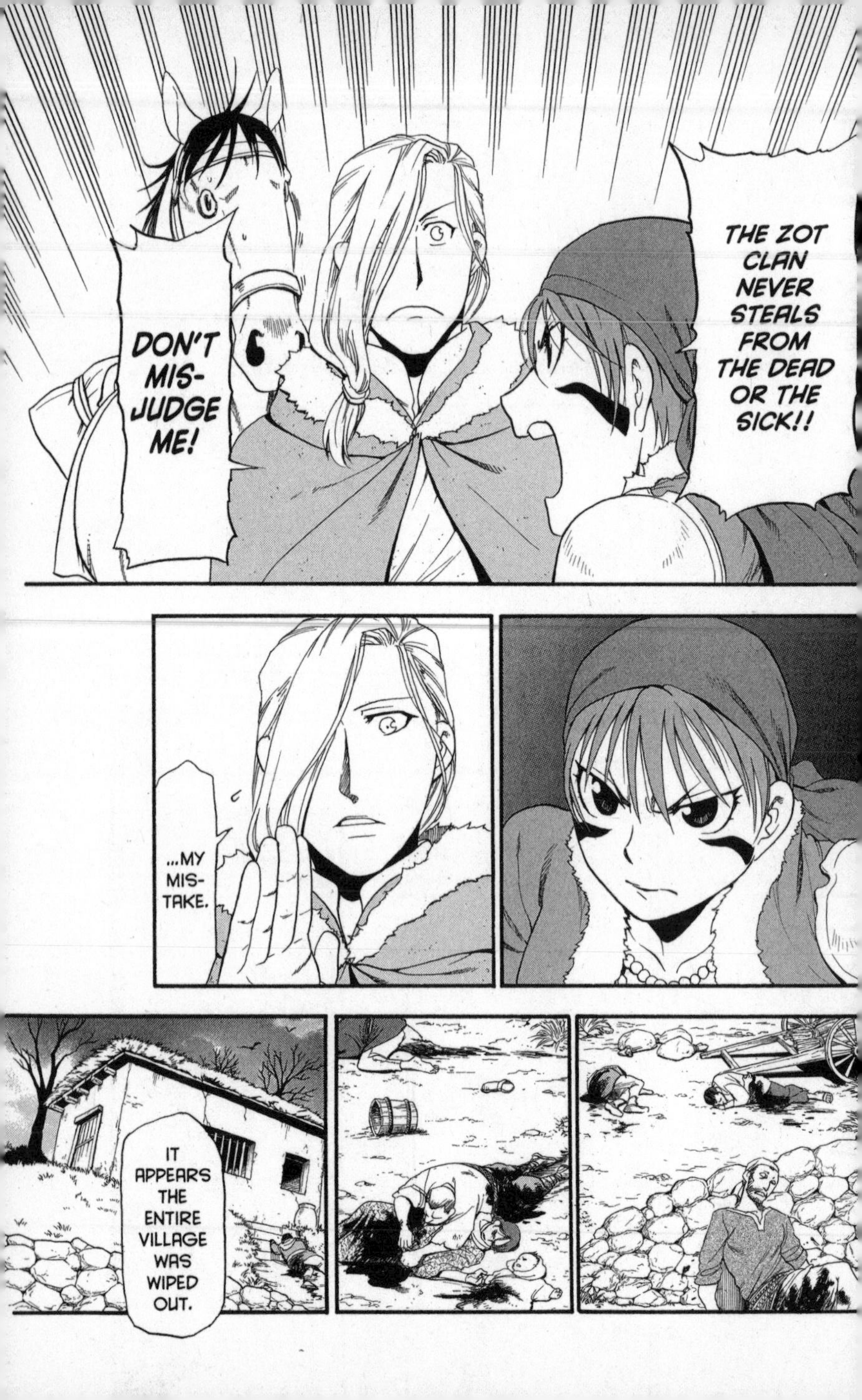
THE ZOT CLAN NEVER STEALS FROM THE DEAD OR THE SICK!!
DON'T MIS-JUDGE ME!
...MY MIS-TAKE.
IT APPEARS THE ENTIRE VILLAGE WAS WIPED OUT.

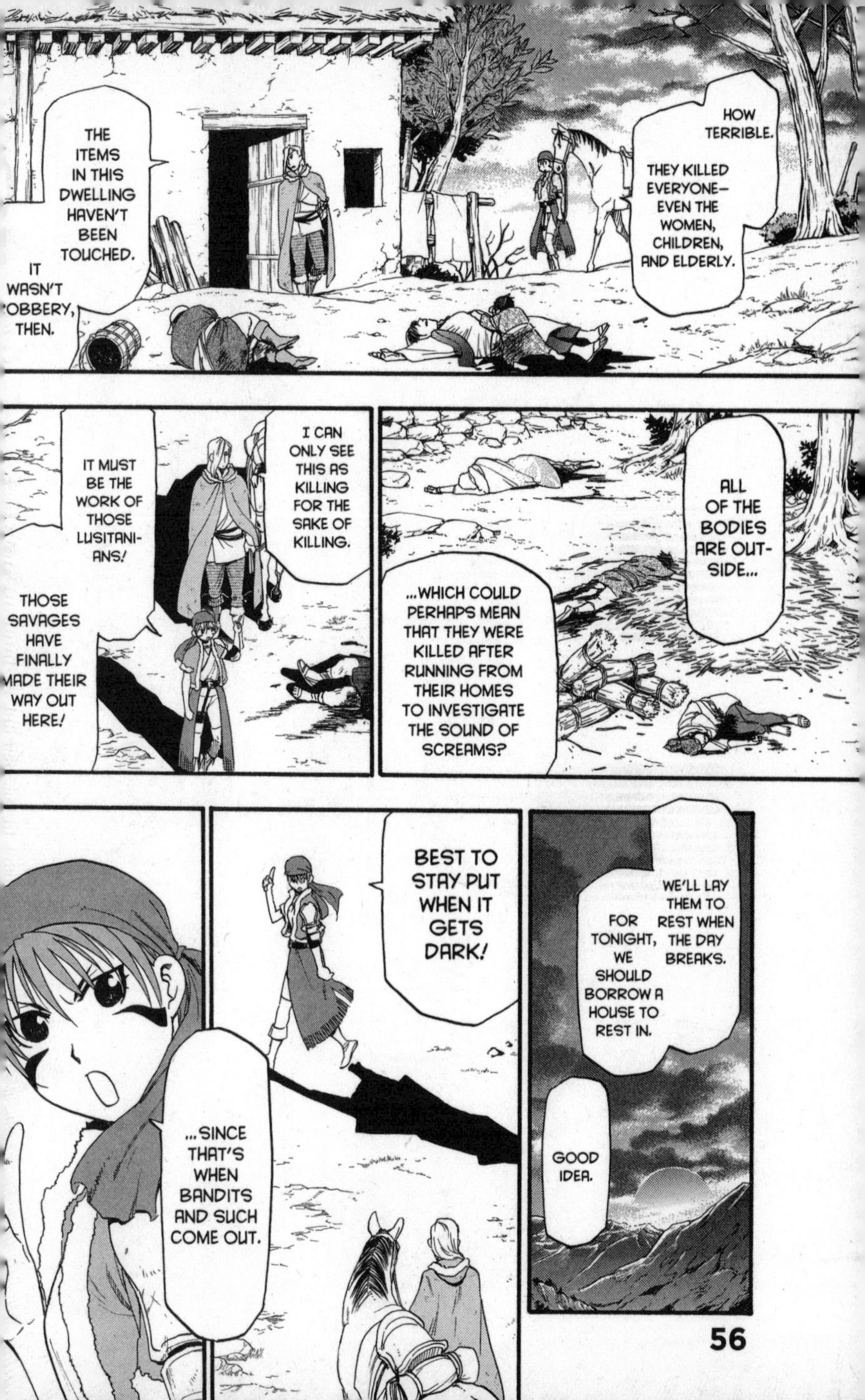
HOW TERRIBLE.
THEY KILLED EVERYONE— EVEN THE WOMEN, CHILDREN, AND ELDERLY.
THE ITEMS IN THIS DWELLING HAVEN'T BEEN TOUCHED.
IT WASN'T OBBERY, THEN.
ALL OF THE BODIES ARE OUT-SIDE...
...WHICH COULD PERHAPS MEAN THAT THEY WERE KILLED AFTER RUNNING FROM THEIR HOMES TO INVESTIGATE THE SOUND OF SCREAMS?
I CAN ONLY SEE THIS AS KILLING FOR THE SAKE OF KILLING.
IT MUST BE THE WORK OF THOSE LUSITANI-ANS!
THOSE SAVAGES HAVE FINALLY MADE THEIR WAY OUT HERE!
WE'LL LAY THEM TO REST WHEN THE DAY BREAKS.
FOR TONIGHT, WE SHOULD BORROW A HOUSE TO REST IN.
GOOD IDEA.
BEST TO STAY PUT WHEN IT GETS DARK!
...SINCE THAT'S WHEN BANDITS AND SUCH COME OUT.

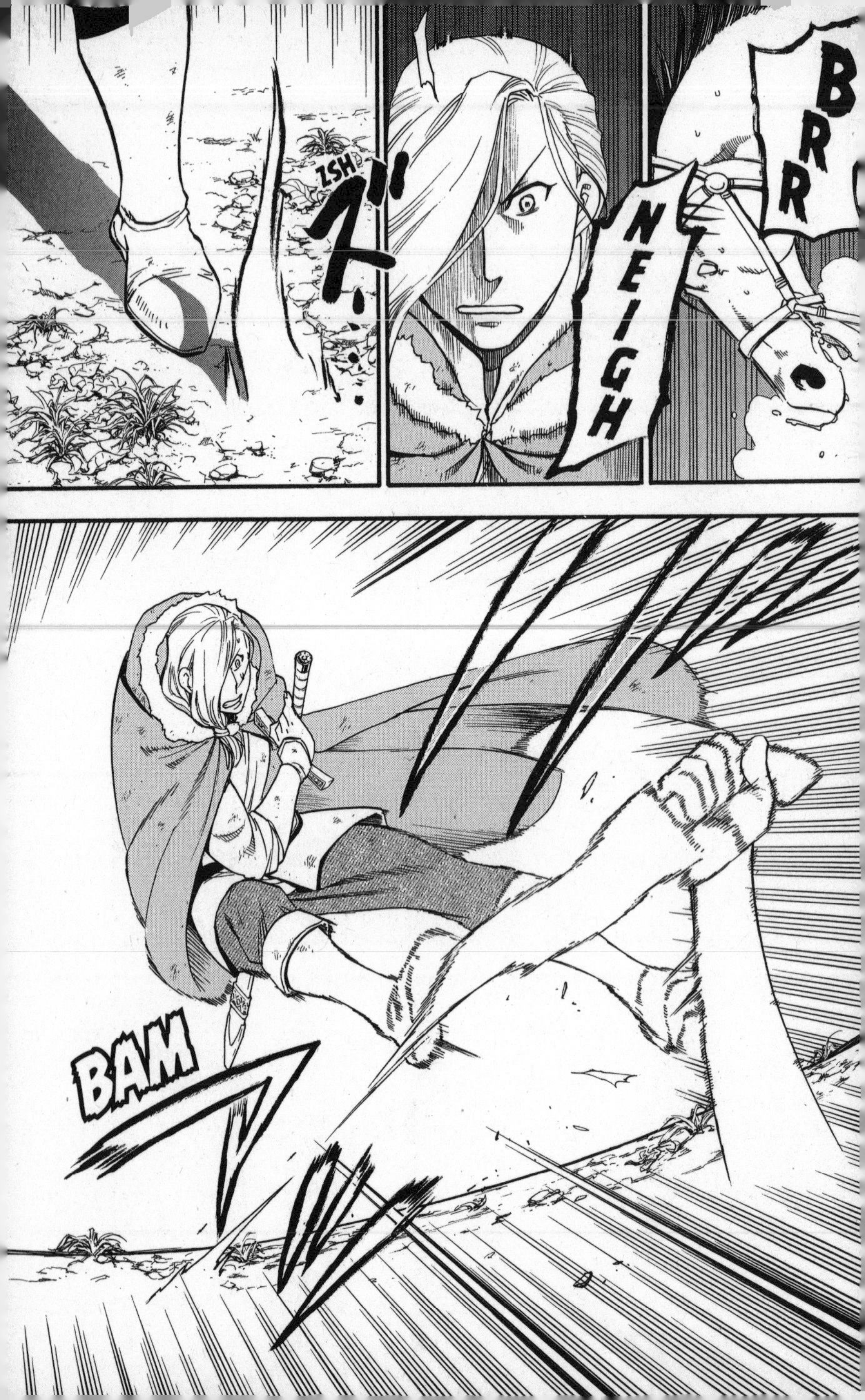
BRRR
NEIGH
ZSH
BAM

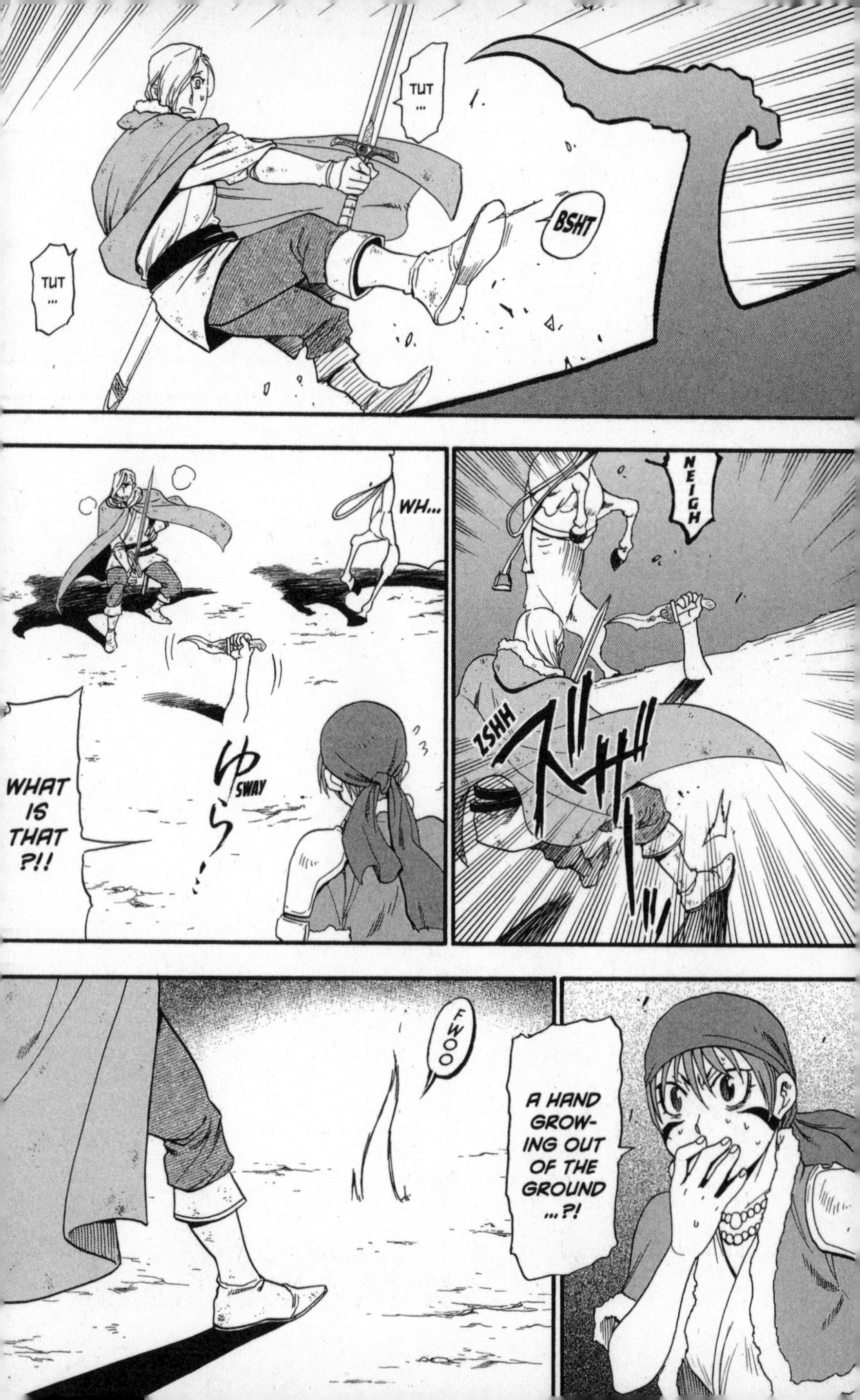
BSHT
TUT ...
TUT ...
NEIGH
ZSHH
WH...
ゆら
SWAY
WHAT IS THAT ?!!
A HAND GROWING OUT OF THE GROUND ...?!
FWOO

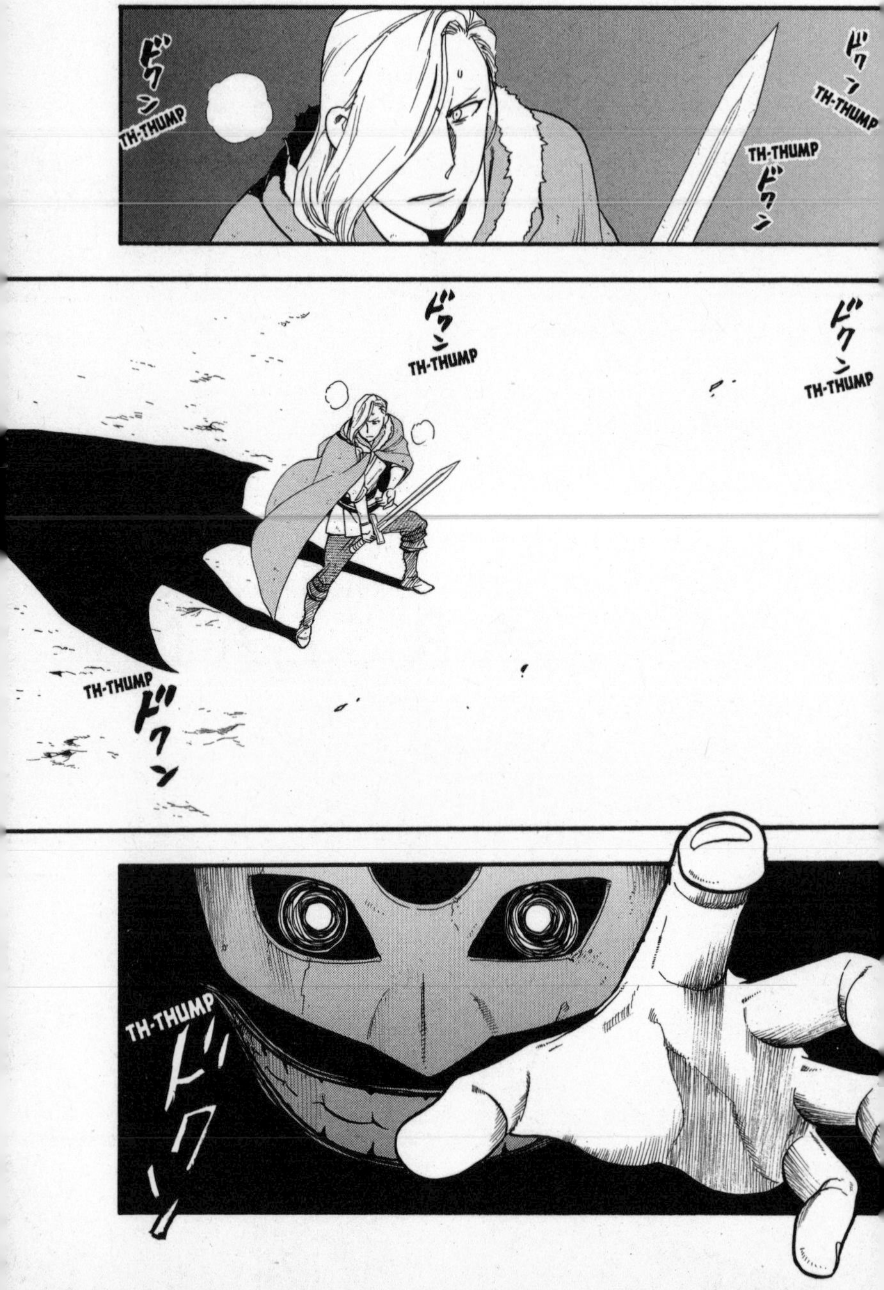
ドクン
TH-THUMP
TH-THUMP
ドクン
ドクン
TH-THUMP
ドクン
TH-THUMP
ドクン
TH-THUMP
TH-THUMP
ドクン
TH-THUMP
ドクン

THE HEROIC LEGEND OF
ARSLAN

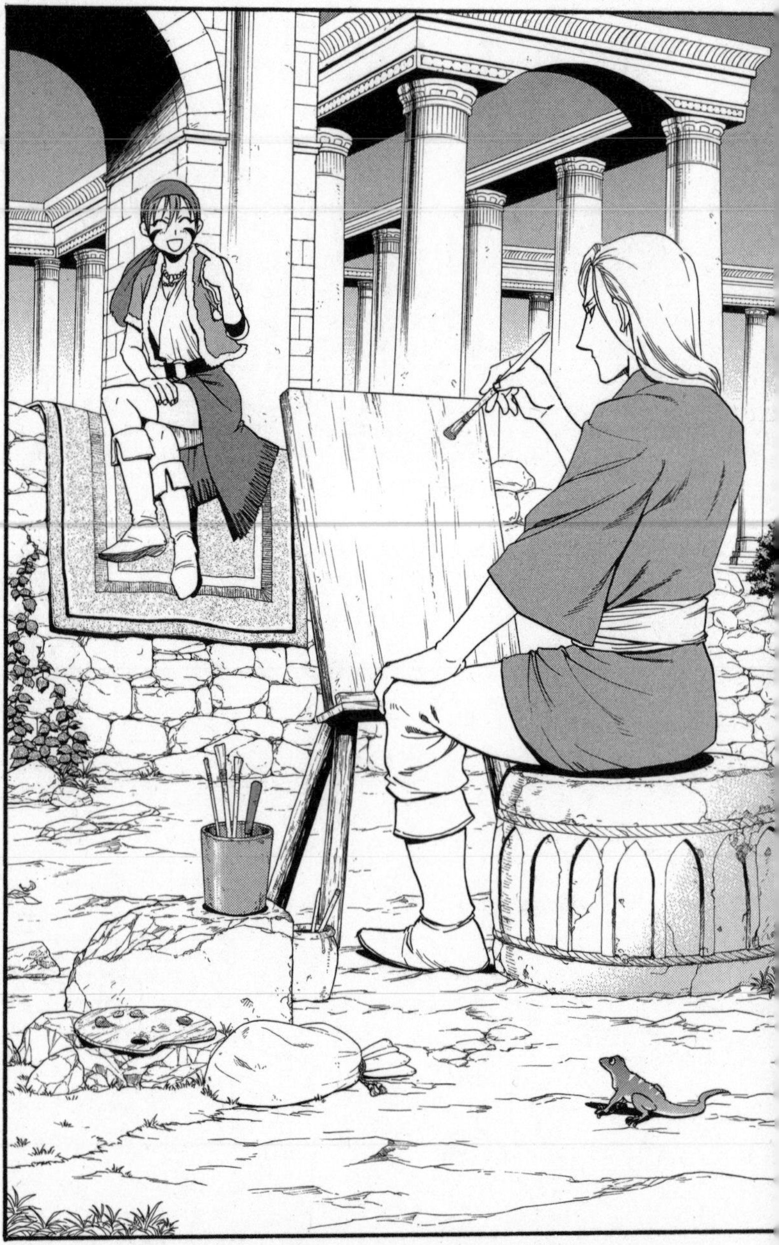

Chapter 30: Shadow of the Snake King

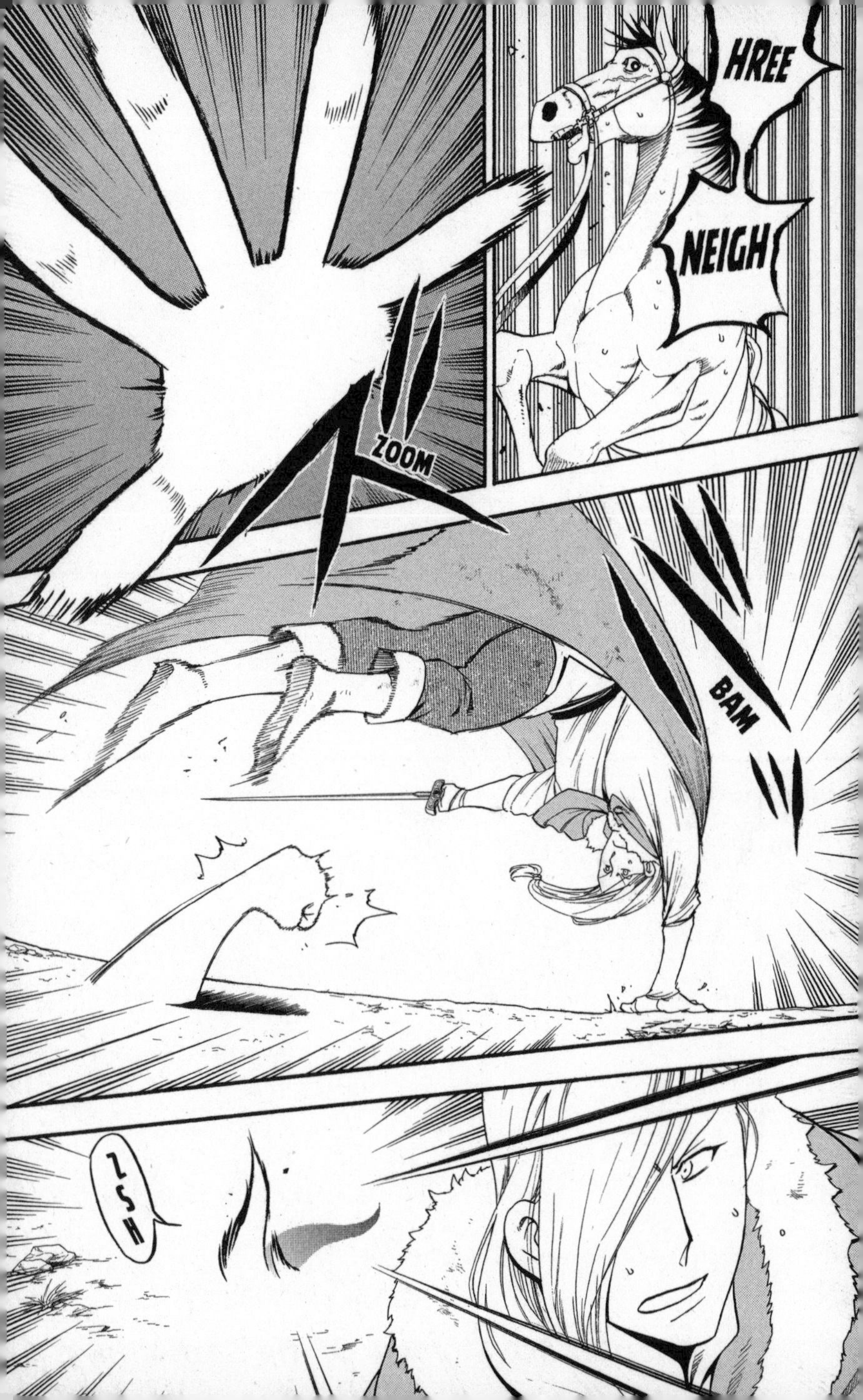
HREE
NEIGH
ZOOM
BAM
ZSH

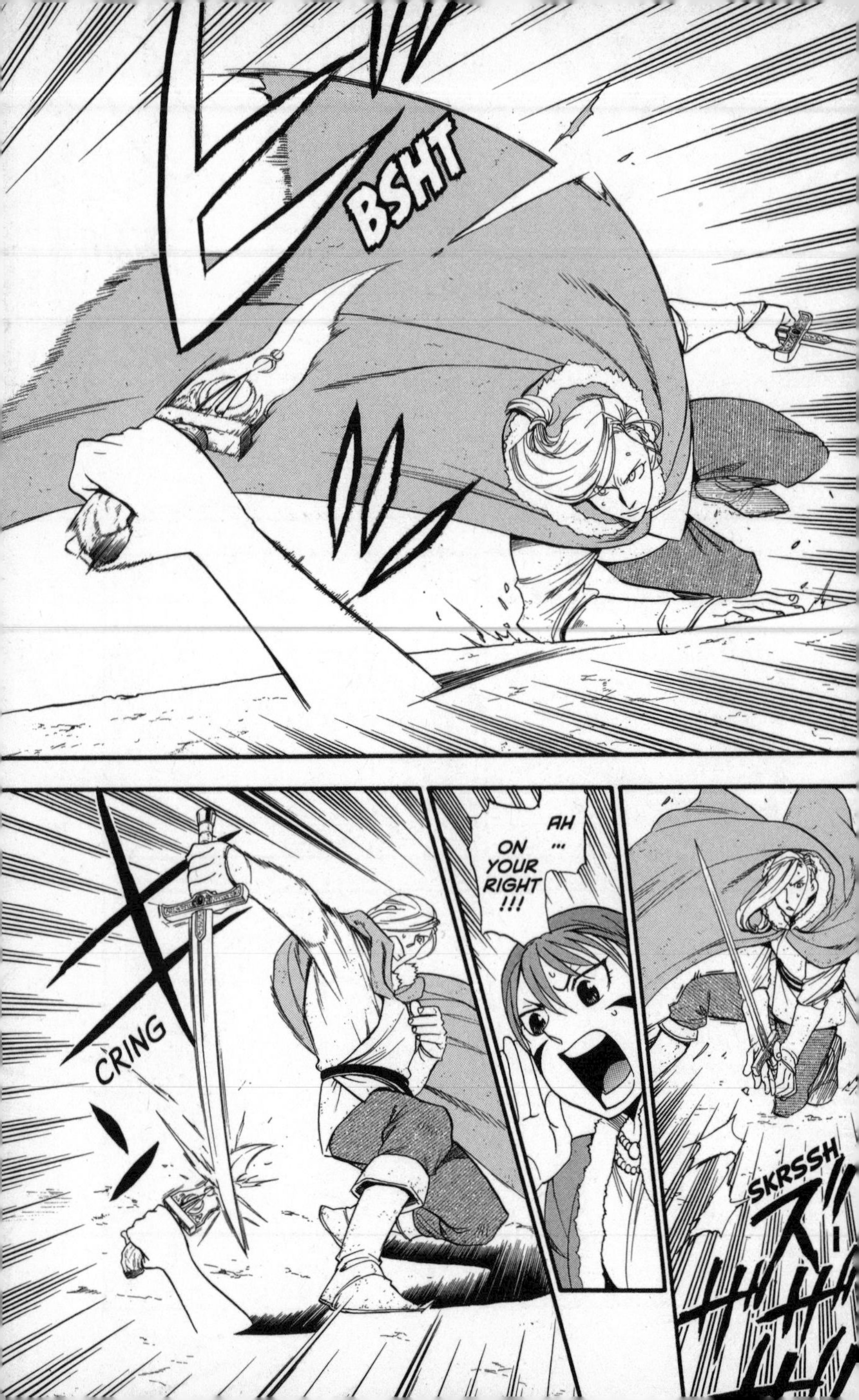
BSHT
SKRSSH
AH ...
ON YOUR RIGHT !!!
CRING

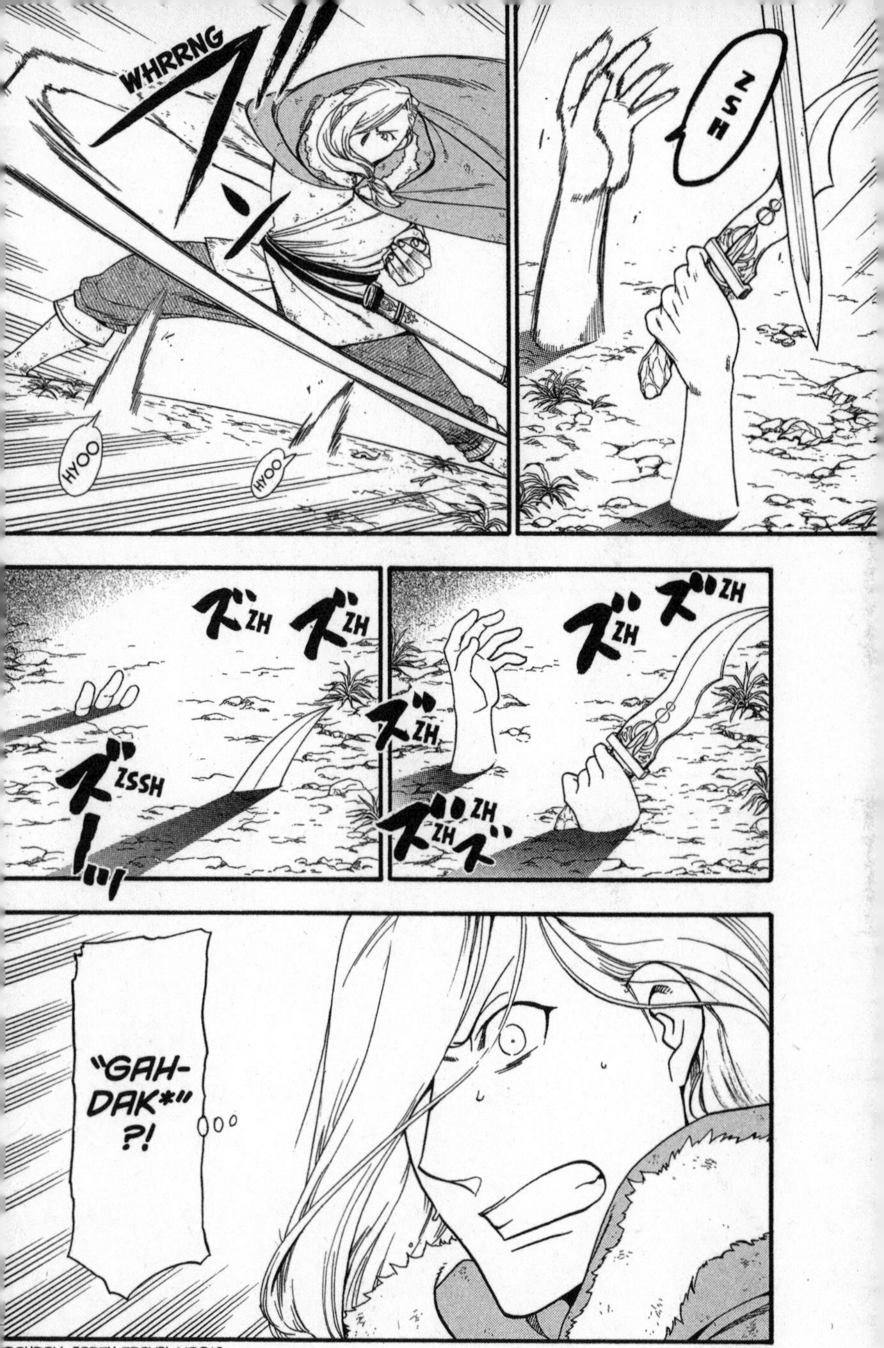
ZSSH
WHRRNG
HYOO
HYOO
ZH
ZH
ZH
ZH ZH
ZH
ZH
ZSSH
"GAH-DAK*"...?!

GAHDAK= EARTH-TRAVEL MAGIC

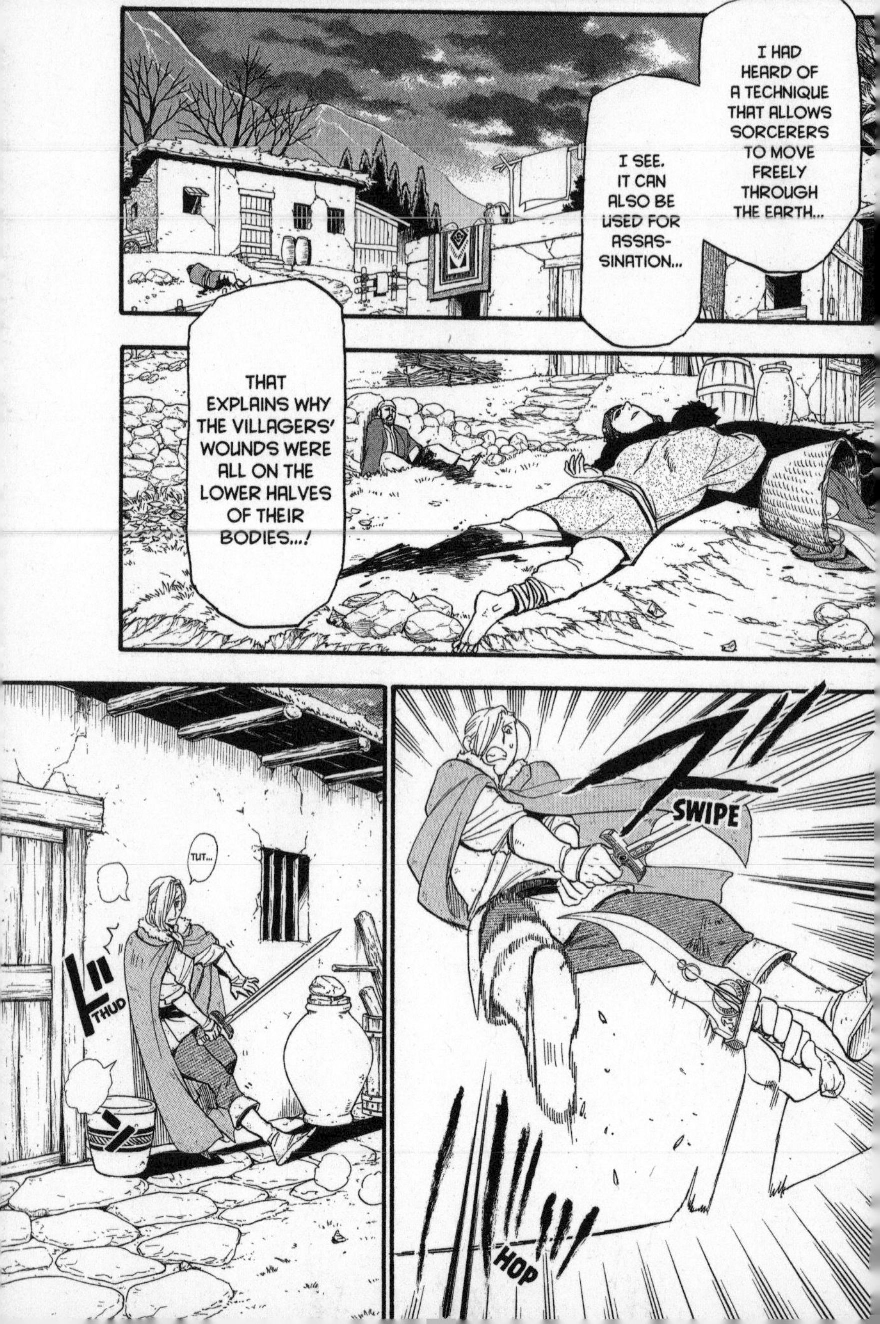
I HAD HEARD OF A TECHNIQUE THAT ALLOWS SORCERERS TO MOVE FREELY THROUGH THE EARTH...
I SEE. IT CAN ALSO BE USED FOR ASSAS-SINATION...
THAT EXPLAINS WHY THE VILLAGERS' WOUNDS WERE ALL ON THE LOWER HALVES OF THEIR BODIES...!
SWIPE
HOP
TUT...
THUD

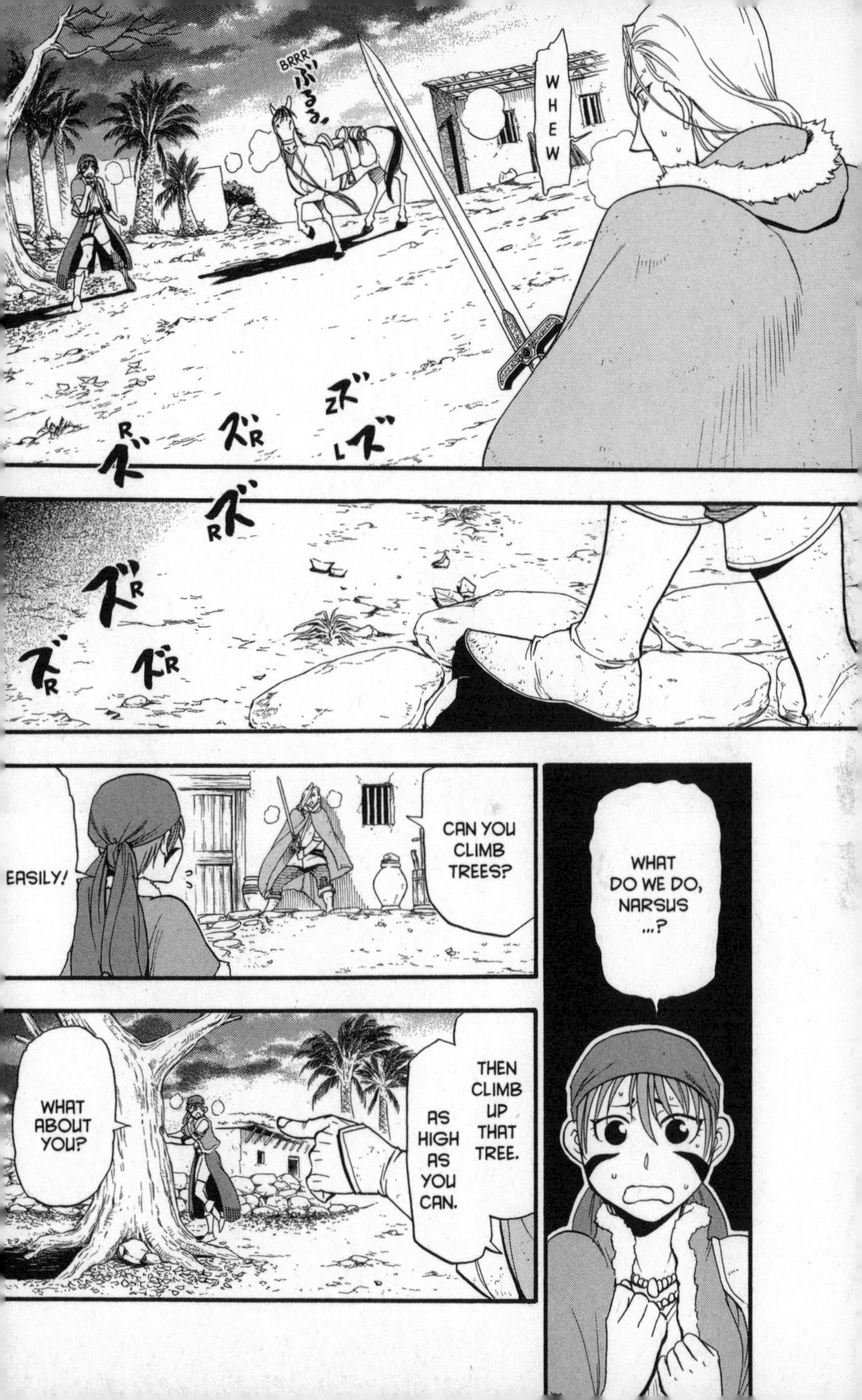
WHEW
BRRR
ぶるる
ZR ズ
ズR
R ズ
RズR
ズR
ズR
ズR
WHAT DO WE DO, NARSUS ...?
CAN YOU CLIMB TREES?
EASILY!
THEN CLIMB UP THAT TREE.
AS HIGH AS YOU CAN.
WHAT ABOUT YOU?

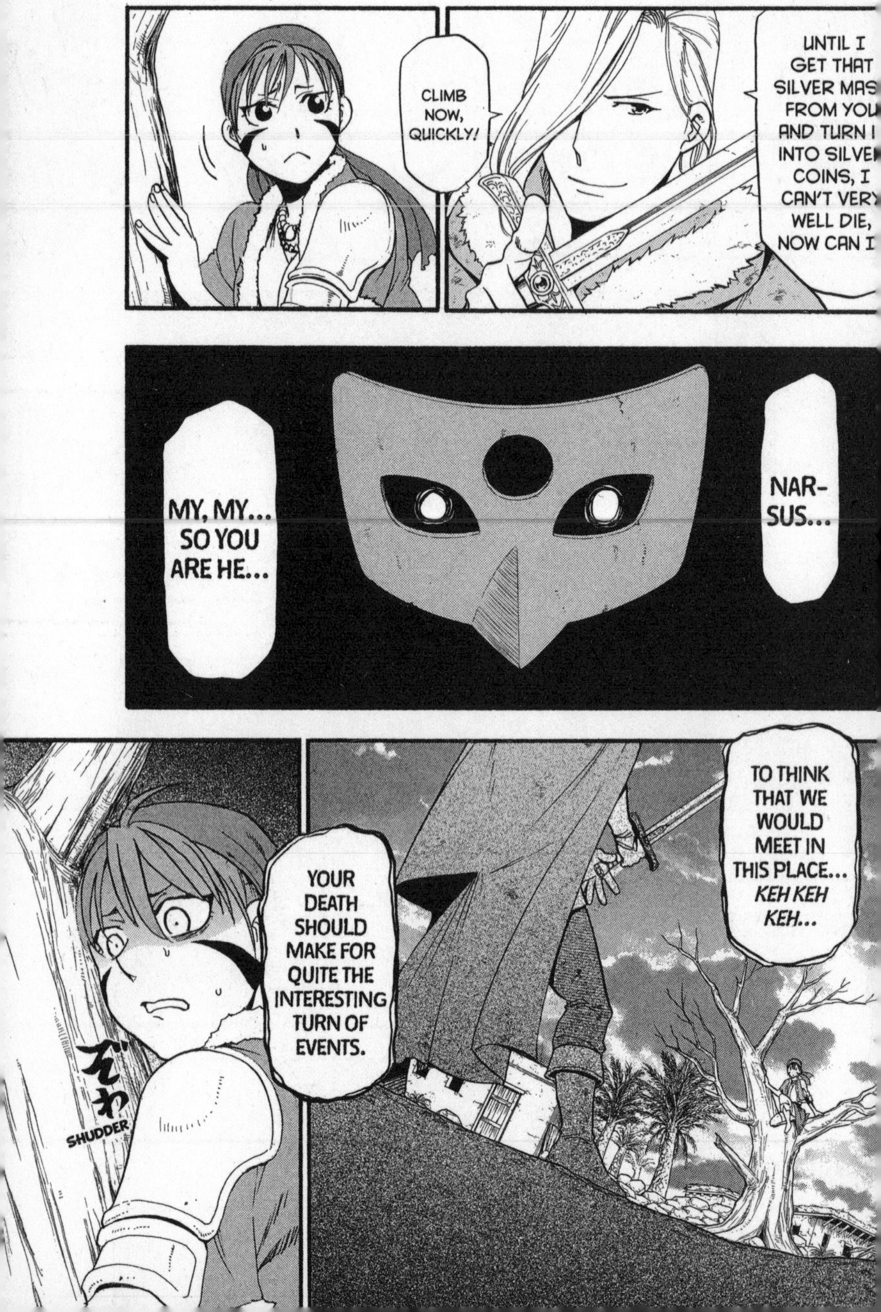
UNTIL I GET THAT SILVER MAS FROM YOU AND TURN I INTO SILVE COINS, I CAN'T VERY WELL DIE, NOW CAN I
CLIMB NOW, QUICKLY!
NAR-SUS...
MY, MY... SO YOU ARE HE...
TO THINK THAT WE WOULD MEET IN THIS PLACE... *KEH KEH KEH...*
YOUR DEATH SHOULD MAKE FOR QUITE THE INTERESTING TURN OF EVENTS.
ぞわ
SHUDDER

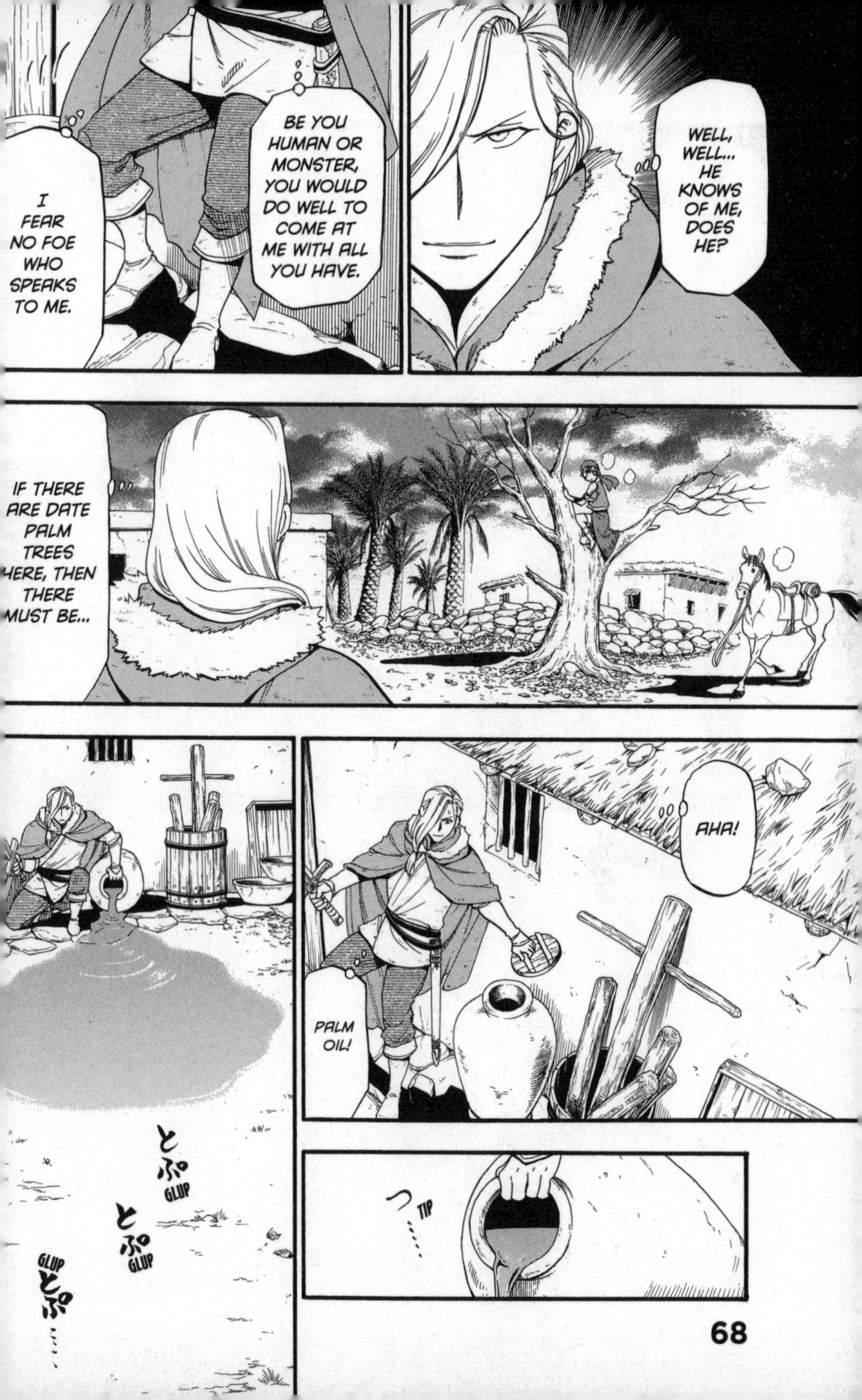
WELL, WELL... HE KNOWS OF ME, DOES HE?
BE YOU HUMAN OR MONSTER, YOU WOULD DO WELL TO COME AT ME WITH ALL YOU HAVE.
I FEAR NO FOE WHO SPEAKS TO ME.
IF THERE ARE DATE PALM TREES HERE, THEN THERE MUST BE...
AHA!
PALM OIL!
TIP
とぷ GLUP
とぷ GLUP
GLUP とぷ……

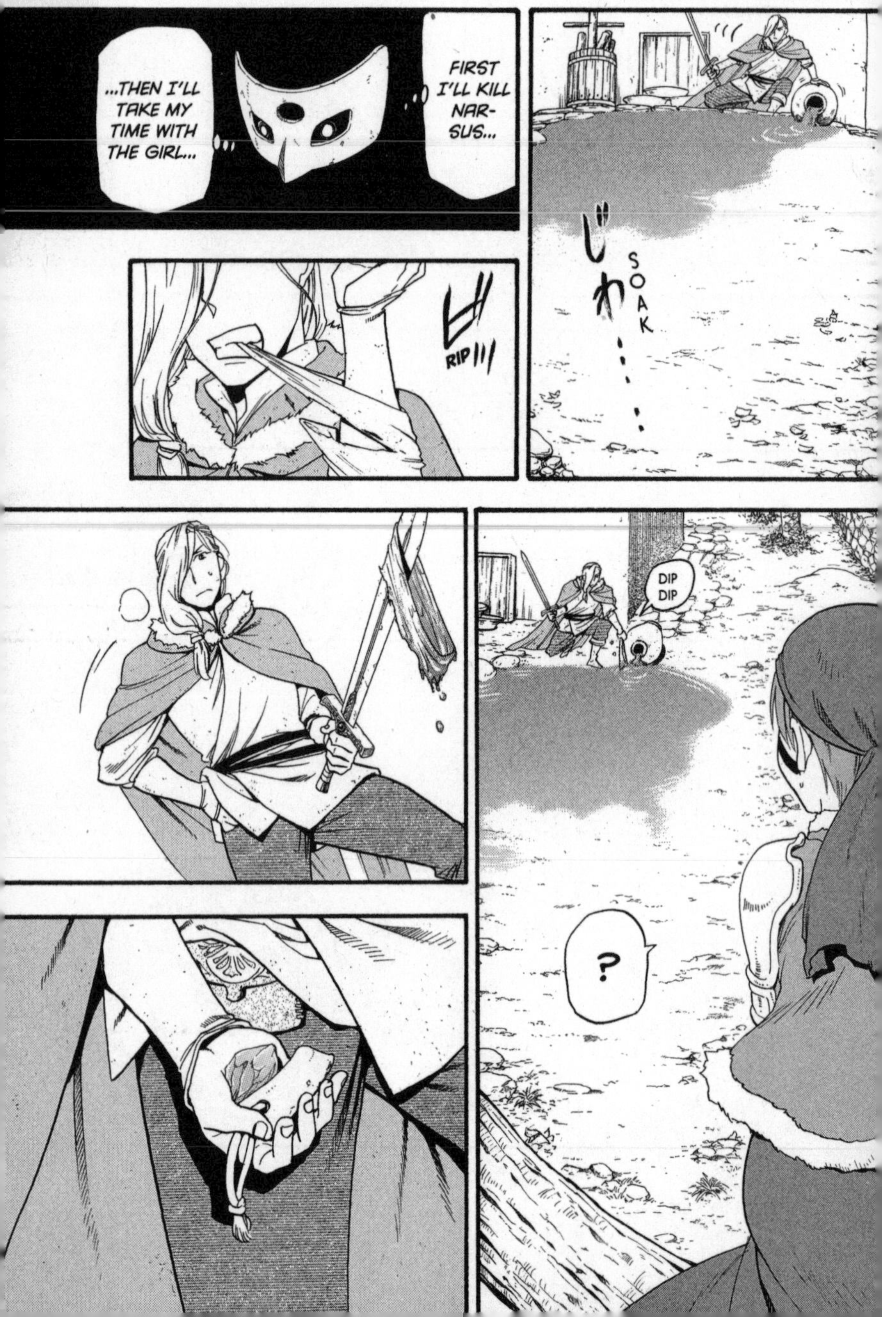
じわ……
SOAK
FIRST I'LL KILL NARSUS...
...THEN I'LL TAKE MY TIME WITH THE GIRL...
RIP
DIP DIP
?

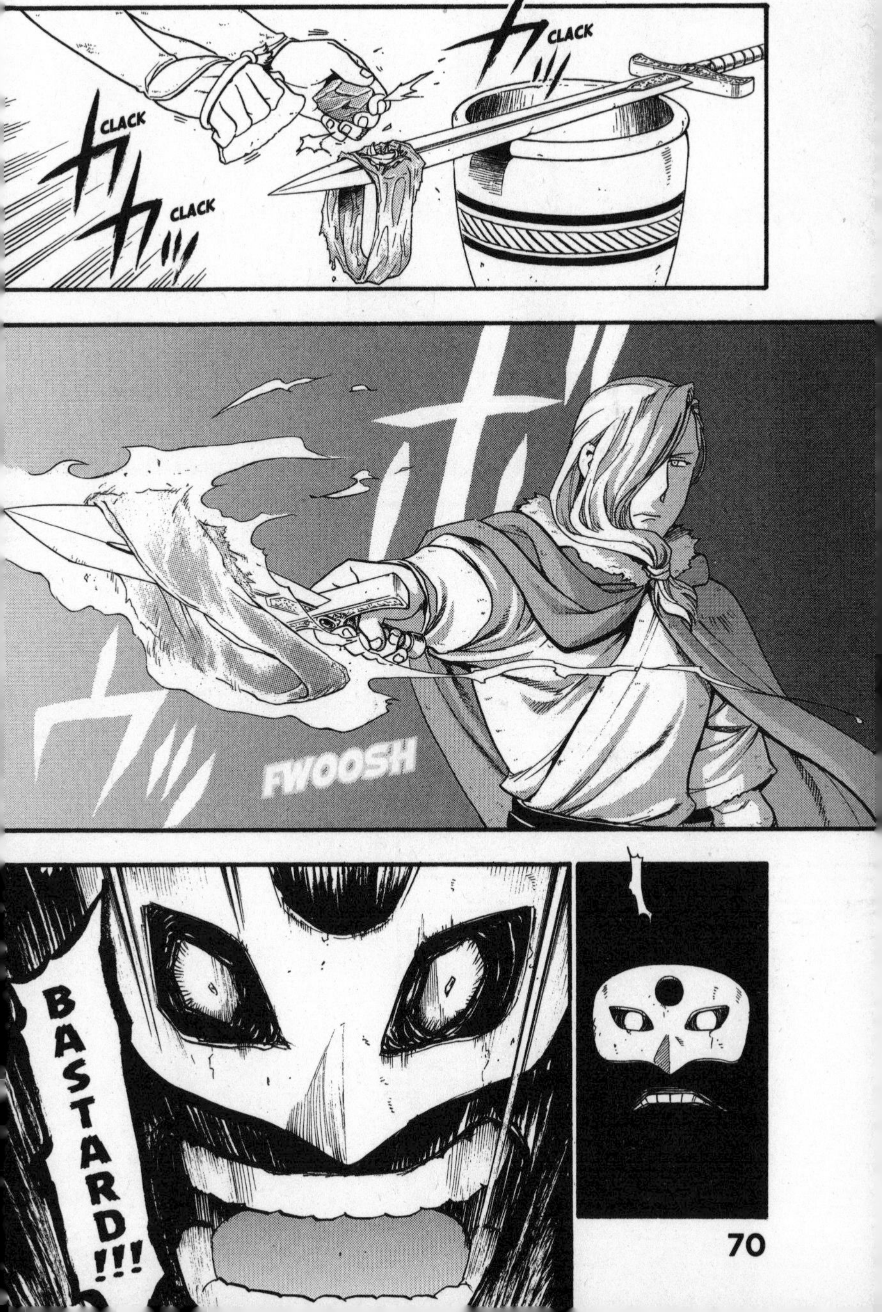
CLACK
CLACK
CLACK
FWOOSH
BASTARD!!!

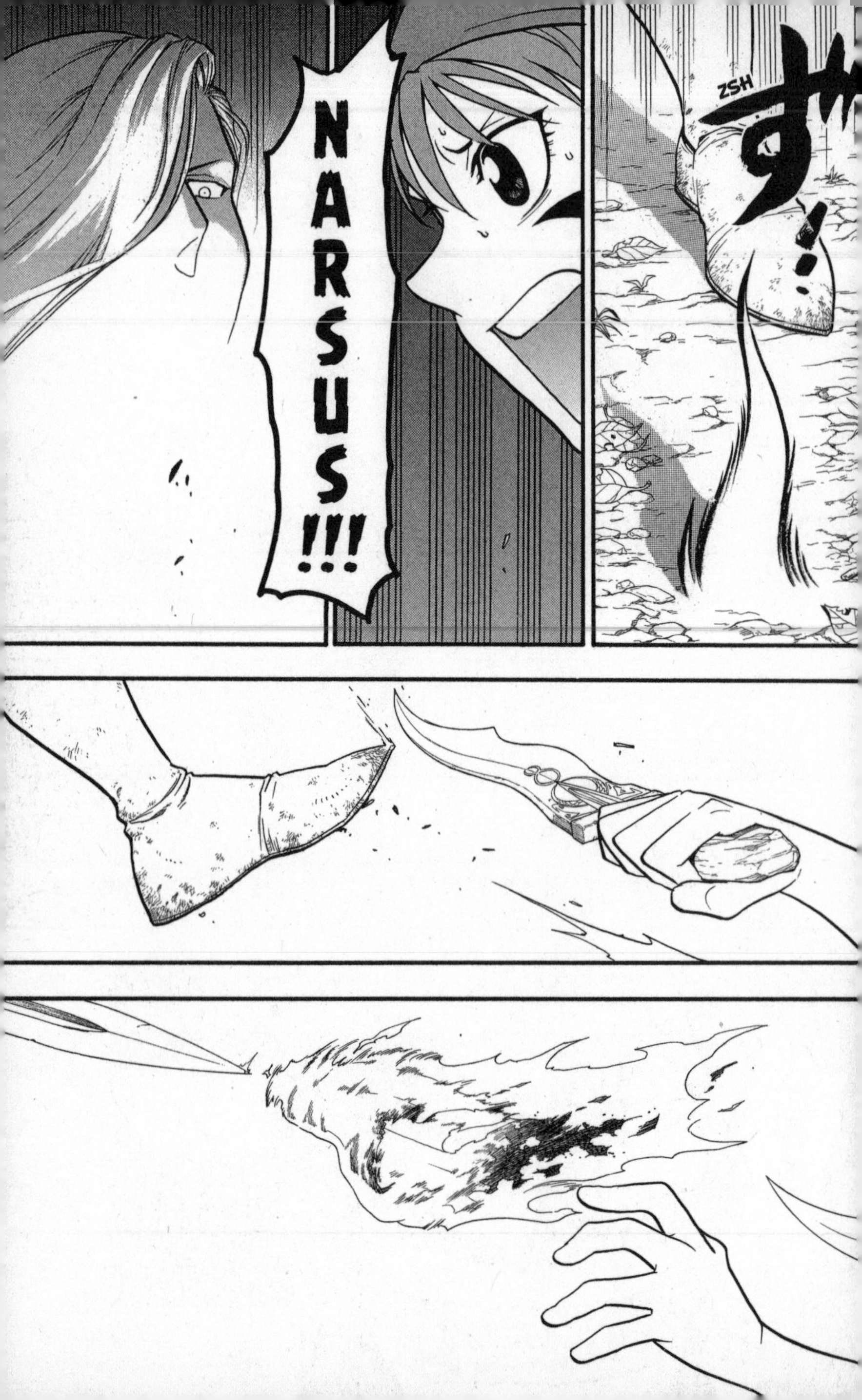
ZSH
すっ
NARSUS!!!

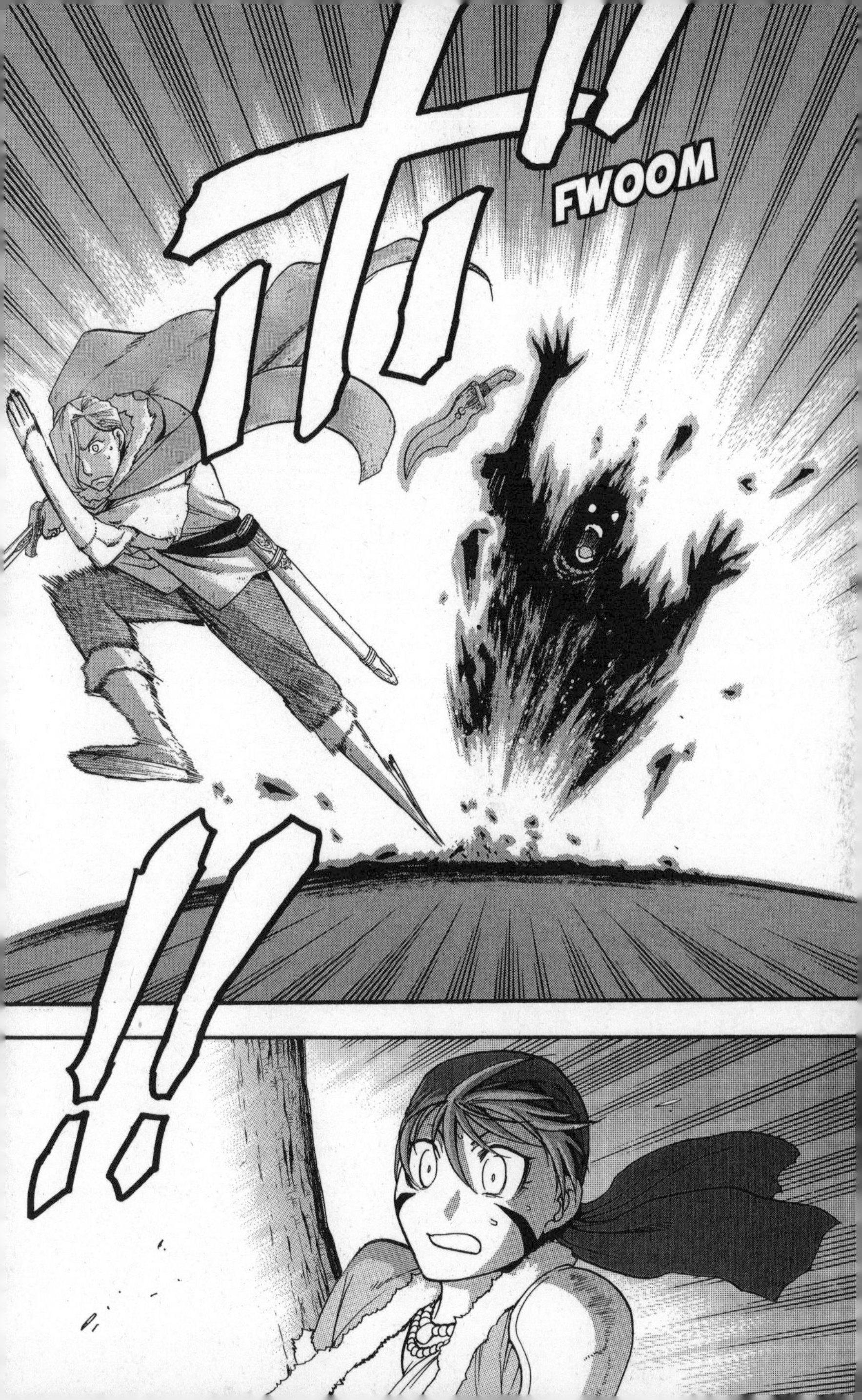
FWOOM

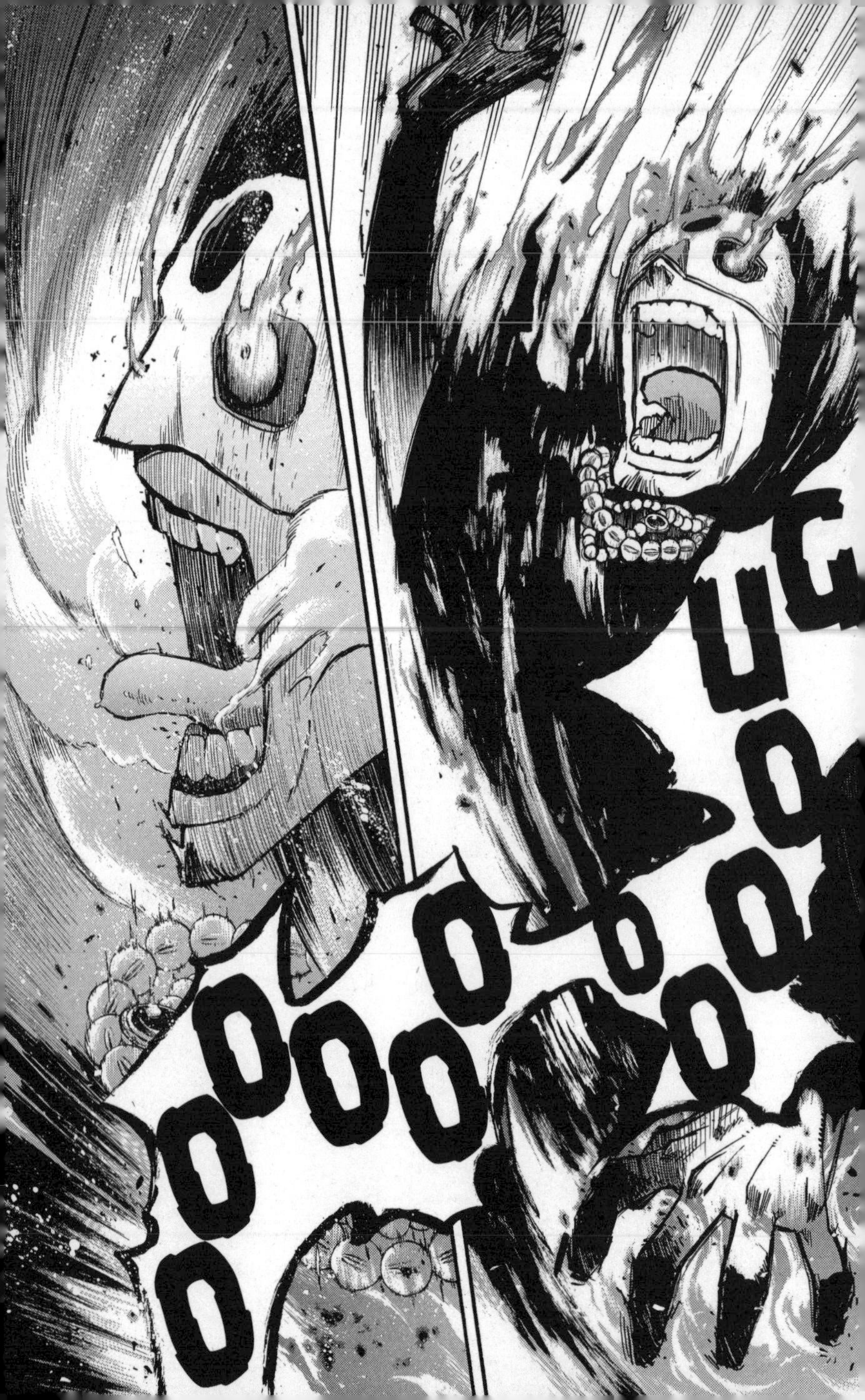
UGOOOOOOOOOOOOOOOO

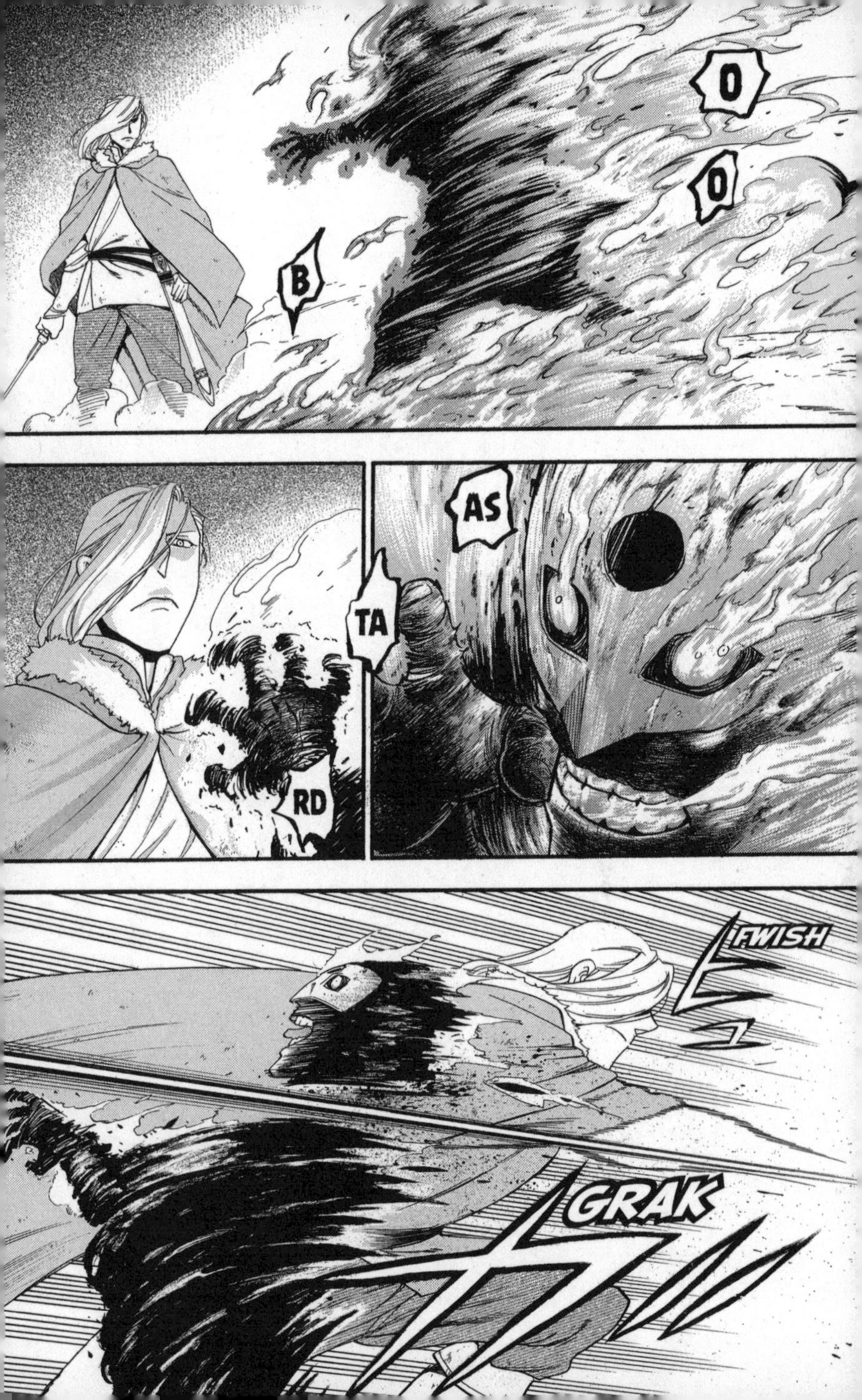
O
O
B
AS
TA
RD
FWISH
GRAK

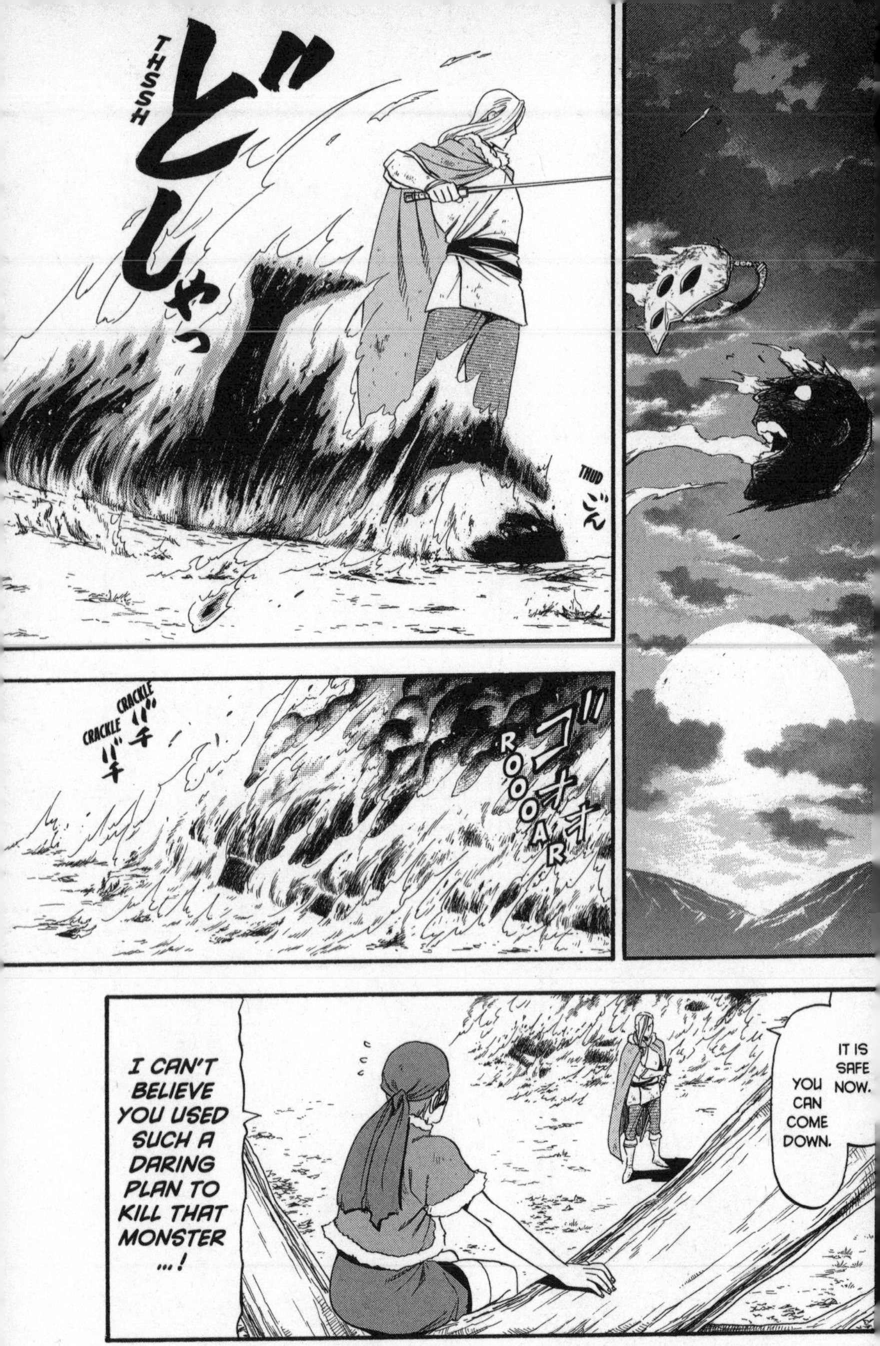
THSSH
どしゃっ
THUD
ごん
ROOOAR
ゴオオ
CRACKLE
バチ
CRACKLE
バチ
IT IS SAFE NOW. YOU CAN COME DOWN.
I CAN'T BELIEVE YOU USED SUCH A DARING PLAN TO KILL THAT MONSTER ...!

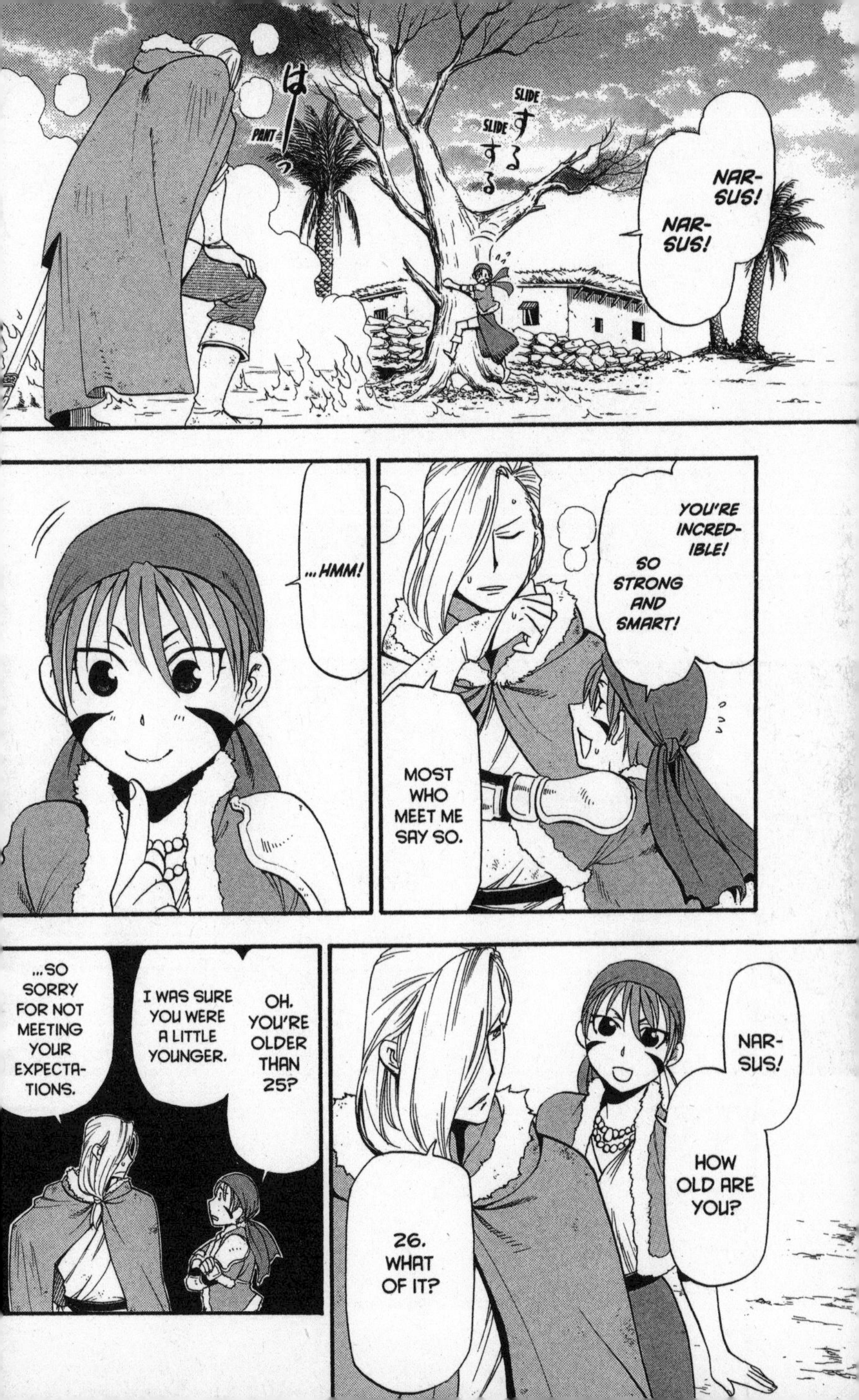
NAR-SUS!
NAR-SUS!
SLIDE する
SLIDE する
PANT はー
YOU'RE INCRED-IBLE!
SO STRONG AND SMART!
MOST WHO MEET ME SAY SO.
...HMM!
NAR-SUS!
HOW OLD ARE YOU?
26. WHAT OF IT?
OH. YOU'RE OLDER THAN 25?
I WAS SURE YOU WERE A LITTLE YOUNGER.
...SO SORRY FOR NOT MEETING YOUR EXPECTA-TIONS.

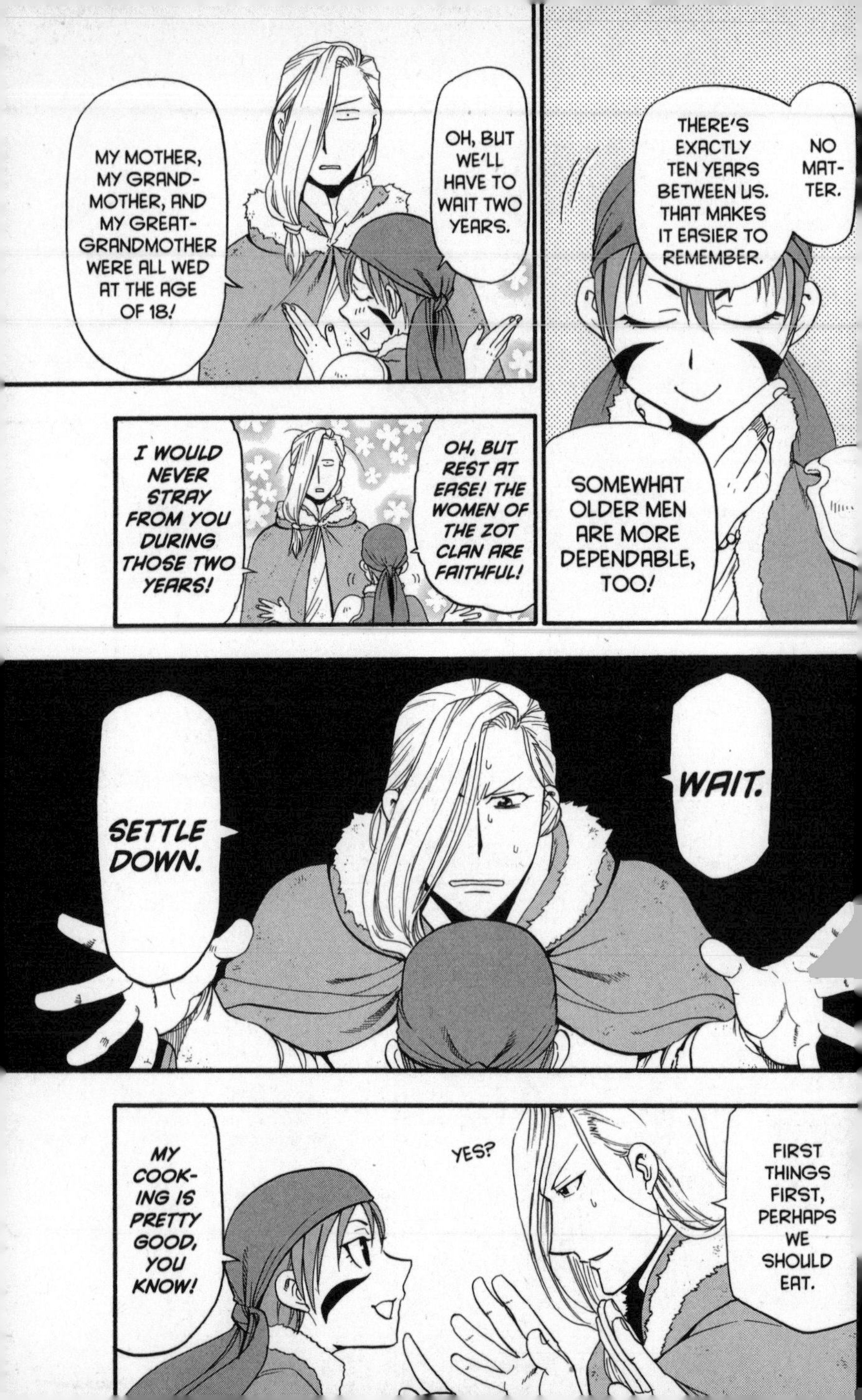
NO MATTER.
THERE'S EXACTLY TEN YEARS BETWEEN US. THAT MAKES IT EASIER TO REMEMBER.
SOMEWHAT OLDER MEN ARE MORE DEPENDABLE, TOO!
OH, BUT WE'LL HAVE TO WAIT TWO YEARS.
MY MOTHER, MY GRANDMOTHER, AND MY GREAT-GRANDMOTHER WERE ALL WED AT THE AGE OF 18!
OH, BUT REST AT EASE! THE WOMEN OF THE ZOT CLAN ARE FAITHFUL!
I WOULD NEVER STRAY FROM YOU DURING THOSE TWO YEARS!
WAIT.
SETTLE DOWN.
FIRST THINGS FIRST, PERHAPS WE SHOULD EAT.
YES?
MY COOKING IS PRETTY GOOD, YOU KNOW!

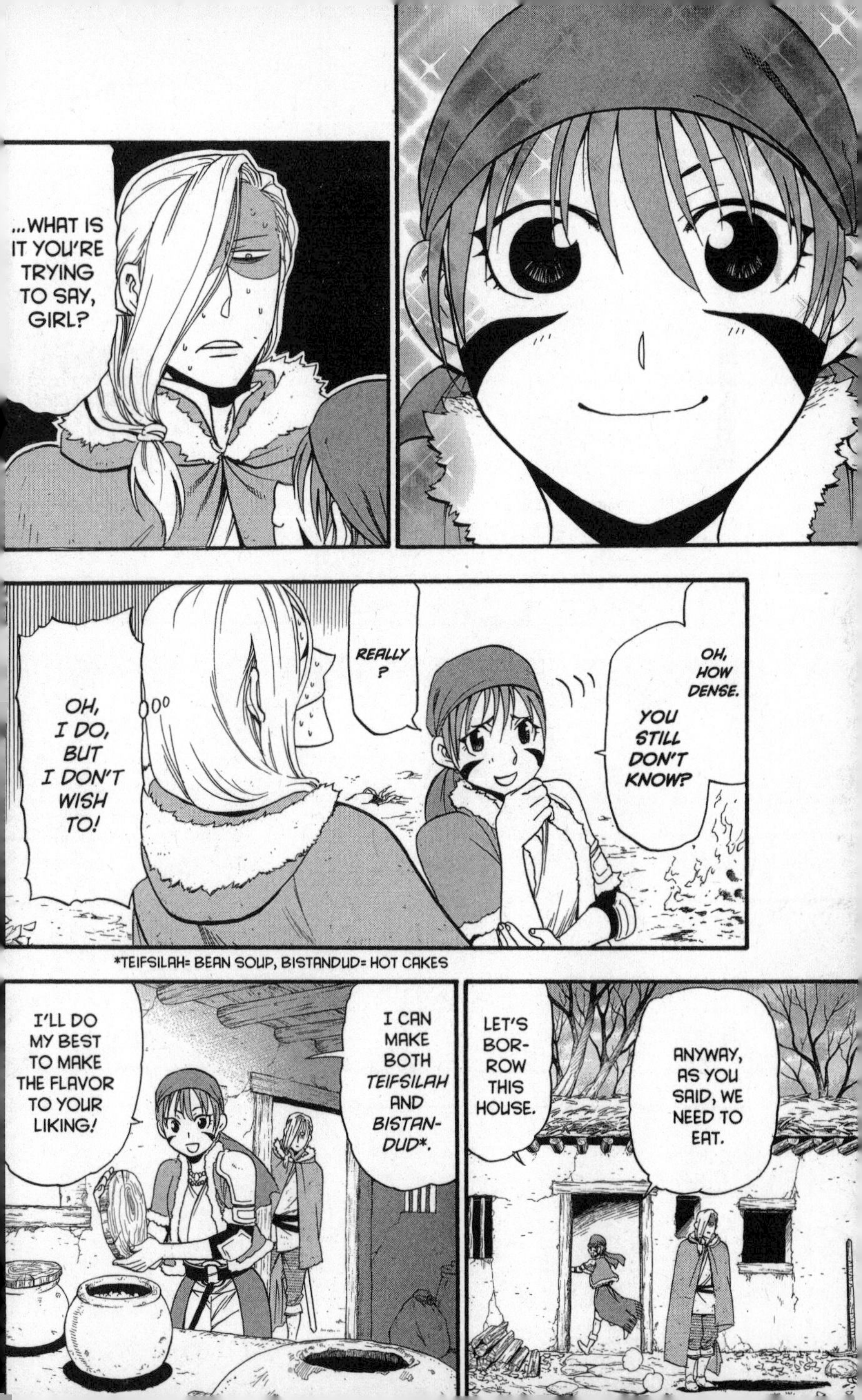
...WHAT IS IT YOU'RE TRYING TO SAY, GIRL?
OH, HOW DENSE.
YOU STILL DON'T KNOW?
REALLY?
OH, I DO, BUT I DON'T WISH TO!
ANYWAY, AS YOU SAID, WE NEED TO EAT.
LET'S BOR-ROW THIS HOUSE.
I CAN MAKE BOTH TEIFSILAH AND BISTAN-DUD*.
I'LL DO MY BEST TO MAKE THE FLAVOR TO YOUR LIKING!

*TEIFSILAH= BEAN SOUP, BISTANDUD= HOT CAKES

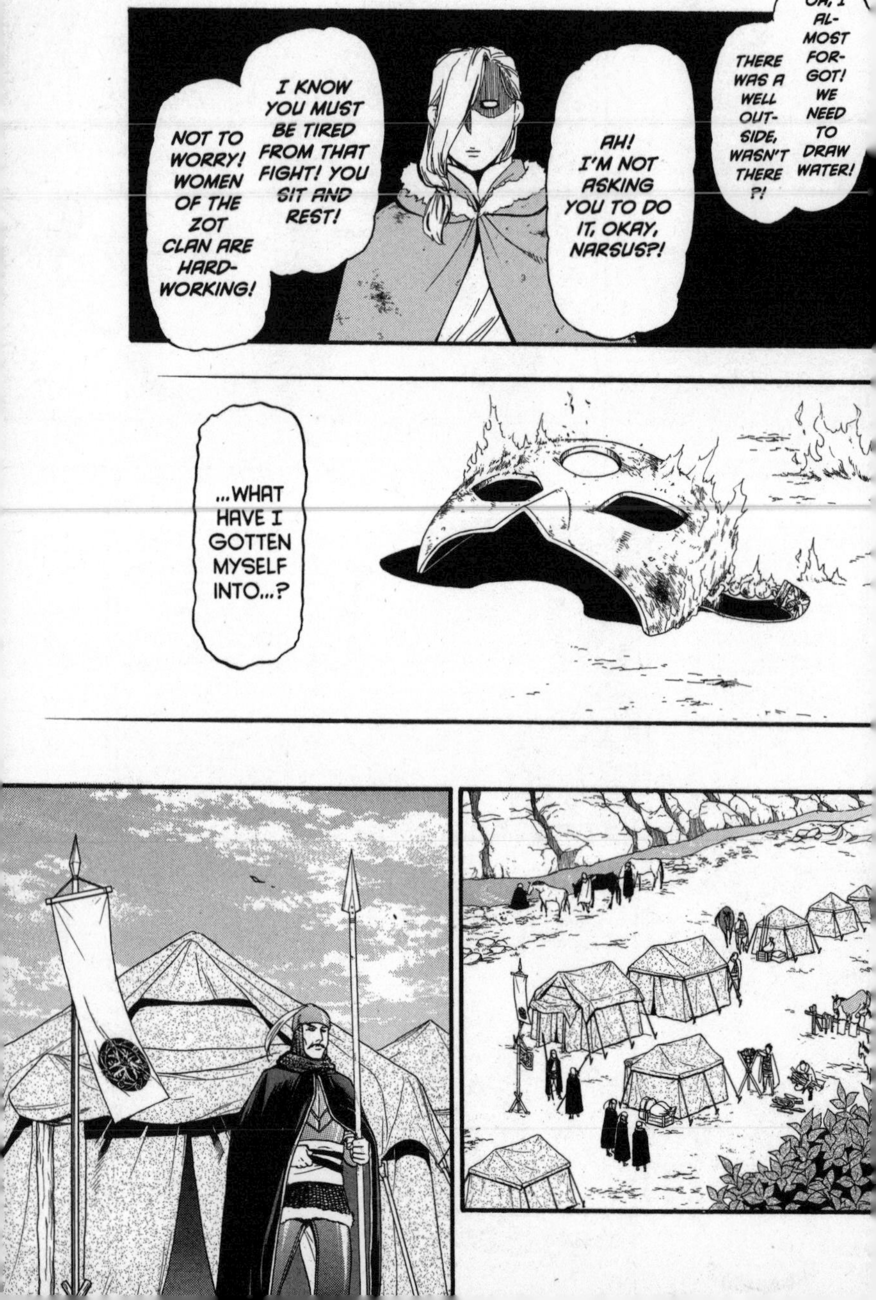
OH, I ALMOST FORGOT! WE NEED TO DRAW WATER!
THERE WAS A WELL OUTSIDE, WASN'T THERE?!
AH! I'M NOT ASKING YOU TO DO IT, OKAY, NARSUS?!
I KNOW YOU MUST BE TIRED FROM THAT FIGHT! YOU SIT AND REST!
NOT TO WORRY! WOMEN OF THE ZOT CLAN ARE HARD-WORKING!
...WHAT HAVE I GOTTEN MYSELF INTO...?

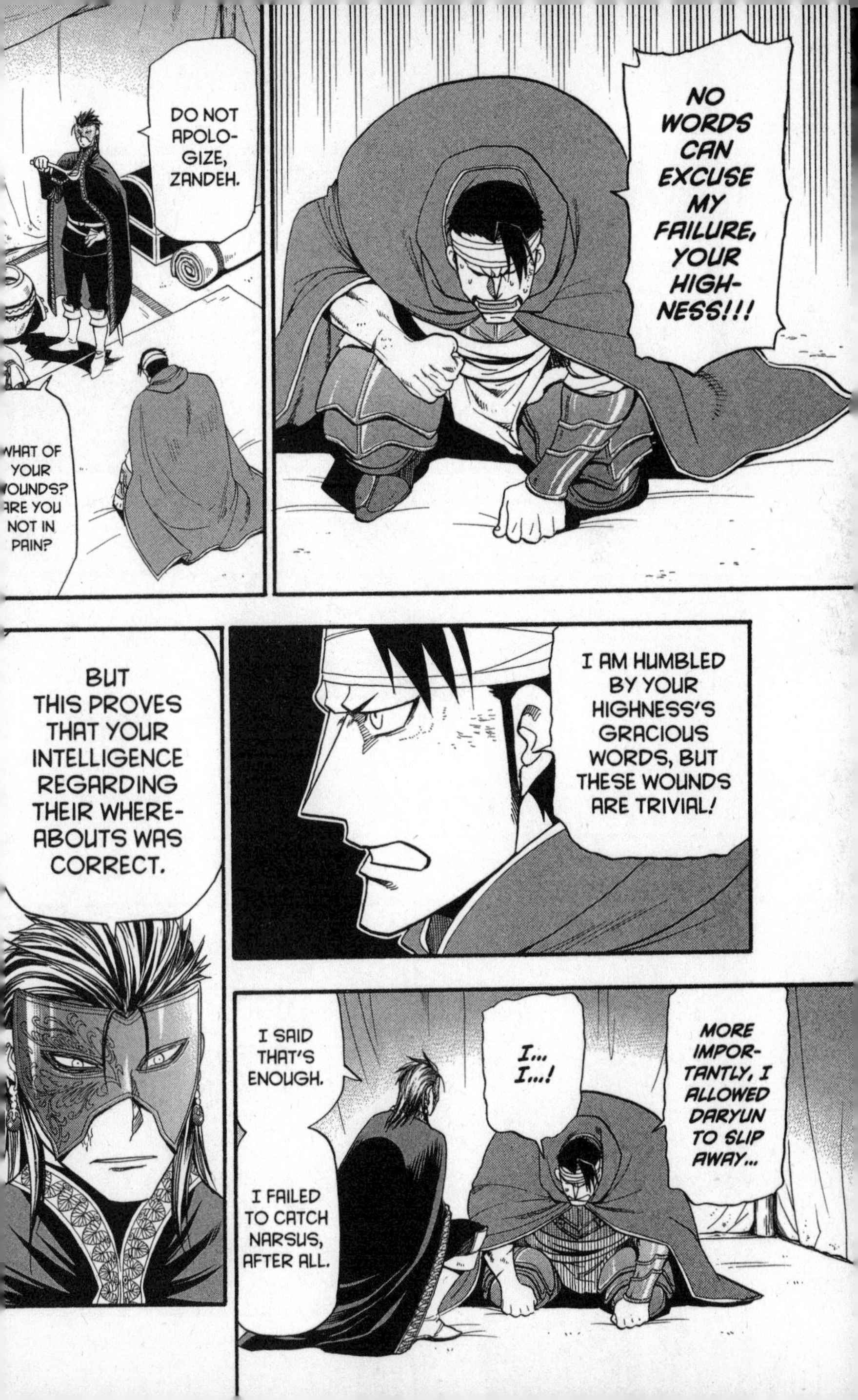
NO WORDS CAN EXCUSE MY FAILURE, YOUR HIGHNESS!!!
DO NOT APOLOGIZE, ZANDEH.
WHAT OF YOUR WOUNDS? ARE YOU NOT IN PAIN?
I AM HUMBLED BY YOUR HIGHNESS'S GRACIOUS WORDS, BUT THESE WOUNDS ARE TRIVIAL!
MORE IMPORTANTLY, I ALLOWED DARYUN TO SLIP AWAY...
I... I...!
I SAID THAT'S ENOUGH.
I FAILED TO CATCH NARSUS, AFTER ALL.
BUT THIS PROVES THAT YOUR INTELLIGENCE REGARDING THEIR WHEREABOUTS WAS CORRECT.

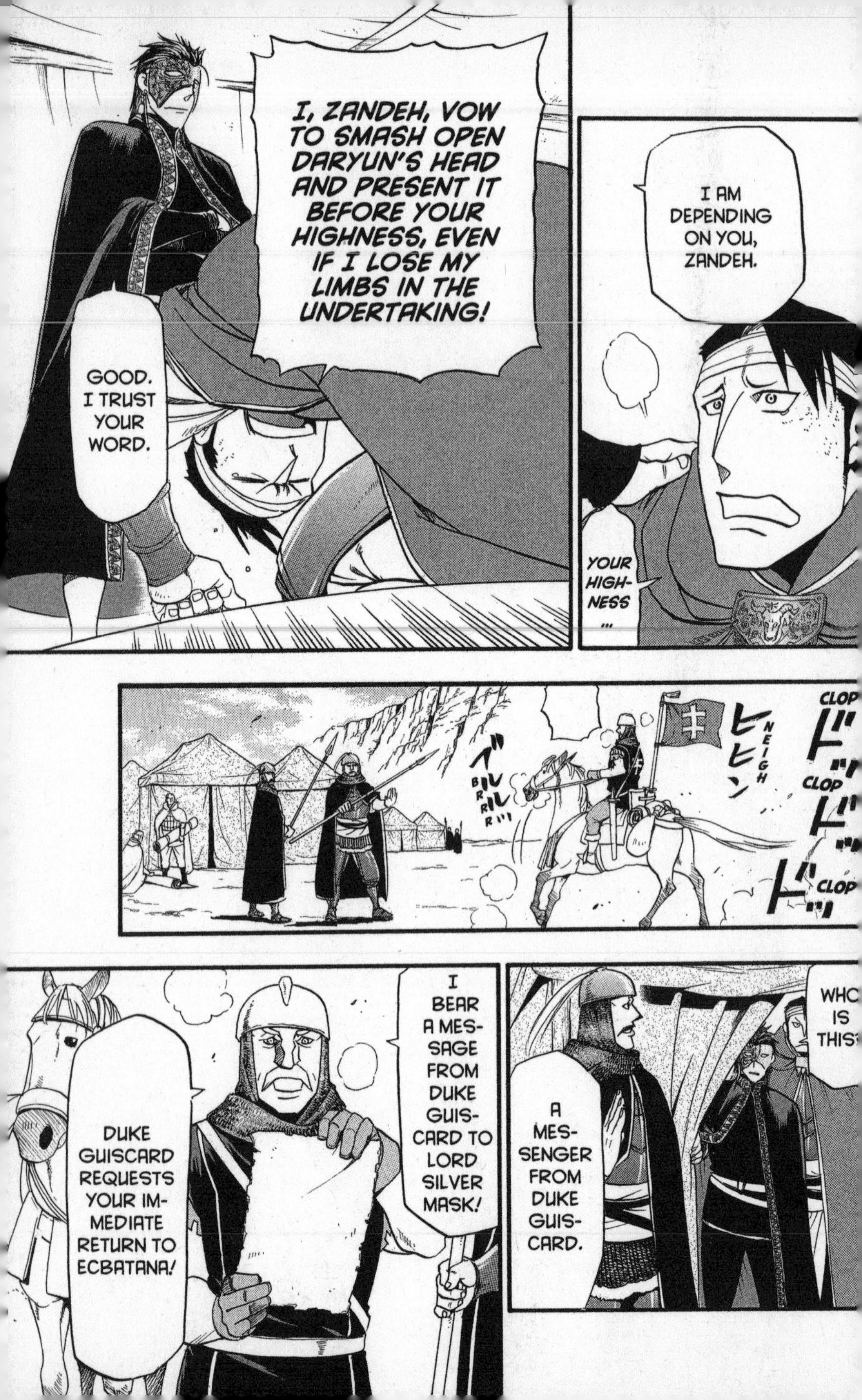
I AM DEPENDING ON YOU, ZANDEH.
YOUR HIGHNESS...
I, ZANDEH, VOW TO SMASH OPEN DARYUN'S HEAD AND PRESENT IT BEFORE YOUR HIGHNESS, EVEN IF I LOSE MY LIMBS IN THE UNDERTAKING!
GOOD. I TRUST YOUR WORD.
ドッ CLOP
ドッ CLOP
ドッ CLOP
ヒヒン NEIGH
ブルルル BRRR
WHO IS THIS?
A MESSENGER FROM DUKE GUISCARD.
I BEAR A MESSAGE FROM DUKE GUISCARD TO LORD SILVER MASK!
DUKE GUISCARD REQUESTS YOUR IMMEDIATE RETURN TO ECBATANA!

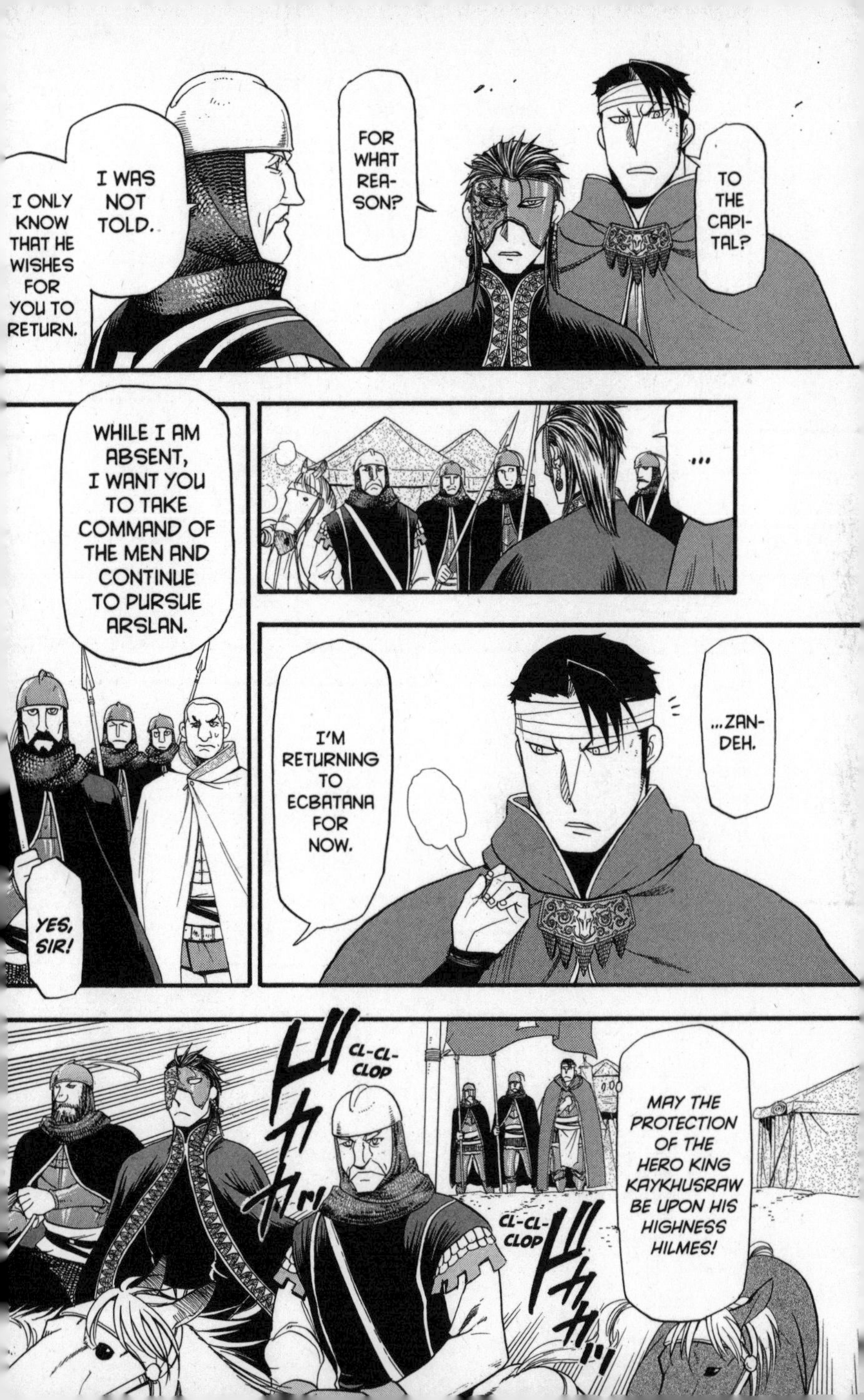
TO THE CAPI-TAL?
FOR WHAT REA-SON?
I WAS NOT TOLD.
I ONLY KNOW THAT HE WISHES FOR YOU TO RETURN.
...
...ZAN-DEH.
I'M RETURNING TO ECBATANA FOR NOW.
WHILE I AM ABSENT, I WANT YOU TO TAKE COMMAND OF THE MEN AND CONTINUE TO PURSUE ARSLAN.
YES, SIR!
MAY THE PROTECTION OF THE HERO KING KAYKHUSRAW BE UPON HIS HIGHNESS HILMES!
CL-CL-CLOP
CL-CL-CLOP

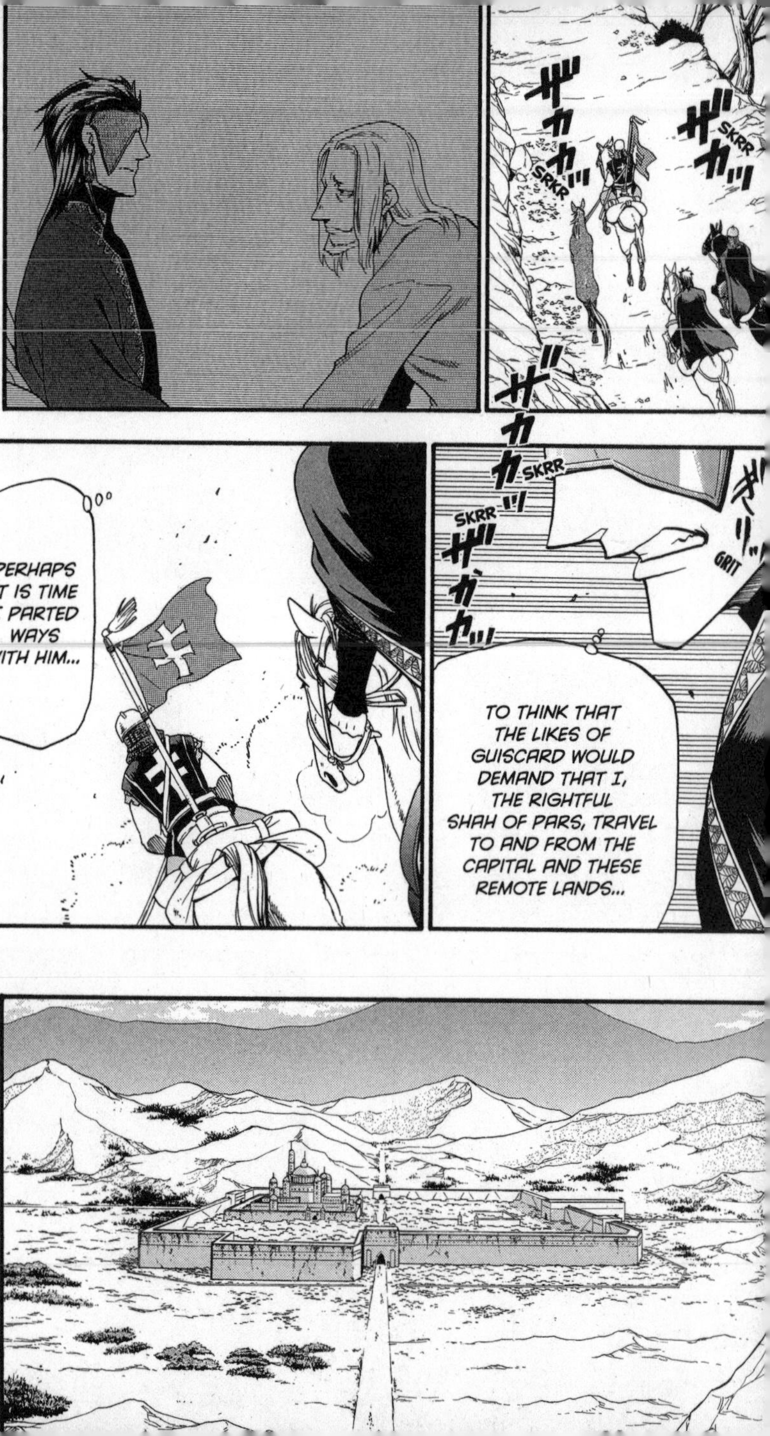
SKRR
SKRR
SKRR
SKRR
GRIT
TO THINK THAT THE LIKES OF GUISCARD WOULD DEMAND THAT I, THE RIGHTFUL SHAH OF PARS, TRAVEL TO AND FROM THE CAPITAL AND THESE REMOTE LANDS...
PERHAPS IT IS TIME I PARTED WAYS WITH HIM...

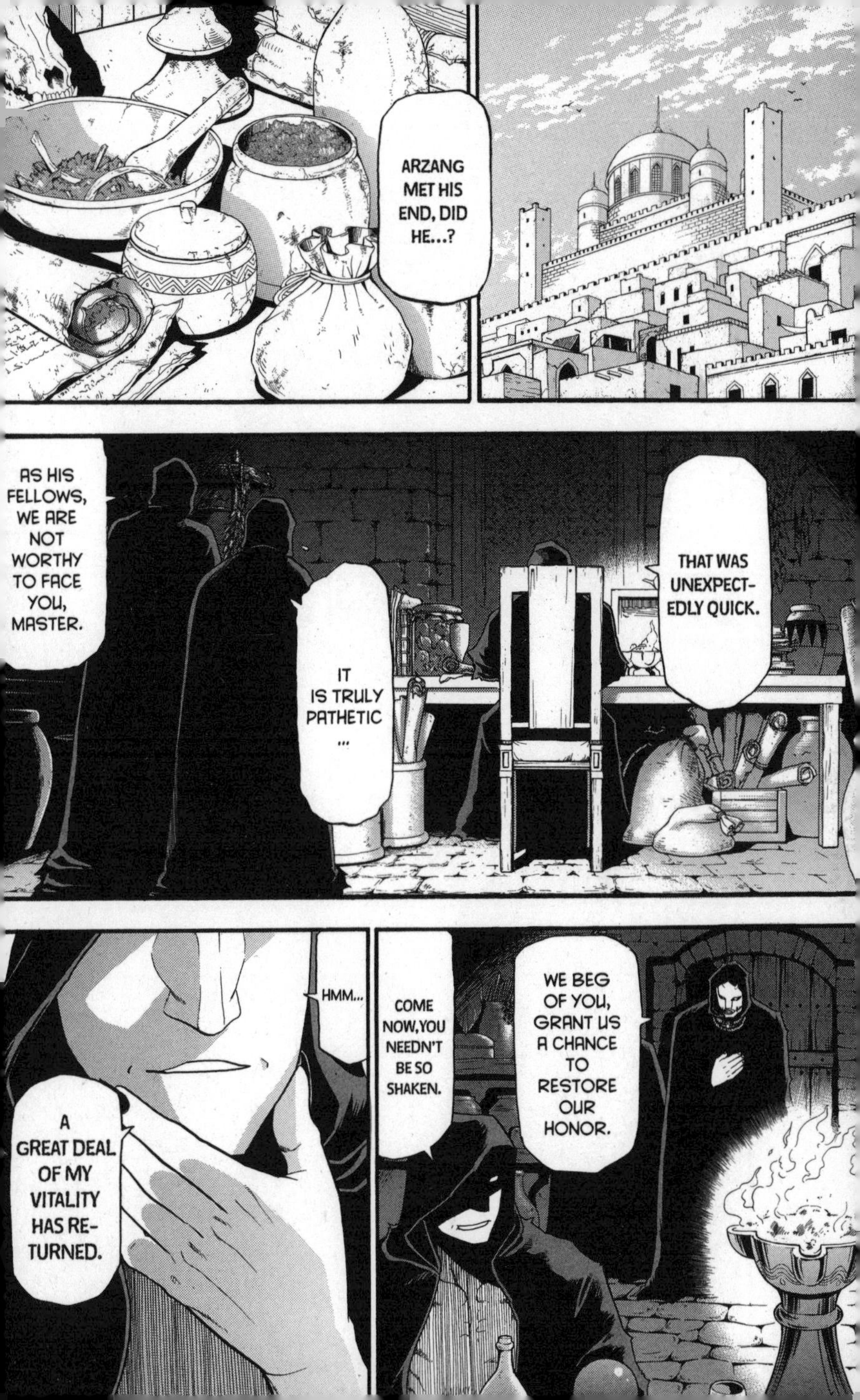
ARZANG MET HIS END, DID HE...?
THAT WAS UNEXPECT-EDLY QUICK.
IT IS TRULY PATHETIC ...
AS HIS FELLOWS, WE ARE NOT WORTHY TO FACE YOU, MASTER.
WE BEG OF YOU, GRANT US A CHANCE TO RESTORE OUR HONOR.
COME NOW, YOU NEEDN'T BE SO SHAKEN.
HMM...
A GREAT DEAL OF MY VITALITY HAS RE-TURNED.

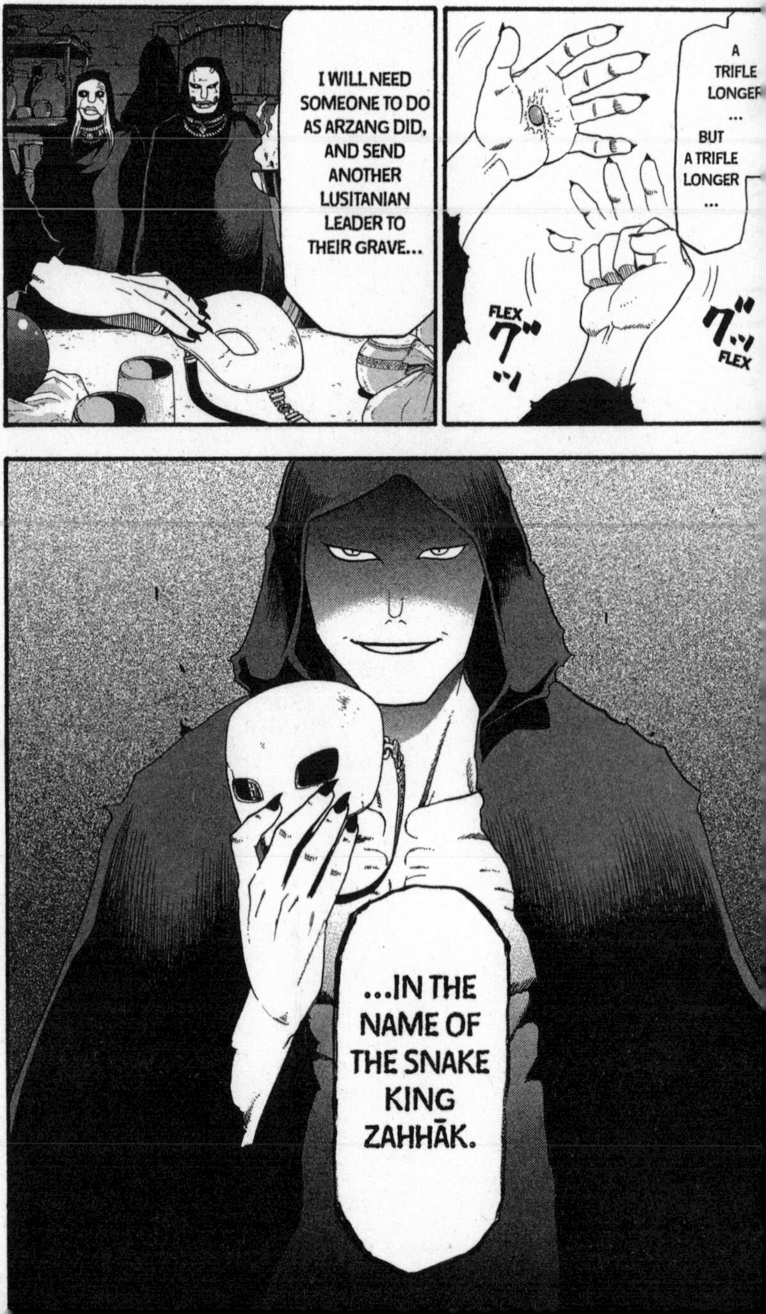
A TRIFLE LONGER ... BUT A TRIFLE LONGER ...
FLEX
FLEX
I WILL NEED SOMEONE TO DO AS ARZANG DID, AND SEND ANOTHER LUSITANIAN LEADER TO THEIR GRAVE...
...IN THE NAME OF THE SNAKE KING ZAHHĀK.

THE HEROIC LEGEND OF
ARSLAN

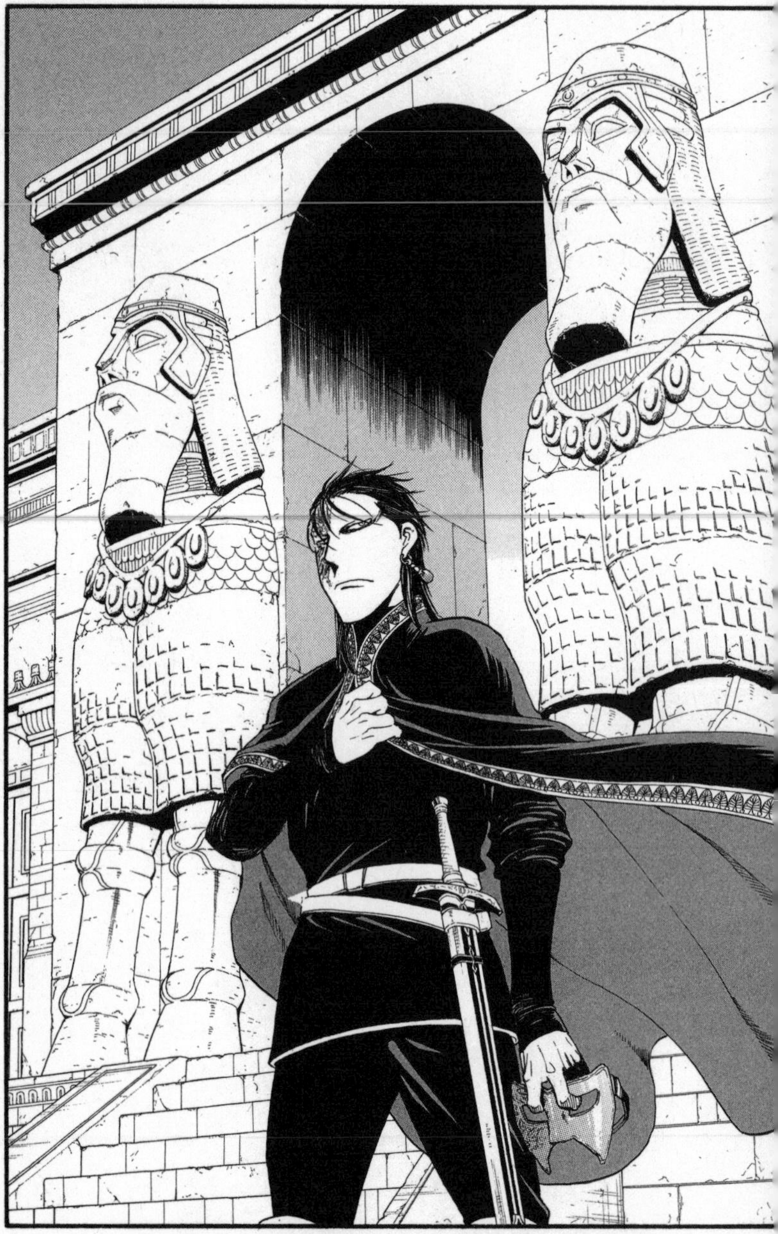

Chapter 31: Behind One's Eyelids

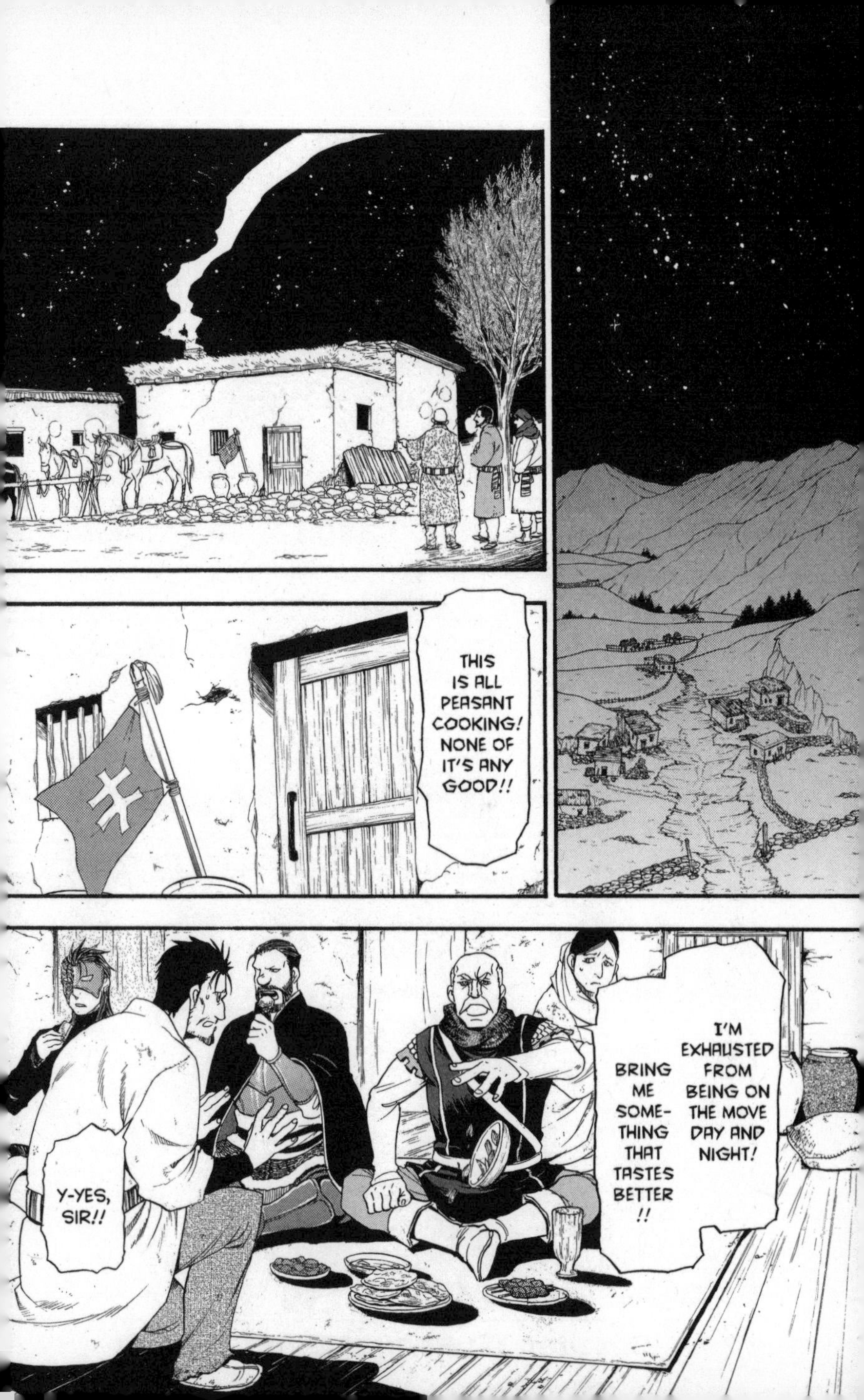
THIS IS ALL PEASANT COOKING! NONE OF IT'S ANY GOOD!!
I'M EXHAUSTED FROM BEING ON THE MOVE DAY AND NIGHT!
BRING ME SOME-THING THAT TASTES BETTER!!
Y-YES, SIR!!

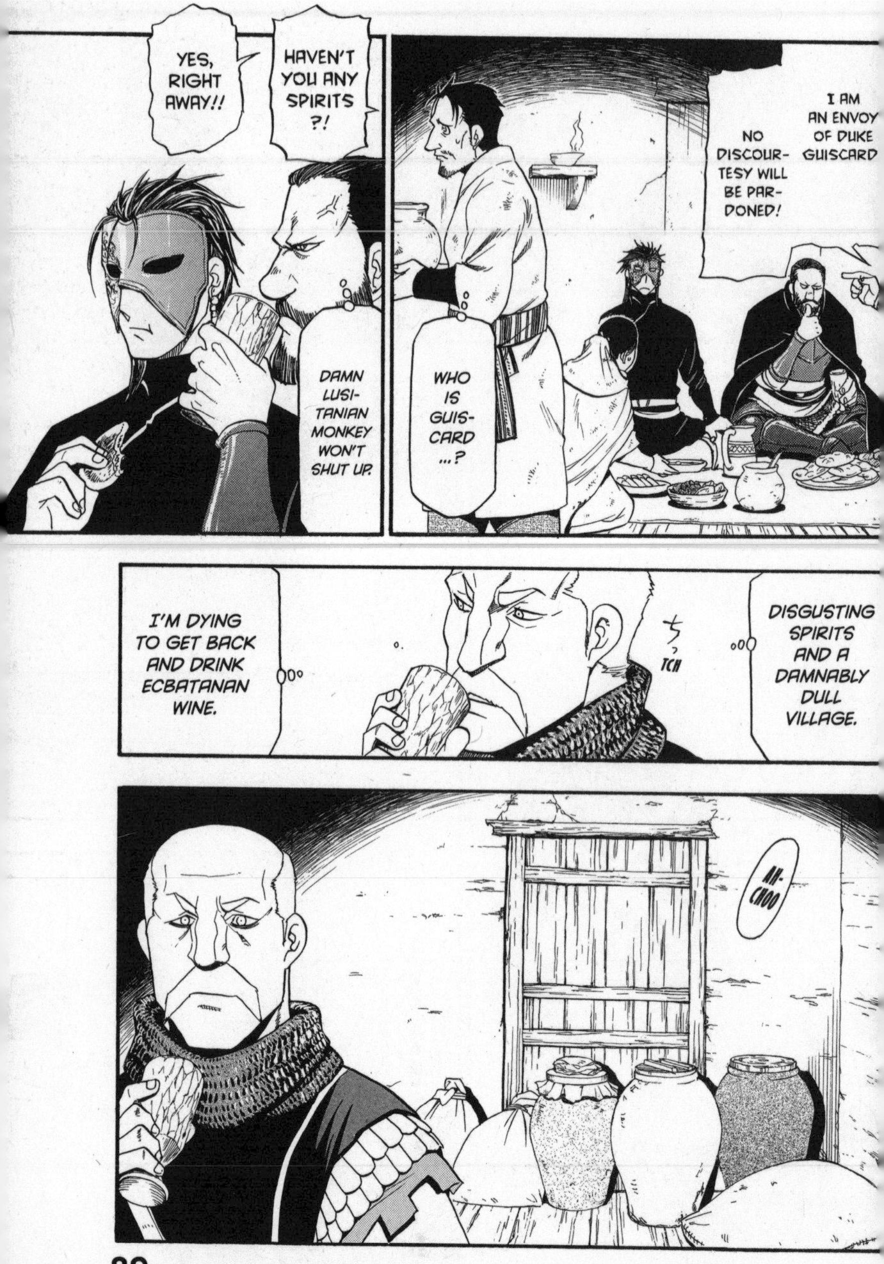
I AM AN ENVOY OF DUKE GUISCARD
NO DISCOURTESY WILL BE PARDONED!
WHO IS GUISCARD ...?
HAVEN'T YOU ANY SPIRITS ?!
YES, RIGHT AWAY!!
DAMN LUSITANIAN MONKEY WON'T SHUT UP.
DISGUSTING SPIRITS AND A DAMNABLY DULL VILLAGE.
TCH
I'M DYING TO GET BACK AND DRINK ECBATANAN WINE.
AH-CHOO

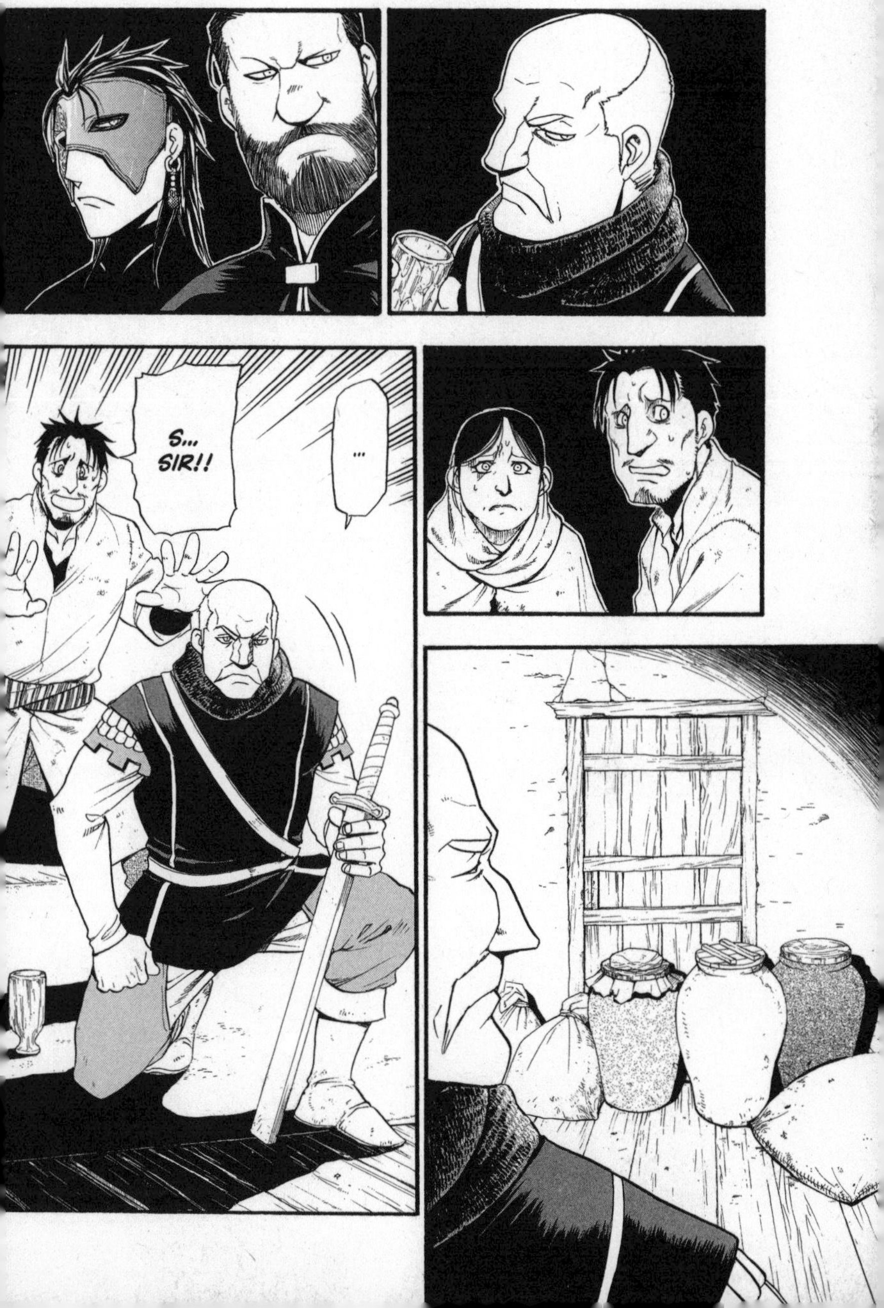
...
S... SIR!!

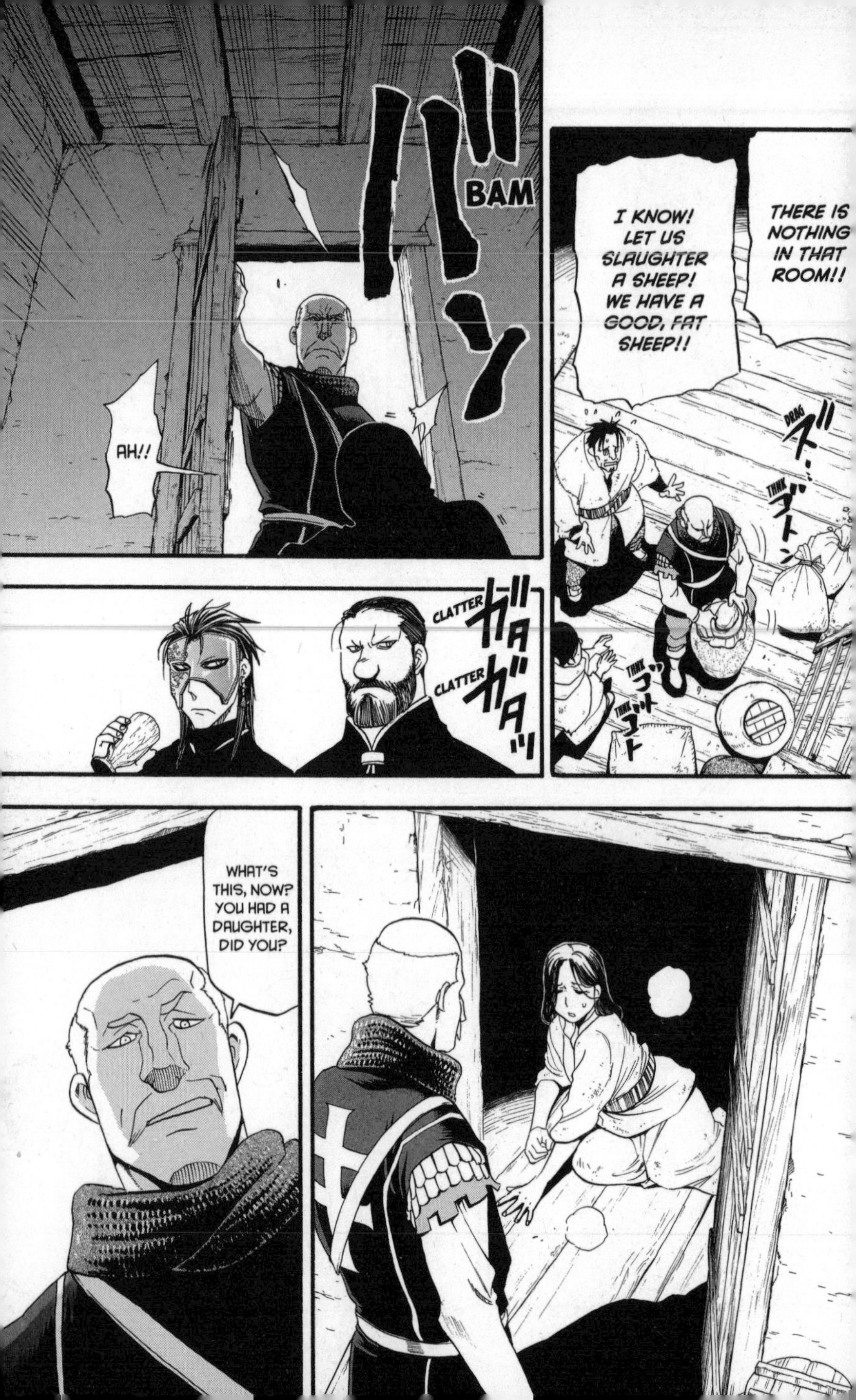

BAM
AH!!
THERE IS NOTHING IN THAT ROOM!!
I KNOW! LET US SLAUGHTER A SHEEP! WE HAVE A GOOD, FAT SHEEP!!
DRAG
THNK
THNK
THNK
CLATTER
CLATTER
WHAT'S THIS, NOW? YOU HAD A DAUGHTER, DID YOU?

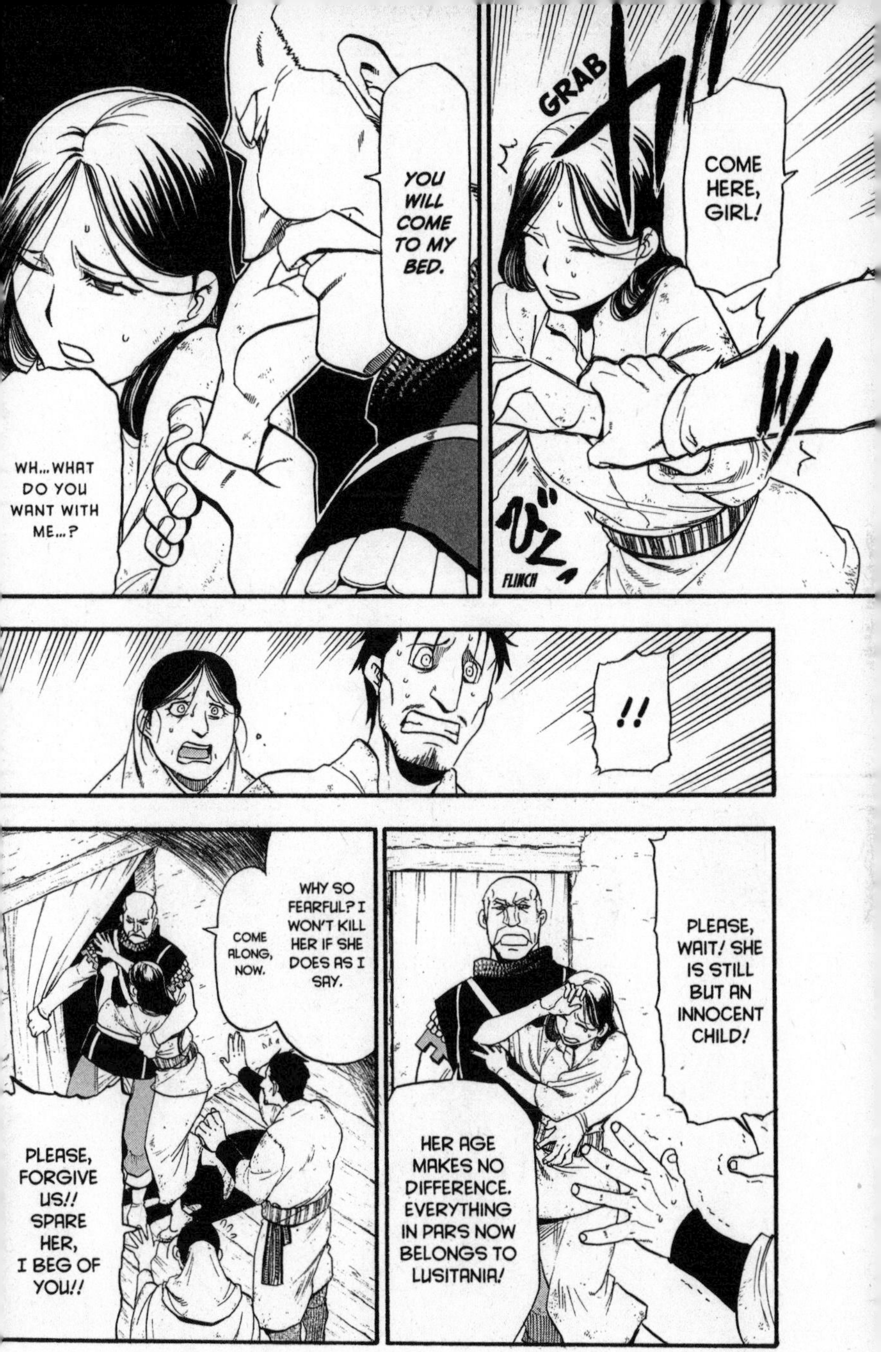
GRAB
COME HERE, GIRL!
FLINCH
YOU WILL COME TO MY BED.
WH...WHAT DO YOU WANT WITH ME...?
!!
PLEASE, WAIT! SHE IS STILL BUT AN INNOCENT CHILD!
HER AGE MAKES NO DIFFERENCE. EVERYTHING IN PARS NOW BELONGS TO LUSITANIA!
WHY SO FEARFUL? I WON'T KILL HER IF SHE DOES AS I SAY.
COME ALONG, NOW.
PLEASE, FORGIVE US!! SPARE HER, I BEG OF YOU!!

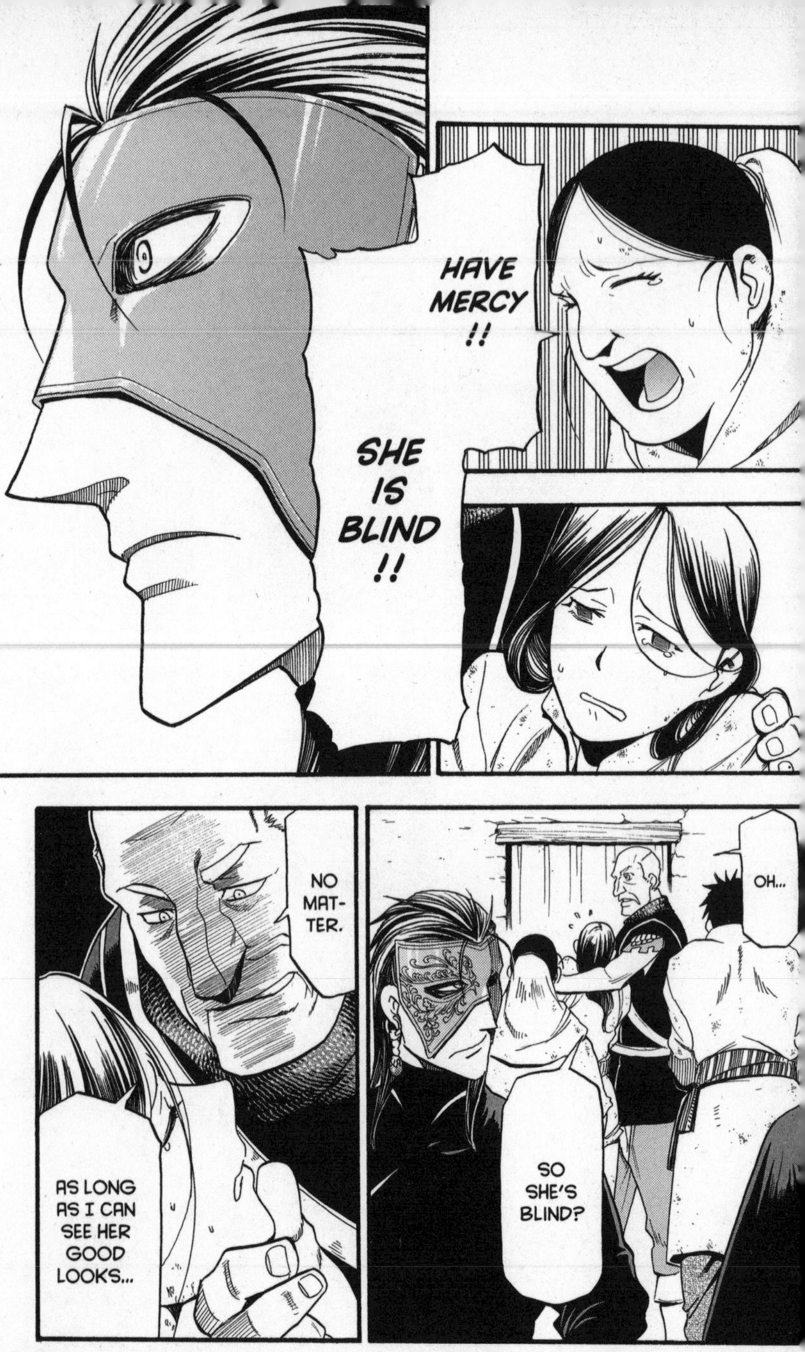
HAVE MERCY!!
SHE IS BLIND!!
OH...
SO SHE'S BLIND?
NO MATTER.
AS LONG AS I CAN SEE HER GOOD LOOKS...

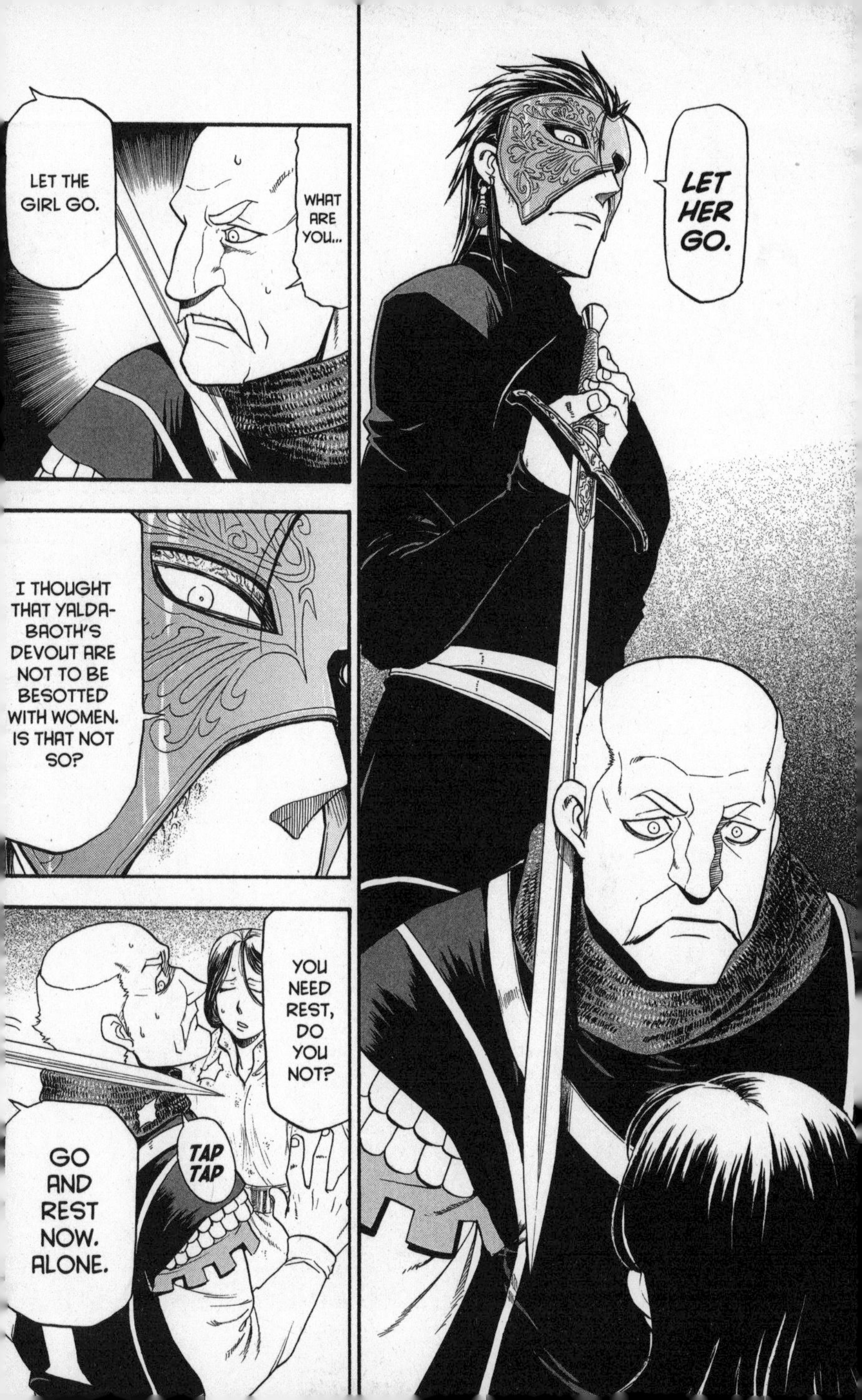
LET HER GO.
WHAT ARE YOU...
LET THE GIRL GO.
I THOUGHT THAT YALDA-BAOTH'S DEVOUT ARE NOT TO BE BESOTTED WITH WOMEN. IS THAT NOT SO?
YOU NEED REST, DO YOU NOT?
TAP TAP
GO AND REST NOW. ALONE.

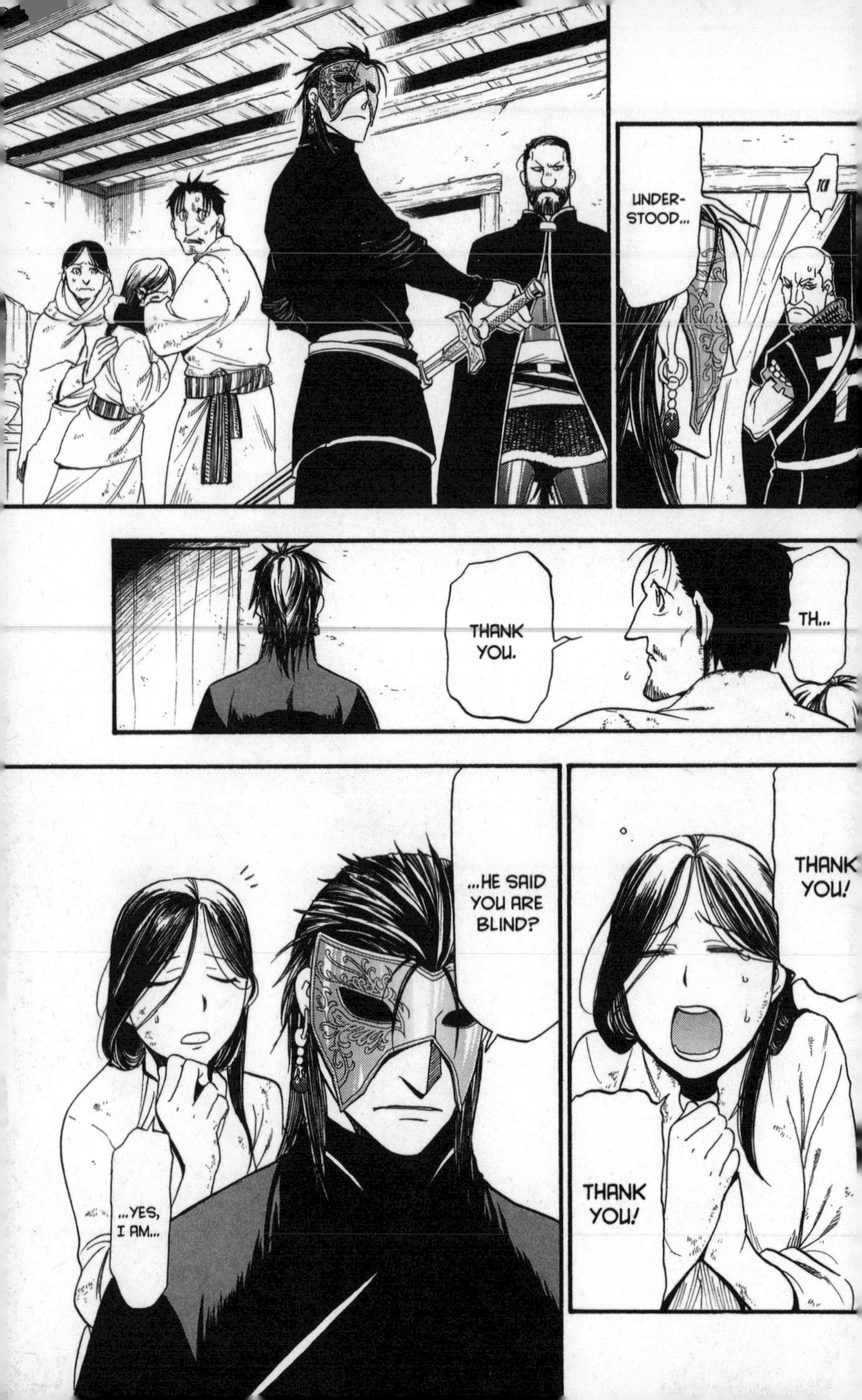
UNDER-STOOD...
TH...
THANK YOU.
THANK YOU!
THANK YOU!
...HE SAID YOU ARE BLIND?
...YES, I AM...

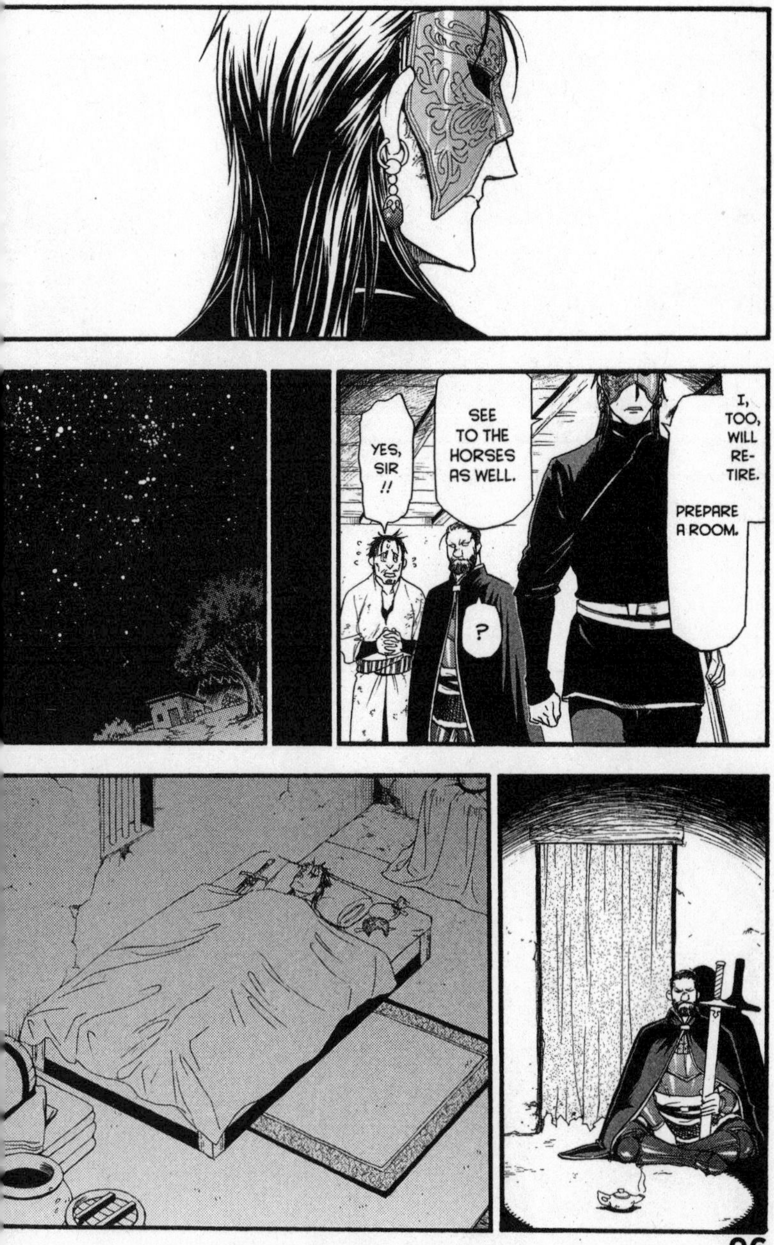
I, TOO, WILL RE-TIRE.
PREPARE A ROOM.
SEE TO THE HORSES AS WELL.
YES, SIR !!
?

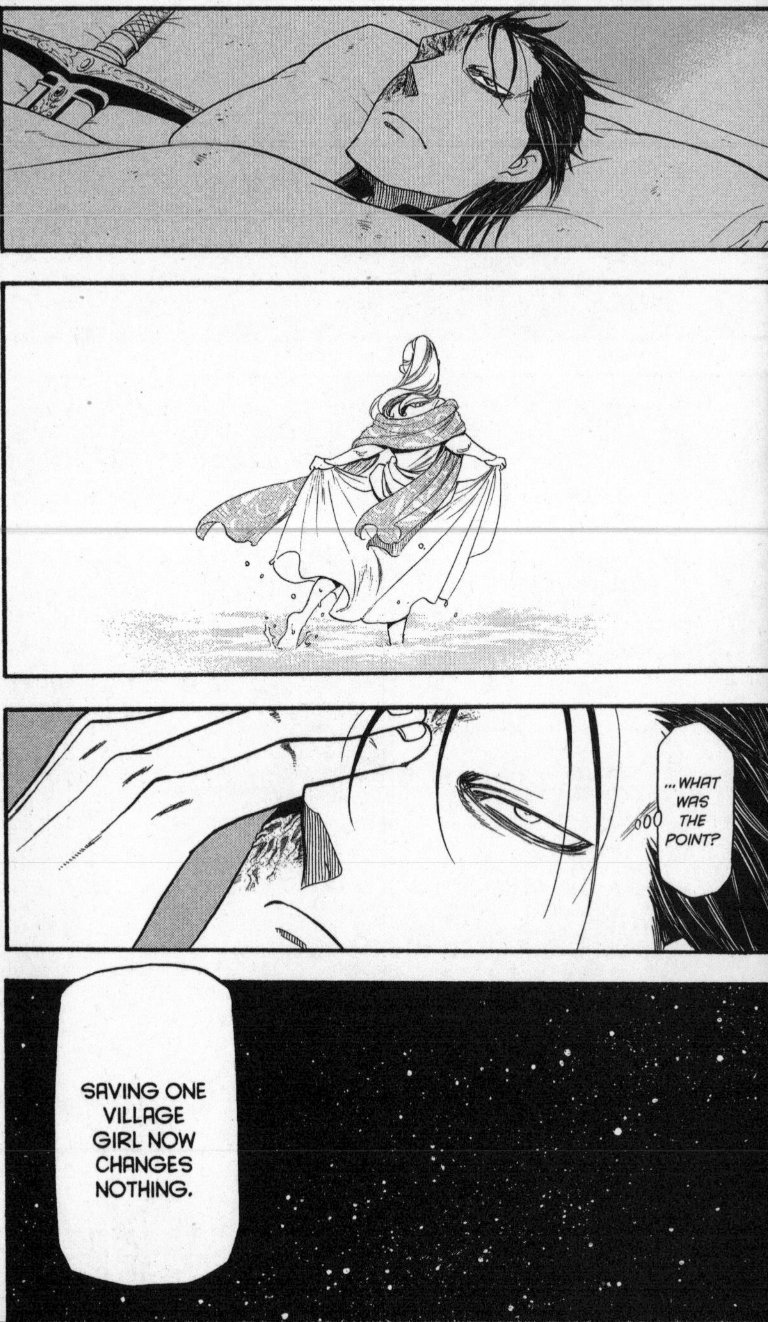
...WHAT WAS THE POINT?
SAVING ONE VILLAGE GIRL NOW CHANGES NOTHING.

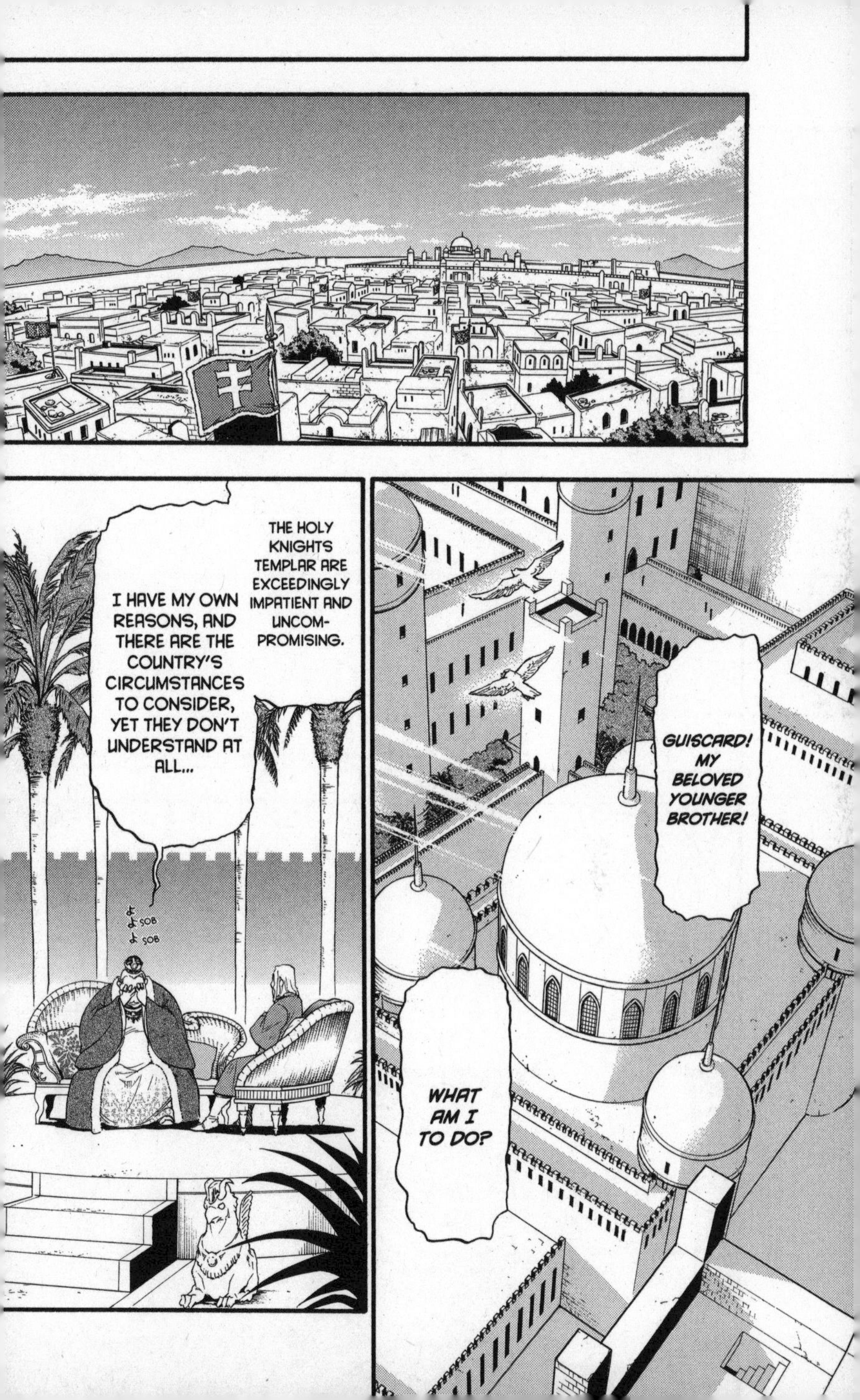
GUISCARD! MY BELOVED YOUNGER BROTHER!
WHAT AM I TO DO?
THE HOLY KNIGHTS TEMPLAR ARE EXCEEDINGLY IMPATIENT AND UNCOM-PROMISING.
I HAVE MY OWN REASONS, AND THERE ARE THE COUNTRY'S CIRCUMSTANCES TO CONSIDER, YET THEY DON'T UNDERSTAND AT ALL...
SOB
SOB

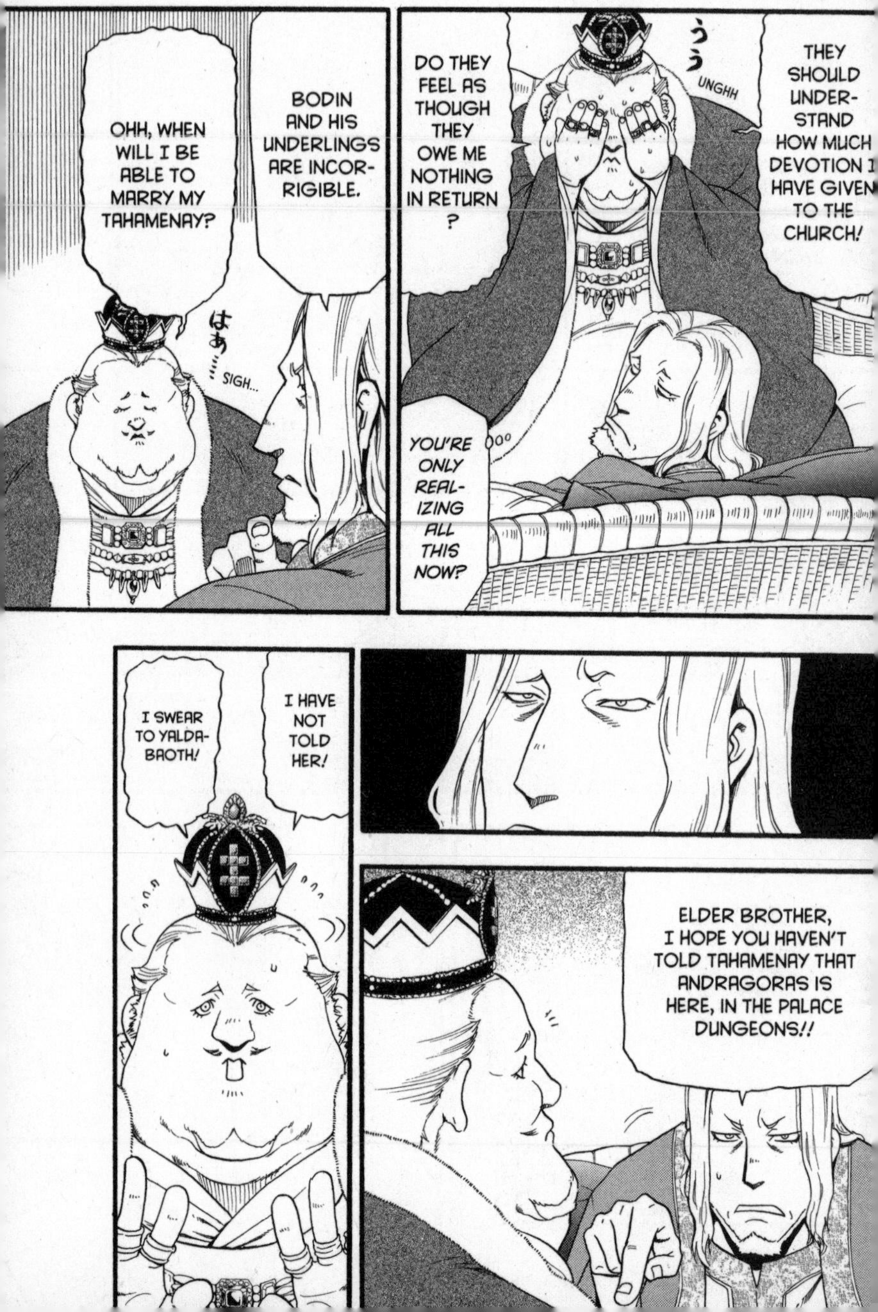
THEY SHOULD UNDER-STAND HOW MUCH DEVOTION I HAVE GIVEN TO THE CHURCH!
うう
UNGHH
DO THEY FEEL AS THOUGH THEY OWE ME NOTHING IN RETURN?
YOU'RE ONLY REAL-IZING ALL THIS NOW?
BODIN AND HIS UNDERLINGS ARE INCOR-RIGIBLE.
OHH, WHEN WILL I BE ABLE TO MARRY MY TAHAMENAY?
はあ
SIGH...
ELDER BROTHER, I HOPE YOU HAVEN'T TOLD TAHAMENAY THAT ANDRAGORAS IS HERE, IN THE PALACE DUNGEONS!!
I HAVE NOT TOLD HER!
I SWEAR TO YALDA-BAOTH!

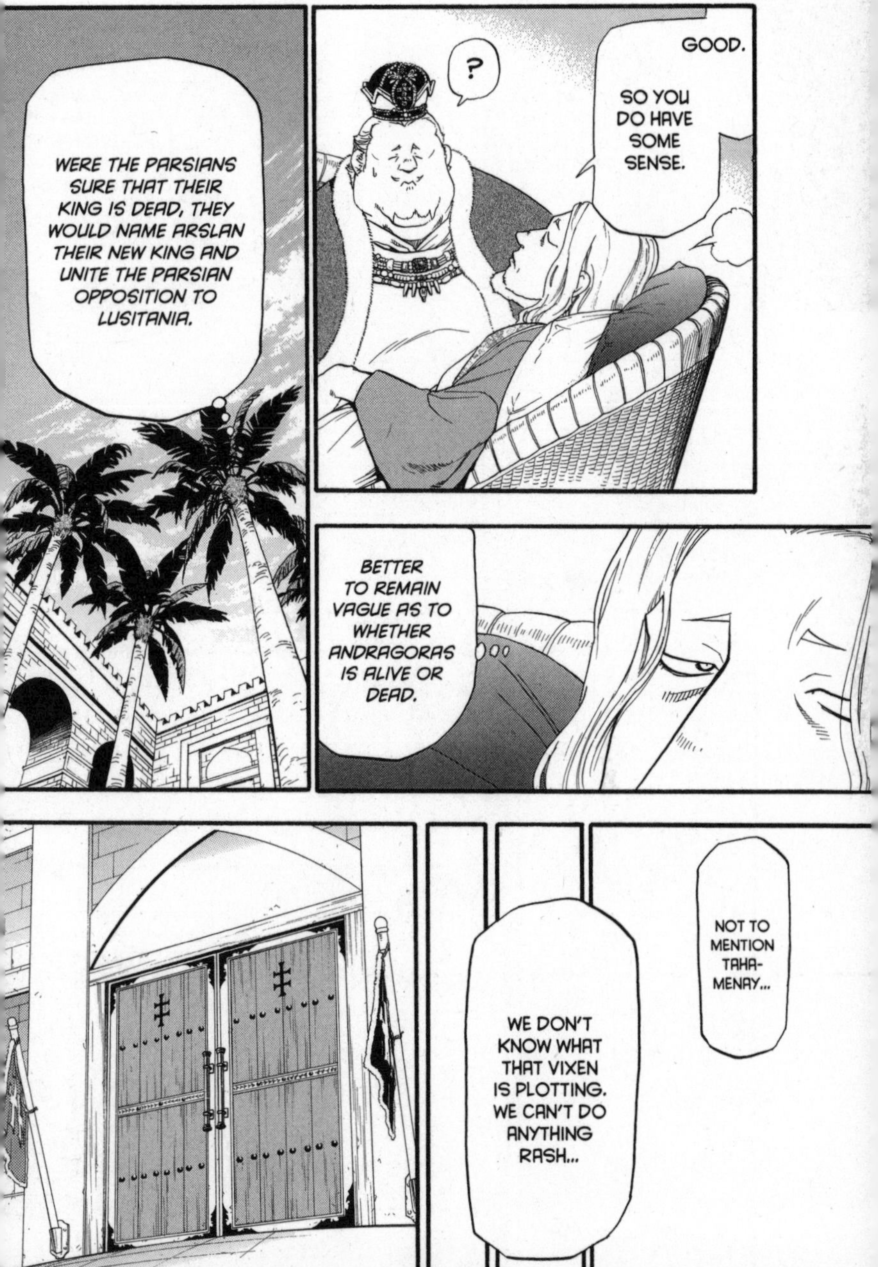
GOOD.
SO YOU DO HAVE SOME SENSE.
?
BETTER TO REMAIN VAGUE AS TO WHETHER ANDRAGORAS IS ALIVE OR DEAD.
WERE THE PARSIANS SURE THAT THEIR KING IS DEAD, THEY WOULD NAME ARSLAN THEIR NEW KING AND UNITE THE PARSIAN OPPOSITION TO LUSITANIA.
NOT TO MENTION TAHA-MENAY...
WE DON'T KNOW WHAT THAT VIXEN IS PLOTTING. WE CAN'T DO ANYTHING RASH...

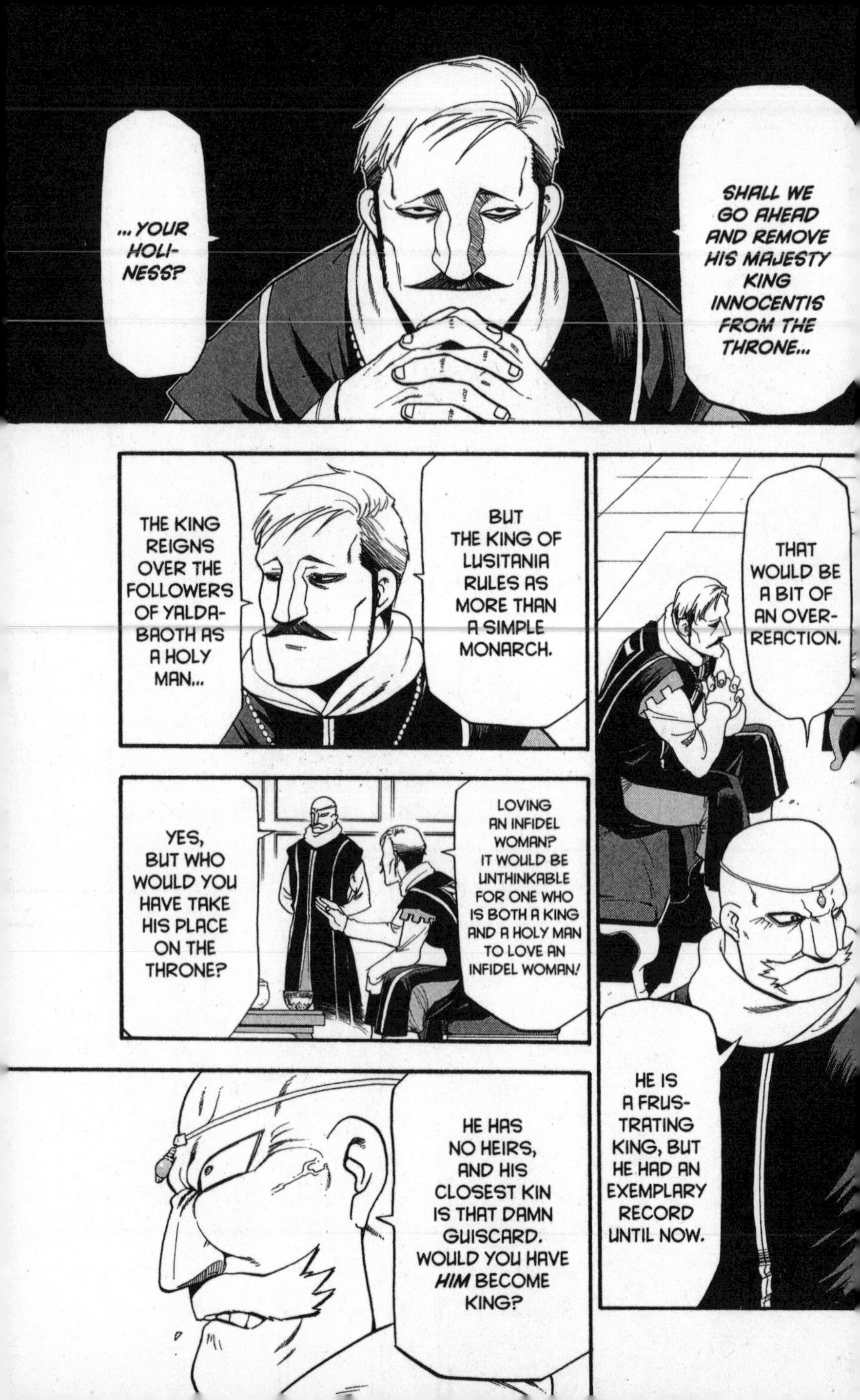
SHALL WE GO AHEAD AND REMOVE HIS MAJESTY KING INNOCENTIS FROM THE THRONE...
...YOUR HOLI-NESS?
THAT WOULD BE A BIT OF AN OVER-REACTION.
HE IS A FRUS-TRATING KING, BUT HE HAD AN EXEMPLARY RECORD UNTIL NOW.
BUT THE KING OF LUSITANIA RULES AS MORE THAN A SIMPLE MONARCH.
THE KING REIGNS OVER THE FOLLOWERS OF YALDA-BAOTH AS A HOLY MAN...
LOVING AN INFIDEL WOMAN? IT WOULD BE UNTHINKABLE FOR ONE WHO IS BOTH A KING AND A HOLY MAN TO LOVE AN INFIDEL WOMAN!
YES, BUT WHO WOULD YOU HAVE TAKE HIS PLACE ON THE THRONE?
HE HAS NO HEIRS, AND HIS CLOSEST KIN IS THAT DAMN GUISCARD. WOULD YOU HAVE *HIM* BECOME KING?

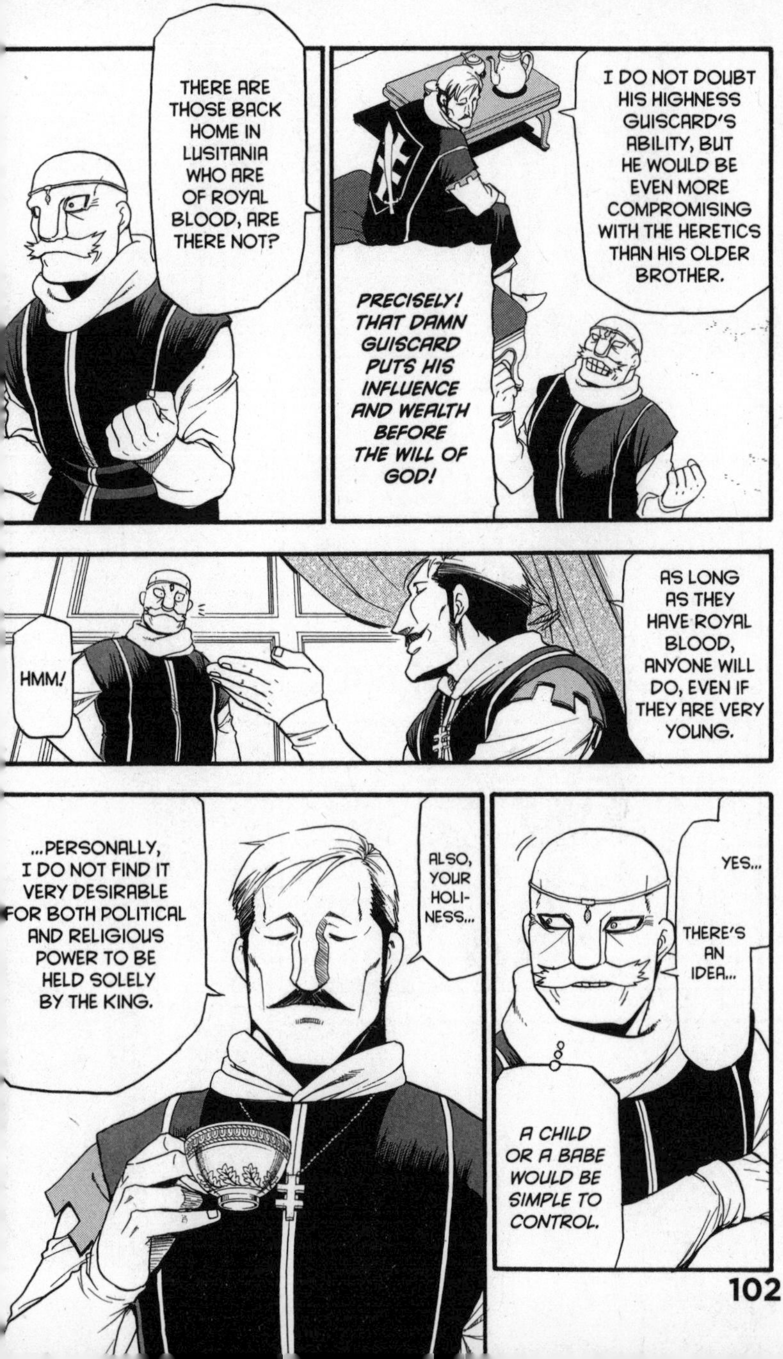
I DO NOT DOUBT HIS HIGHNESS GUISCARD'S ABILITY, BUT HE WOULD BE EVEN MORE COMPROMISING WITH THE HERETICS THAN HIS OLDER BROTHER.
PRECISELY! THAT DAMN GUISCARD PUTS HIS INFLUENCE AND WEALTH BEFORE THE WILL OF GOD!
THERE ARE THOSE BACK HOME IN LUSITANIA WHO ARE OF ROYAL BLOOD, ARE THERE NOT?
AS LONG AS THEY HAVE ROYAL BLOOD, ANYONE WILL DO, EVEN IF THEY ARE VERY YOUNG.
HMM!
YES...
THERE'S AN IDEA...
A CHILD OR A BABE WOULD BE SIMPLE TO CONTROL.
ALSO, YOUR HOLI-NESS...
...PERSONALLY, I DO NOT FIND IT VERY DESIRABLE FOR BOTH POLITICAL AND RELIGIOUS POWER TO BE HELD SOLELY BY THE KING.

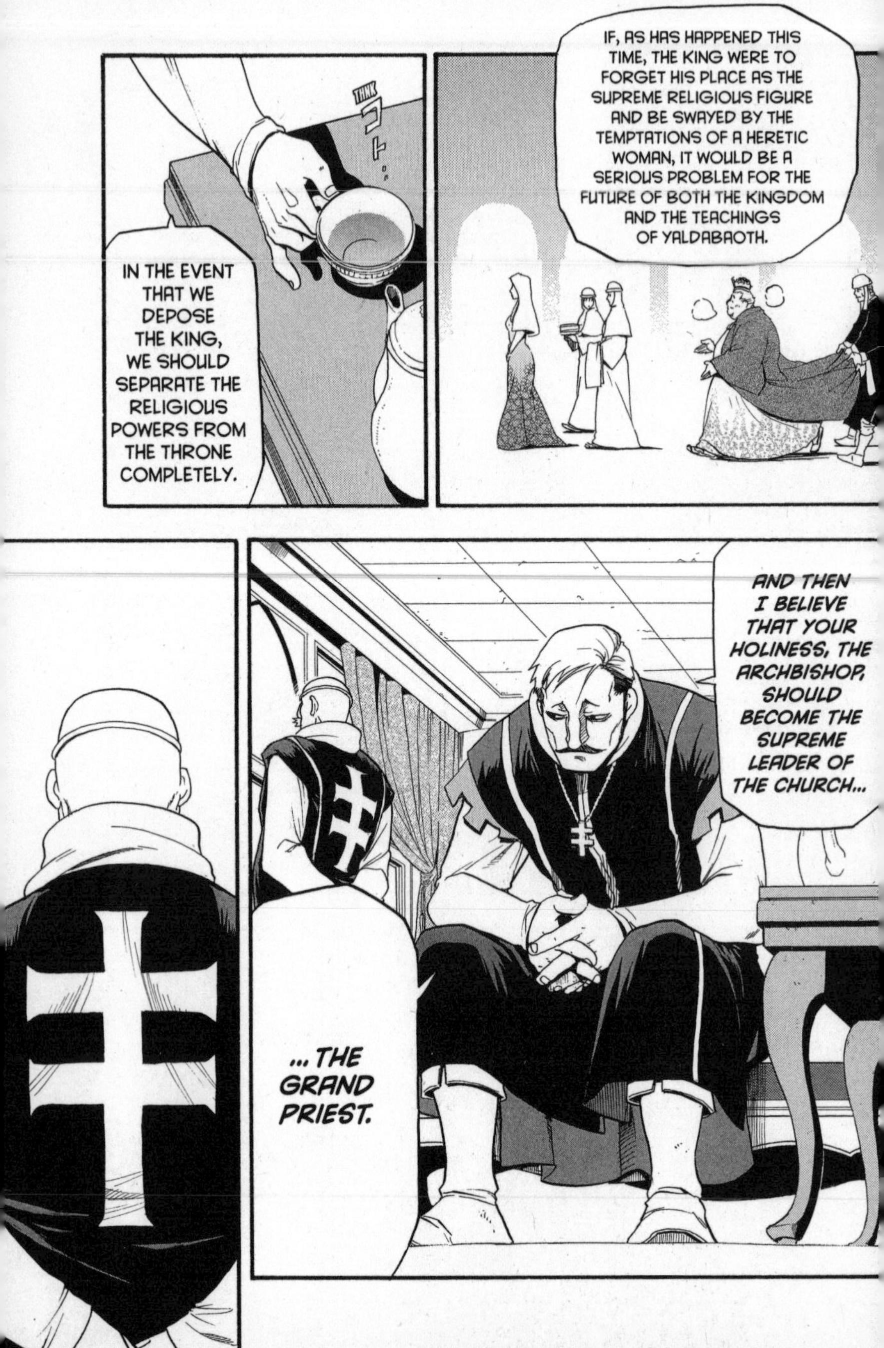
IF, AS HAS HAPPENED THIS TIME, THE KING WERE TO FORGET HIS PLACE AS THE SUPREME RELIGIOUS FIGURE AND BE SWAYED BY THE TEMPTATIONS OF A HERETIC WOMAN, IT WOULD BE A SERIOUS PROBLEM FOR THE FUTURE OF BOTH THE KINGDOM AND THE TEACHINGS OF YALDABAOTH.
THNK
コト
IN THE EVENT THAT WE DEPOSE THE KING, WE SHOULD SEPARATE THE RELIGIOUS POWERS FROM THE THRONE COMPLETELY.
AND THEN I BELIEVE THAT YOUR HOLINESS, THE ARCHBISHOP, SHOULD BECOME THE SUPREME LEADER OF THE CHURCH...
...THE GRAND PRIEST.

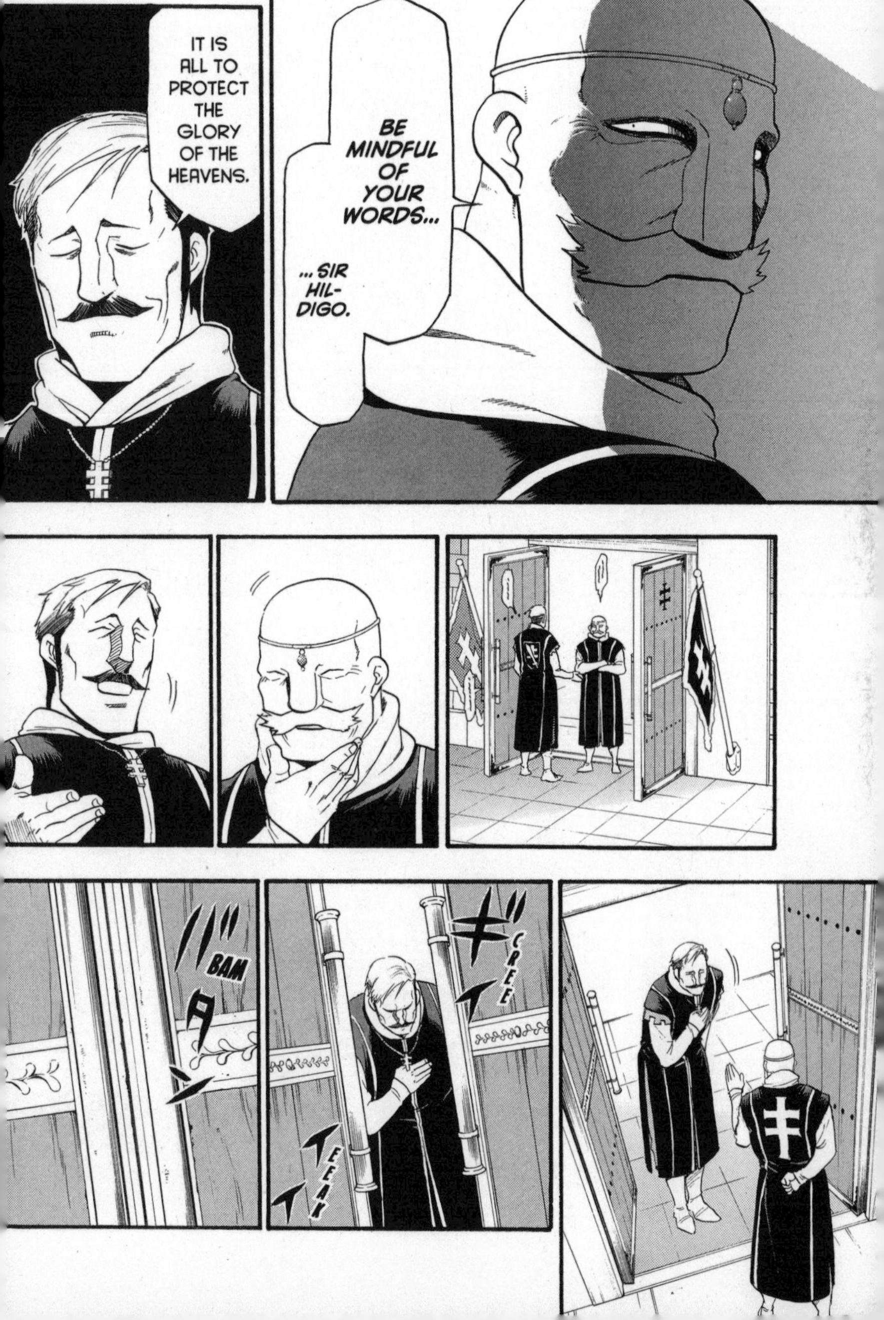
BE MINDFUL OF YOUR WORDS...
...SIR HIL-DIGO.
IT IS ALL TO PROTECT THE GLORY OF THE HEAVENS.
CREE
EEEAK
BAM

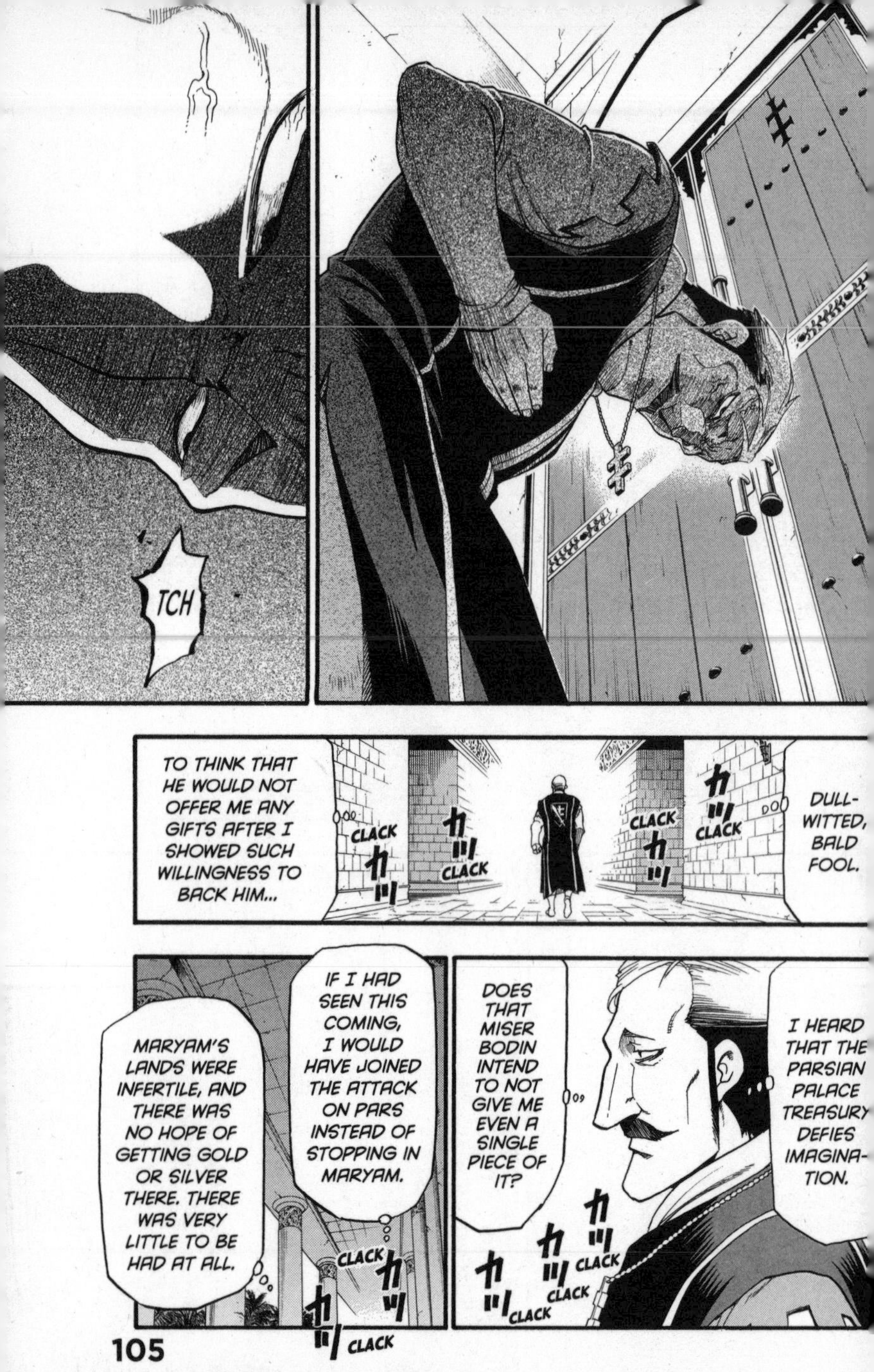
TCH
DULL-WITTED, BALD FOOL.
カッ CLACK
カッ CLACK
カッ CLACK
カッ CLACK
TO THINK THAT HE WOULD NOT OFFER ME ANY GIFTS AFTER I SHOWED SUCH WILLINGNESS TO BACK HIM...
I HEARD THAT THE PARSIAN PALACE TREASURY DEFIES IMAGINATION.
DOES THAT MISER BODIN INTEND TO NOT GIVE ME EVEN A SINGLE PIECE OF IT?
カッ CLACK
カッ CLACK
カッ CLACK
IF I HAD SEEN THIS COMING, I WOULD HAVE JOINED THE ATTACK ON PARS INSTEAD OF STOPPING IN MARYAM.
MARYAM'S LANDS WERE INFERTILE, AND THERE WAS NO HOPE OF GETTING GOLD OR SILVER THERE. THERE WAS VERY LITTLE TO BE HAD AT ALL.
カッ CLACK
カッ CLACK

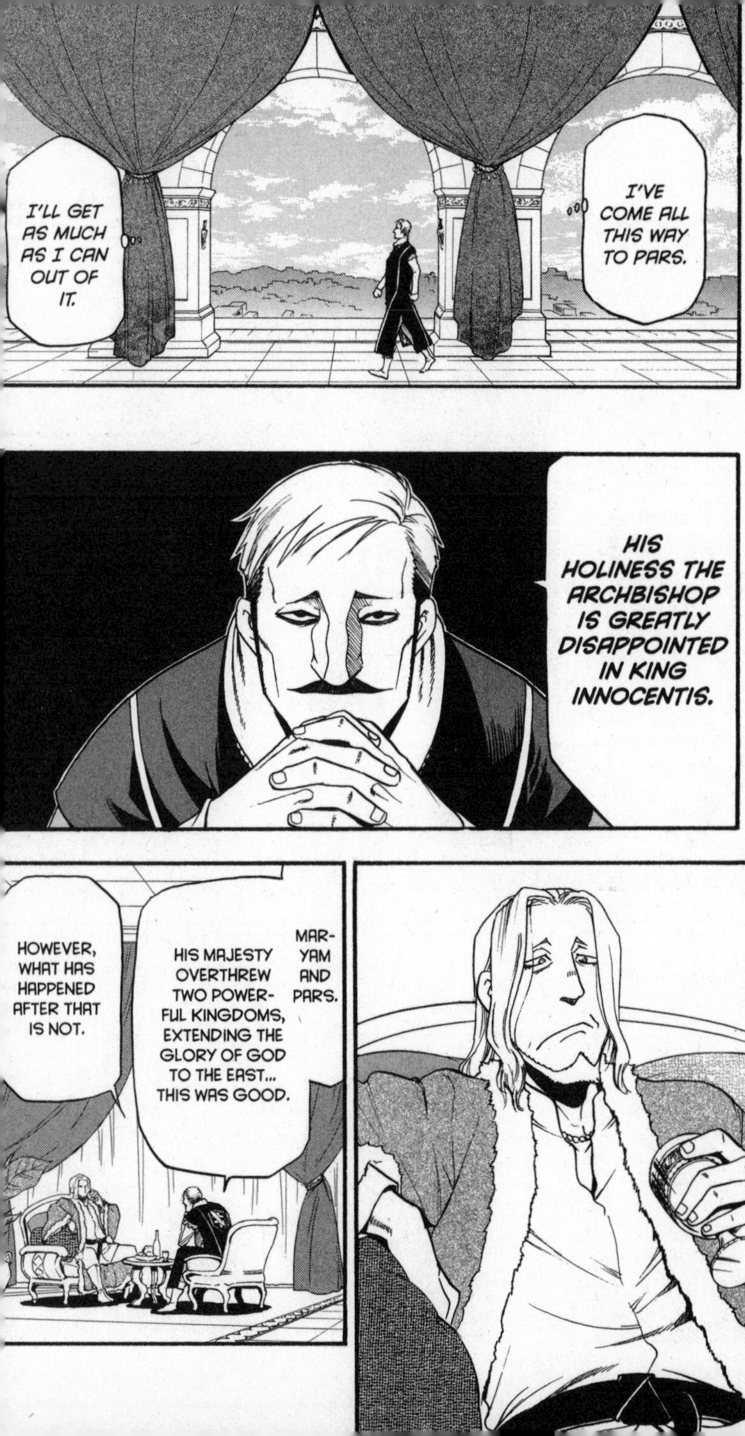
I'VE COME ALL THIS WAY TO PARS.
I'LL GET AS MUCH AS I CAN OUT OF IT.
HIS HOLINESS THE ARCHBISHOP IS GREATLY DISAPPOINTED IN KING INNOCENTIS.
MAR-YAM AND PARS.
HIS MAJESTY OVERTHREW TWO POWER-FUL KINGDOMS, EXTENDING THE GLORY OF GOD TO THE EAST... THIS WAS GOOD.
HOWEVER, WHAT HAS HAPPENED AFTER THAT IS NOT.

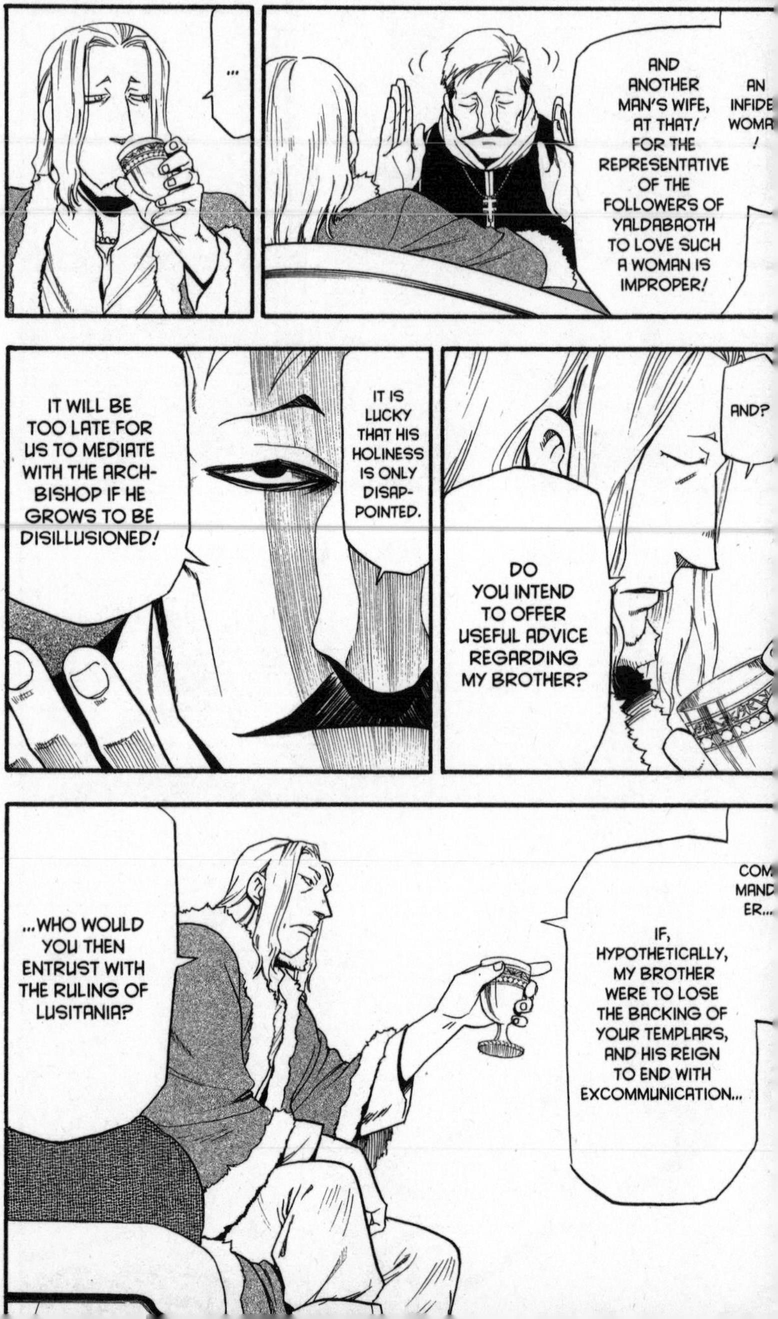
AN INFIDE WOMA!
AND ANOTHER MAN'S WIFE, AT THAT! FOR THE REPRESENTATIVE OF THE FOLLOWERS OF YALDABAOTH TO LOVE SUCH A WOMAN IS IMPROPER!
...
AND?
DO YOU INTEND TO OFFER USEFUL ADVICE REGARDING MY BROTHER?
IT IS LUCKY THAT HIS HOLINESS IS ONLY DISAPPOINTED.
IT WILL BE TOO LATE FOR US TO MEDIATE WITH THE ARCHBISHOP IF HE GROWS TO BE DISILLUSIONED!
COMMANDER...
IF, HYPOTHETICALLY, MY BROTHER WERE TO LOSE THE BACKING OF YOUR TEMPLARS, AND HIS REIGN TO END WITH EXCOMMUNICATION...
...WHO WOULD YOU THEN ENTRUST WITH THE RULING OF LUSITANIA?

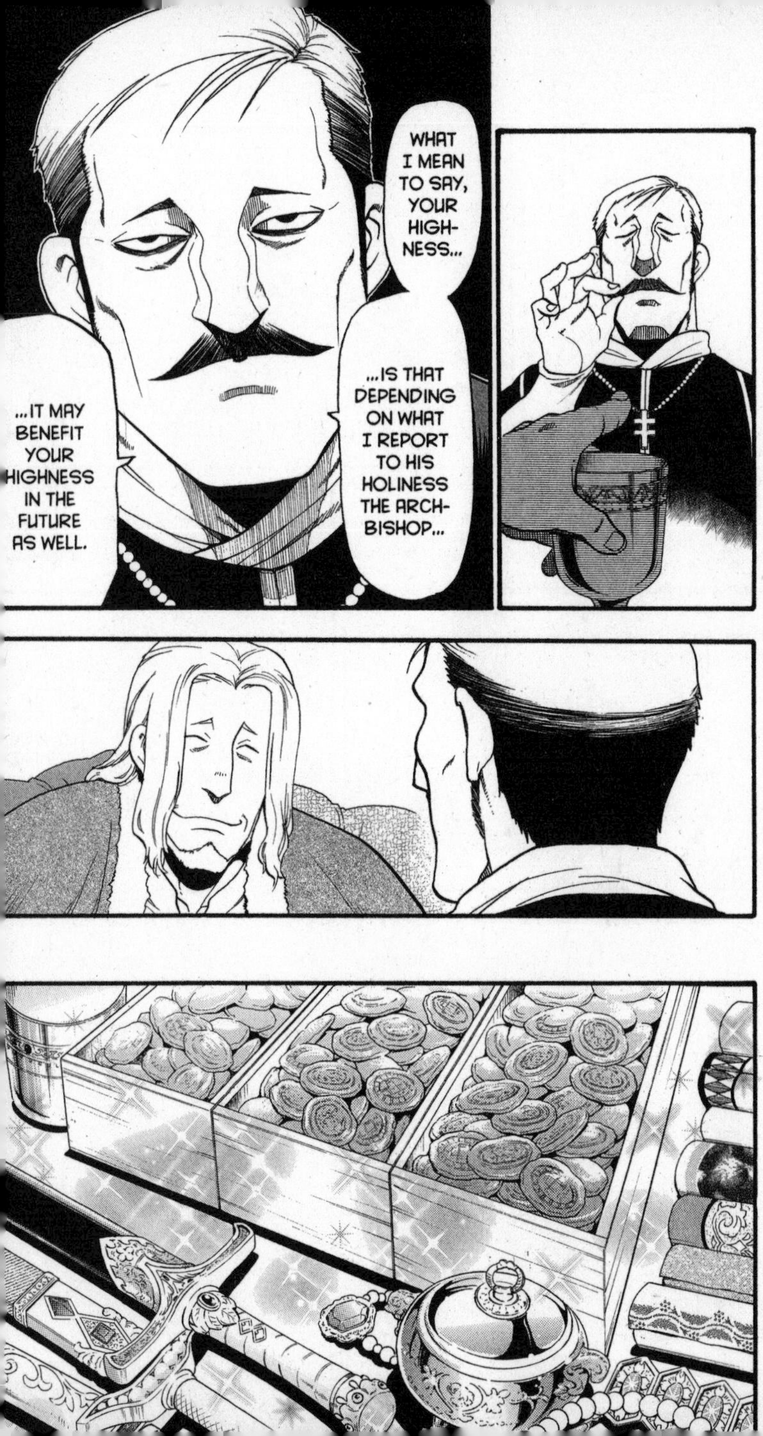
WHAT I MEAN TO SAY, YOUR HIGHNESS...
...IS THAT DEPENDING ON WHAT I REPORT TO HIS HOLINESS THE ARCHBISHOP...
...IT MAY BENEFIT YOUR HIGHNESS IN THE FUTURE AS WELL.

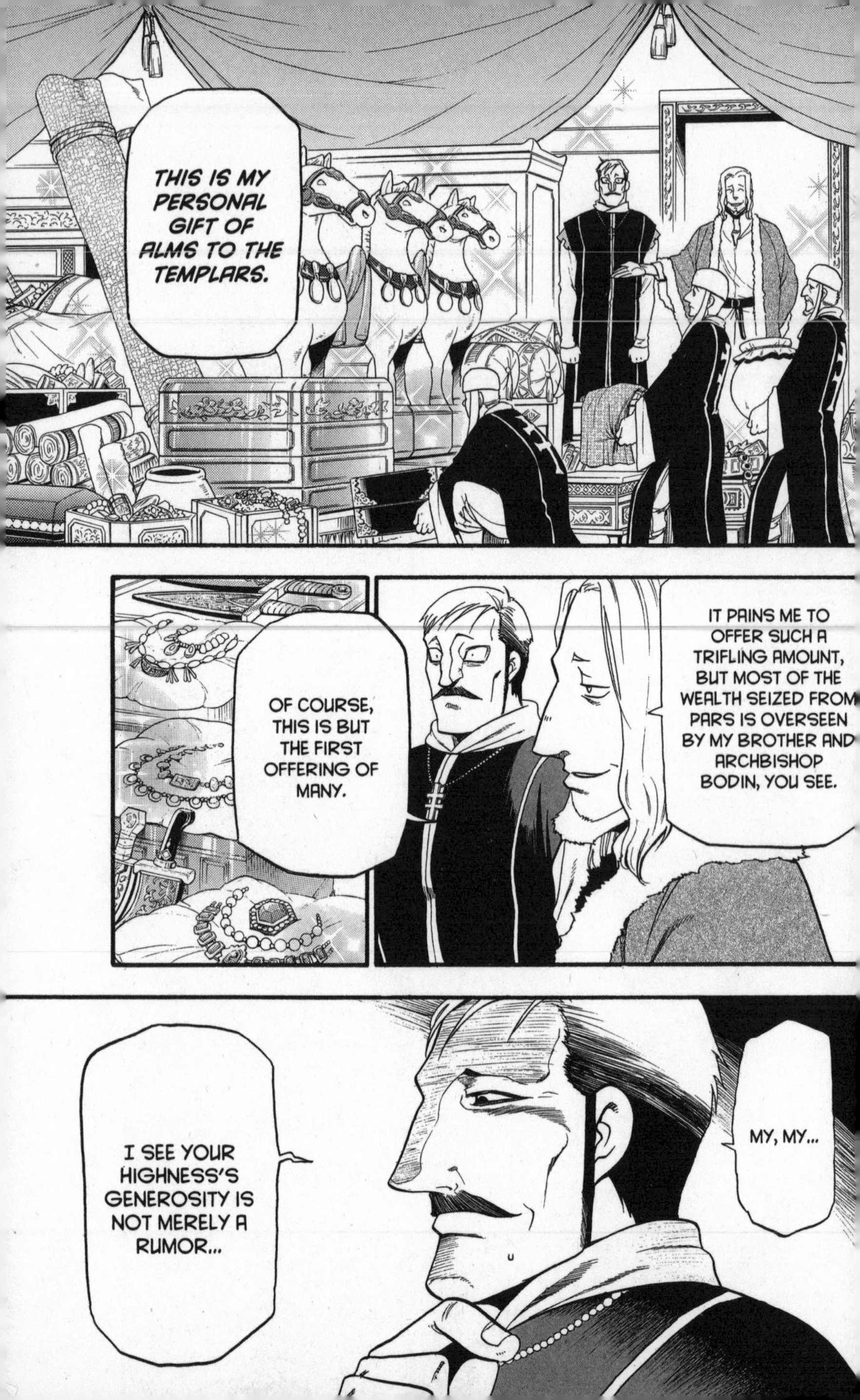
THIS IS MY PERSONAL GIFT OF ALMS TO THE TEMPLARS.
IT PAINS ME TO OFFER SUCH A TRIFLING AMOUNT, BUT MOST OF THE WEALTH SEIZED FROM PARS IS OVERSEEN BY MY BROTHER AND ARCHBISHOP BODIN, YOU SEE.
OF COURSE, THIS IS BUT THE FIRST OFFERING OF MANY.
MY, MY...
I SEE YOUR HIGHNESS'S GENEROSITY IS NOT MERELY A RUMOR...

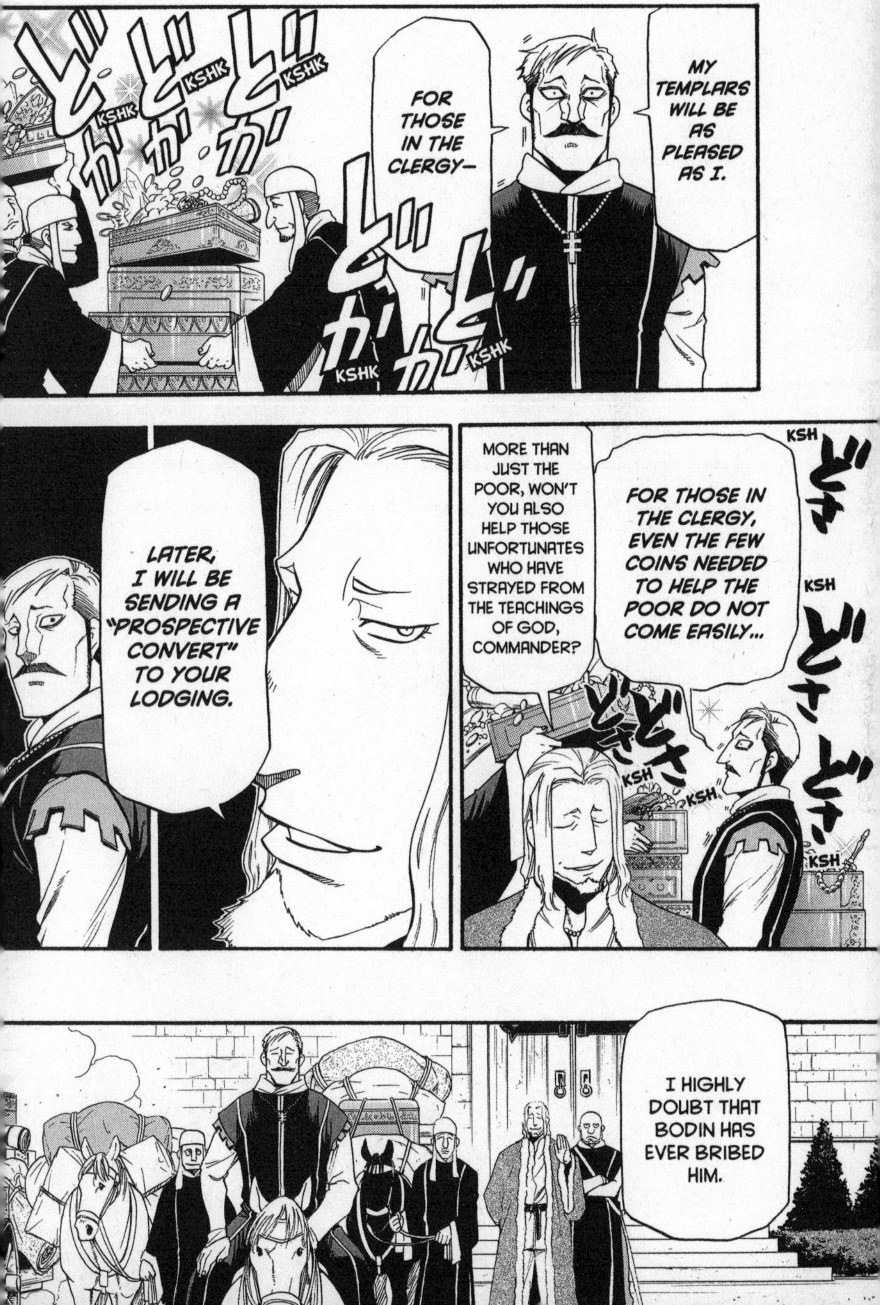
MY TEMPLARS WILL BE AS PLEASED AS I.
FOR THOSE IN THE CLERGY—
KSHK
KSHK
KSHK
KSHK
KSHK
FOR THOSE IN THE CLERGY, EVEN THE FEW COINS NEEDED TO HELP THE POOR DO NOT COME EASILY...
MORE THAN JUST THE POOR, WON'T YOU ALSO HELP THOSE UNFORTUNATES WHO HAVE STRAYED FROM THE TEACHINGS OF GOD, COMMANDER?
KSH
KSH
KSH
KSH
KSH
LATER, I WILL BE SENDING A "PROSPECTIVE CONVERT" TO YOUR LODGING.
I HIGHLY DOUBT THAT BODIN HAS EVER BRIBED HIM.

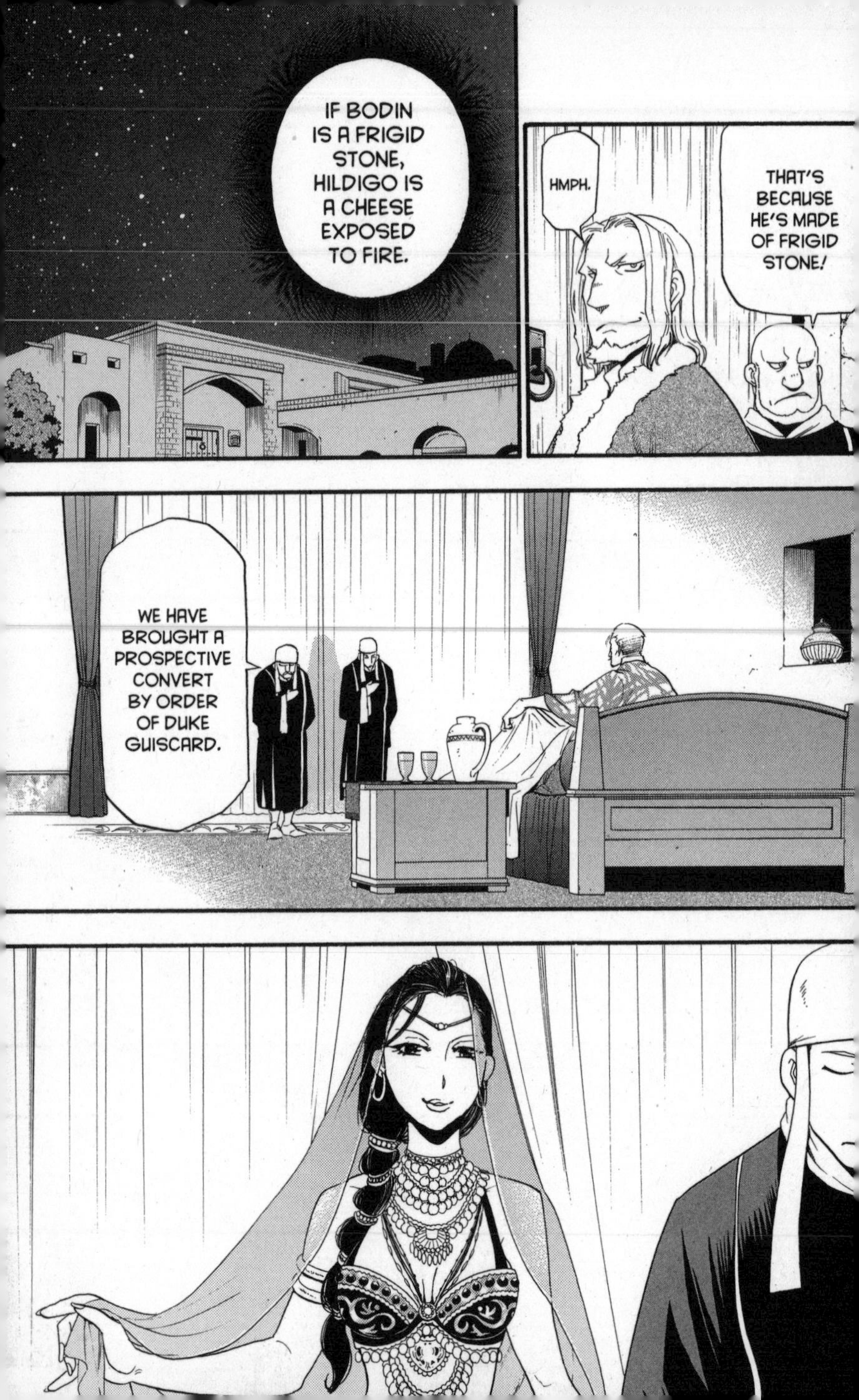
THAT'S BECAUSE HE'S MADE OF FRIGID STONE!
HMPH.
IF BODIN IS A FRIGID STONE, HILDIGO IS A CHEESE EXPOSED TO FIRE.
WE HAVE BROUGHT A PROSPECTIVE CONVERT BY ORDER OF DUKE GUISCARD.

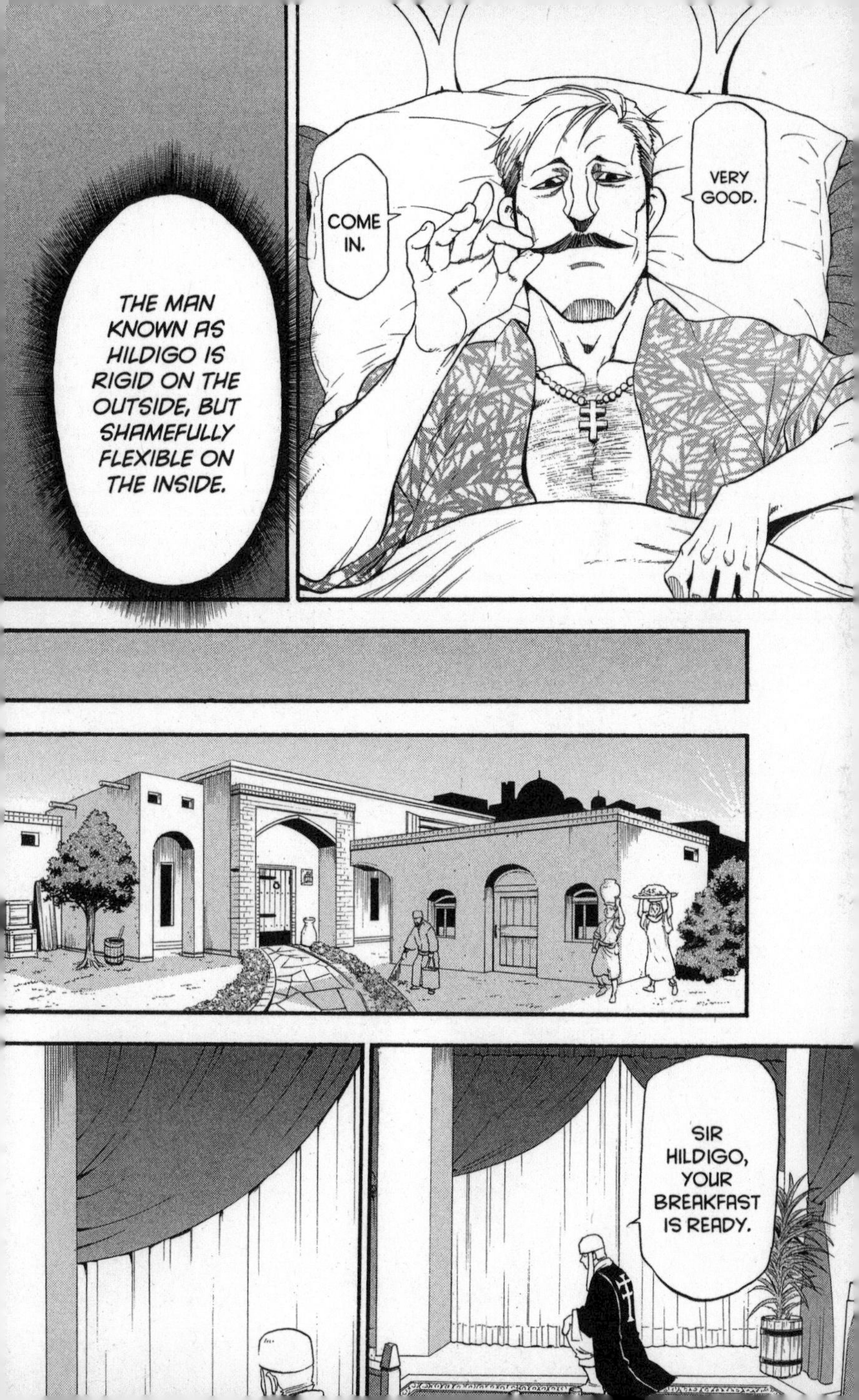
VERY GOOD.
COME IN.
THE MAN KNOWN AS HILDIGO IS RIGID ON THE OUTSIDE, BUT SHAMEFULLY FLEXIBLE ON THE INSIDE.
SIR HILDIGO, YOUR BREAKFAST IS READY.

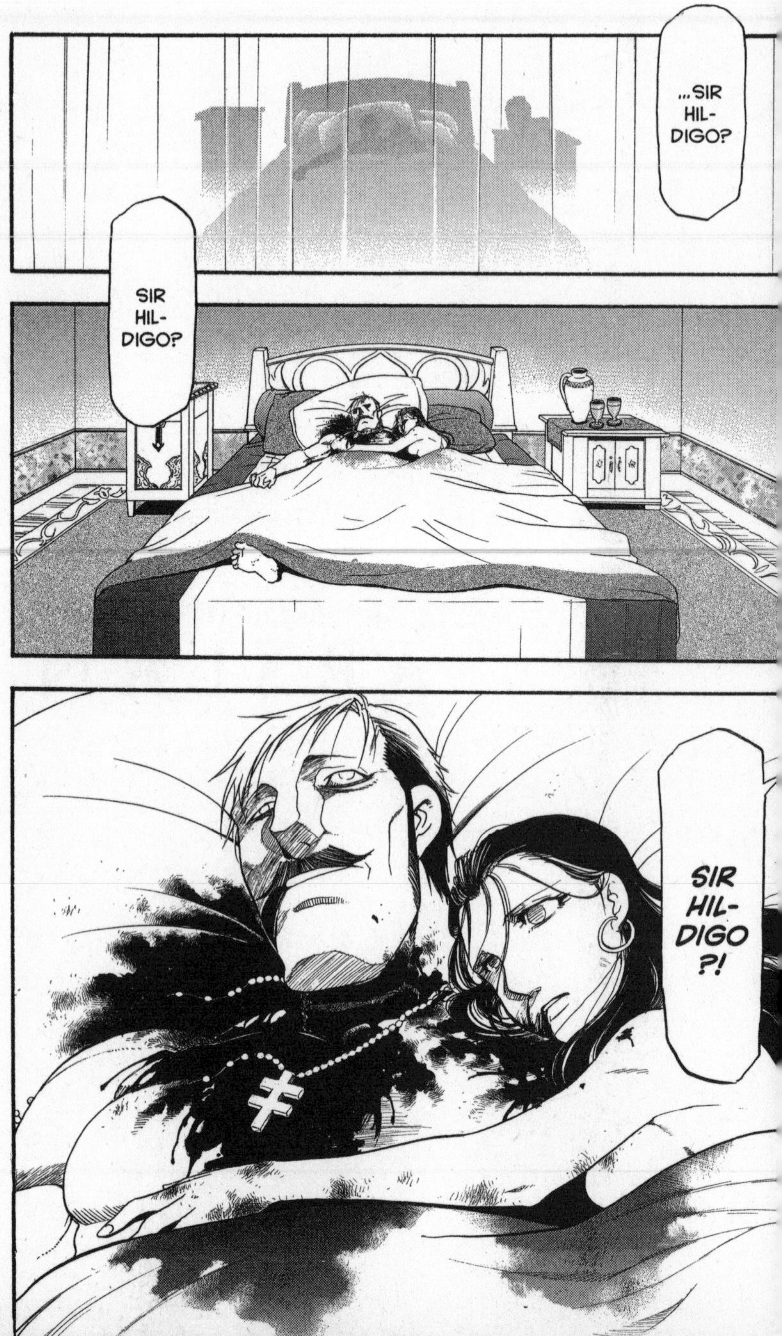
...SIR HIL-DIGO?
SIR HIL-DIGO?
SIR HIL-DIGO?!

THE HEROIC LEGEND OF
ARSLAN

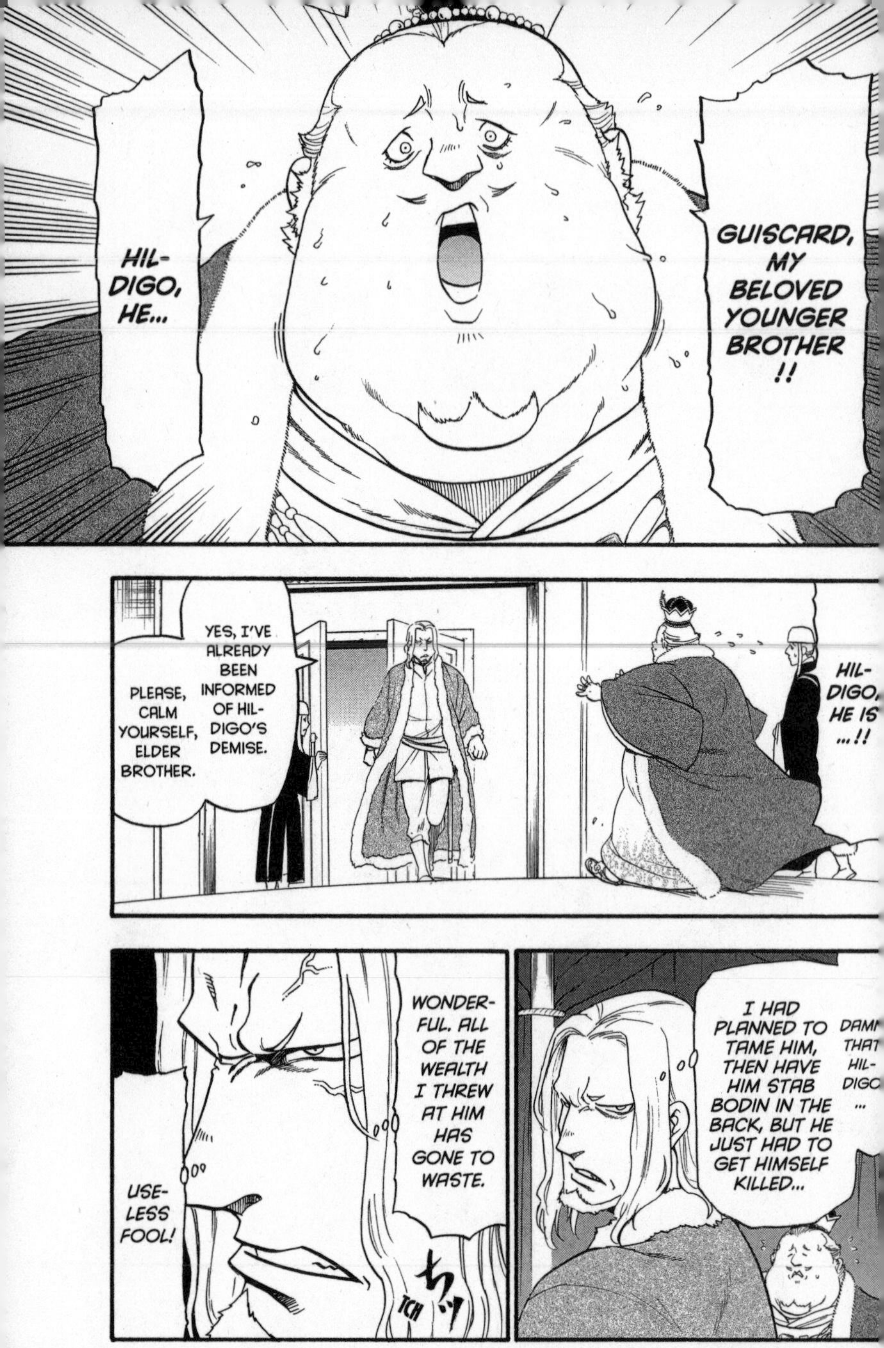
GUISCARD, MY BELOVED YOUNGER BROTHER!!
HIL-DIGO, HE...
HIL-DIGO, HE IS ...!!
YES, I'VE ALREADY BEEN INFORMED OF HIL-DIGO'S DEMISE.
PLEASE, CALM YOURSELF, ELDER BROTHER.
DAM THAT HIL-DIGO ...
I HAD PLANNED TO TAME HIM, THEN HAVE HIM STAB BODIN IN THE BACK, BUT HE JUST HAD TO GET HIMSELF KILLED...
WONDER-FUL. ALL OF THE WEALTH I THREW AT HIM HAS GONE TO WASTE.
USE-LESS FOOL!
TCH

Chapter 32: Return of the Warrior

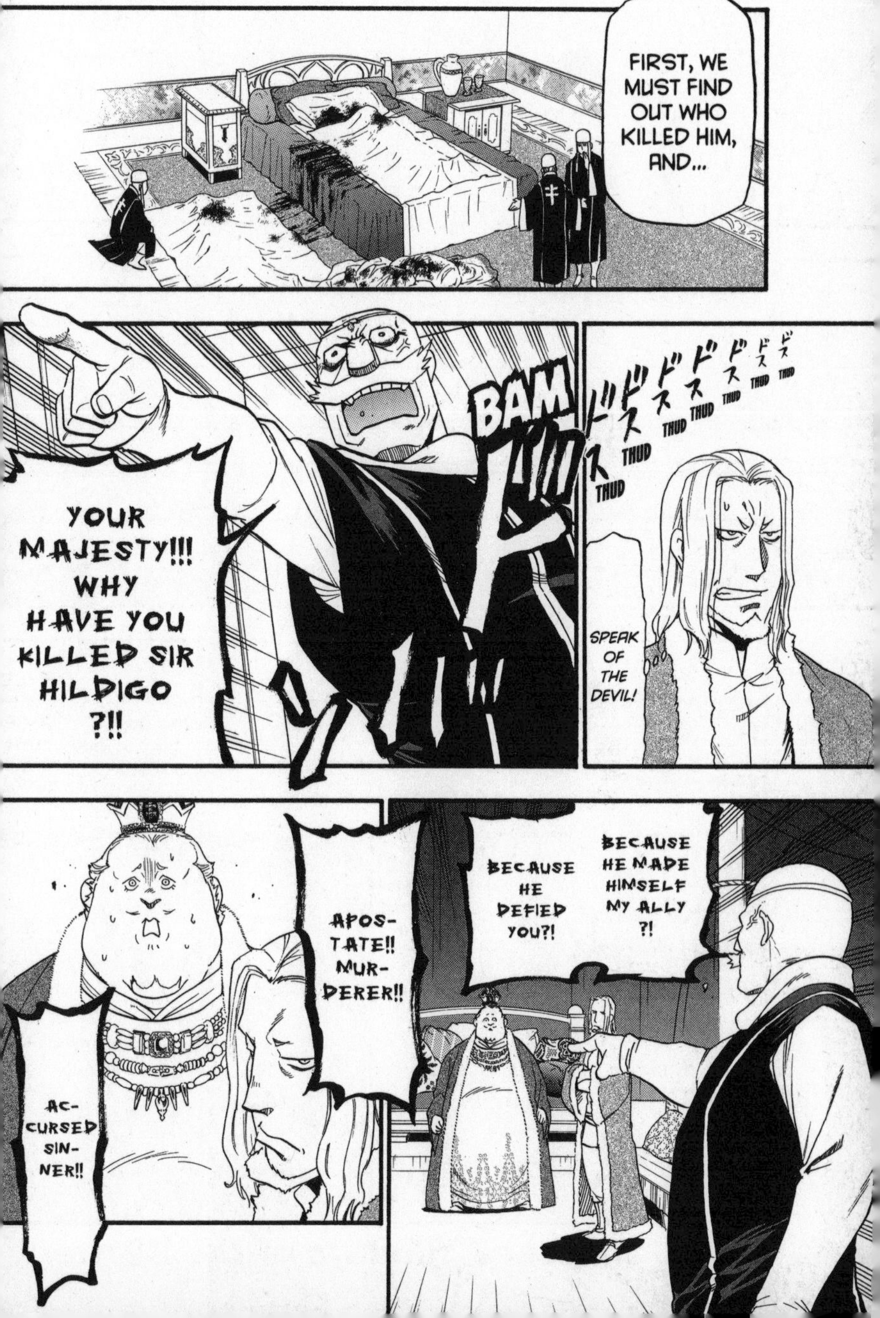
FIRST, WE MUST FIND OUT WHO KILLED HIM, AND...
ドスドスドスドスドスドス
THUD THUD THUD THUD THUD THUD
SPEAK OF THE DEVIL!
BAM
YOUR MAJESTY!!! WHY HAVE YOU KILLED SIR HILDIGO?!!
BECAUSE HE MADE HIMSELF MY ALLY?!
BECAUSE HE DEFIED YOU?!
APOS-TATE!! MUR-DERER!!
AC-CURSED SIN-NER!!

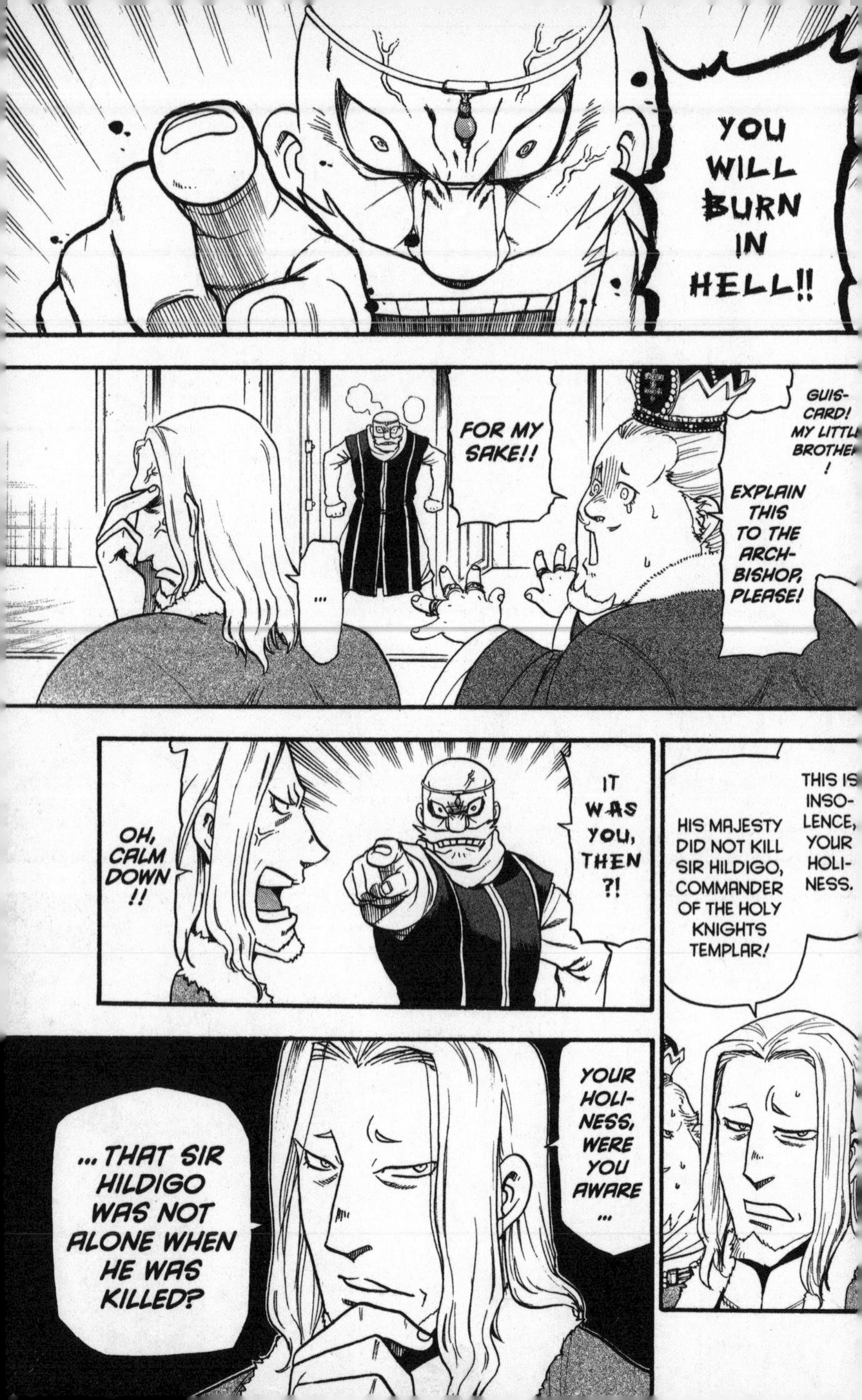
YOU WILL BURN IN HELL!!
GUIS-CARD! MY LITTL BROTHE!
EXPLAIN THIS TO THE ARCH-BISHOP, PLEASE!
FOR MY SAKE!!
...
THIS IS INSO-LENCE, YOUR HOLI-NESS.
HIS MAJESTY DID NOT KILL SIR HILDIGO, COMMANDER OF THE HOLY KNIGHTS TEMPLAR!
IT WAS YOU, THEN?!
OH, CALM DOWN!!
YOUR HOLI-NESS, WERE YOU AWARE...
...THAT SIR HILDIGO WAS NOT ALONE WHEN HE WAS KILLED?

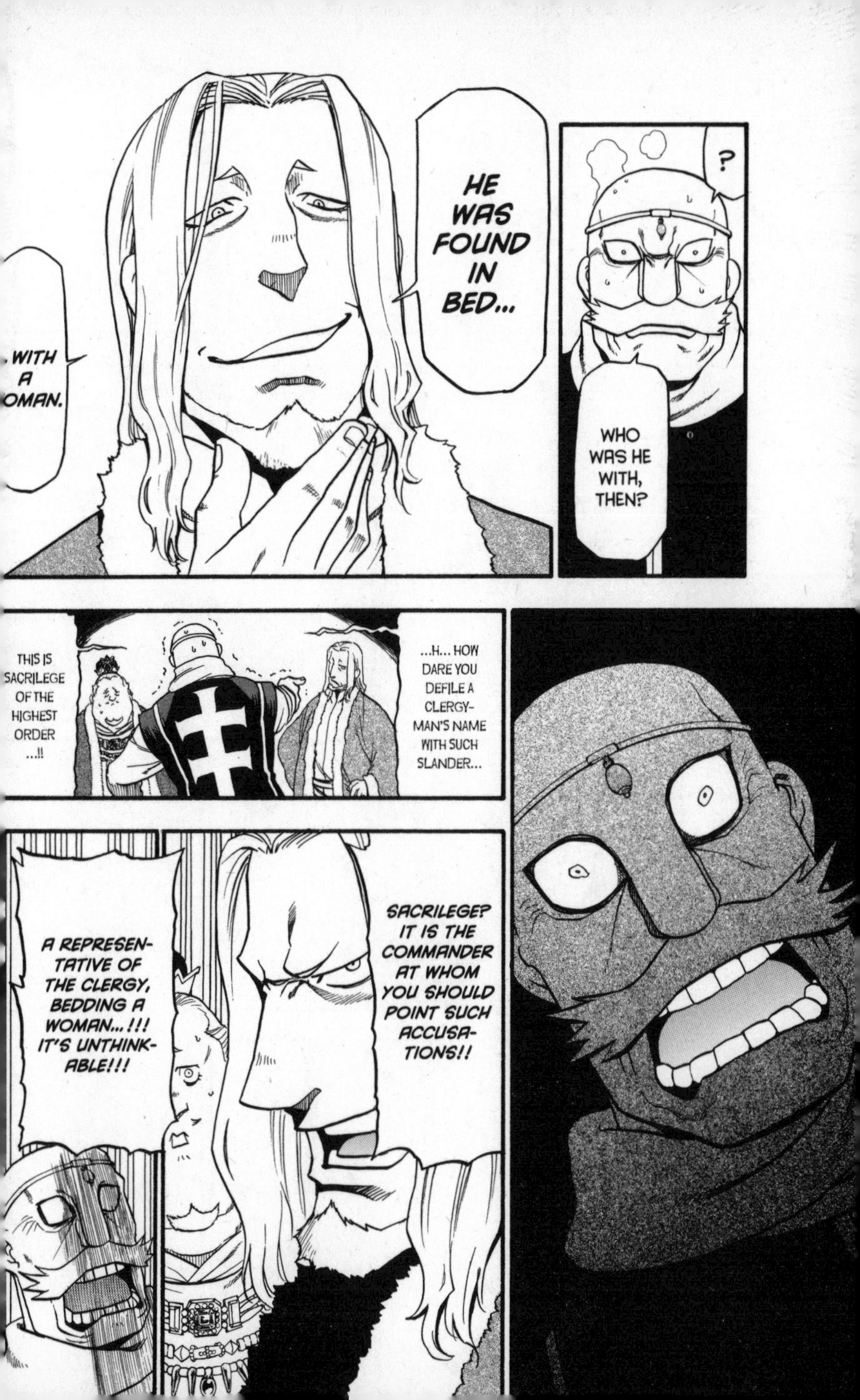

?
WHO WAS HE WITH, THEN?
HE WAS FOUND IN BED...
WITH A OMAN.
...H... HOW DARE YOU DEFILE A CLERGY-MAN'S NAME WITH SUCH SLANDER...
THIS IS SACRILEGE OF THE HIGHEST ORDER ...!!
SACRILEGE? IT IS THE COMMANDER AT WHOM YOU SHOULD POINT SUCH ACCUSA-TIONS!!
A REPRESEN-TATIVE OF THE CLERGY, BEDDING A WOMAN...!!! IT'S UNTHINK-ABLE!!!

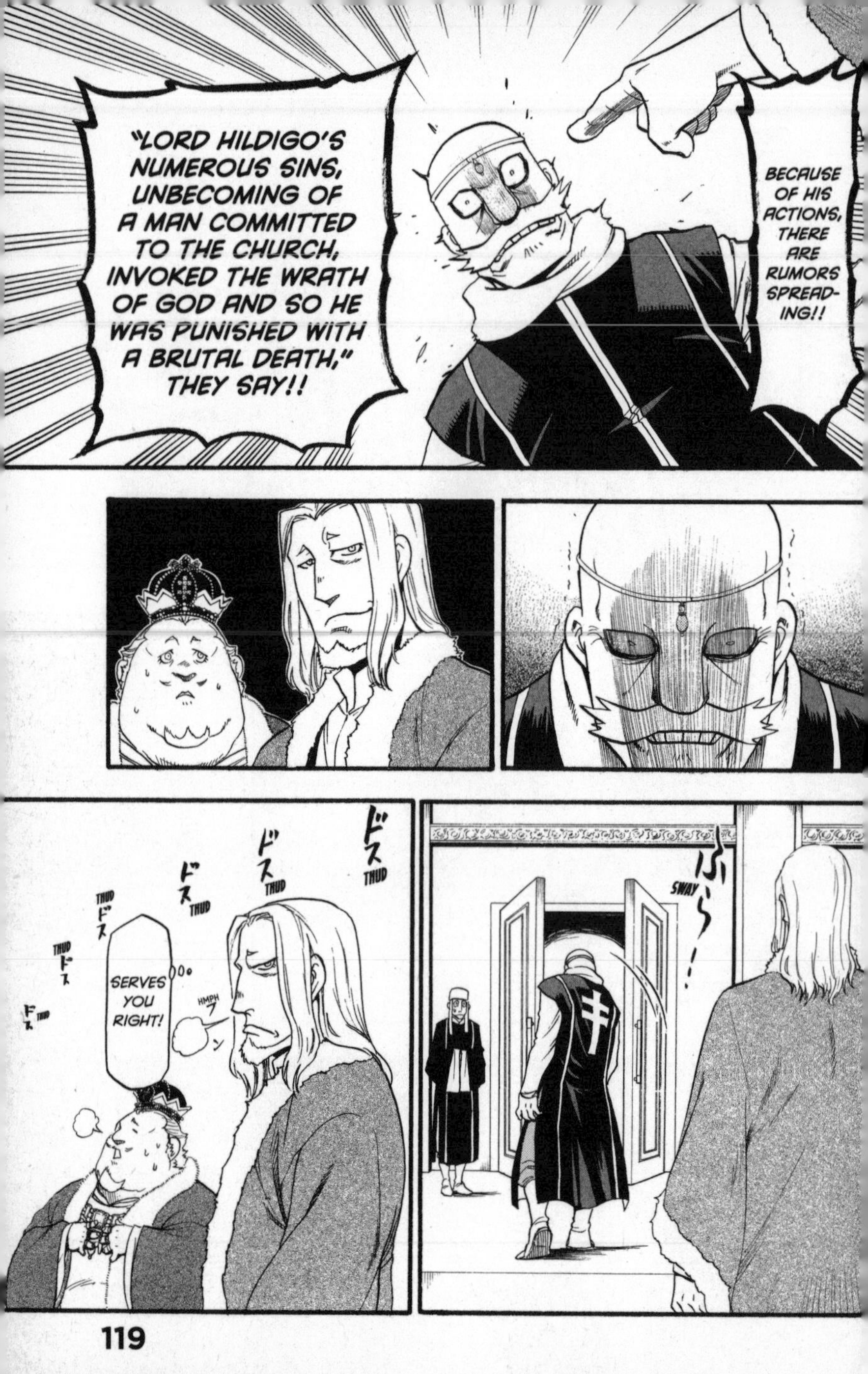
BECAUSE OF HIS ACTIONS, THERE ARE RUMORS SPREADING!!
"LORD HILDIGO'S NUMEROUS SINS, UNBECOMING OF A MAN COMMITTED TO THE CHURCH, INVOKED THE WRATH OF GOD AND SO HE WAS PUNISHED WITH A BRUTAL DEATH," THEY SAY!!
ふら SWAY
ドス THUD
ドス THUD
ドス THUD
ドス THUD
ドス THUD
ドス THUD
フン HMPH
SERVES YOU RIGHT!

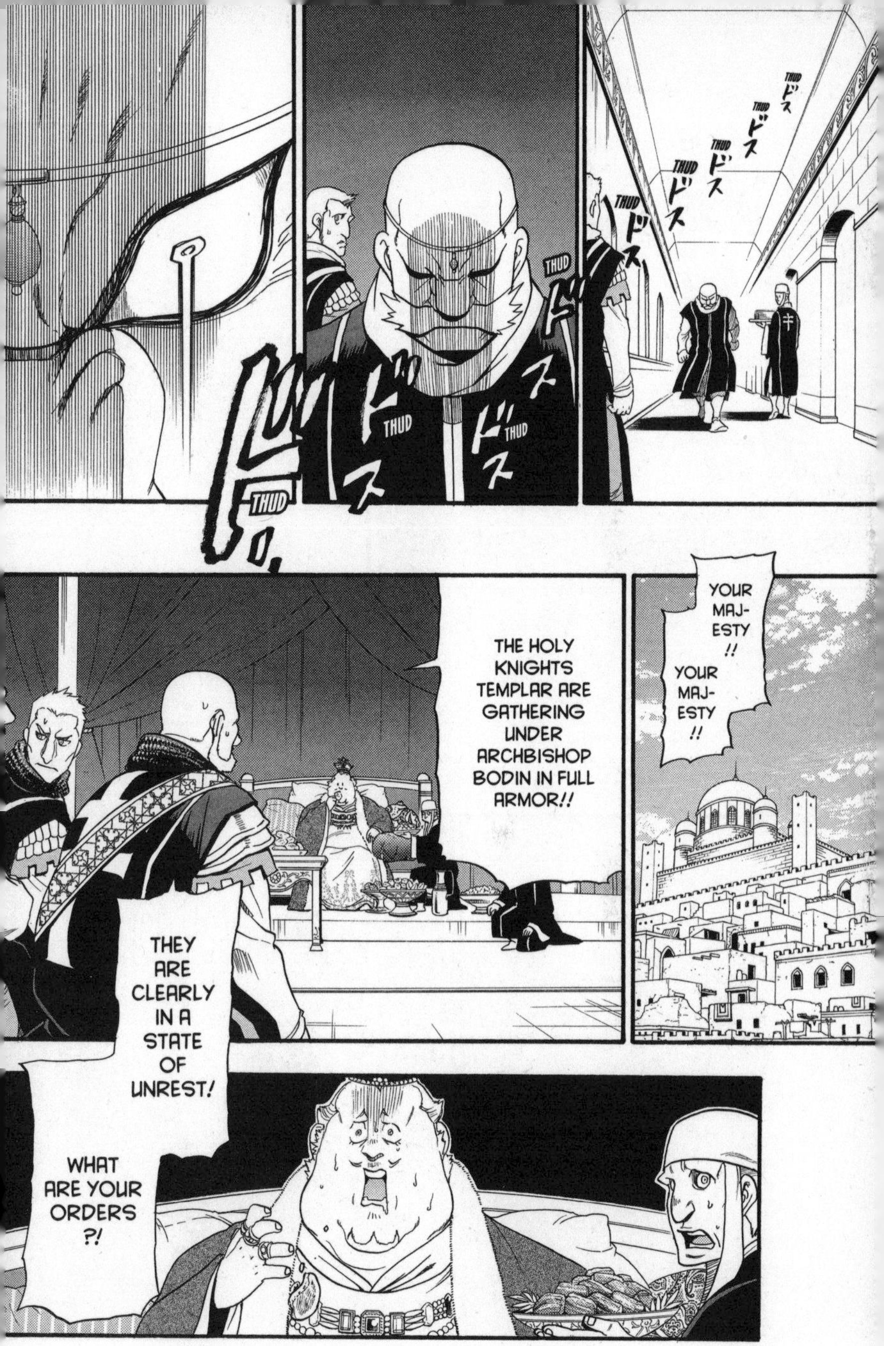
THUD ドス
THUD ドス
THUD ドス
THUD ドス
THUD ドス
THUD ド
THUD ドス
THUD ドス
THUD
YOUR MAJ-ESTY!!
YOUR MAJ-ESTY!!
THE HOLY KNIGHTS TEMPLAR ARE GATHERING UNDER ARCHBISHOP BODIN IN FULL ARMOR!!
THEY ARE CLEARLY IN A STATE OF UNREST!
WHAT ARE YOUR ORDERS?!

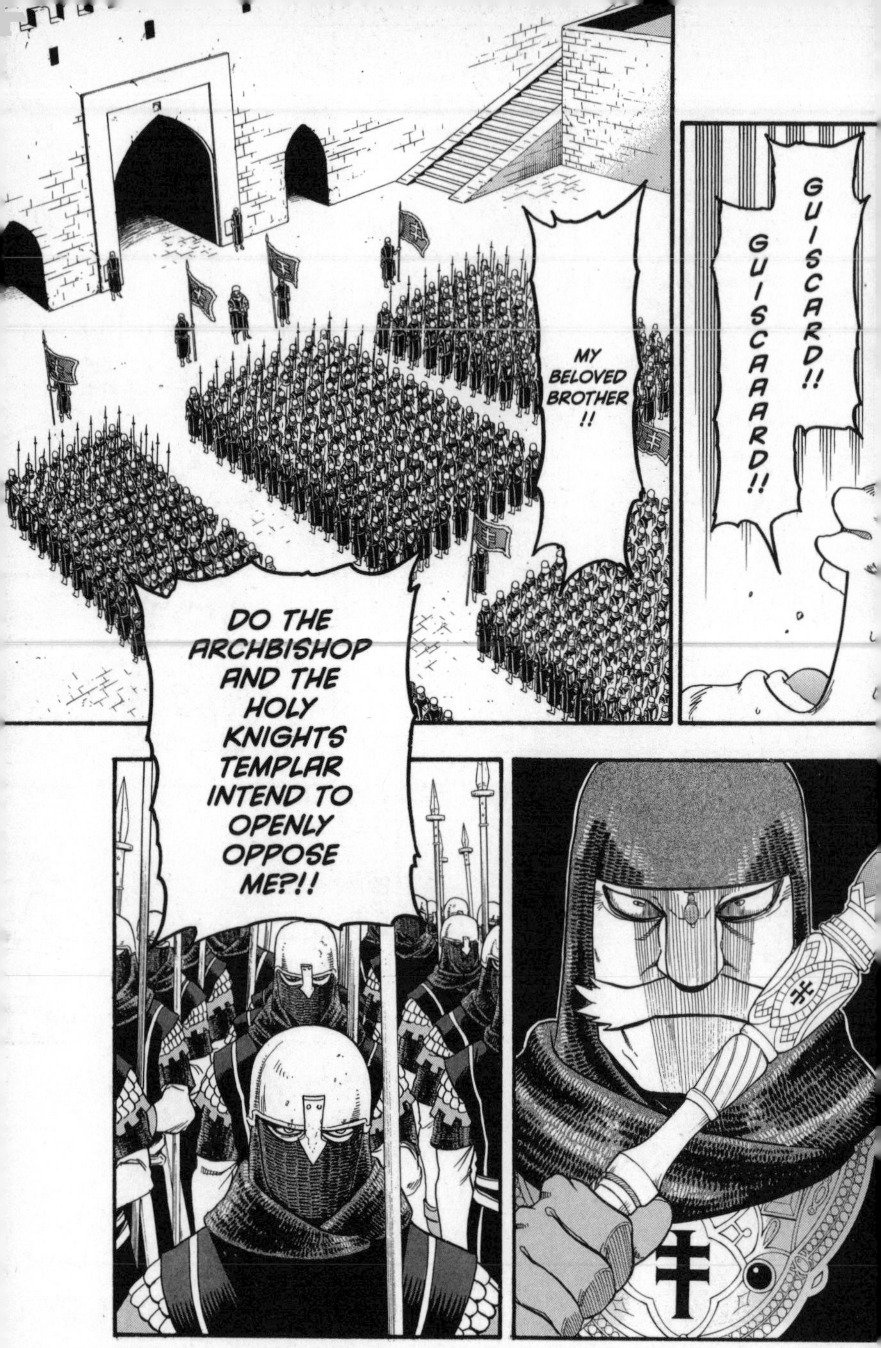
GUISCARD!!
GUISCAAARD!!
MY BELOVED BROTHER!!
DO THE ARCHBISHOP AND THE HOLY KNIGHTS TEMPLAR INTEND TO OPENLY OPPOSE ME?!!

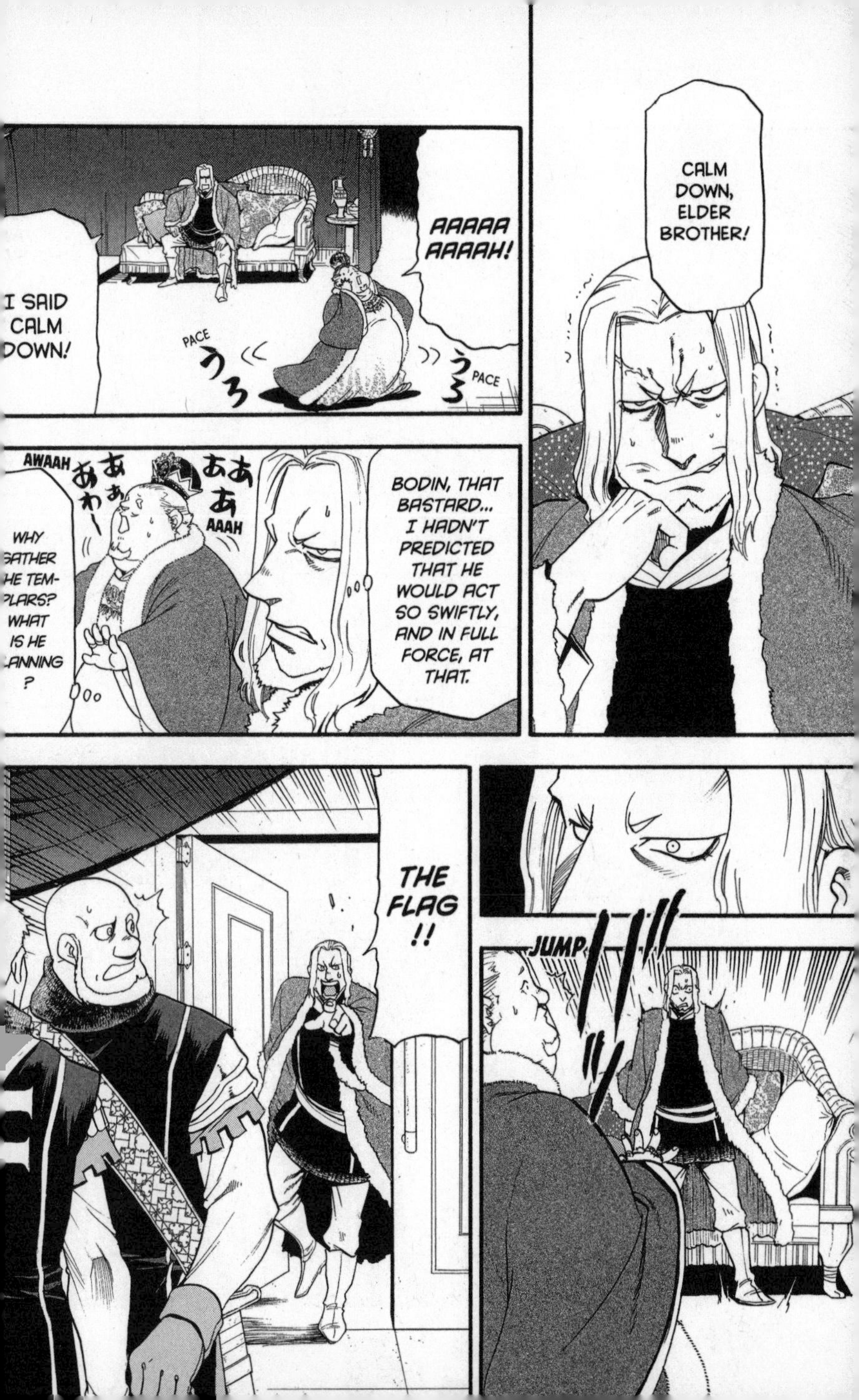

CALM DOWN, ELDER BROTHER!
AAAAA AAAAH!
PACE うろ
PACE うろ
I SAID CALM DOWN!
ああ ああ あ AAAH
あわ〜 AWAAAH
BODIN, THAT BASTARD... I HADN'T PREDICTED THAT HE WOULD ACT SO SWIFTLY, AND IN FULL FORCE, AT THAT.
WHY GATHER HE TEM-PLARS? WHAT IS HE LANNING?
JUMP
THE FLAG!!

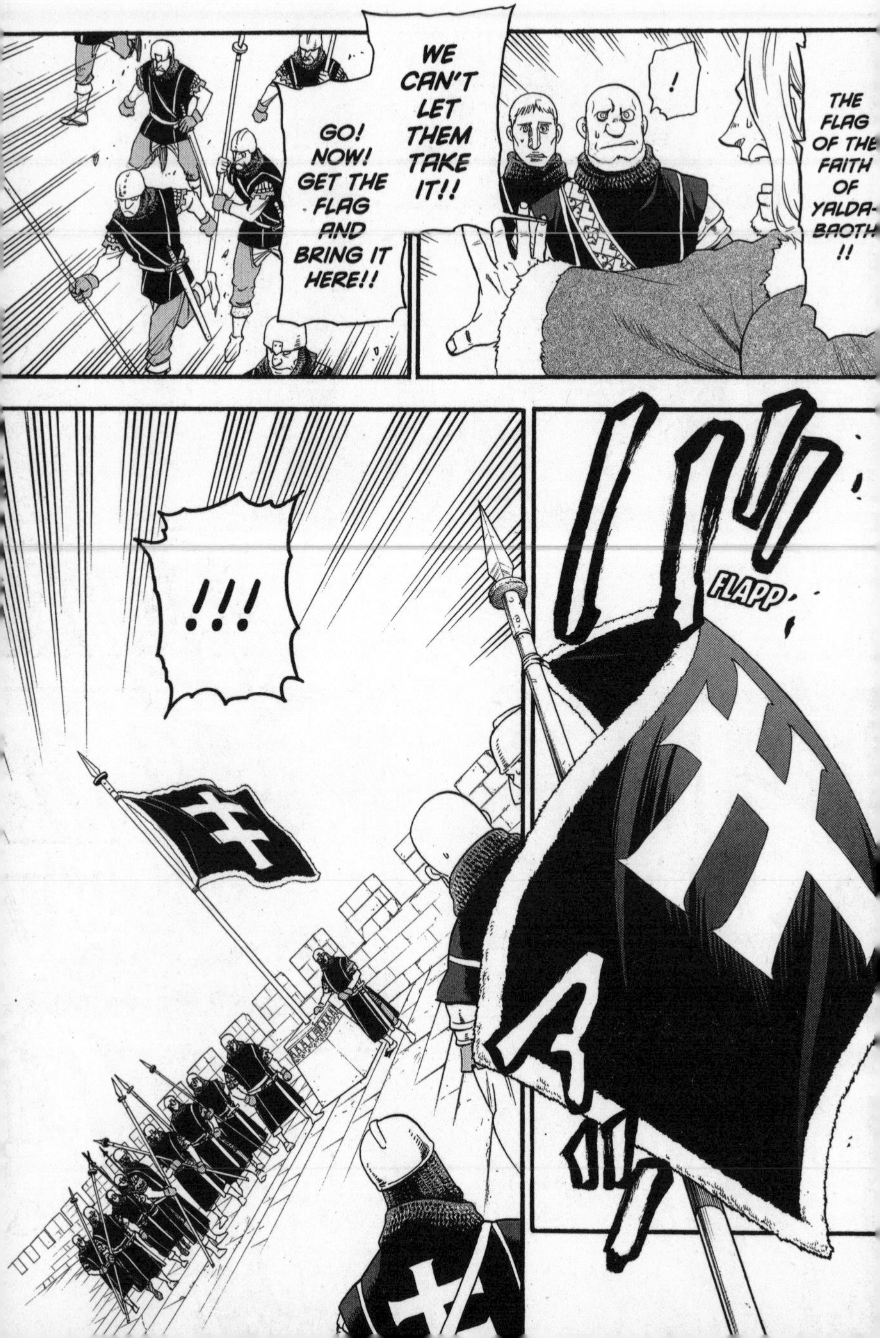
!
THE FLAG OF THE FAITH OF YALDA-BAOTH!!
WE CAN'T LET THEM TAKE IT!!
GO! NOW! GET THE FLAG AND BRING IT HERE!!
FLAPP
!!!

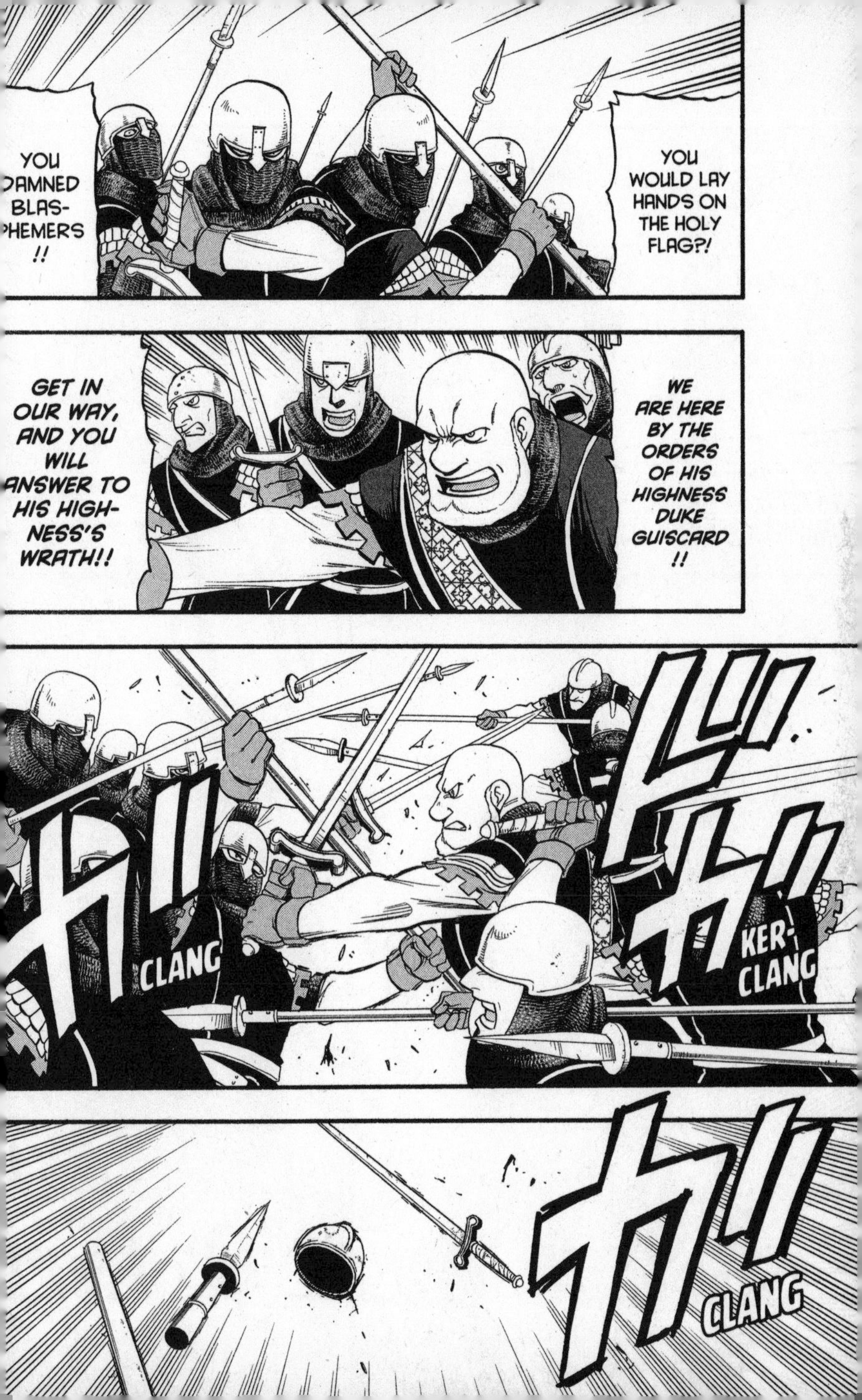
YOU WOULD LAY HANDS ON THE HOLY FLAG?!
YOU DAMNED BLAS-PHEMERS !!
WE ARE HERE BY THE ORDERS OF HIS HIGHNESS DUKE GUISCARD !!
GET IN OUR WAY, AND YOU WILL ANSWER TO HIS HIGH-NESS'S WRATH!!
KER-CLANG
CLANG
CLANG

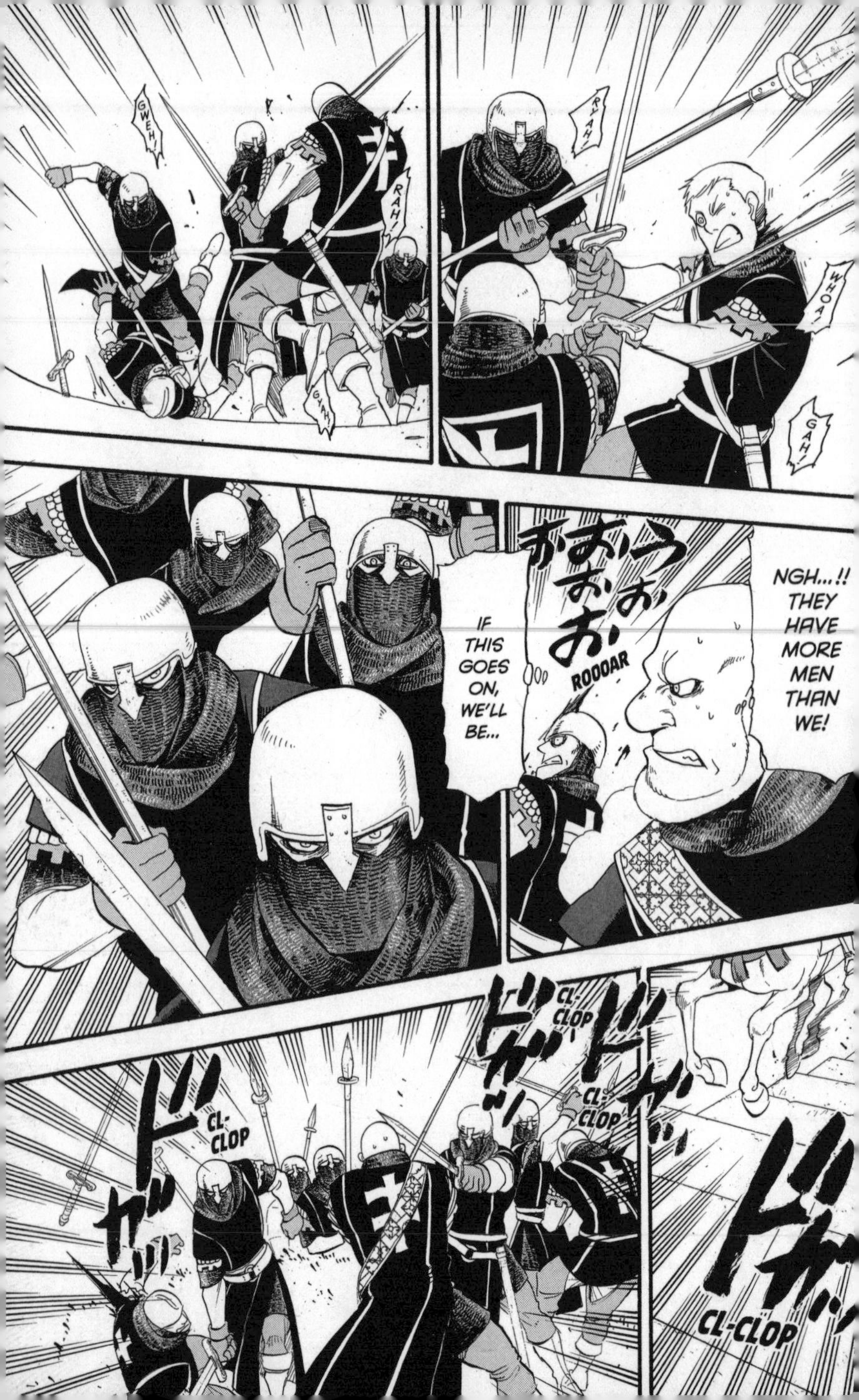
RYAH!
WHOA!
GAH!
GWEH!
RAH!
GAH!
NGH...!! THEY HAVE MORE MEN THAN WE!
ROOOAR
IF THIS GOES ON, WE'LL BE...
CL-CLOP
CL-CLOP
CL-CLOP
CL-CLOP

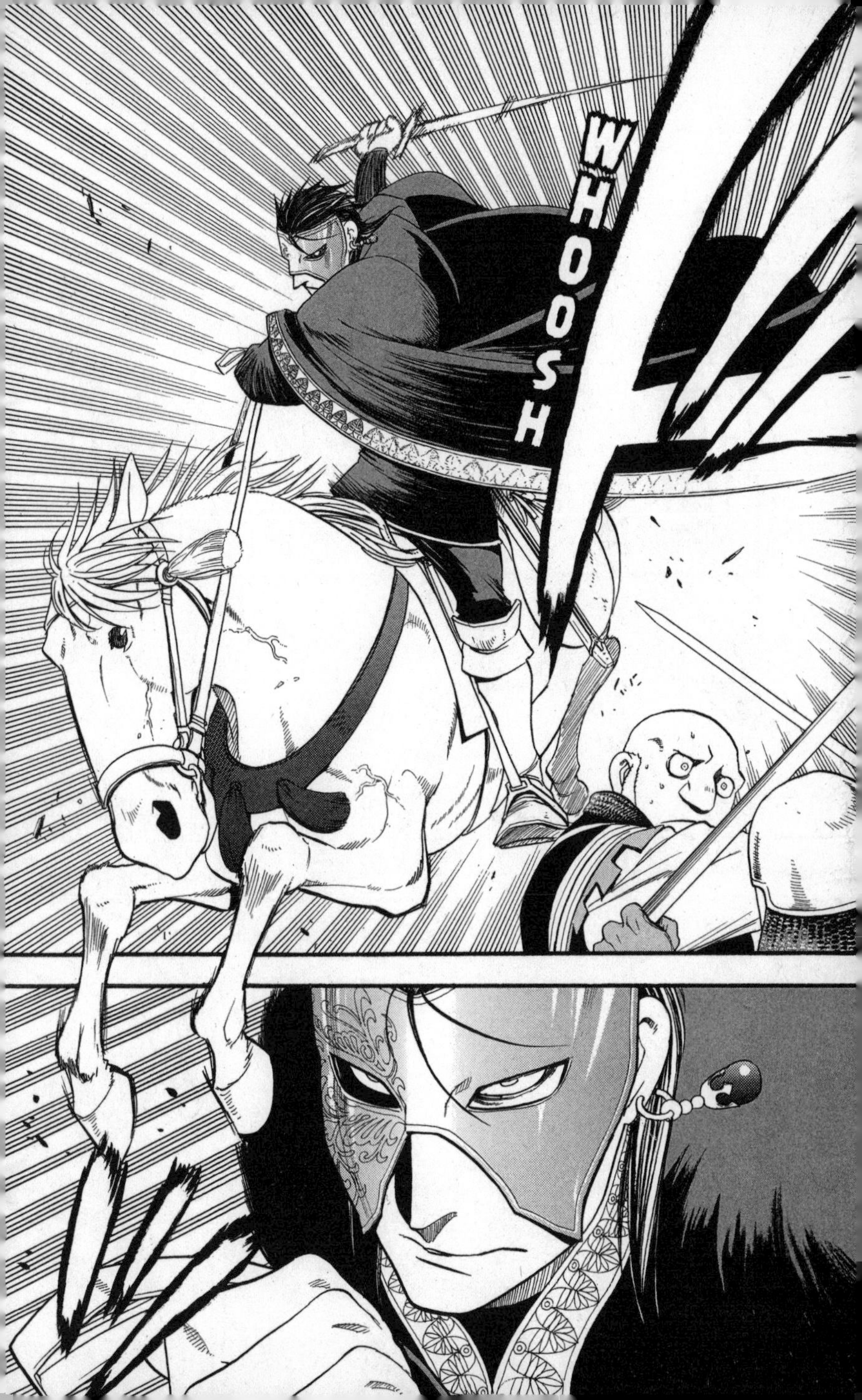
WHOOSH

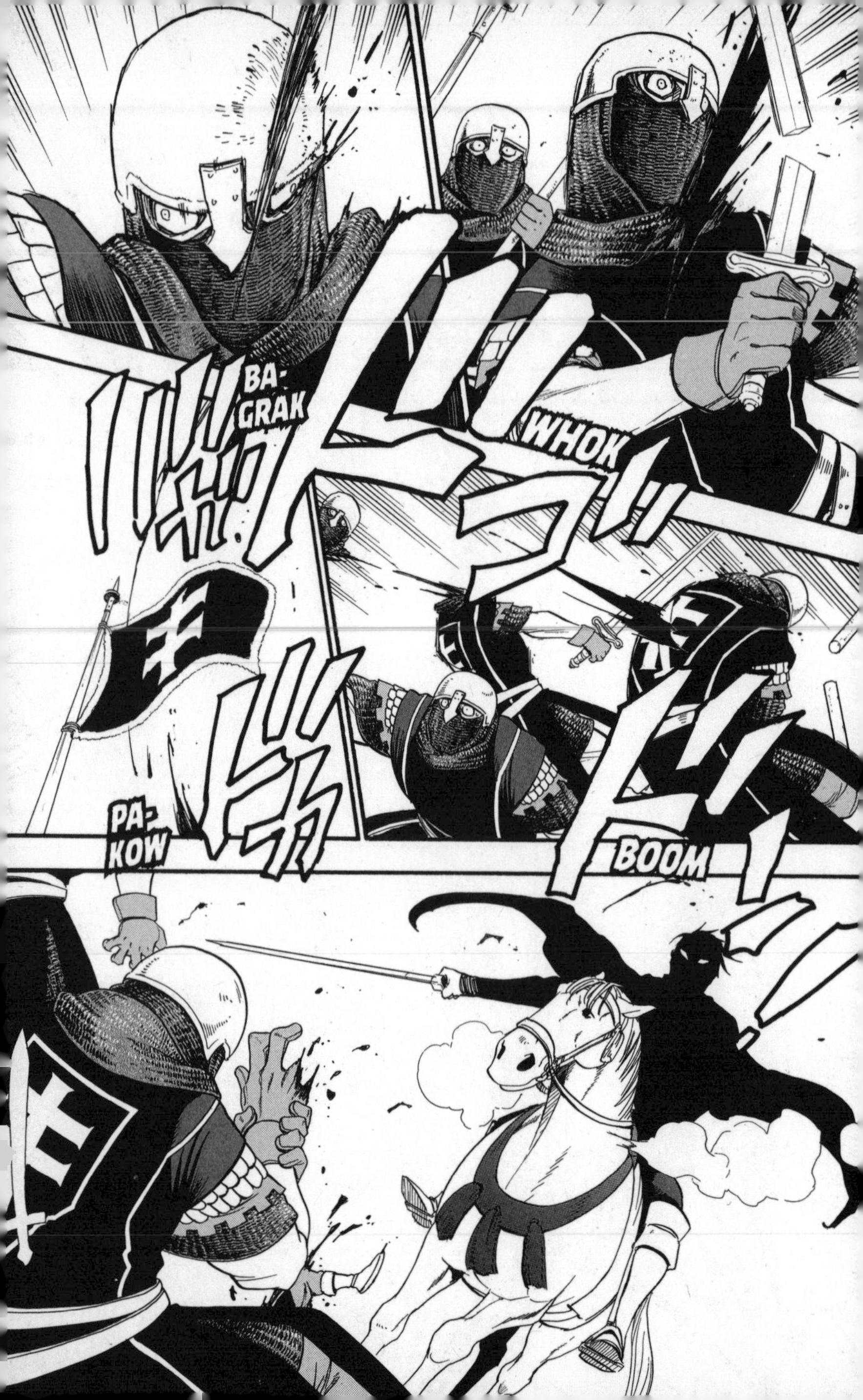

BA-GRAK
WHOK
BOOM
PA-KOW

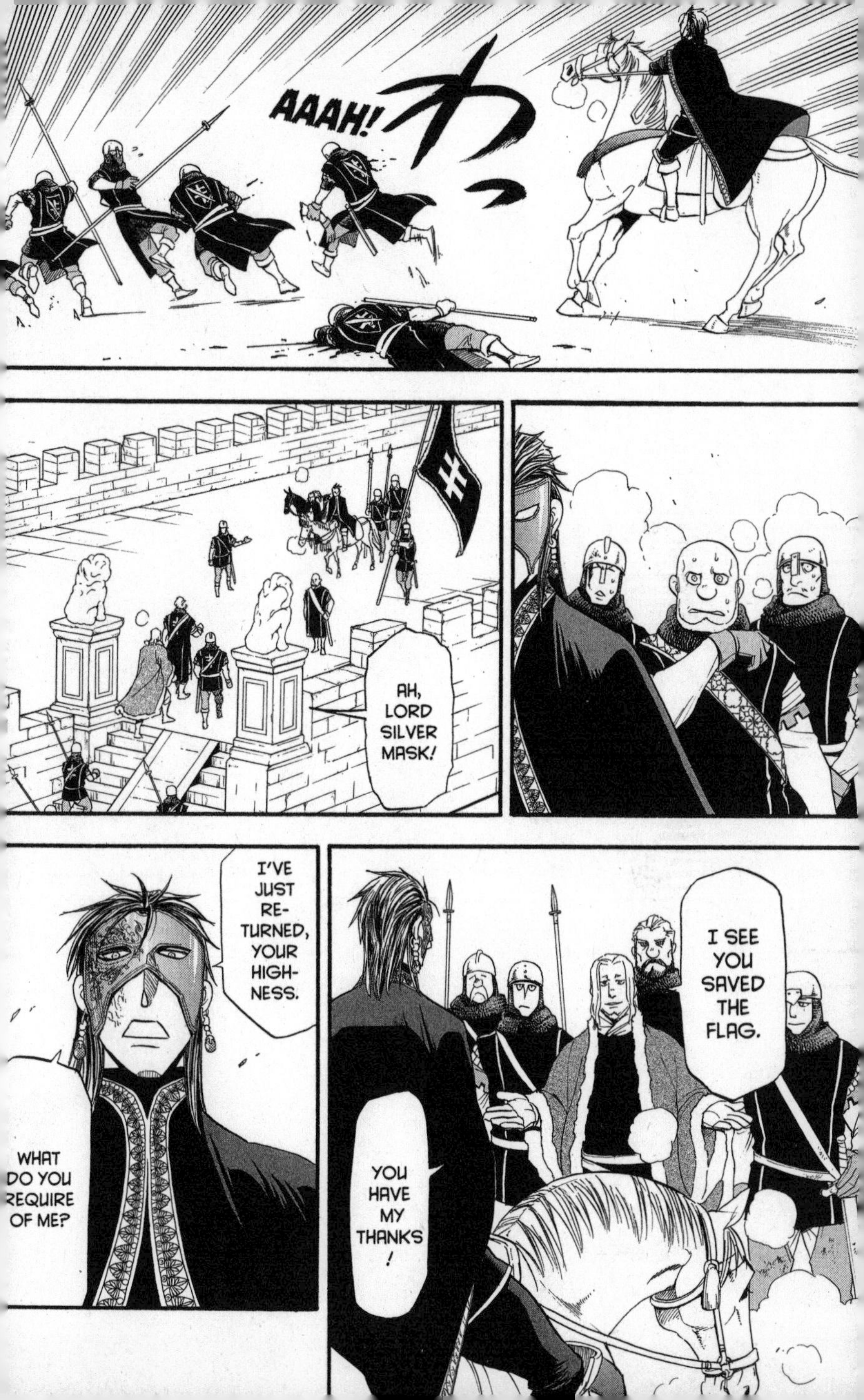
AAAH!
わっ
AH, LORD SILVER MASK!
I SEE YOU SAVED THE FLAG.
YOU HAVE MY THANKS!
I'VE JUST RETURNED, YOUR HIGHNESS.
WHAT DO YOU REQUIRE OF ME?

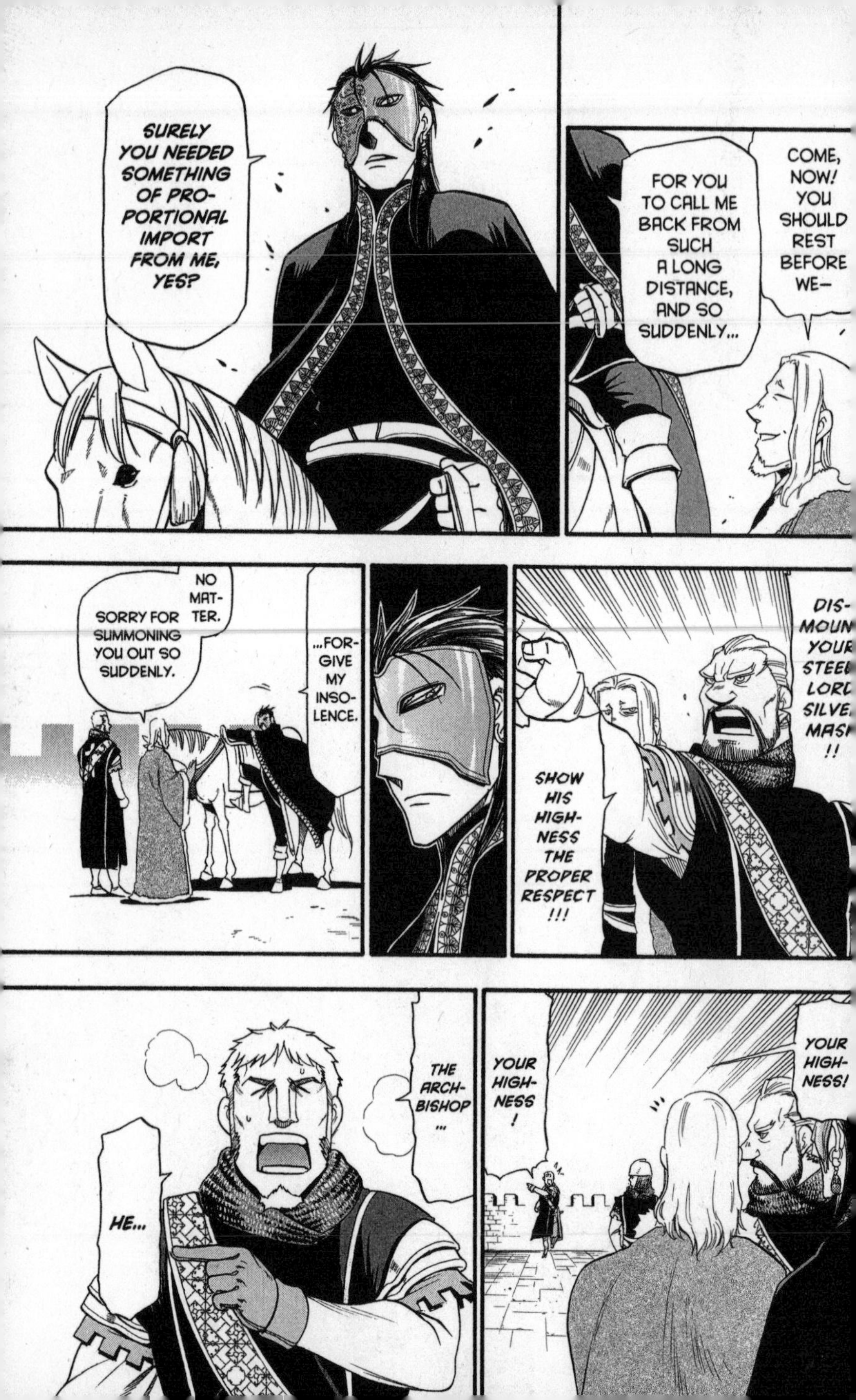
COME, NOW! YOU SHOULD REST BEFORE WE—
FOR YOU TO CALL ME BACK FROM SUCH A LONG DISTANCE, AND SO SUDDENLY...
SURELY YOU NEEDED SOMETHING OF PROPORTIONAL IMPORT FROM ME, YES?
DIS- MOUN YOUR STEEL LORD SILVE MASI !!
SHOW HIS HIGHNESS THE PROPER RESPECT!!!
...FORGIVE MY INSOLENCE.
NO MATTER.
SORRY FOR SUMMONING YOU OUT SO SUDDENLY.
YOUR HIGHNESS!
YOUR HIGHNESS!
THE ARCHBISHOP...
HE...

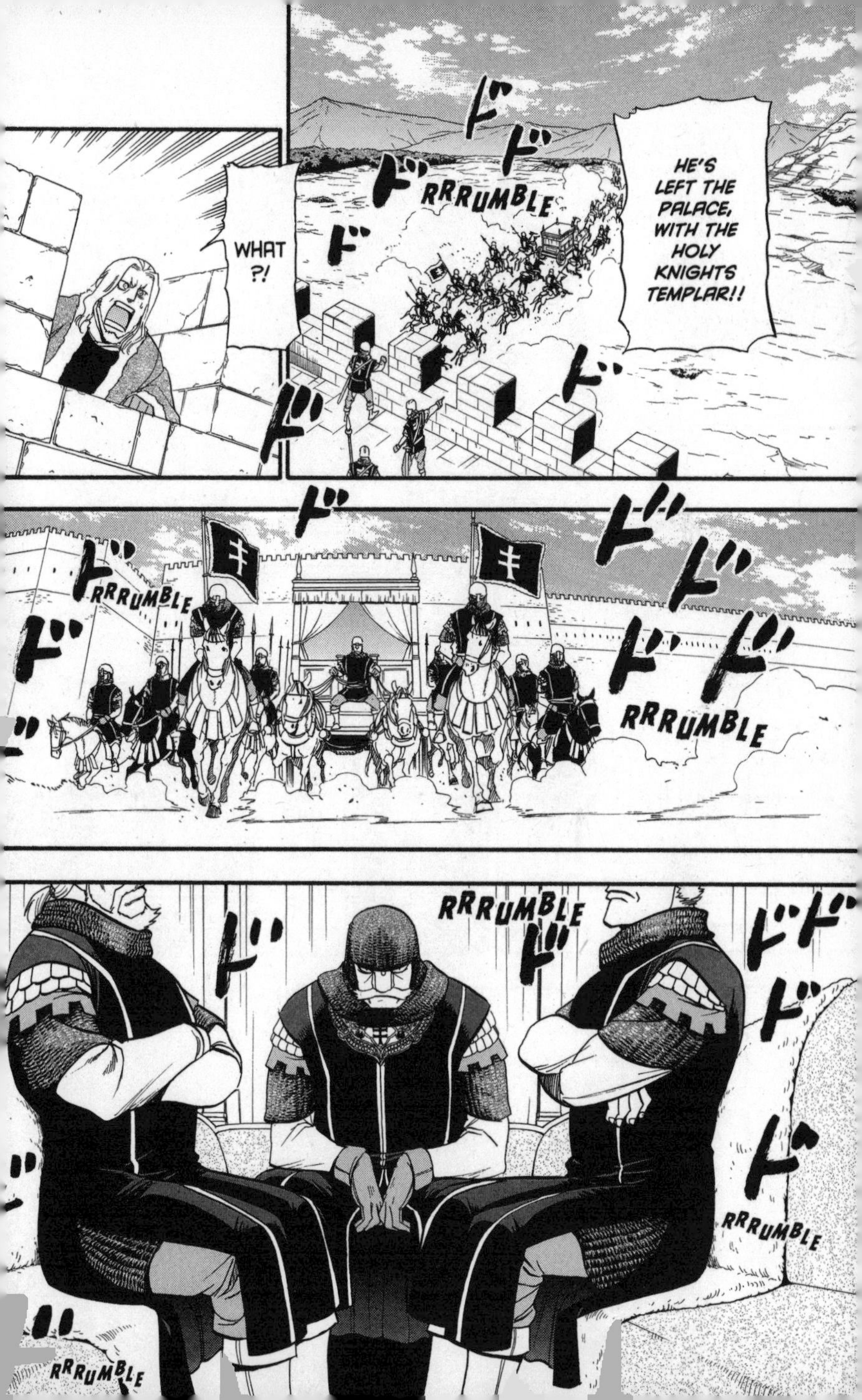
HE'S LEFT THE PALACE, WITH THE HOLY KNIGHTS TEMPLAR!!
ドドド
RRRUMBLE
ド
ド
ド
WHAT ?!
ドドドドド
RRRUMBLE
ド
ドRRRUMBLE
ド
ドドドド
RRRUMBLE
RRRUMBLE
ド
ド
RRRUMBLE

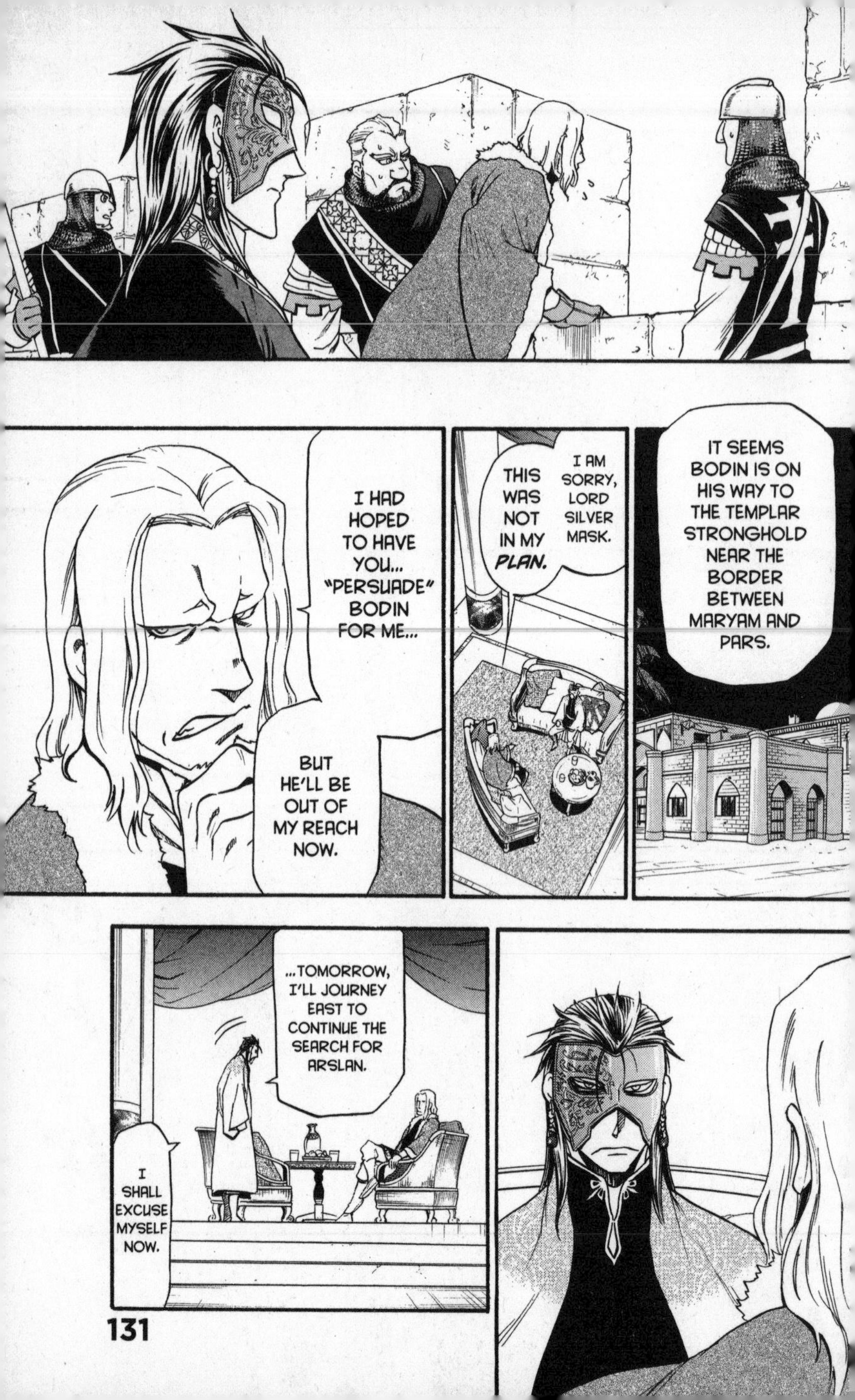
IT SEEMS BODIN IS ON HIS WAY TO THE TEMPLAR STRONGHOLD NEAR THE BORDER BETWEEN MARYAM AND PARS.
I AM SORRY, LORD SILVER MASK.
THIS WAS NOT IN MY *PLAN.*
I HAD HOPED TO HAVE YOU... "PERSUADE" BODIN FOR ME...
BUT HE'LL BE OUT OF MY REACH NOW.
...TOMORROW, I'LL JOURNEY EAST TO CONTINUE THE SEARCH FOR ARSLAN.
I SHALL EXCUSE MYSELF NOW.

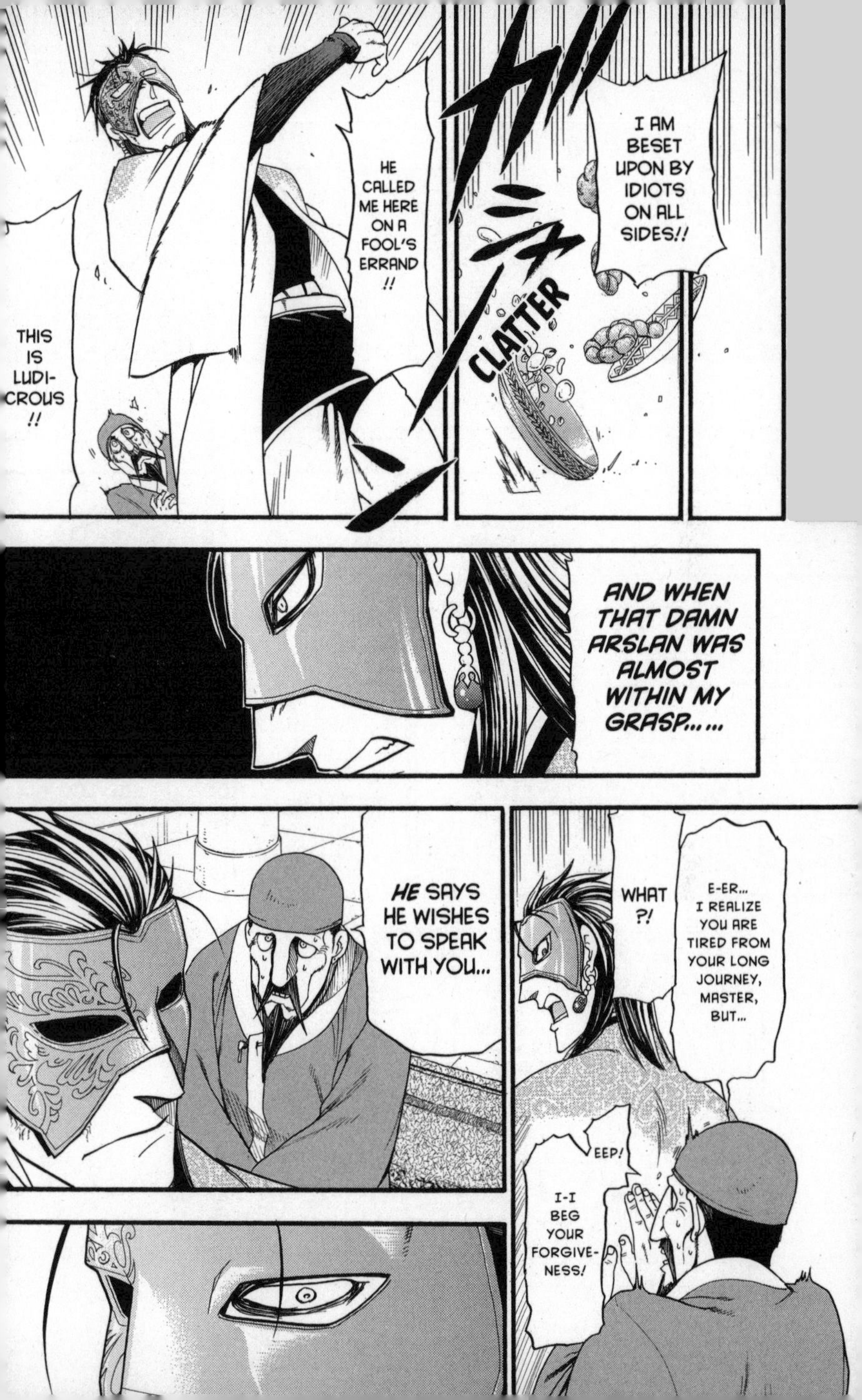
I AM BESET UPON BY IDIOTS ON ALL SIDES!!
CLATTER
HE CALLED ME HERE ON A FOOL'S ERRAND!!
THIS IS LUDICROUS!!
AND WHEN THAT DAMN ARSLAN WAS ALMOST WITHIN MY GRASP......
WHAT?!
E-ER... I REALIZE YOU ARE TIRED FROM YOUR LONG JOURNEY, MASTER, BUT...
EEP!
I-I BEG YOUR FORGIVENESS!
HE SAYS HE WISHES TO SPEAK WITH YOU...

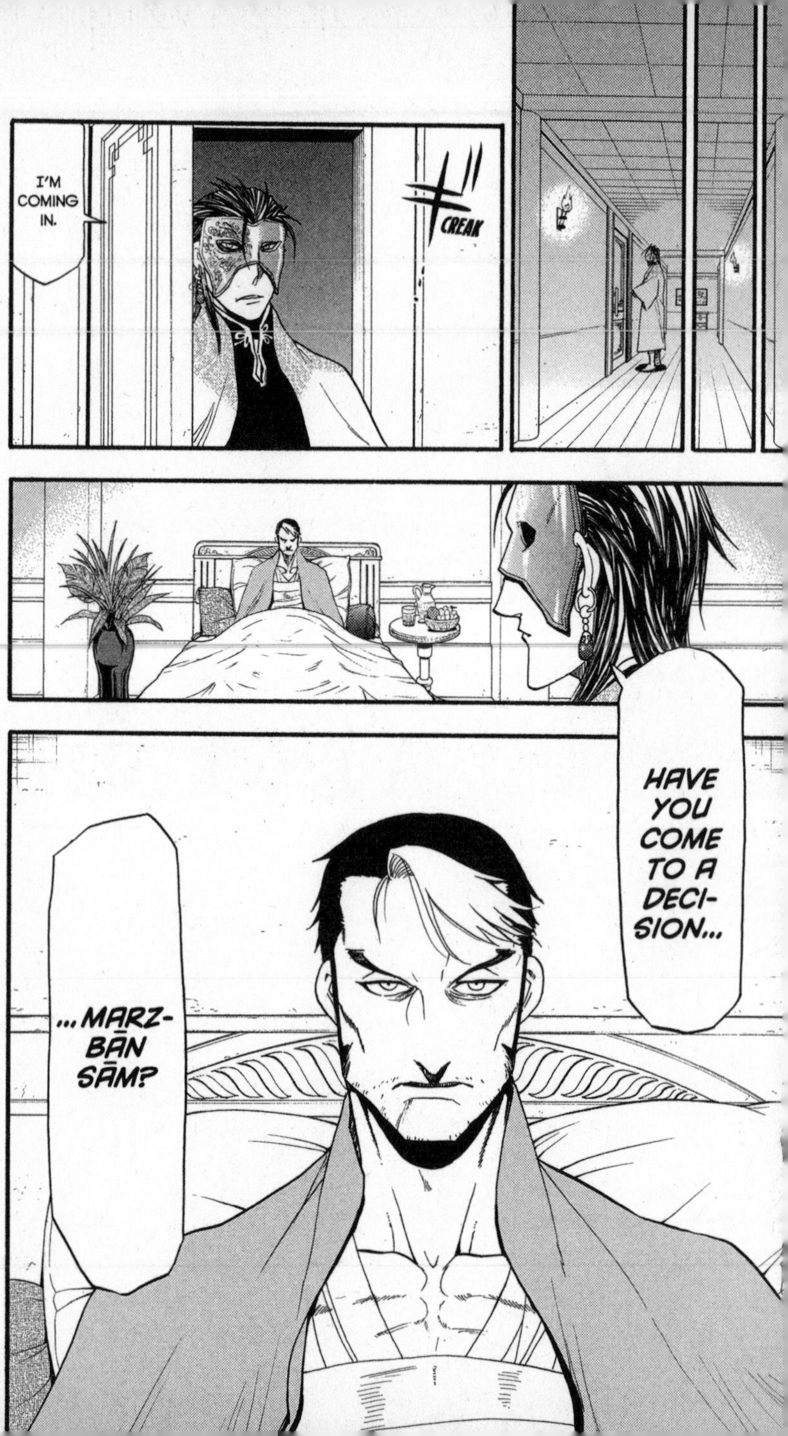
CREAK
I'M COMING IN.
HAVE YOU COME TO A DECISION...
...MARZBĀN SĀM?

THE HEROIC LEGEND OF
ARSLAN

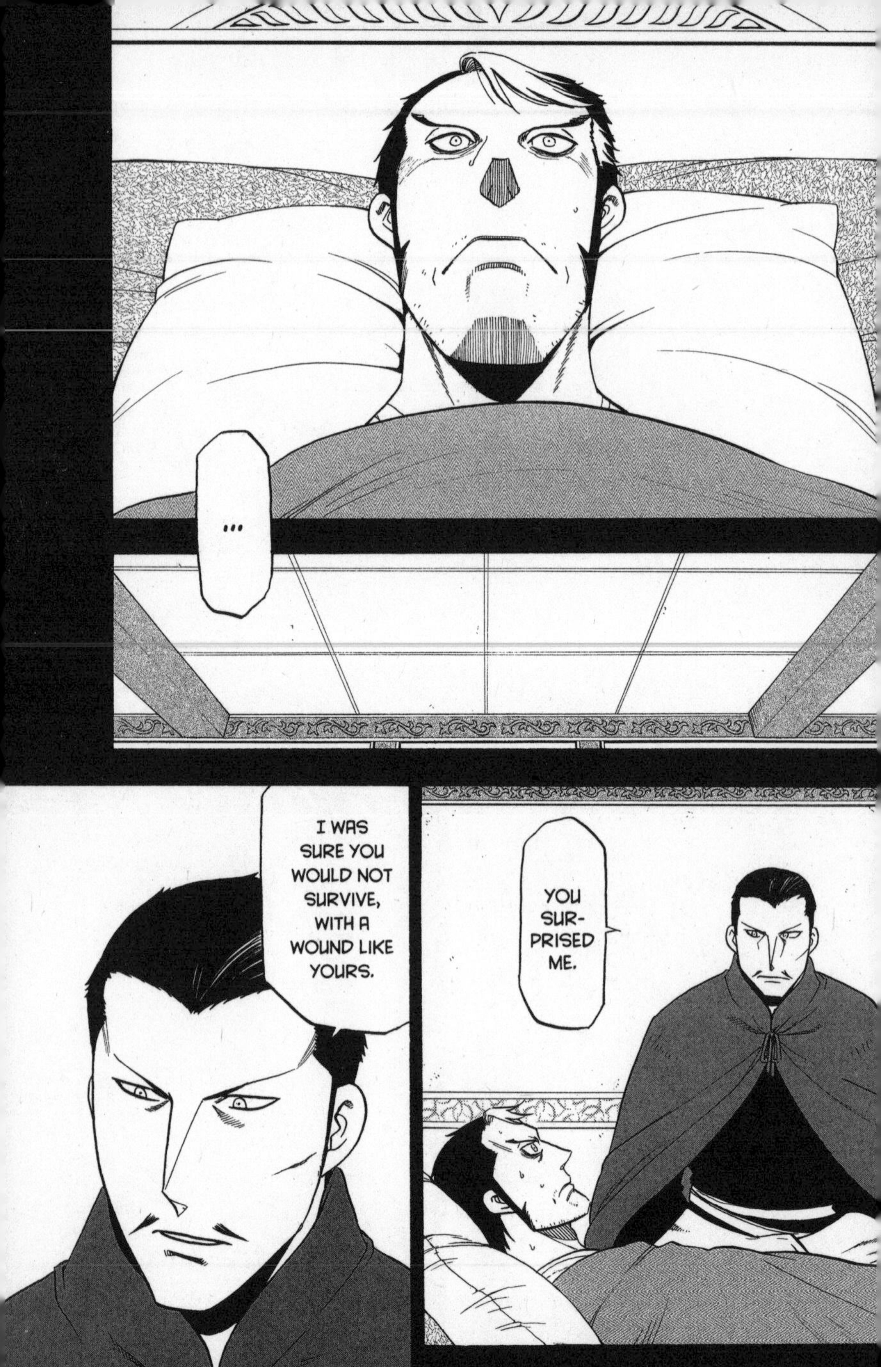
...
YOU SURPRISED ME.
I WAS SURE YOU WOULD NOT SURVIVE, WITH A WOUND LIKE YOURS.

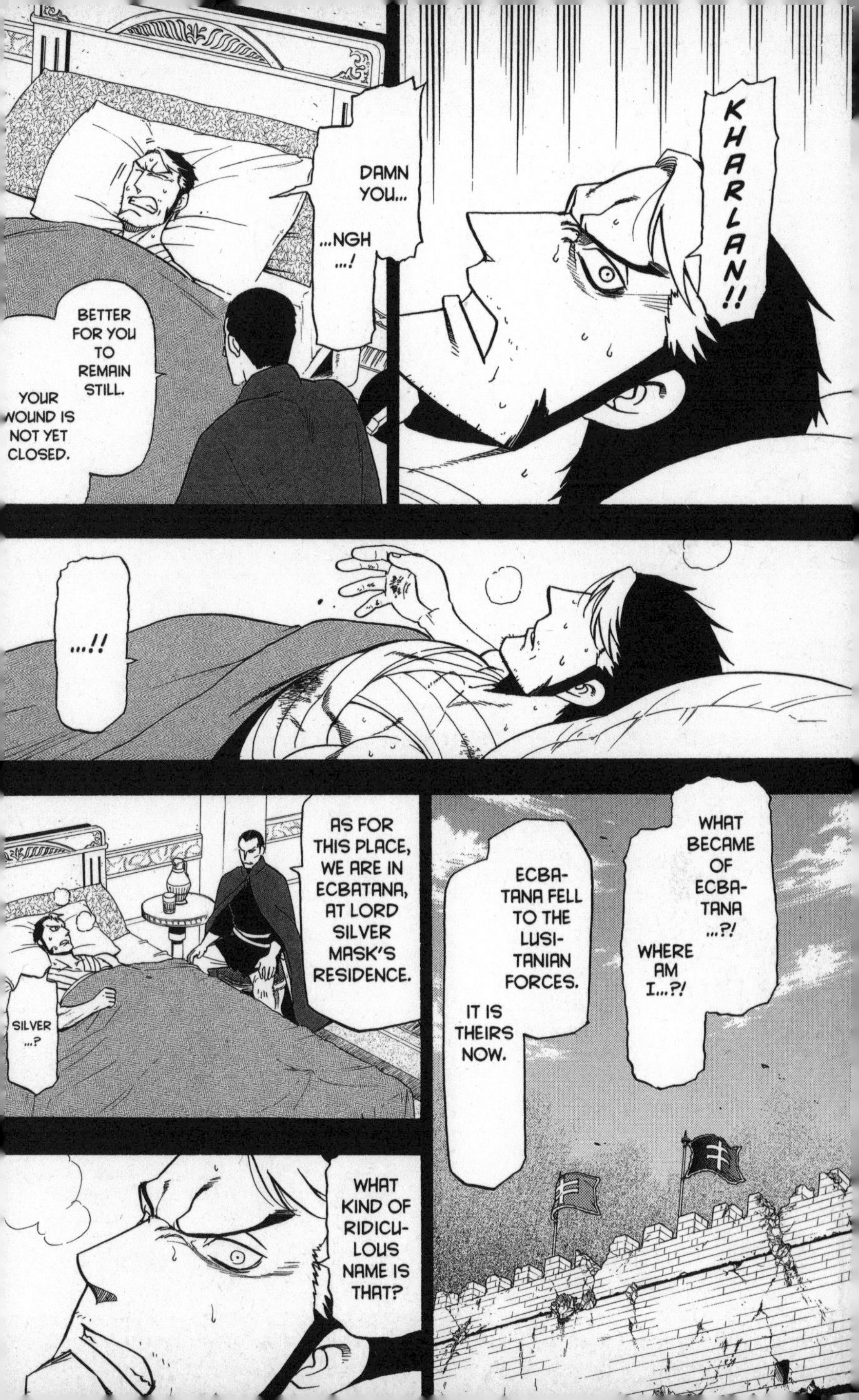
KHARLAN!!
DAMN YOU... ...NGH ...!
BETTER FOR YOU TO REMAIN STILL.
YOUR WOUND IS NOT YET CLOSED.
...!!
WHAT BECAME OF ECBATANA ...?!
WHERE AM I...?!
ECBATANA FELL TO THE LUSITANIAN FORCES.
IT IS THEIRS NOW.
AS FOR THIS PLACE, WE ARE IN ECBATANA, AT LORD SILVER MASK'S RESIDENCE.
SILVER ...?
WHAT KIND OF RIDICULOUS NAME IS THAT?

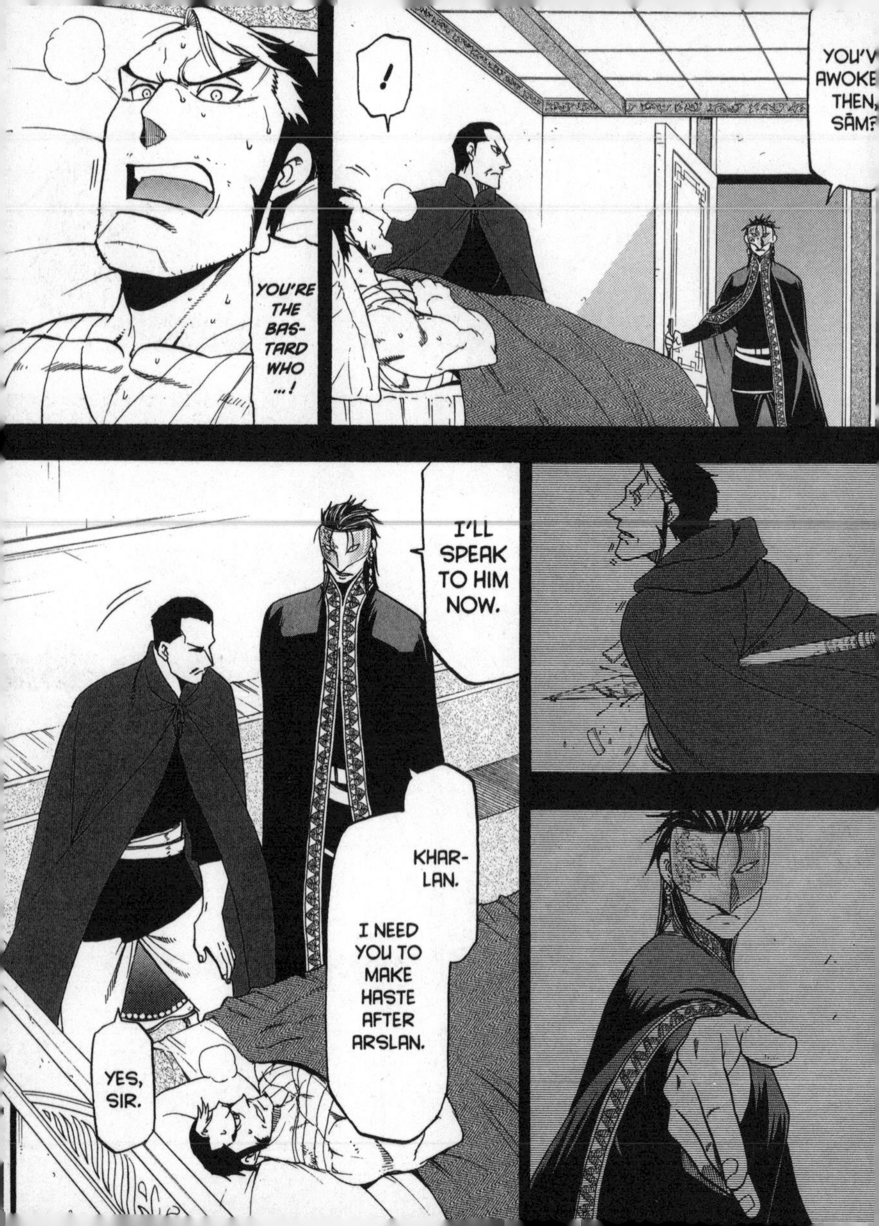
YOU'V AWOKE THEN, SĀM?
!
YOU'RE THE BAS-TARD WHO ...!
I'LL SPEAK TO HIM NOW.
KHAR-LAN.
I NEED YOU TO MAKE HASTE AFTER ARSLAN.
YES, SIR.

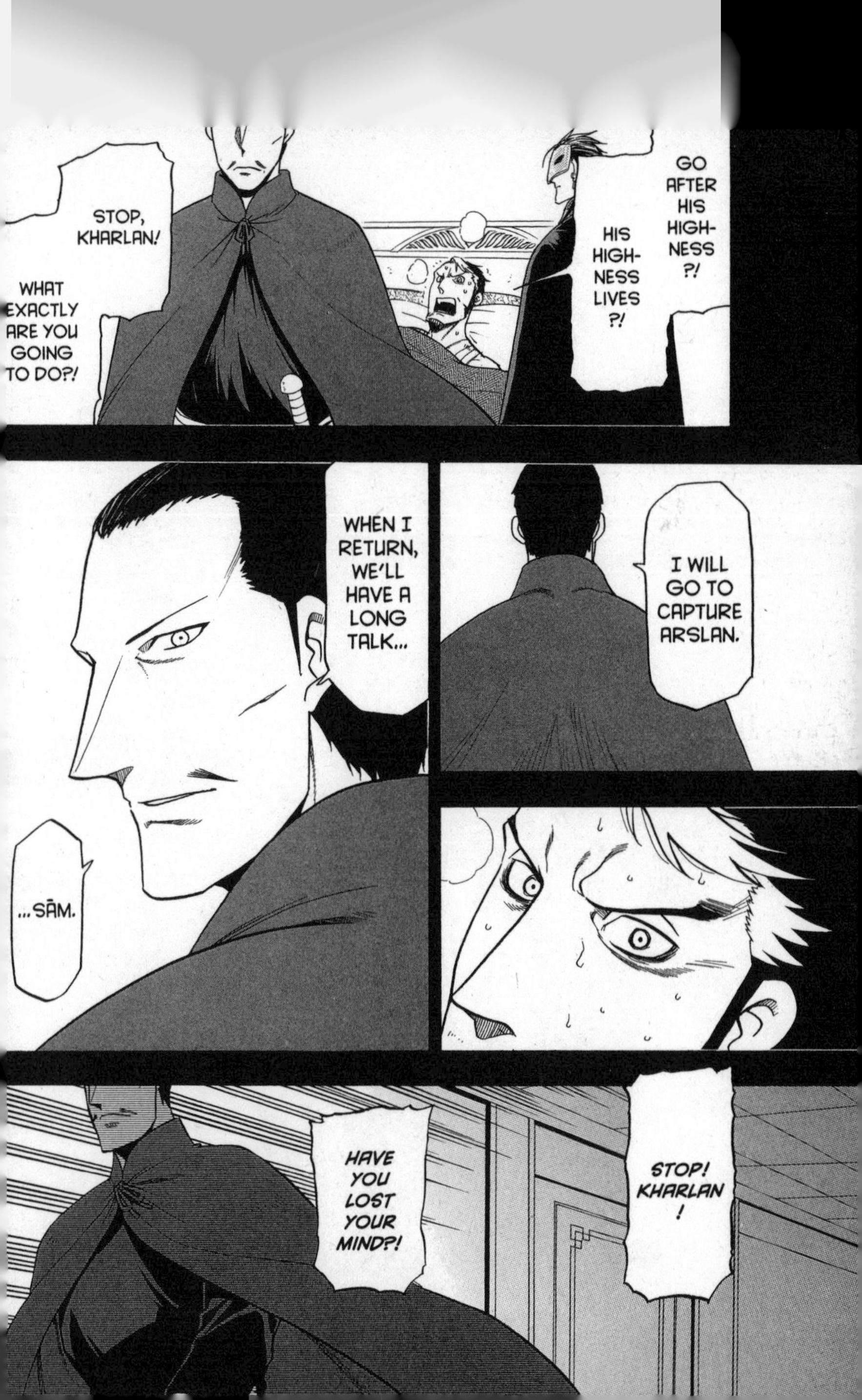
GO AFTER HIS HIGHNESS?!
HIS HIGHNESS LIVES?!
STOP, KHARLAN!
WHAT EXACTLY ARE YOU GOING TO DO?!
I WILL GO TO CAPTURE ARSLAN.
WHEN I RETURN, WE'LL HAVE A LONG TALK...
...SĀM.
STOP! KHARLAN!
HAVE YOU LOST YOUR MIND?!

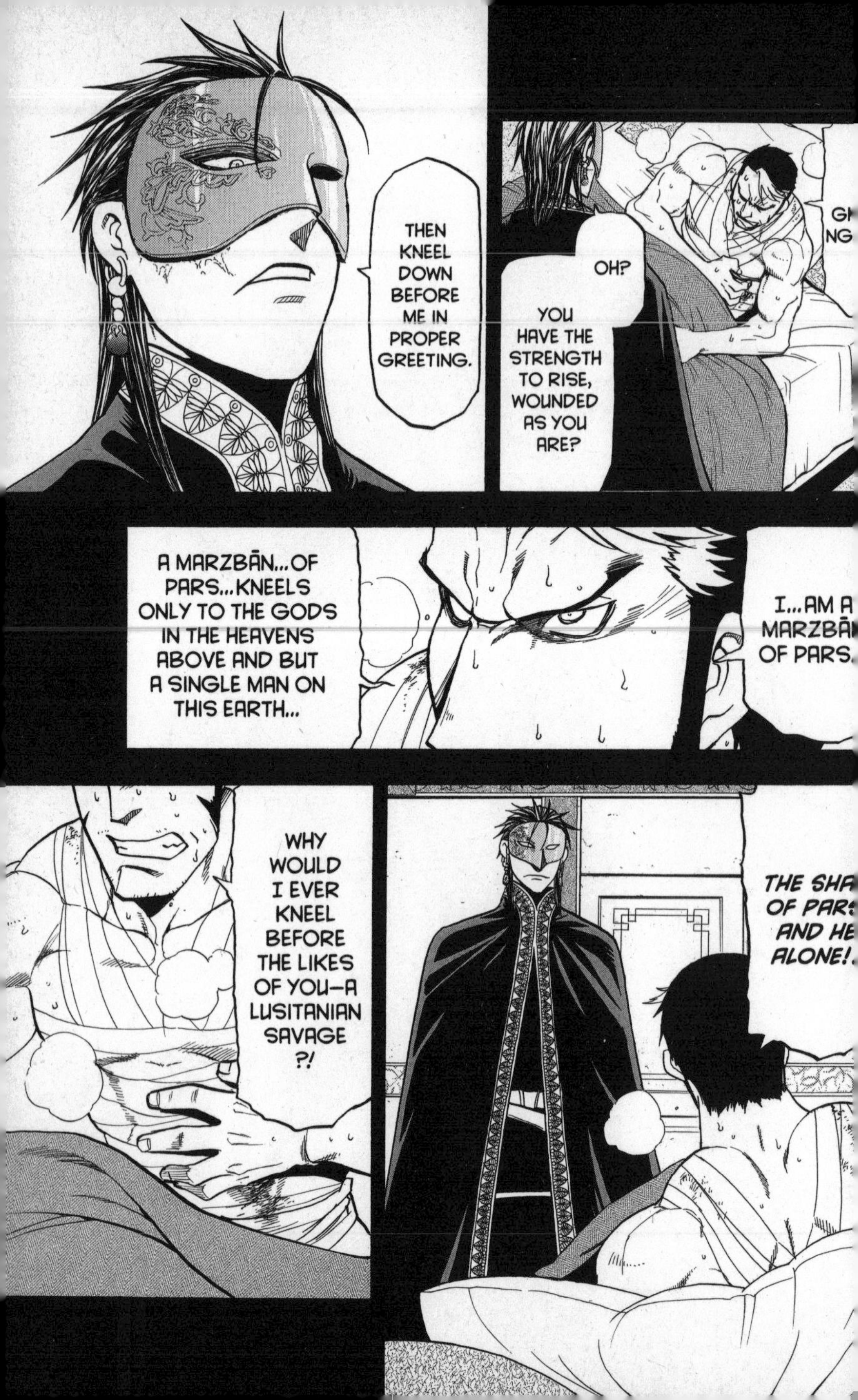
OH?
YOU HAVE THE STRENGTH TO RISE, WOUNDED AS YOU ARE?
THEN KNEEL DOWN BEFORE ME IN PROPER GREETING.
I...AM A MARZBĀ OF PARS.
A MARZBĀN...OF PARS...KNEELS ONLY TO THE GODS IN THE HEAVENS ABOVE AND BUT A SINGLE MAN ON THIS EARTH...
THE SHA OF PARS AND HE ALONE!..
WHY WOULD I EVER KNEEL BEFORE THE LIKES OF YOU—A LUSITANIAN SAVAGE ?!

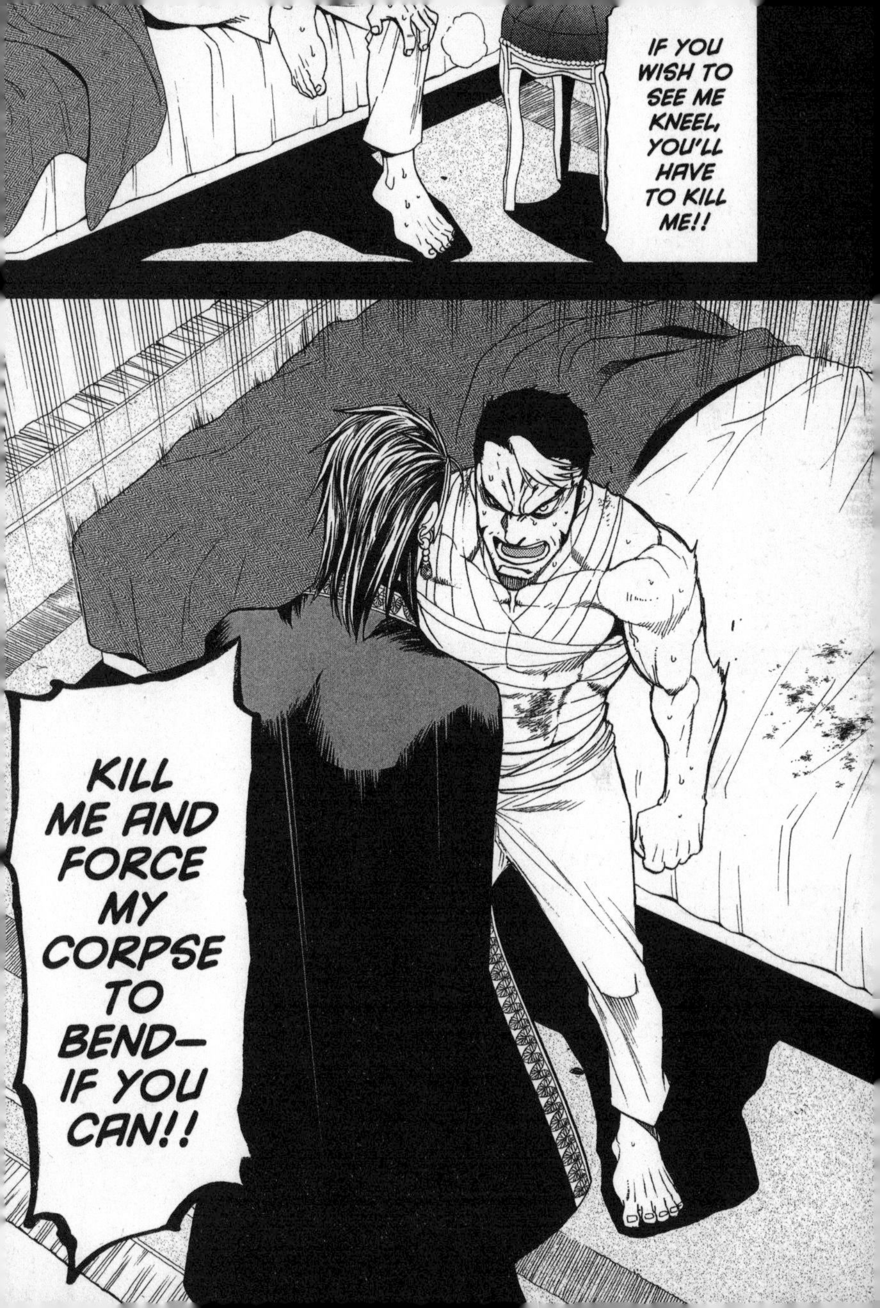
IF YOU WISH TO SEE ME KNEEL, YOU'LL HAVE TO KILL ME!!
KILL ME AND FORCE MY CORPSE TO BEND— IF YOU CAN!!

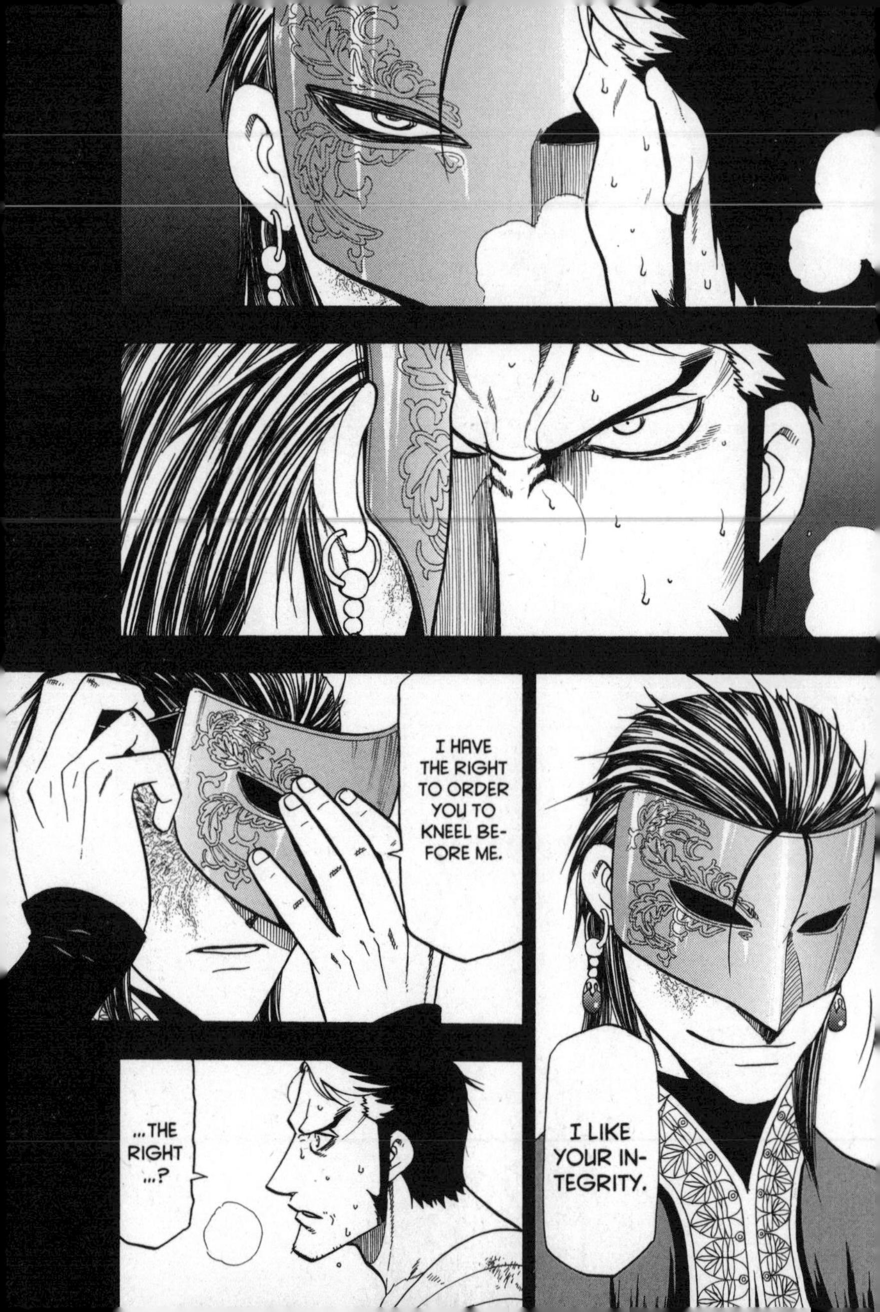
I LIKE YOUR INTEGRITY.
I HAVE THE RIGHT TO ORDER YOU TO KNEEL BEFORE ME.
...THE RIGHT ...?

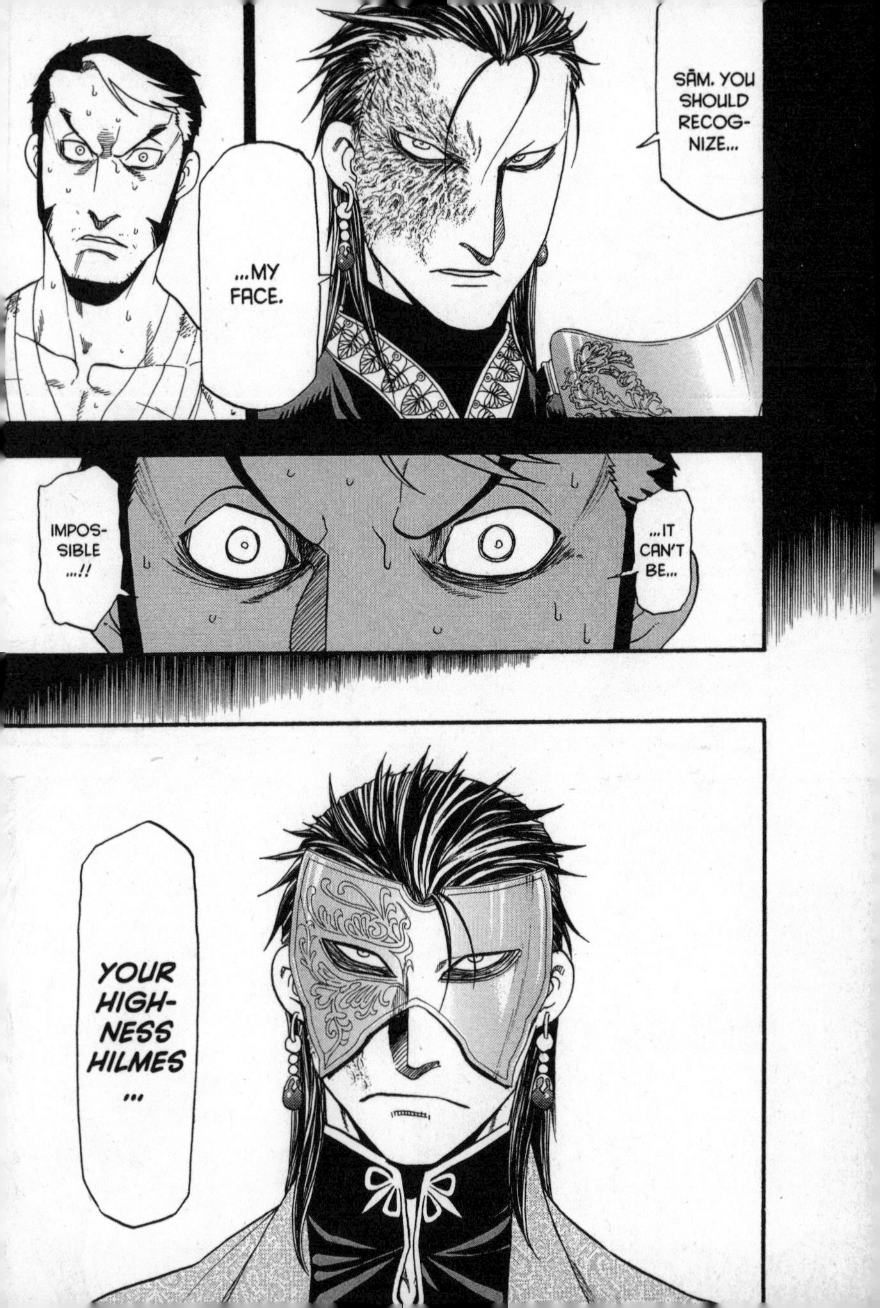
SĀM. YOU SHOULD RECOG-NIZE...
...MY FACE.
...IT CAN'T BE...
IMPOS-SIBLE ...!!
YOUR HIGH-NESS HILMES ...

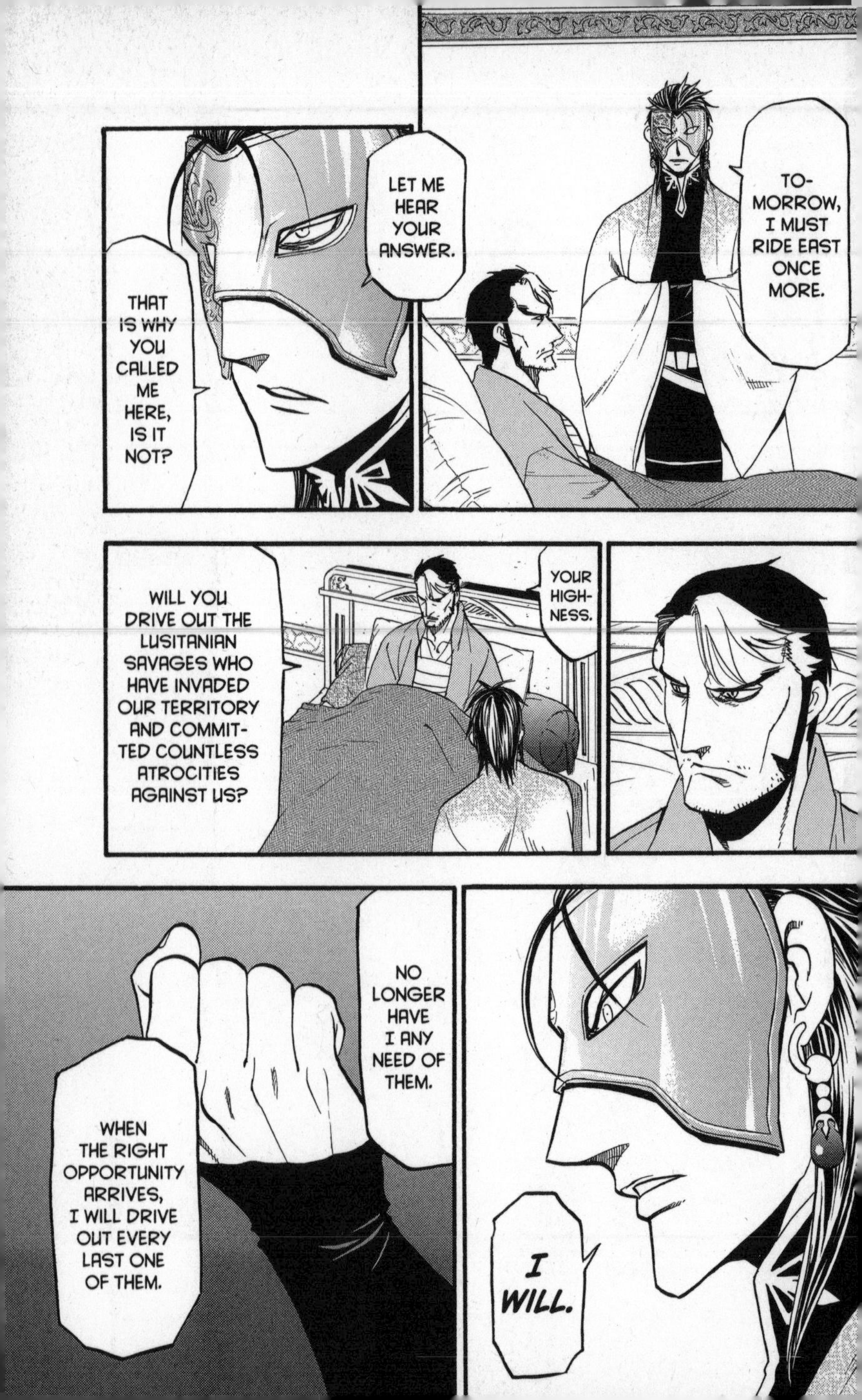
TO-MORROW, I MUST RIDE EAST ONCE MORE.
LET ME HEAR YOUR ANSWER.
THAT IS WHY YOU CALLED ME HERE, IS IT NOT?
YOUR HIGHNESS.
WILL YOU DRIVE OUT THE LUSITANIAN SAVAGES WHO HAVE INVADED OUR TERRITORY AND COMMIT-TED COUNTLESS ATROCITIES AGAINST US?
I WILL.
NO LONGER HAVE I ANY NEED OF THEM.
WHEN THE RIGHT OPPORTUNITY ARRIVES, I WILL DRIVE OUT EVERY LAST ONE OF THEM.

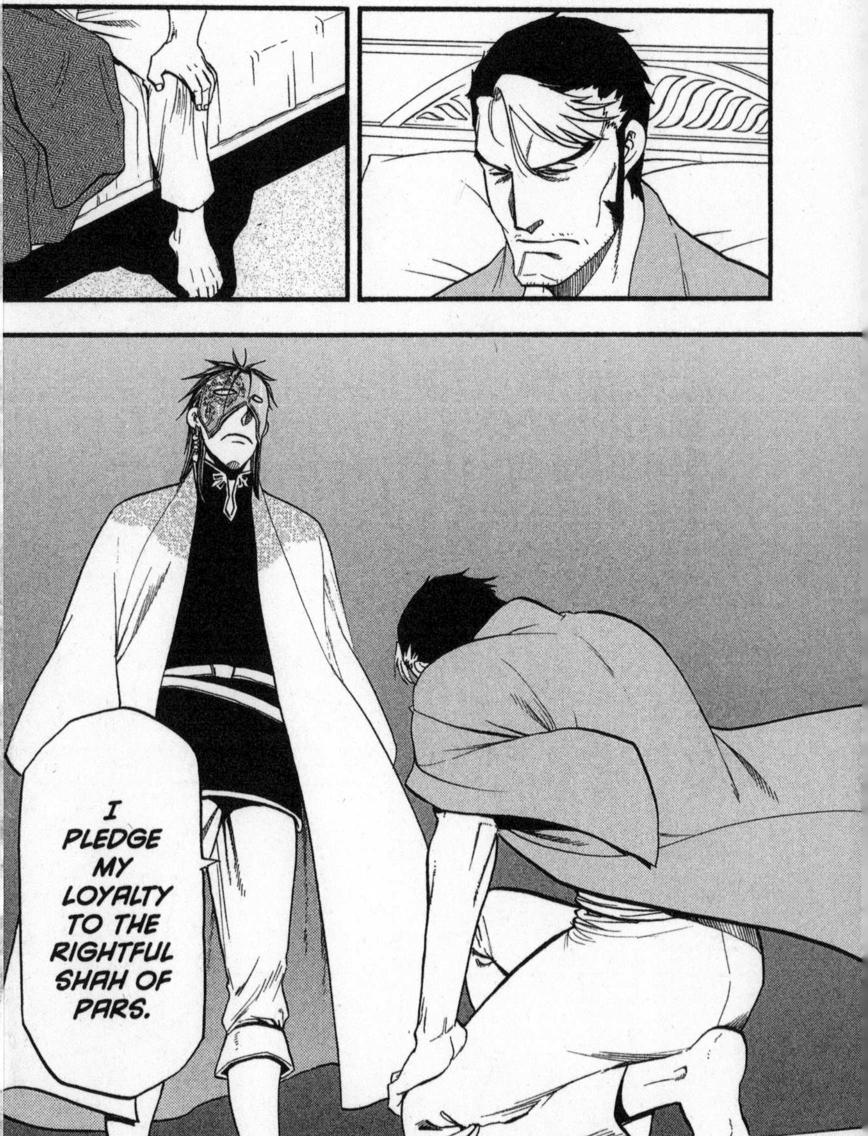
I PLEDGE MY LOYALTY TO THE RIGHTFUL SHAH OF PARS.

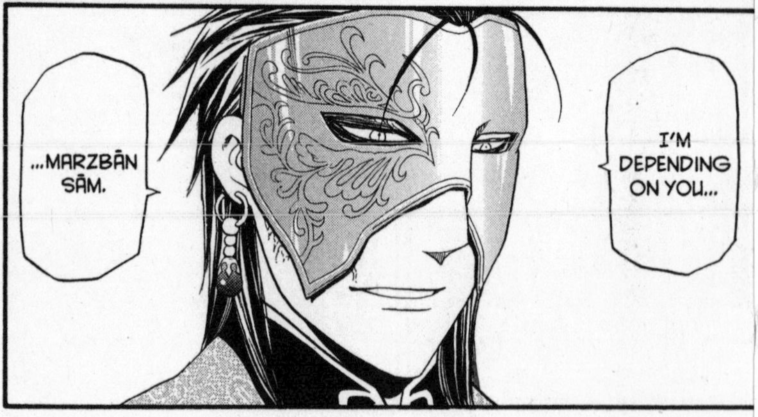
I'M DEPENDING ON YOU...
...MARZBĀN SĀM.

Chapter 33: Sām's Submission

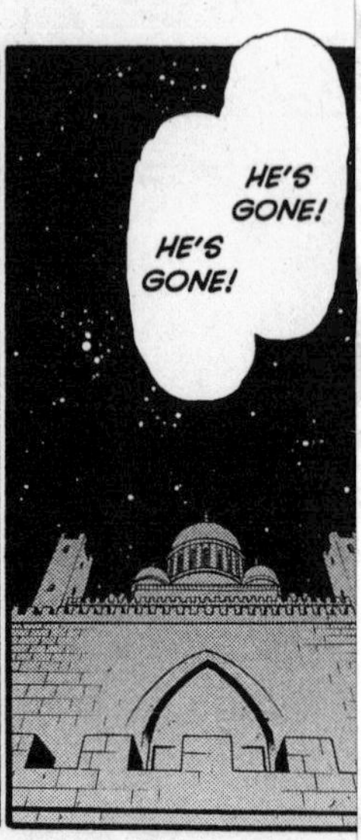
HE'S GONE!
HE'S GONE!

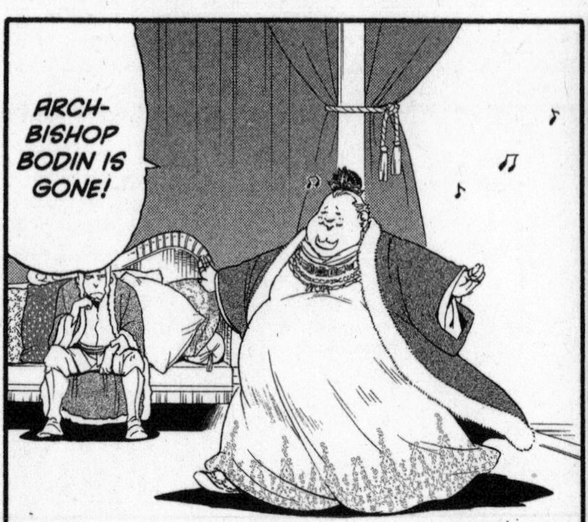
ARCH-BISHOP BODIN IS GONE!

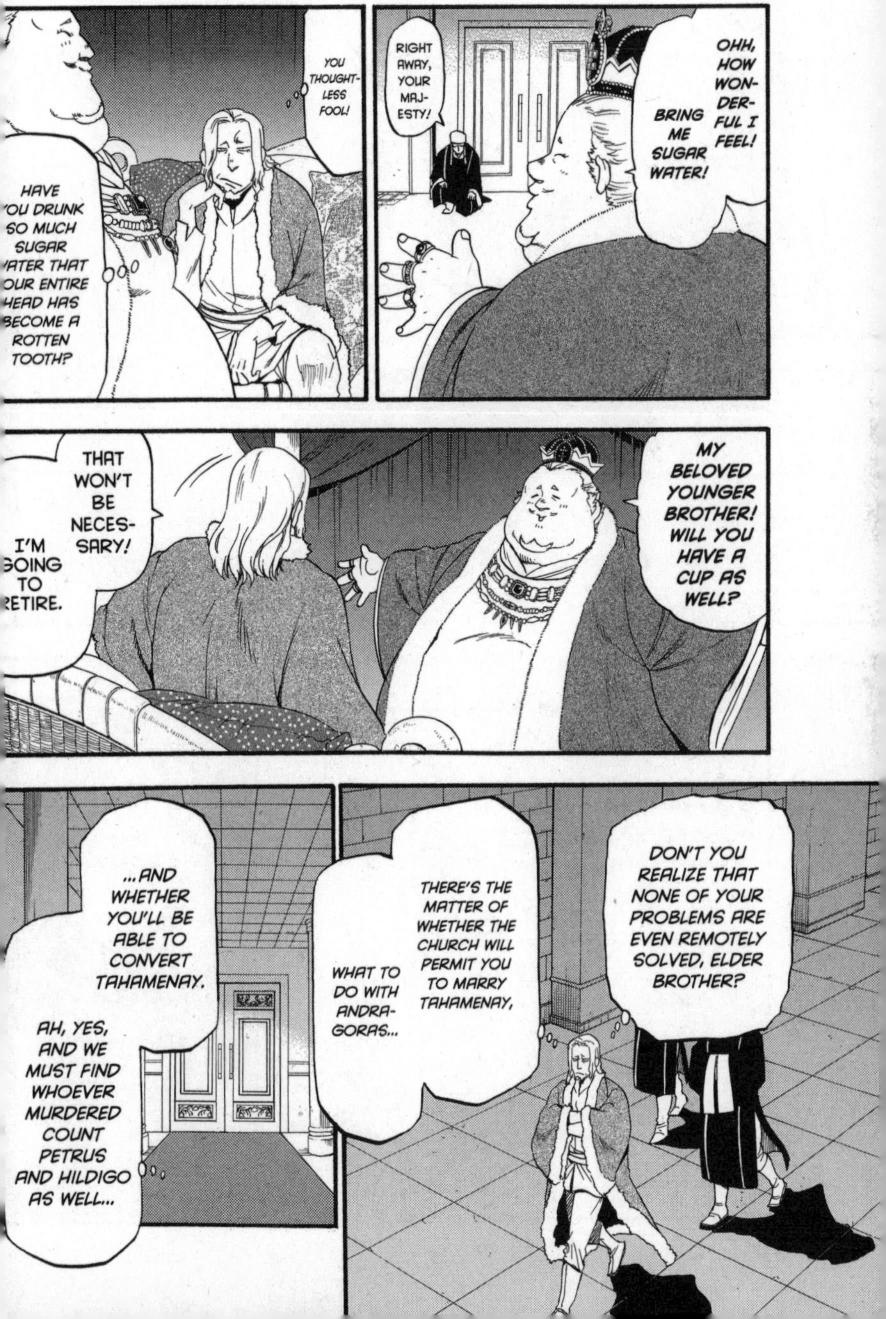
OHH, HOW WONDERFUL I FEEL!
BRING ME SUGAR WATER!
RIGHT AWAY, YOUR MAJESTY!
YOU THOUGHTLESS FOOL!
HAVE OU DRUNK SO MUCH SUGAR ATER THAT OUR ENTIRE HEAD HAS ECOME A ROTTEN TOOTH?
MY BELOVED YOUNGER BROTHER! WILL YOU HAVE A CUP AS WELL?
THAT WON'T BE NECESSARY!
I'M OING TO ETIRE.
DON'T YOU REALIZE THAT NONE OF YOUR PROBLEMS ARE EVEN REMOTELY SOLVED, ELDER BROTHER?
THERE'S THE MATTER OF WHETHER THE CHURCH WILL PERMIT YOU TO MARRY TAHAMENAY,
WHAT TO DO WITH ANDRAGORAS...
...AND WHETHER YOU'LL BE ABLE TO CONVERT TAHAMENAY.
AH, YES, AND WE MUST FIND WHOEVER MURDERED COUNT PETRUS AND HILDIGO AS WELL...

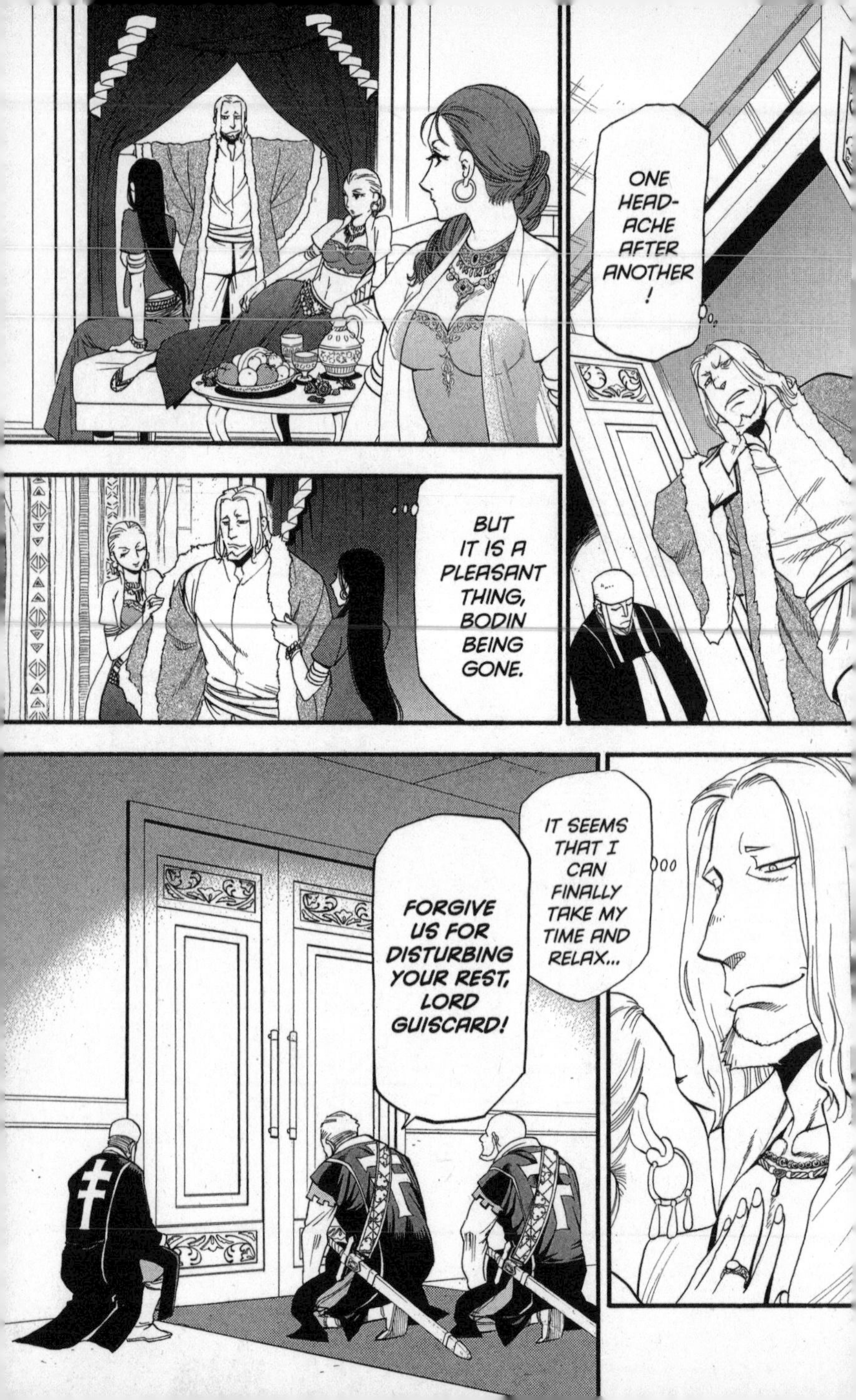
ONE HEAD-ACHE AFTER ANOTHER!
"...
BUT IT IS A PLEASANT THING, BODIN BEING GONE.
IT SEEMS THAT I CAN FINALLY TAKE MY TIME AND RELAX...
FORGIVE US FOR DISTURBING YOUR REST, LORD GUISCARD!

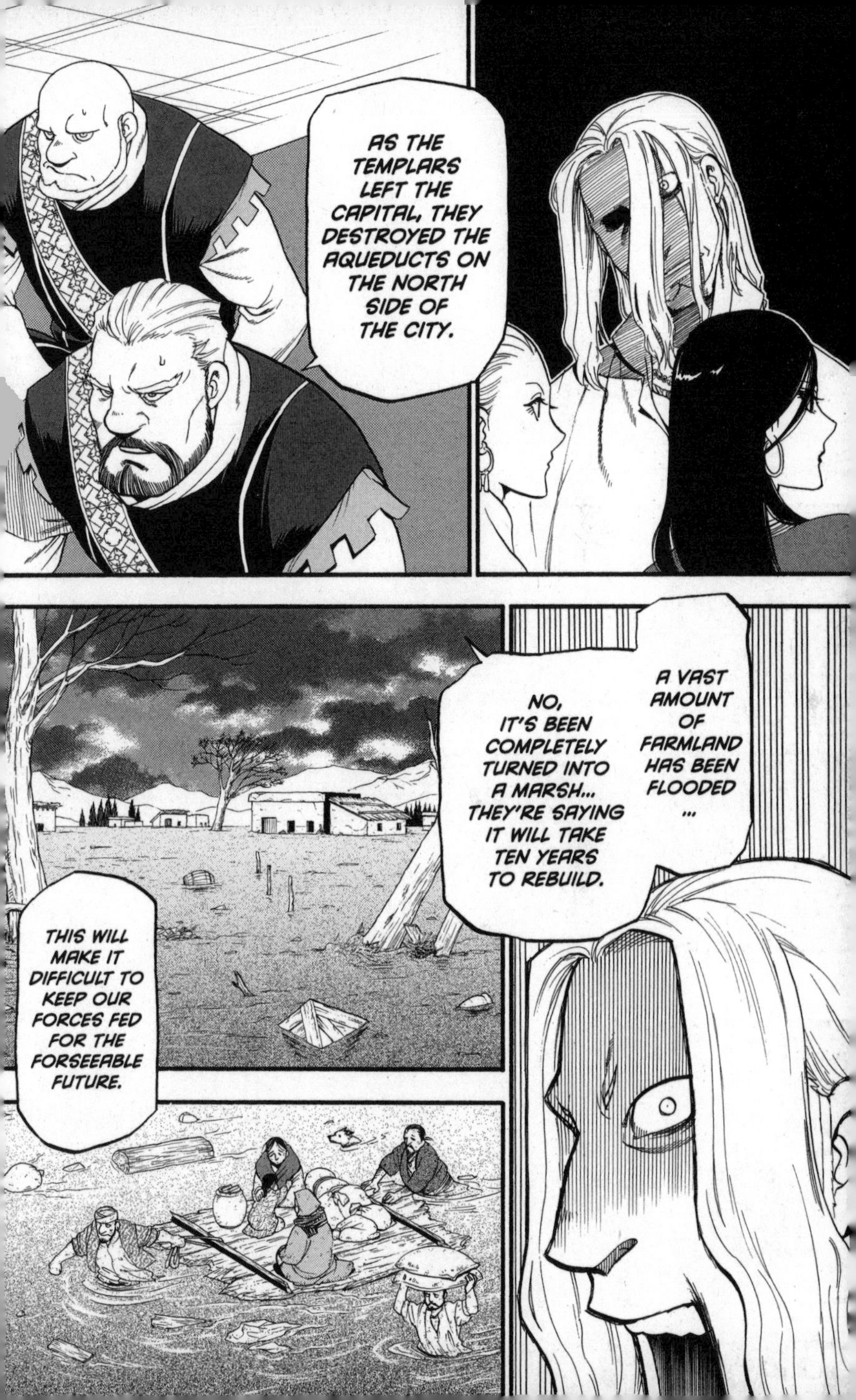
AS THE TEMPLARS LEFT THE CAPITAL, THEY DESTROYED THE AQUEDUCTS ON THE NORTH SIDE OF THE CITY.
A VAST AMOUNT OF FARMLAND HAS BEEN FLOODED...
NO, IT'S BEEN COMPLETELY TURNED INTO A MARSH... THEY'RE SAYING IT WILL TAKE TEN YEARS TO REBUILD.
THIS WILL MAKE IT DIFFICULT TO KEEP OUR FORCES FED FOR THE FORSEEABLE FUTURE.

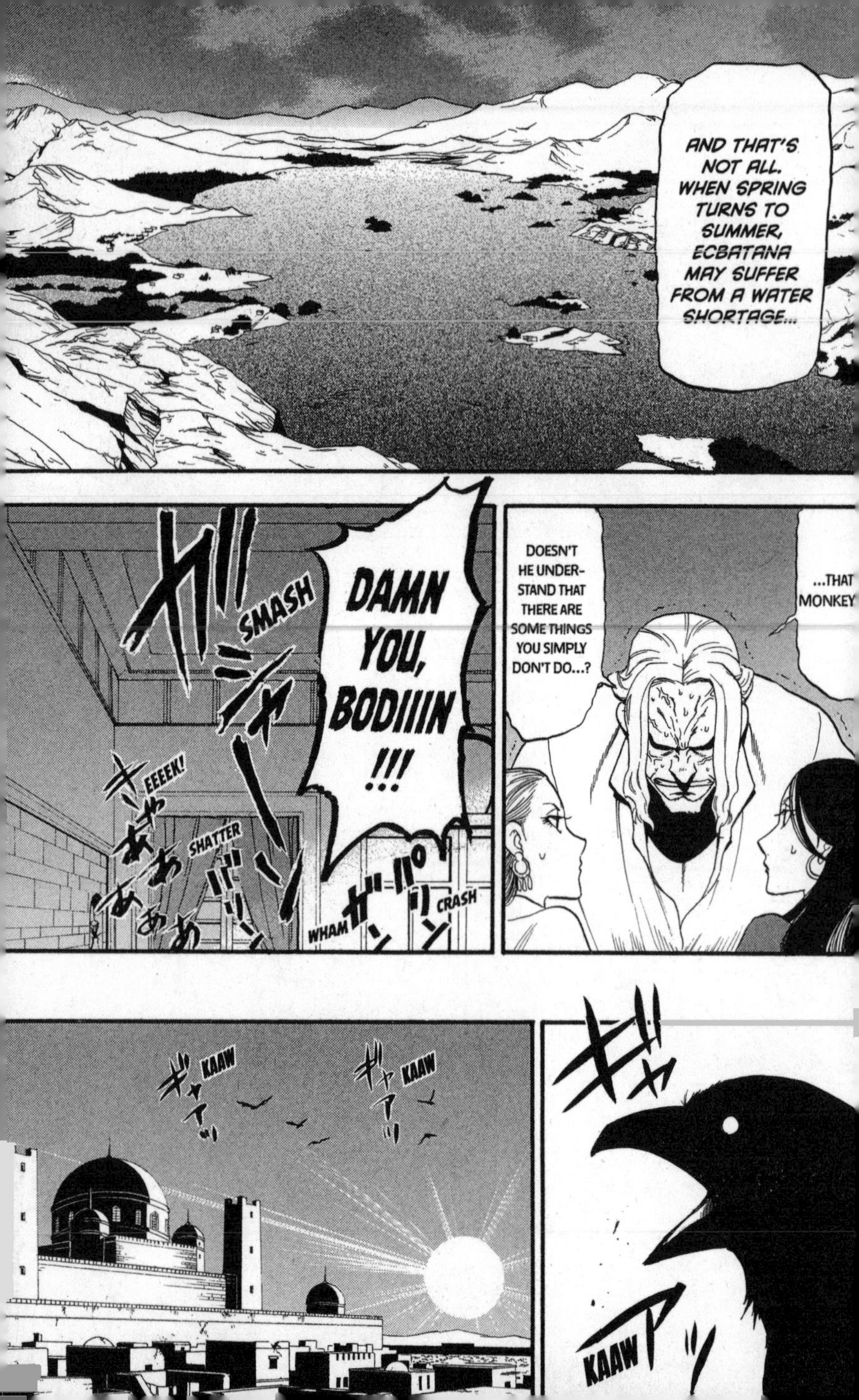
AND THAT'S NOT ALL. WHEN SPRING TURNS TO SUMMER, ECBATANA MAY SUFFER FROM A WATER SHORTAGE...
...THAT MONKEY
DOESN'T HE UNDER-STAND THAT THERE ARE SOME THINGS YOU SIMPLY DON'T DO...?
DAMN YOU, BODIIIN!!!
SMASH
EEEEK!
SHATTER
CRASH
WHAM
KAAW
KAAW
KAAW

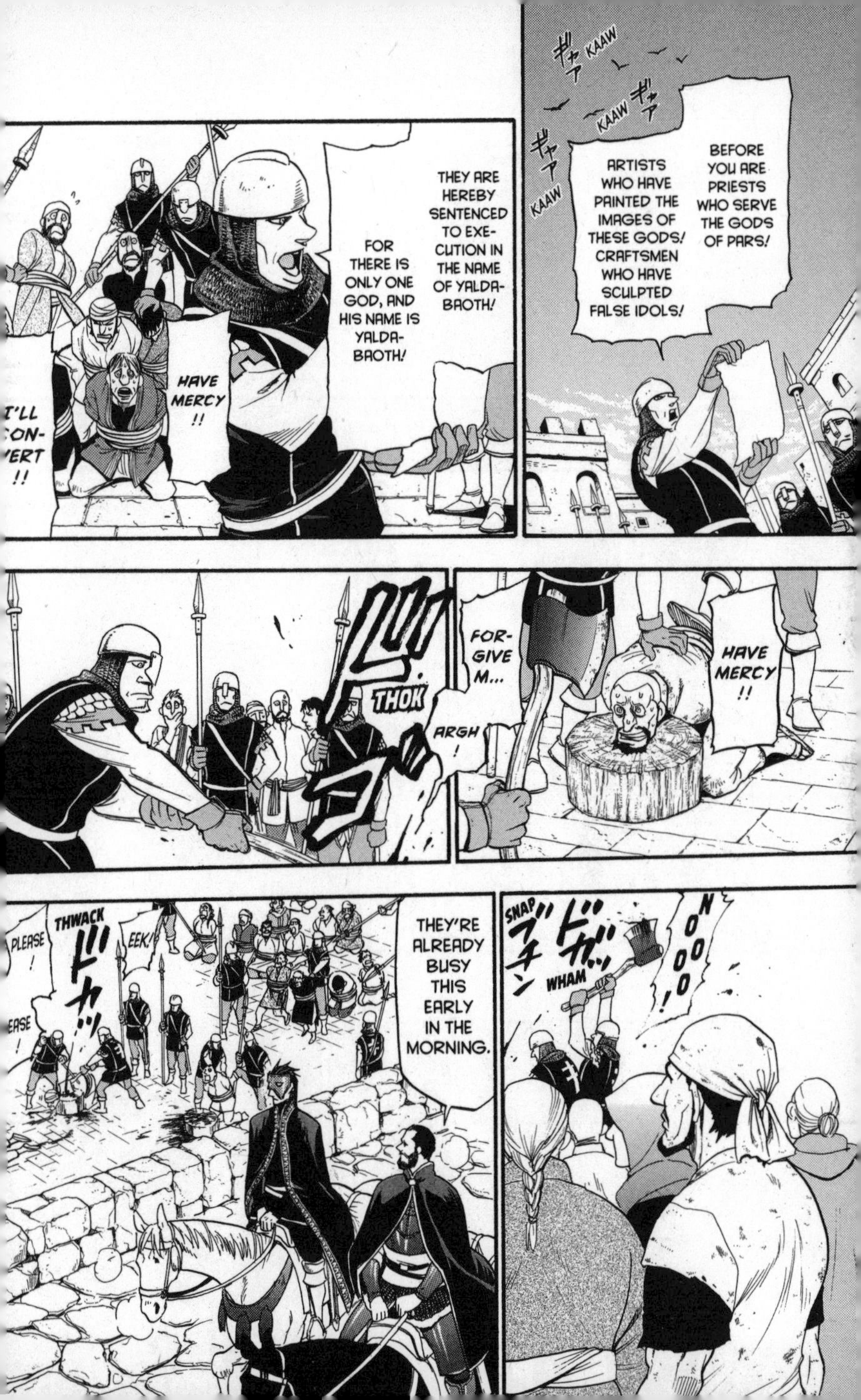
KAAW
KAAW
KAAW
BEFORE YOU ARE PRIESTS WHO SERVE THE GODS OF PARS!
ARTISTS WHO HAVE PAINTED THE IMAGES OF THESE GODS! CRAFTSMEN WHO HAVE SCULPTED FALSE IDOLS!
THEY ARE HEREBY SENTENCED TO EXE-CUTION IN THE NAME OF YALDA-BAOTH!
FOR THERE IS ONLY ONE GOD, AND HIS NAME IS YALDA-BAOTH!
HAVE MERCY!!
I'LL CON-VERT!!
HAVE MERCY!!
FOR-GIVE M...
THOK
ARGH!
SNAP
WHAM
NOOOOO!
THEY'RE ALREADY BUSY THIS EARLY IN THE MORNING.
THWACK
EEK!
PLEASE!
EASE!

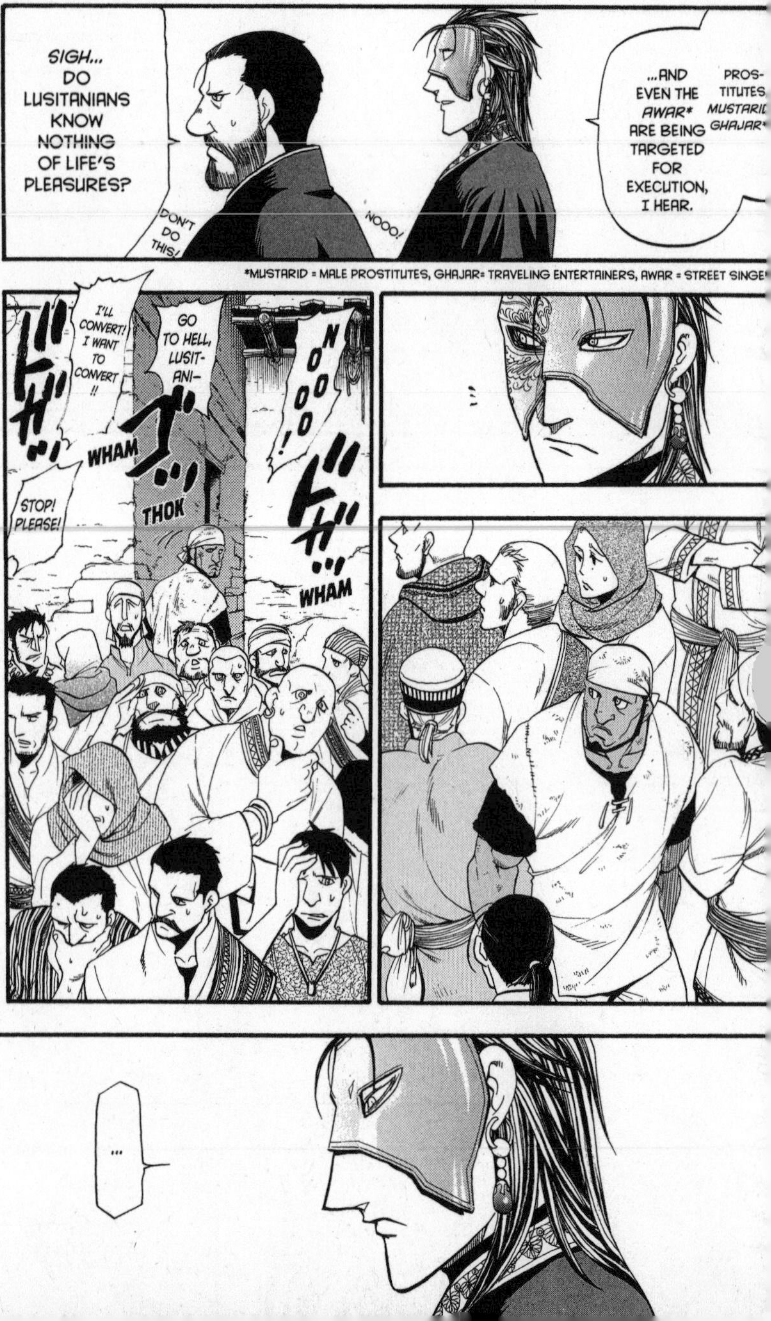
PROS-TITUTES, MUSTARID GHAJAR*
...AND EVEN THE AWAR* ARE BEING TARGETED FOR EXECUTION, I HEAR.
NOOO!
SIGH... DO LUSITANIANS KNOW NOTHING OF LIFE'S PLEASURES?
DON'T DO THIS!
*MUSTARID = MALE PROSTITUTES, GHAJAR= TRAVELING ENTERTAINERS, AWAR = STREET SINGE
NOOOOOO!
WHAM
GO TO HELL, LUSIT-ANI-
THOK
I'LL CONVERT! I WANT TO CONVERT!!
WHAM
STOP! PLEASE!
...

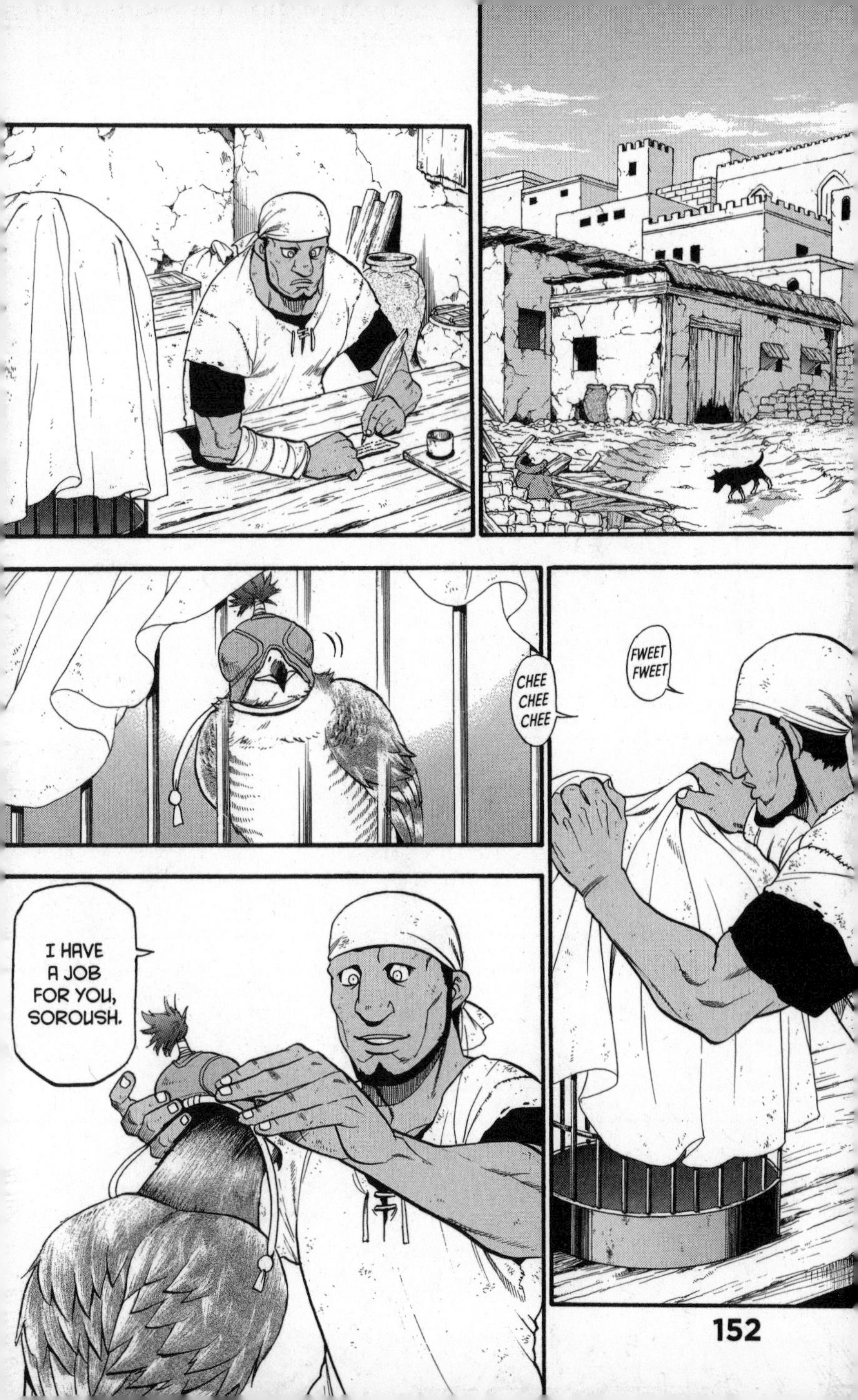
FWEET FWEET
CHEE CHEE CHEE
I HAVE A JOB FOR YOU, SOROUSH.

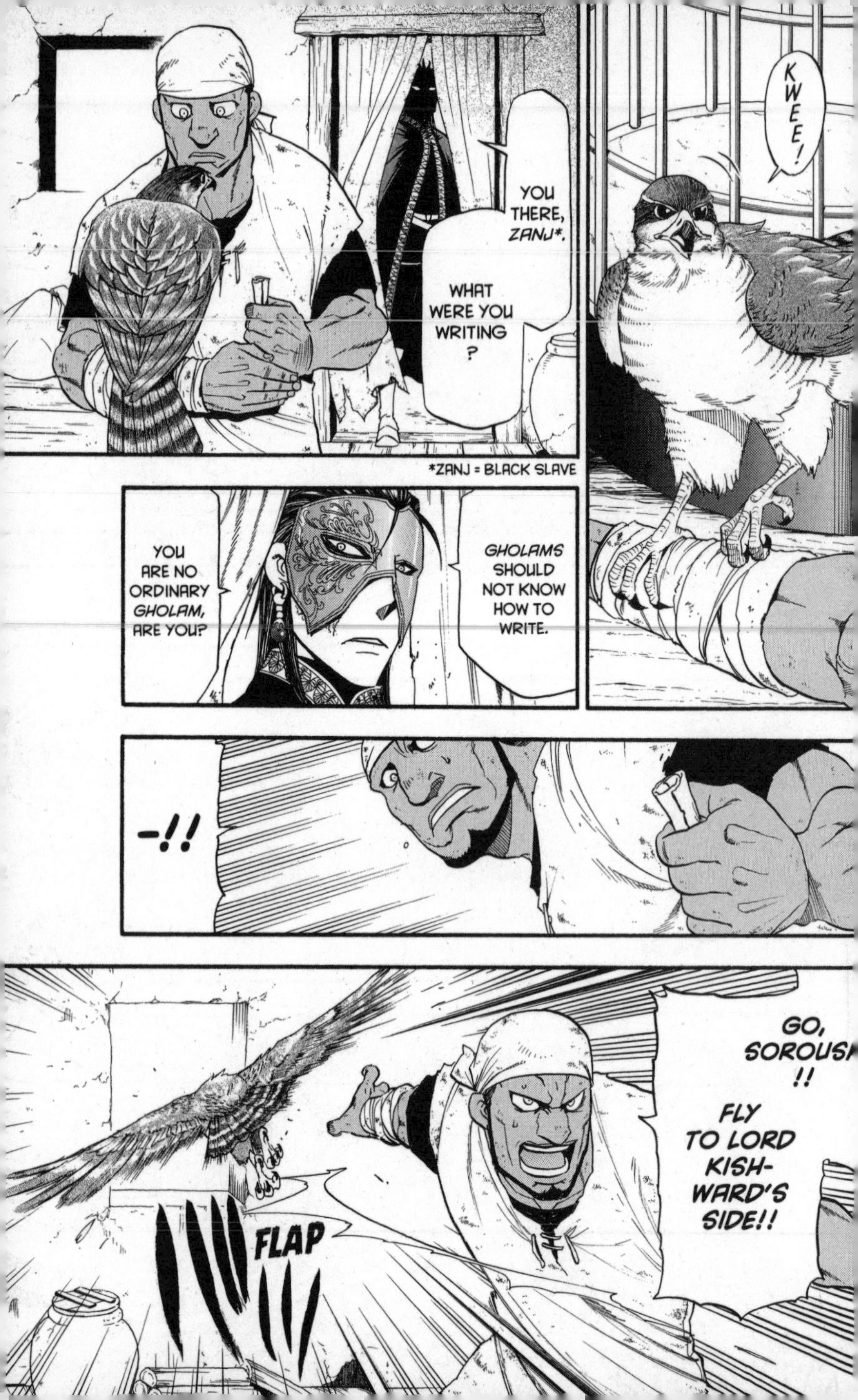
KWEE!
YOU THERE, ZANJ*.
WHAT WERE YOU WRITING?
*ZANJ = BLACK SLAVE
GHOLAMS SHOULD NOT KNOW HOW TO WRITE.
YOU ARE NO ORDINARY GHOLAM, ARE YOU?
-!!
GO, SOROUSH!!
FLY TO LORD KISH-WARD'S SIDE!!
FLAP

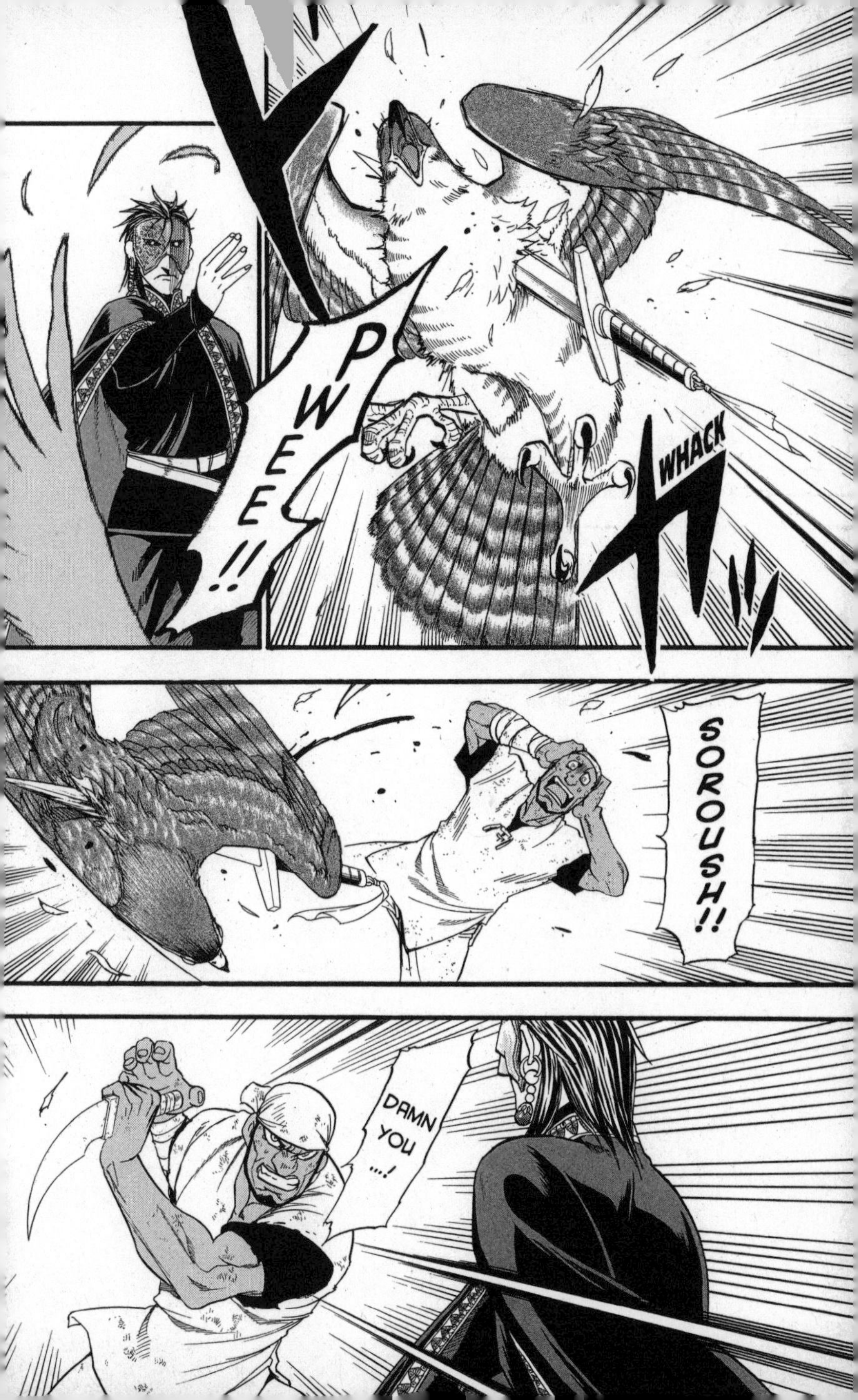
WHACK
PWEEE!!
SOROUSH!!
DAMN YOU ...!

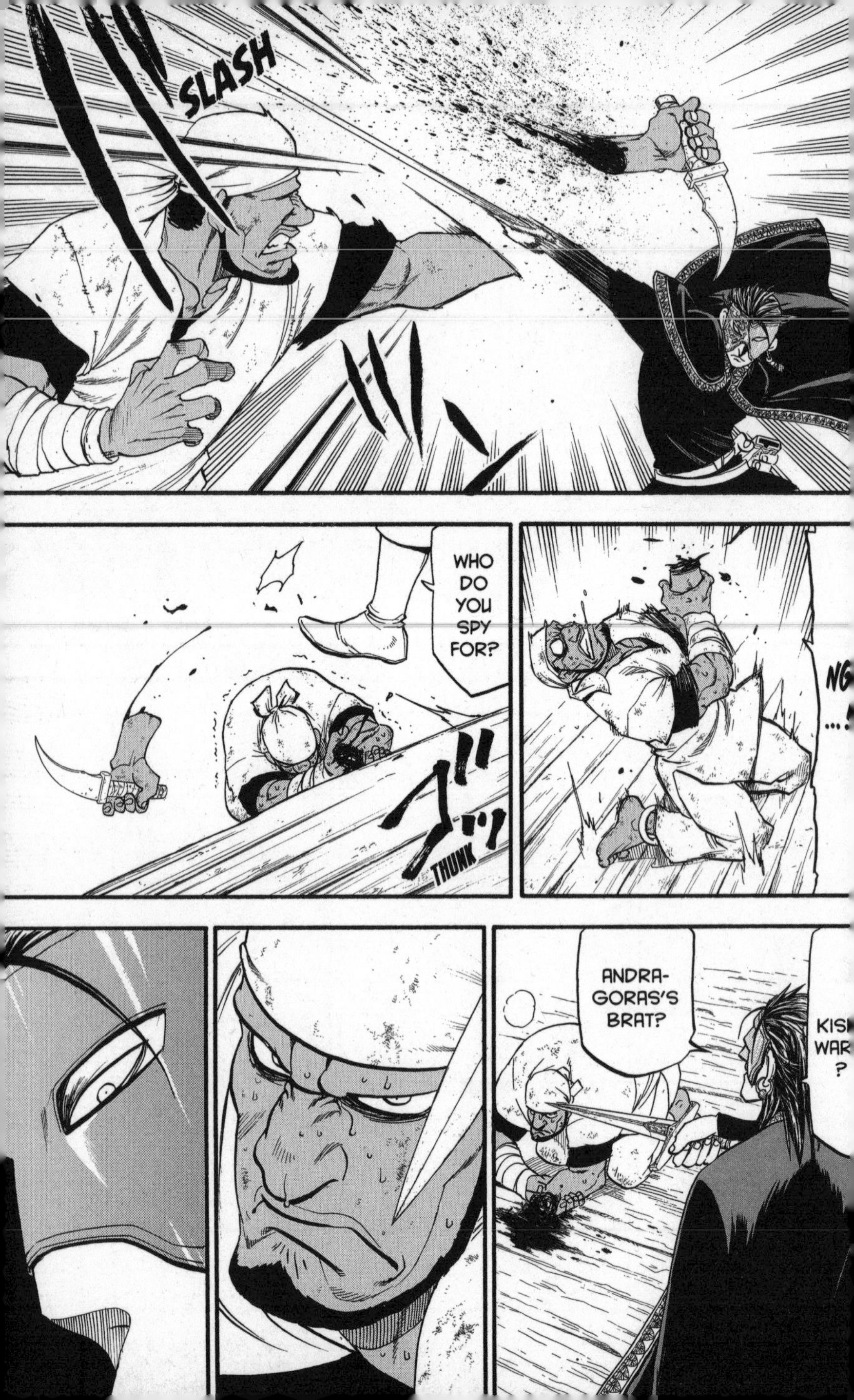
SLASH
NG...!
WHO DO YOU SPY FOR?
THUNK
KIS WAR ?
ANDRA-GORAS'S BRAT?

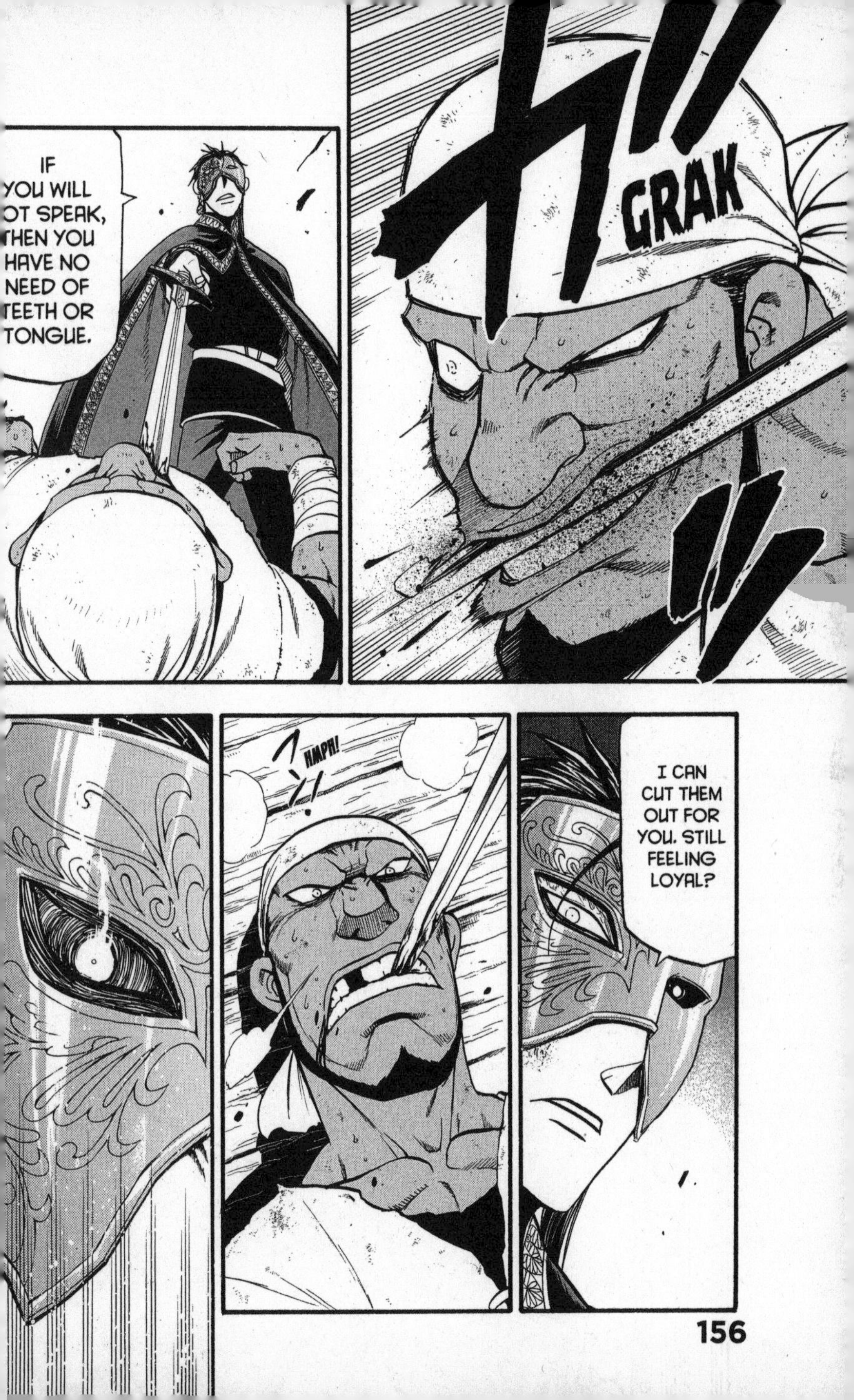
GRAK
IF YOU WILL OT SPEAK, THEN YOU HAVE NO NEED OF TEETH OR TONGUE.
I CAN CUT THEM OUT FOR YOU. STILL FEELING LOYAL?
HMPH!

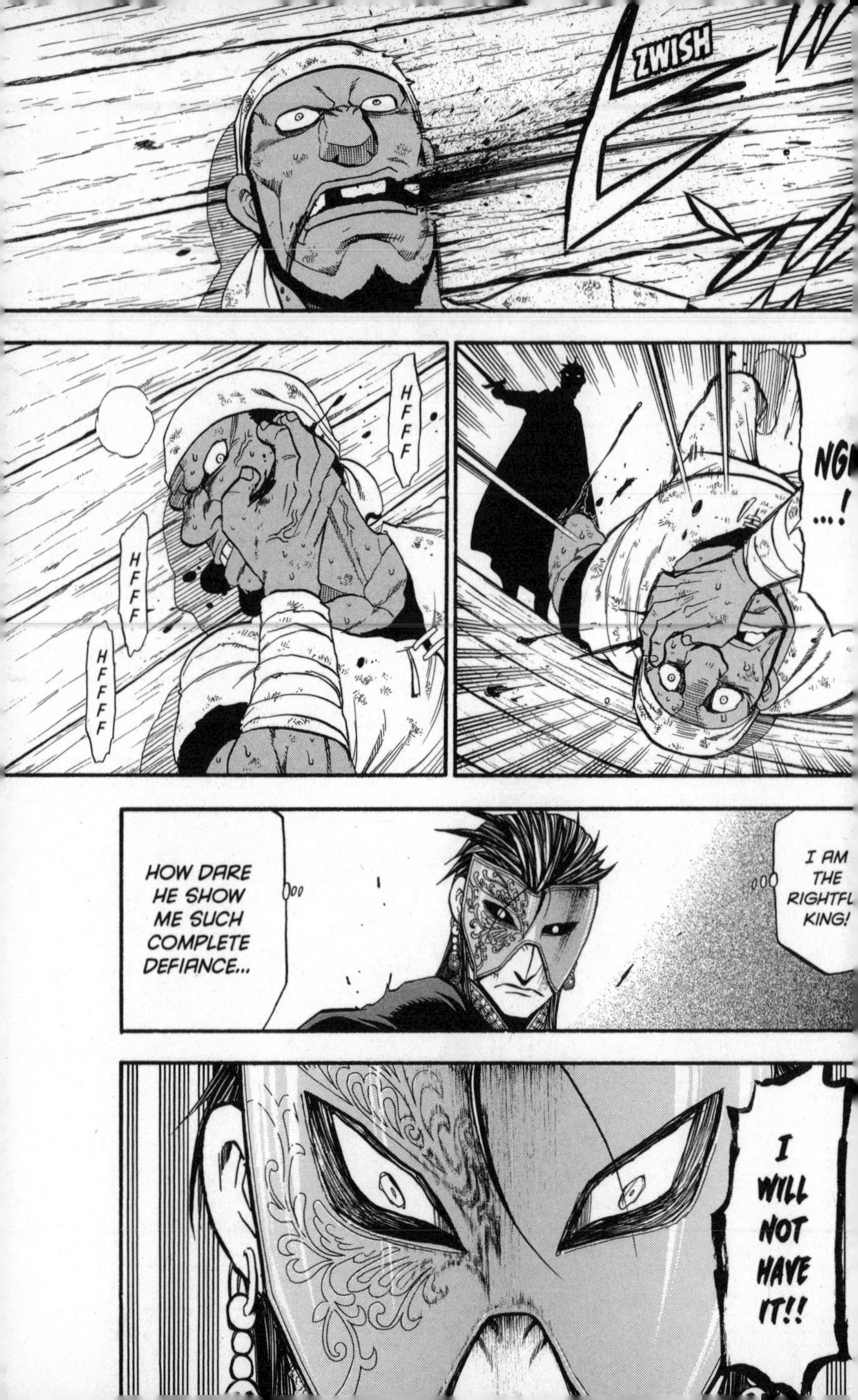
ZWISH
NG! ...!
HFFF
HFFF
HFFFF
I AM THE RIGHTFU KING!
HOW DARE HE SHOW ME SUCH COMPLETE DEFIANCE...
I WILL NOT HAVE IT!!

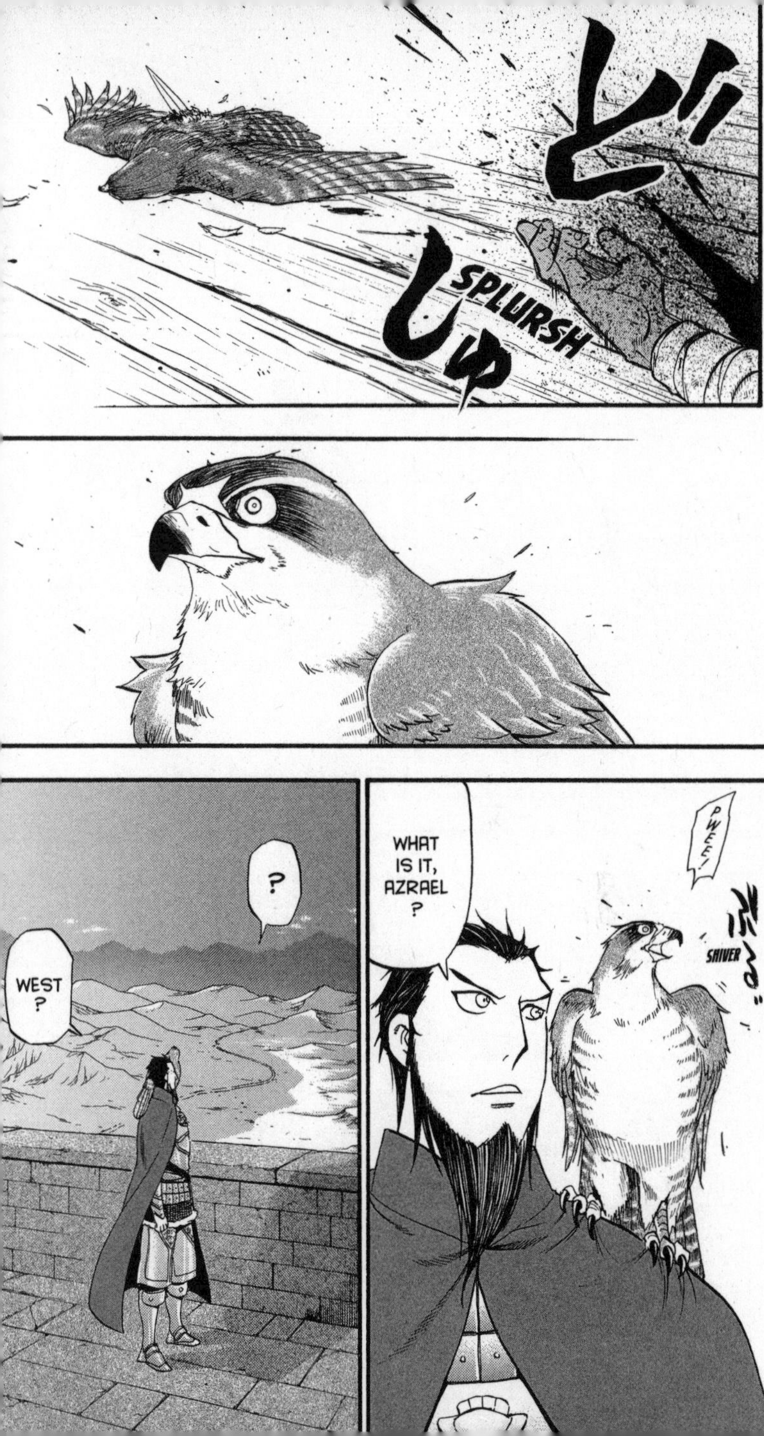
SPLURSH
WHAT IS IT, AZRAEL?
PWEE!
SHIVER
?
WEST?

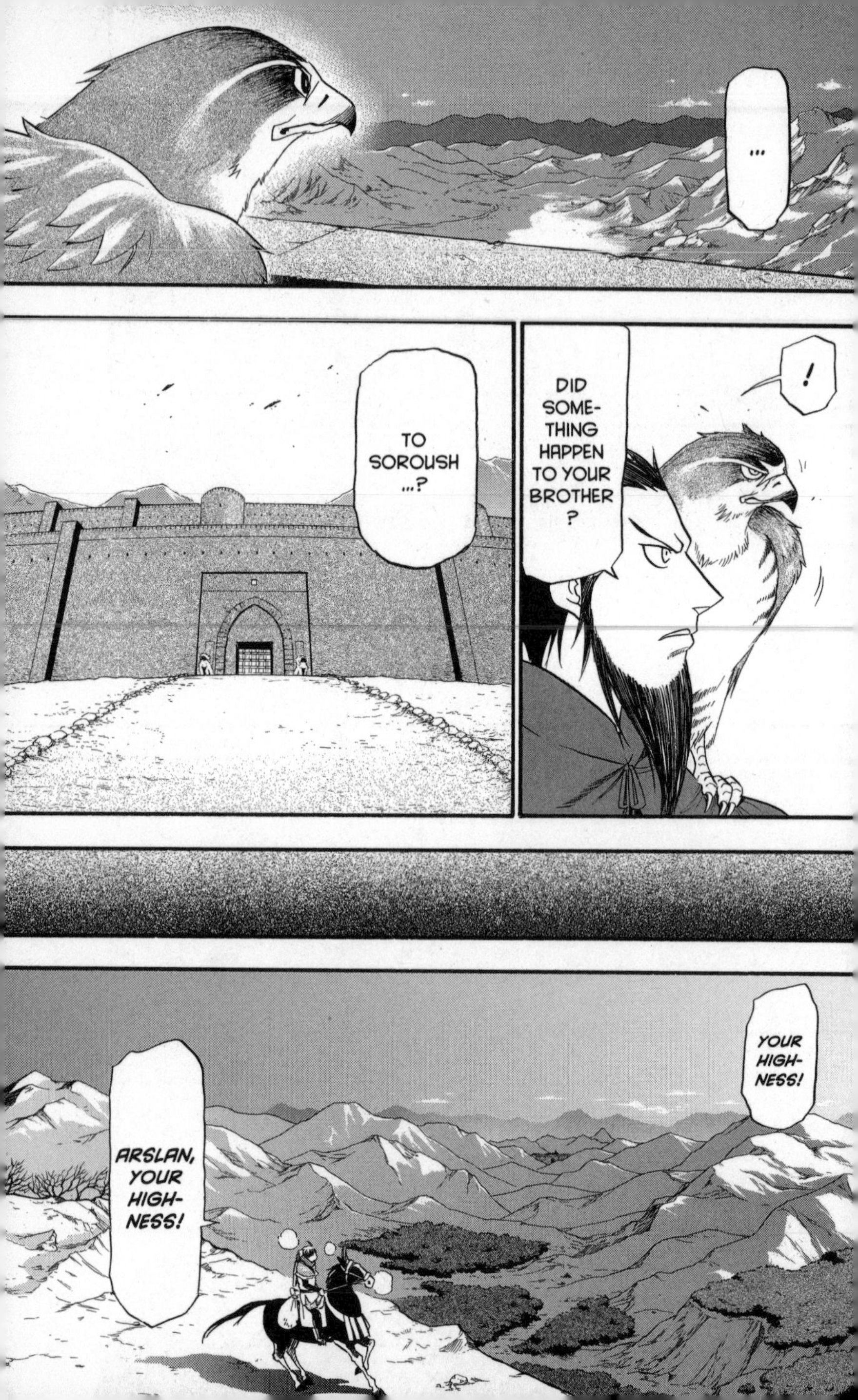
...
!
DID SOMETHING HAPPEN TO YOUR BROTHER?
TO SOROUSH ...?
YOUR HIGHNESS!
ARSLAN, YOUR HIGHNESS!

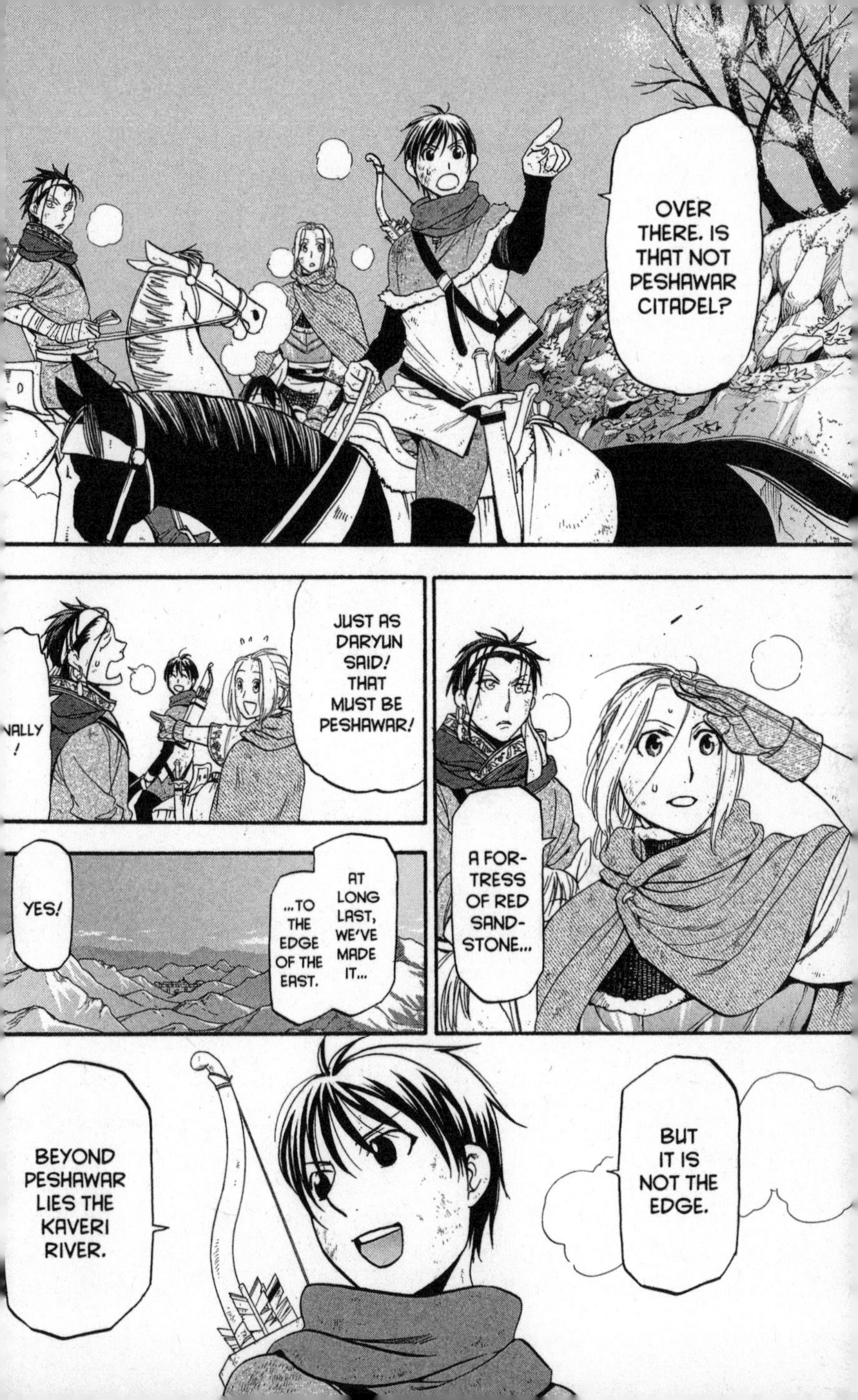
OVER THERE. IS THAT NOT PESHAWAR CITADEL?
A FOR-TRESS OF RED SAND-STONE...
JUST AS DARYUN SAID! THAT MUST BE PESHAWAR!
NALLY!
AT LONG LAST, WE'VE MADE IT...
...TO THE EDGE OF THE EAST.
YES!
BUT IT IS NOT THE EDGE.
BEYOND PESHAWAR LIES THE KAVERI RIVER.

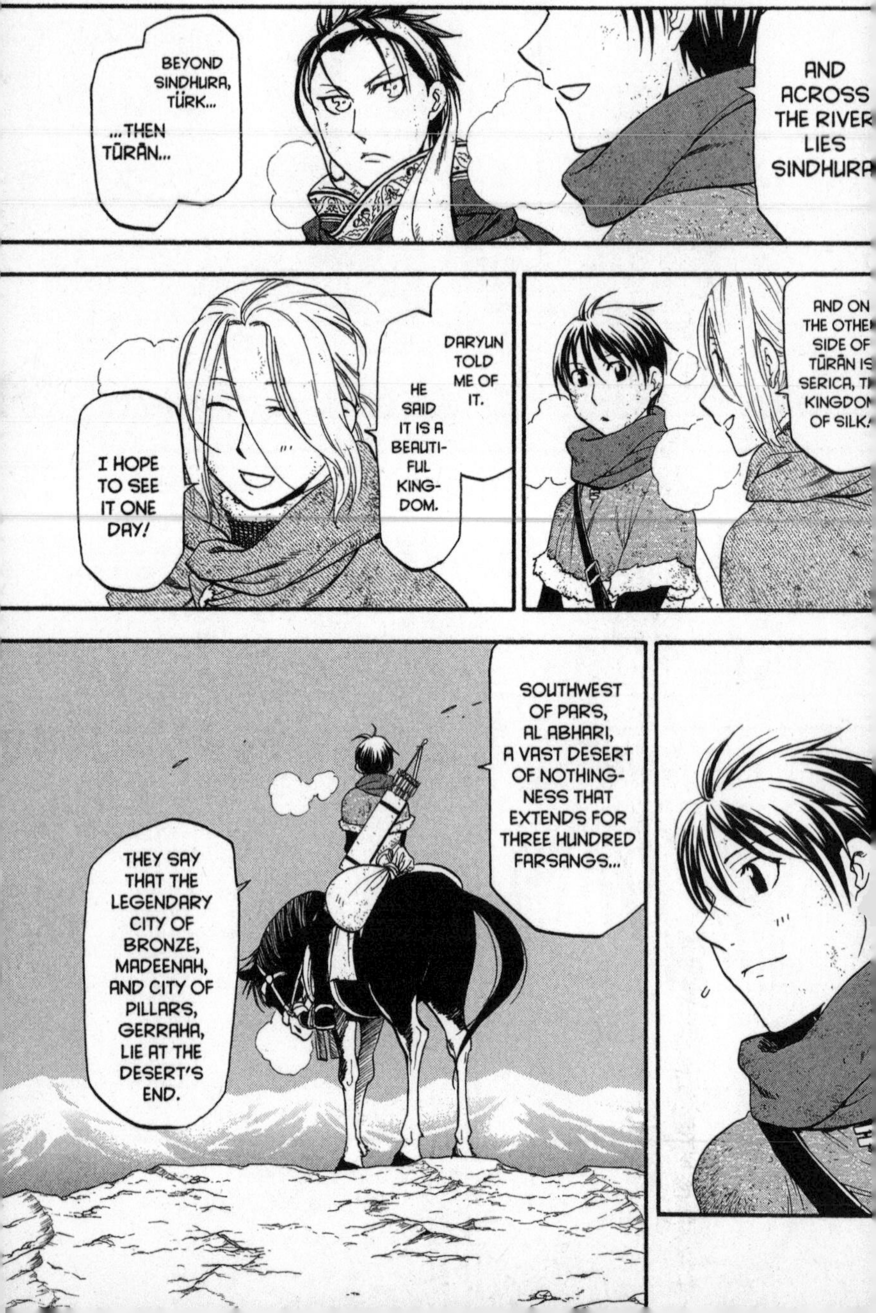
AND ACROSS THE RIVER LIES SINDHURA
BEYOND SINDHURA, TÜRK...
...THEN TŪRĀN...
AND ON THE OTHE SIDE OF TŪRĀN IS SERICA, T KINGDON OF SILK.
DARYUN TOLD ME OF IT.
HE SAID IT IS A BEAUTI-FUL KING-DOM.
I HOPE TO SEE IT ONE DAY!
SOUTHWEST OF PARS, AL ABHARI, A VAST DESERT OF NOTHING-NESS THAT EXTENDS FOR THREE HUNDRED FARSANGS...
THEY SAY THAT THE LEGENDARY CITY OF BRONZE, MADEENAH, AND CITY OF PILLARS, GERRAHA, LIE AT THE DESERT'S END.

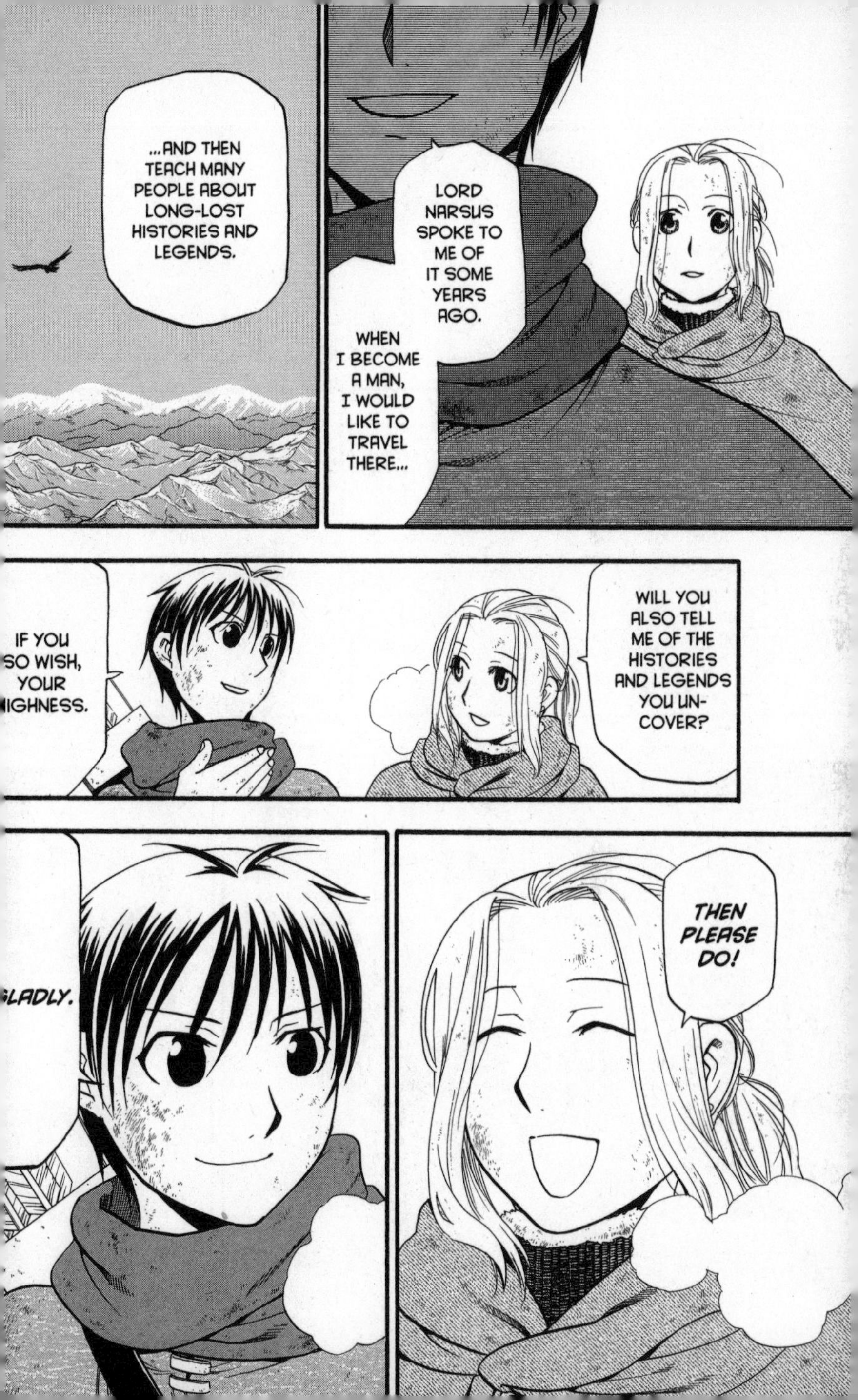
LORD NARSUS SPOKE TO ME OF IT SOME YEARS AGO.
WHEN I BECOME A MAN, I WOULD LIKE TO TRAVEL THERE...
...AND THEN TEACH MANY PEOPLE ABOUT LONG-LOST HISTORIES AND LEGENDS.
WILL YOU ALSO TELL ME OF THE HISTORIES AND LEGENDS YOU UN-COVER?
IF YOU SO WISH, YOUR IGHNESS.
THEN PLEASE DO!
LADLY.

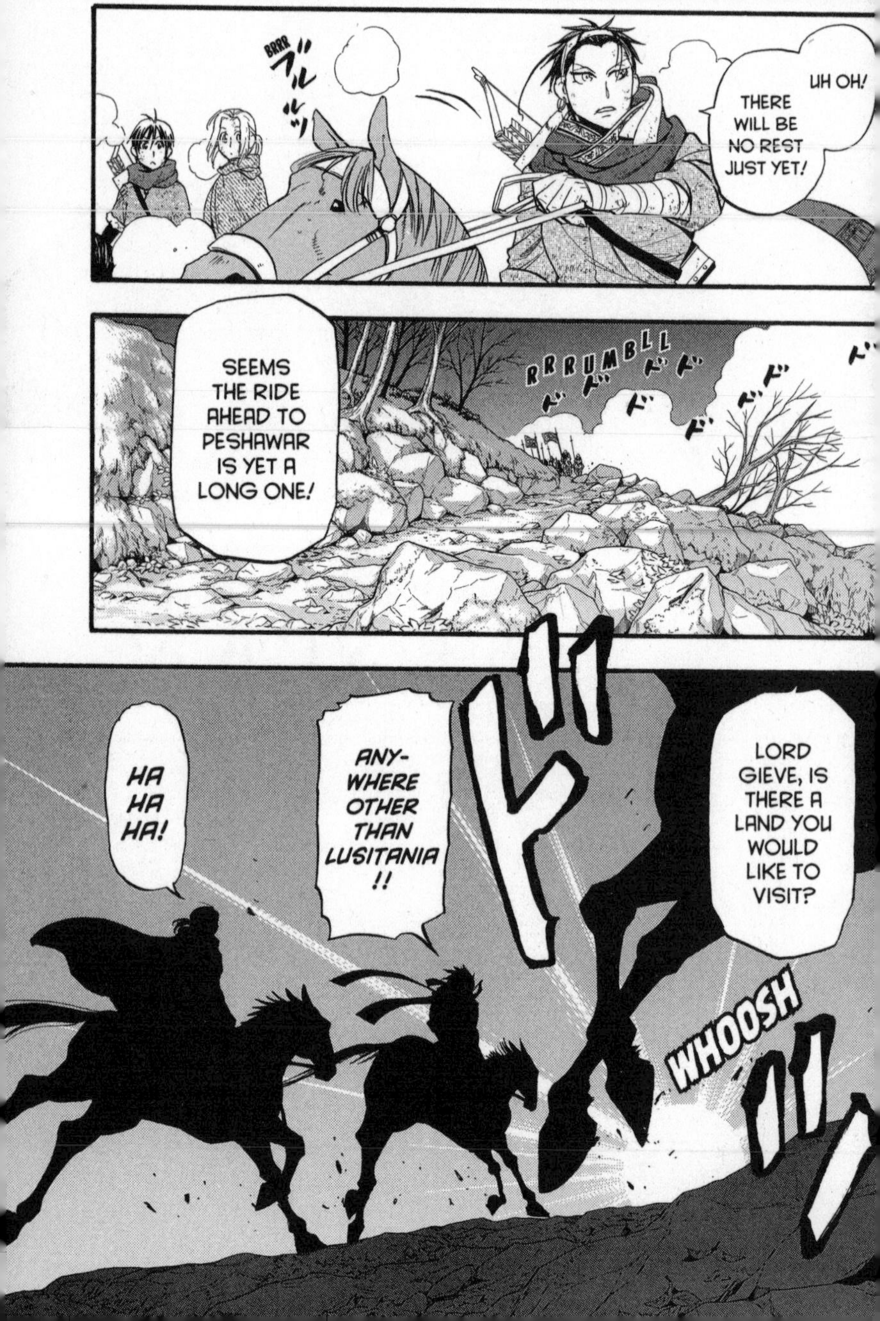
UH OH! THERE WILL BE NO REST JUST YET!
BRRR
RRRUMBLL
SEEMS THE RIDE AHEAD TO PESHAWAR IS YET A LONG ONE!
LORD GIEVE, IS THERE A LAND YOU WOULD LIKE TO VISIT?
ANY-WHERE OTHER THAN LUSITANIA!!
HA HA HA!
WHOOSH

THE HEROIC LEGEND OF
ARSLAN

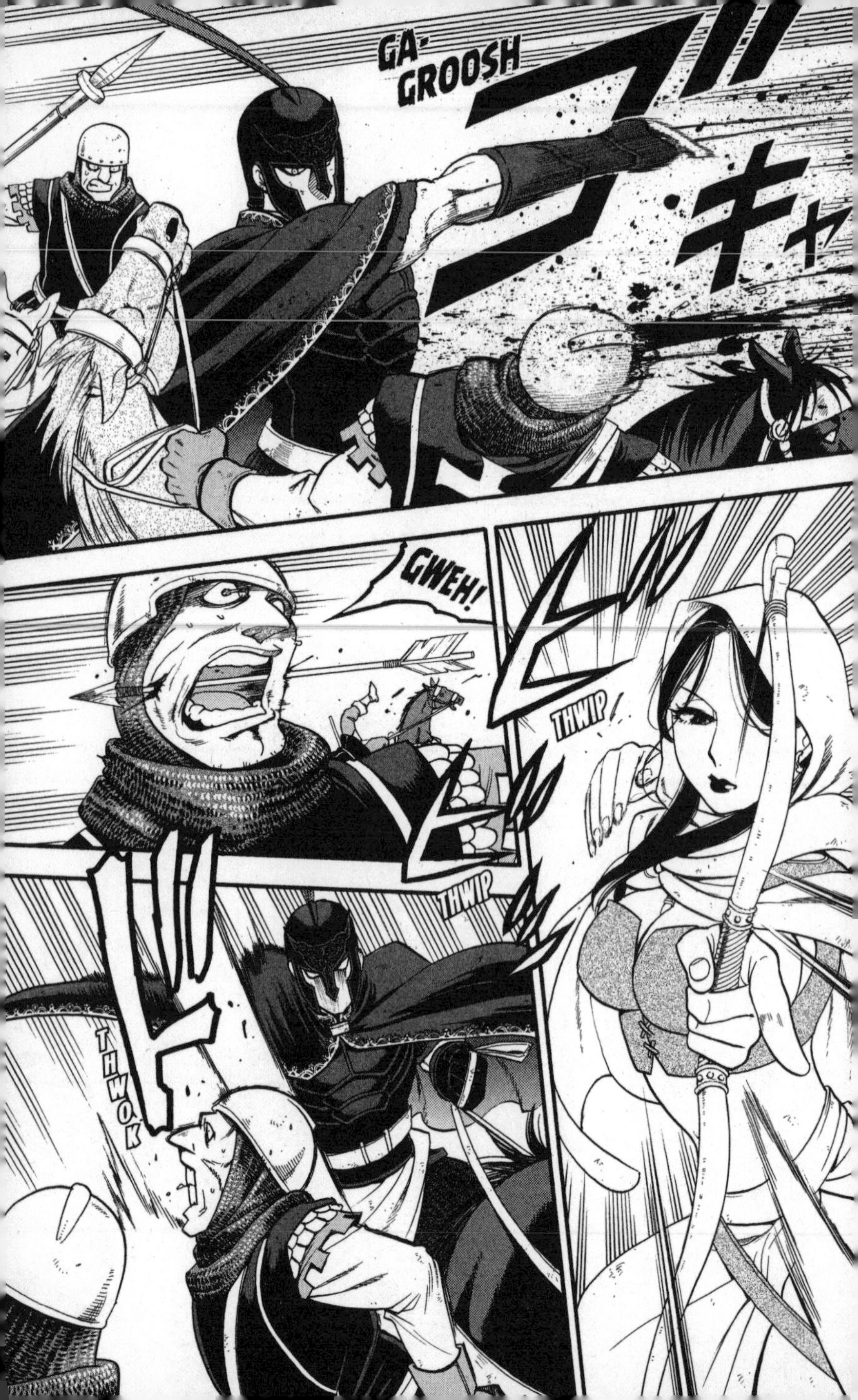

GA-GROOSH
THWIP
GWEH!
THWIP
THWOK

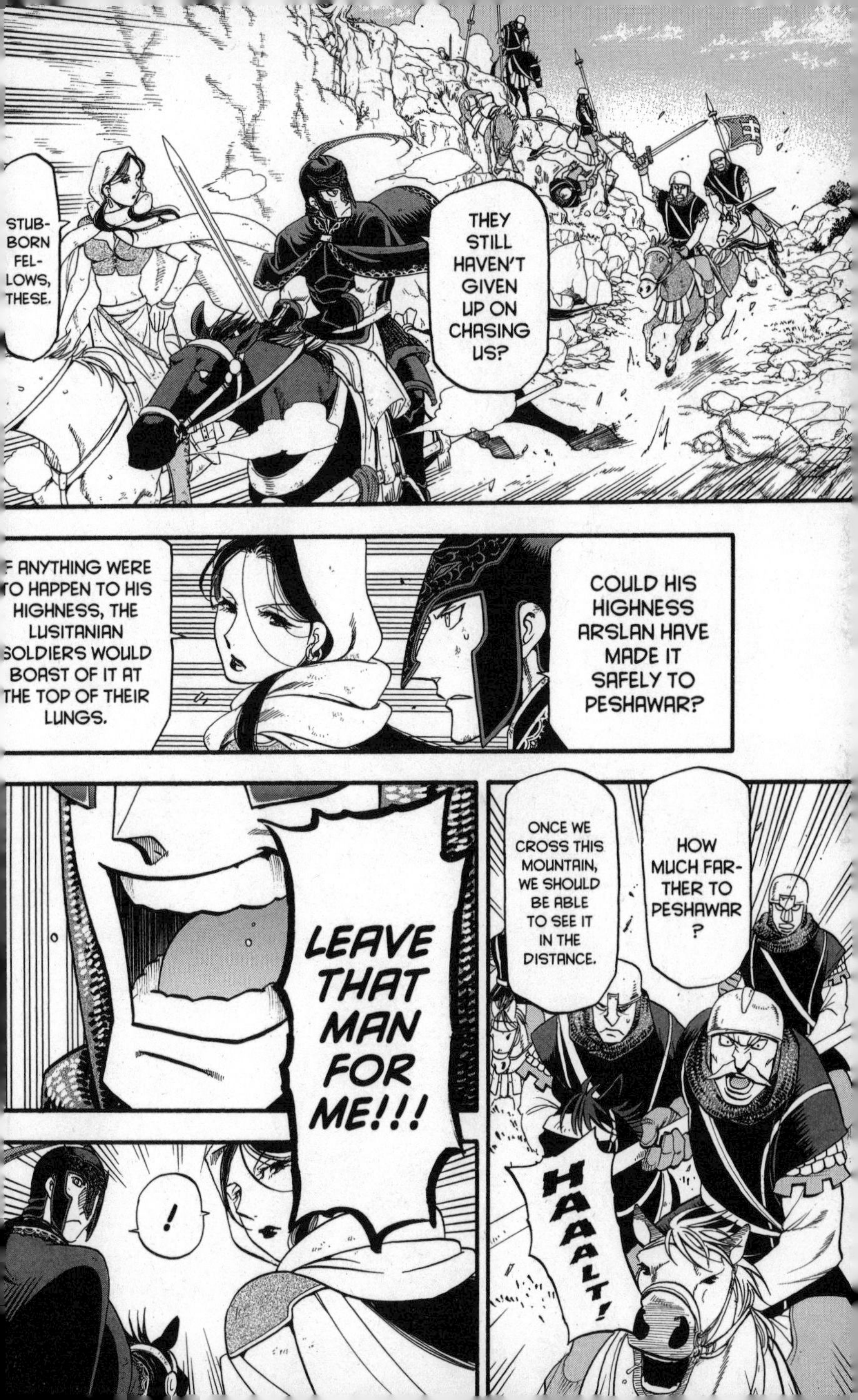
THEY STILL HAVEN'T GIVEN UP ON CHASING US?
STUB-BORN FEL-LOWS, THESE.
COULD HIS HIGHNESS ARSLAN HAVE MADE IT SAFELY TO PESHAWAR?
IF ANYTHING WERE TO HAPPEN TO HIS HIGHNESS, THE LUSITANIAN SOLDIERS WOULD BOAST OF IT AT THE TOP OF THEIR LUNGS.
HOW MUCH FAR-THER TO PESHAWAR?
ONCE WE CROSS THIS MOUNTAIN, WE SHOULD BE ABLE TO SEE IT IN THE DISTANCE.
HAAALT!
LEAVE THAT MAN FOR ME!!!
!

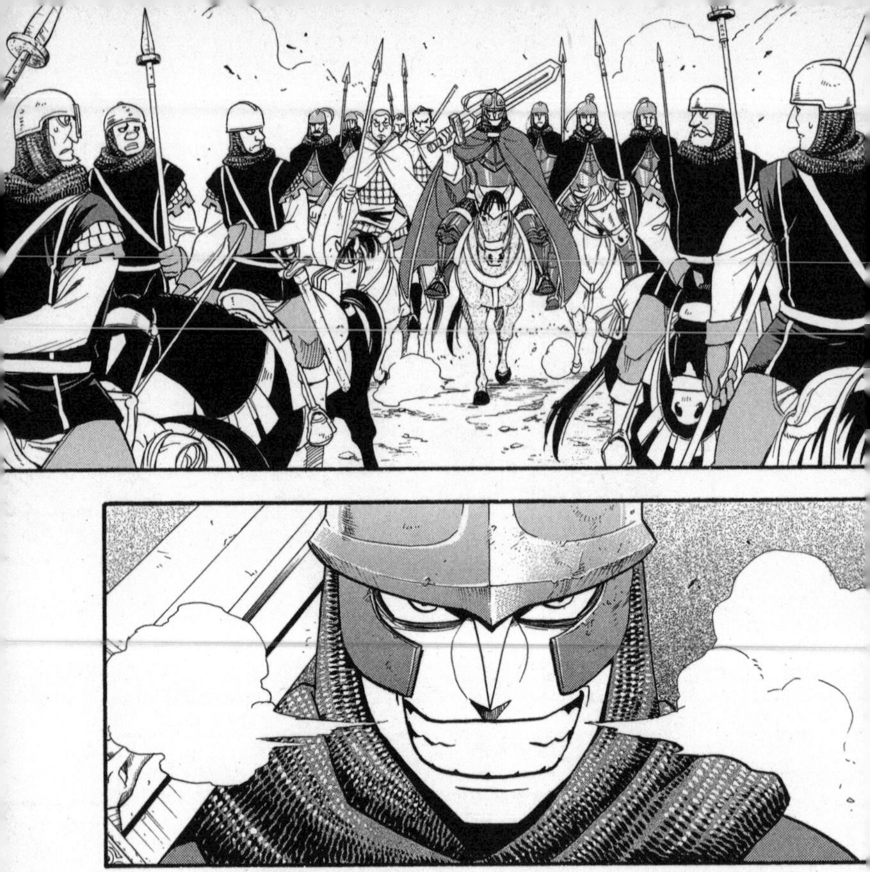

Chapter 34: The Magic Mountain

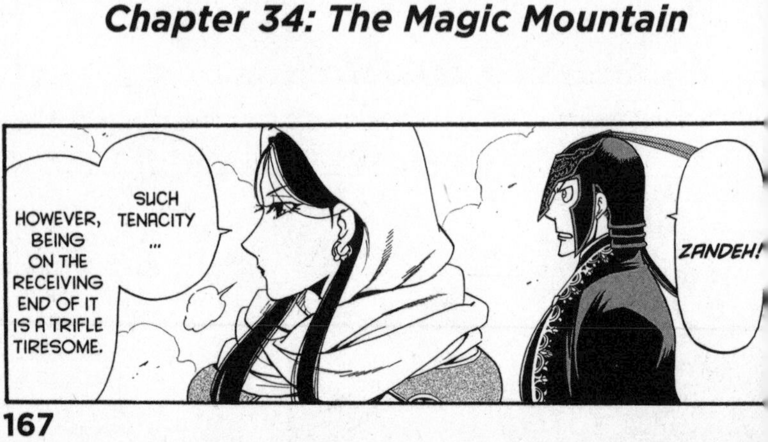
ZANDEH!
SUCH TENACITY ...
HOWEVER, BEING ON THE RECEIVING END OF IT IS A TRIFLE TIRESOME.

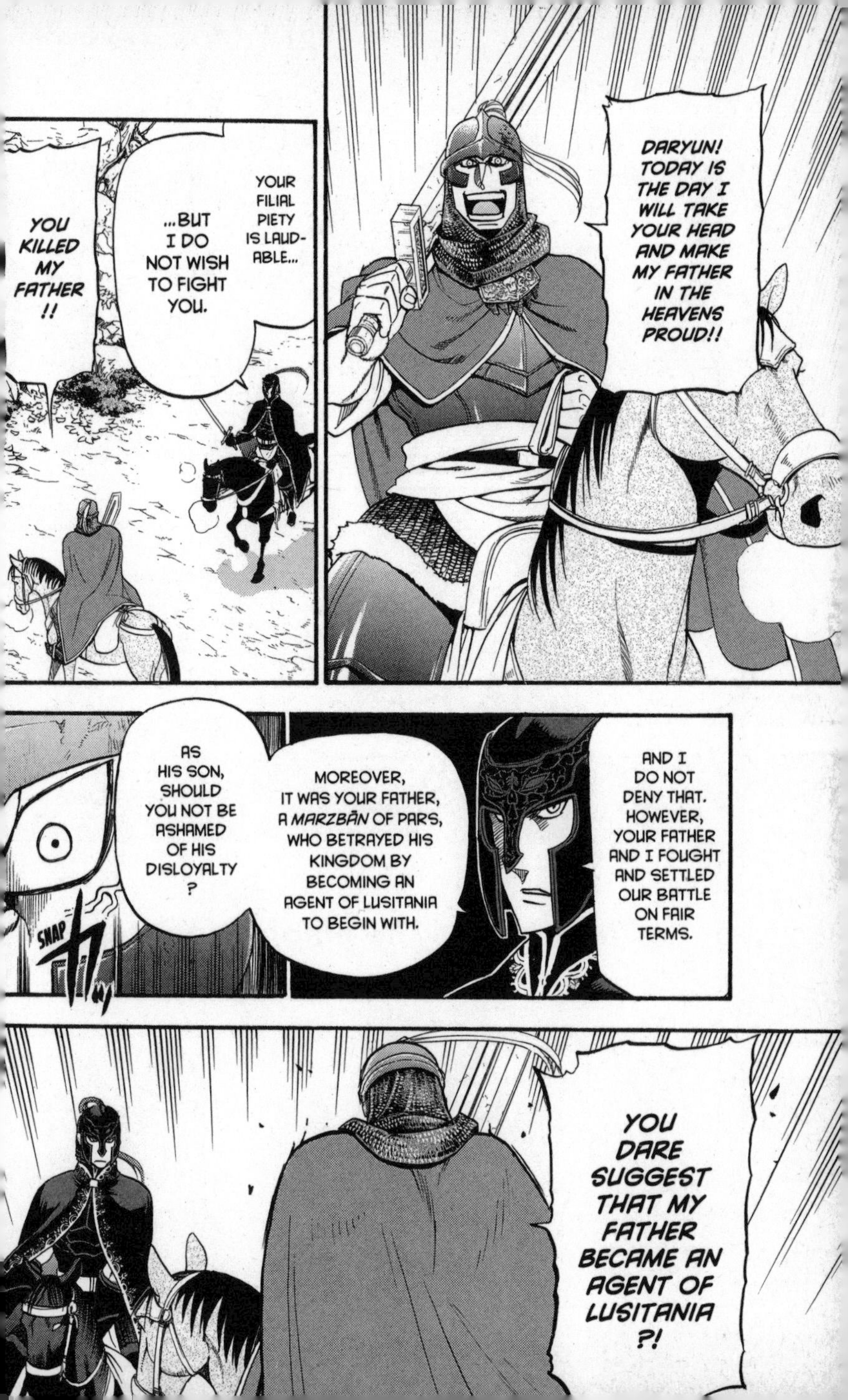
DARYUN! TODAY IS THE DAY I WILL TAKE YOUR HEAD AND MAKE MY FATHER IN THE HEAVENS PROUD!!
YOUR FILIAL PIETY IS LAUD-ABLE...
...BUT I DO NOT WISH TO FIGHT YOU.
YOU KILLED MY FATHER!!
AND I DO NOT DENY THAT. HOWEVER, YOUR FATHER AND I FOUGHT AND SETTLED OUR BATTLE ON FAIR TERMS.
MOREOVER, IT WAS YOUR FATHER, A MARZBĀN OF PARS, WHO BETRAYED HIS KINGDOM BY BECOMING AN AGENT OF LUSITANIA TO BEGIN WITH.
AS HIS SON, SHOULD YOU NOT BE ASHAMED OF HIS DISLOYALTY?
SNAP
YOU DARE SUGGEST THAT MY FATHER BECAME AN AGENT OF LUSITANIA?!

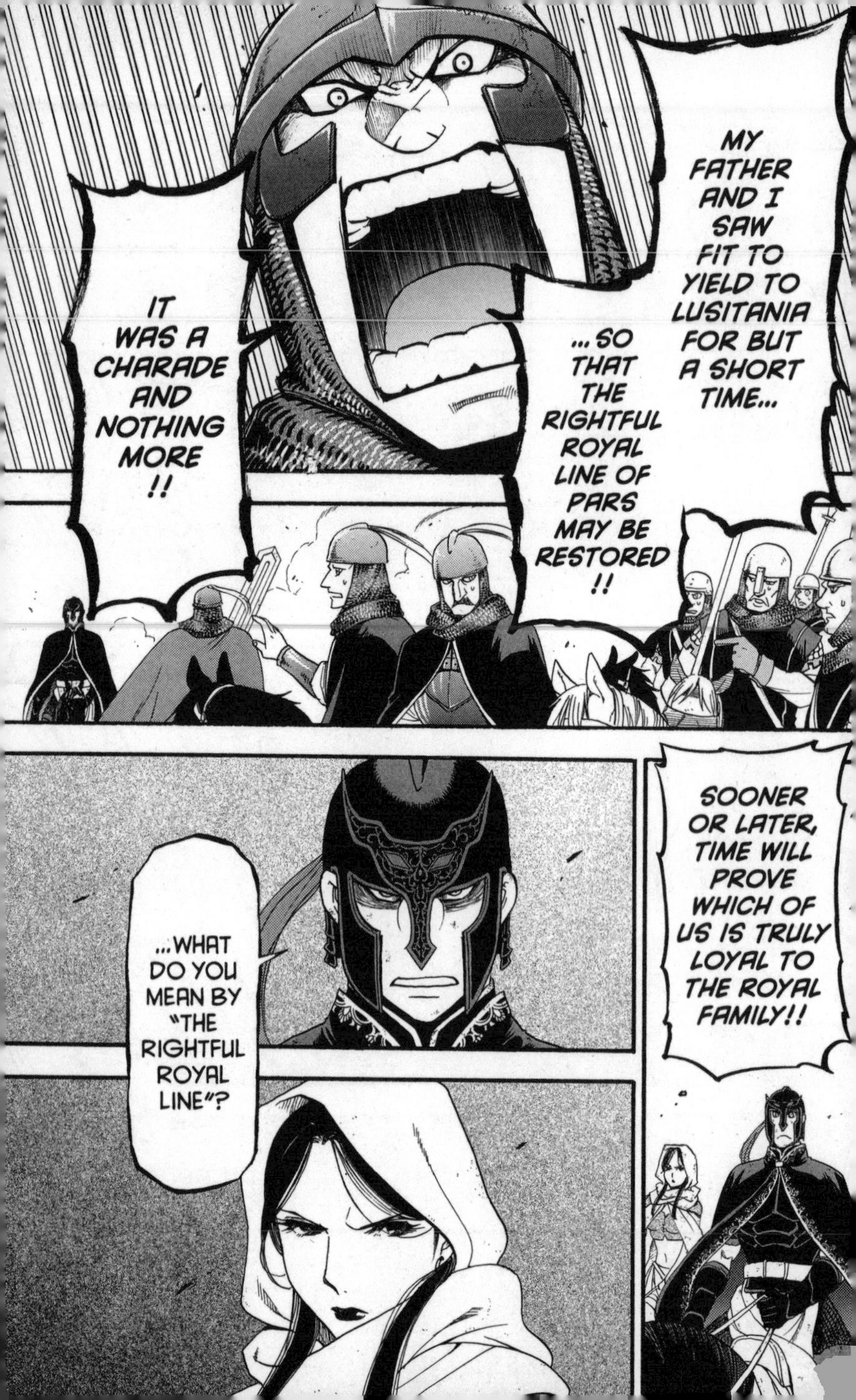
MY FATHER AND I SAW FIT TO YIELD TO LUSITANIA FOR BUT A SHORT TIME...
...SO THAT THE RIGHTFUL ROYAL LINE OF PARS MAY BE RESTORED!!
IT WAS A CHARADE AND NOTHING MORE!!
SOONER OR LATER, TIME WILL PROVE WHICH OF US IS TRULY LOYAL TO THE ROYAL FAMILY!!
...WHAT DO YOU MEAN BY "THE RIGHTFUL ROYAL LINE"?

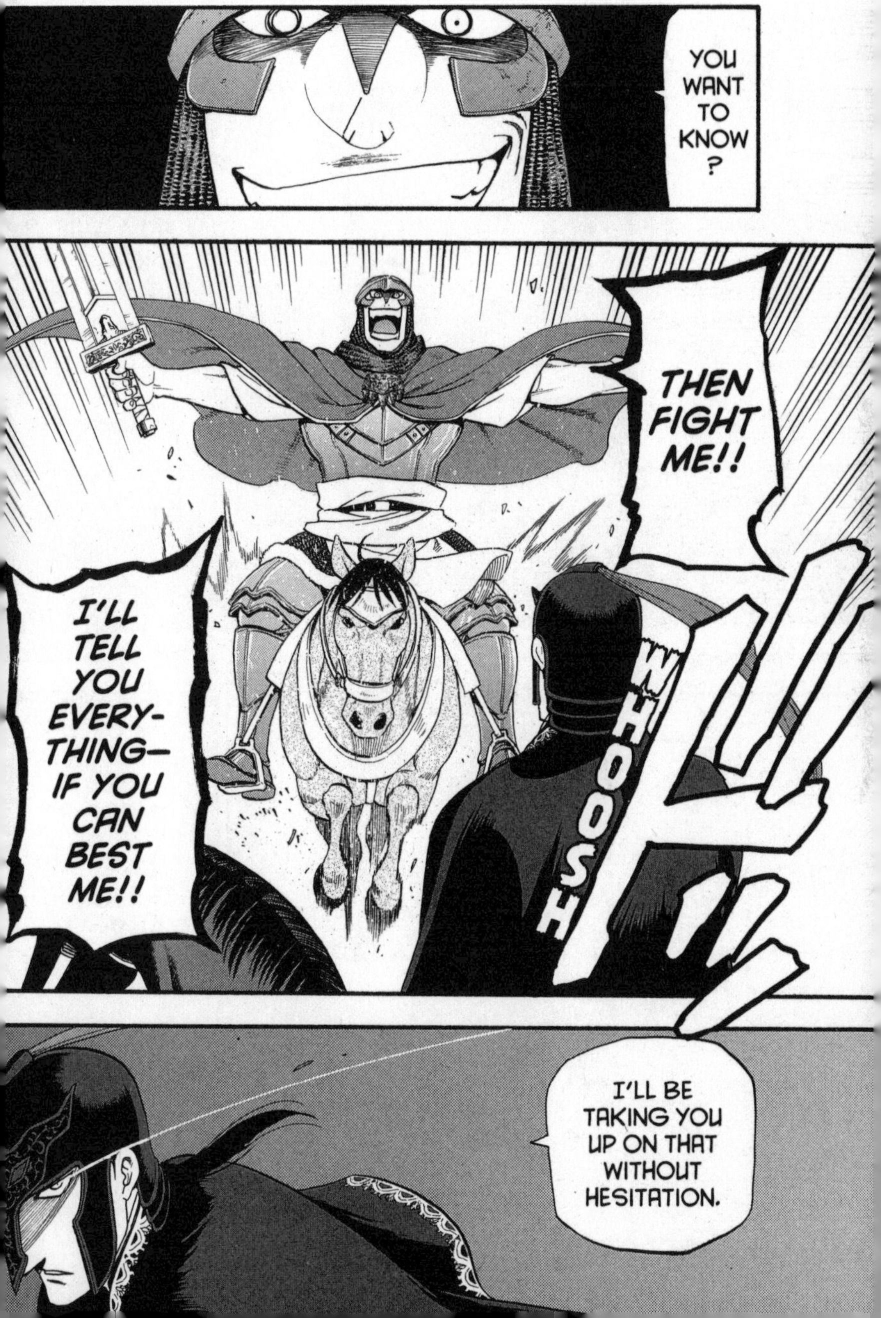
YOU WANT TO KNOW?
THEN FIGHT ME!!
I'LL TELL YOU EVERYTHING— IF YOU CAN BEST ME!!
WHOOSH
I'LL BE TAKING YOU UP ON THAT WITHOUT HESITATION.

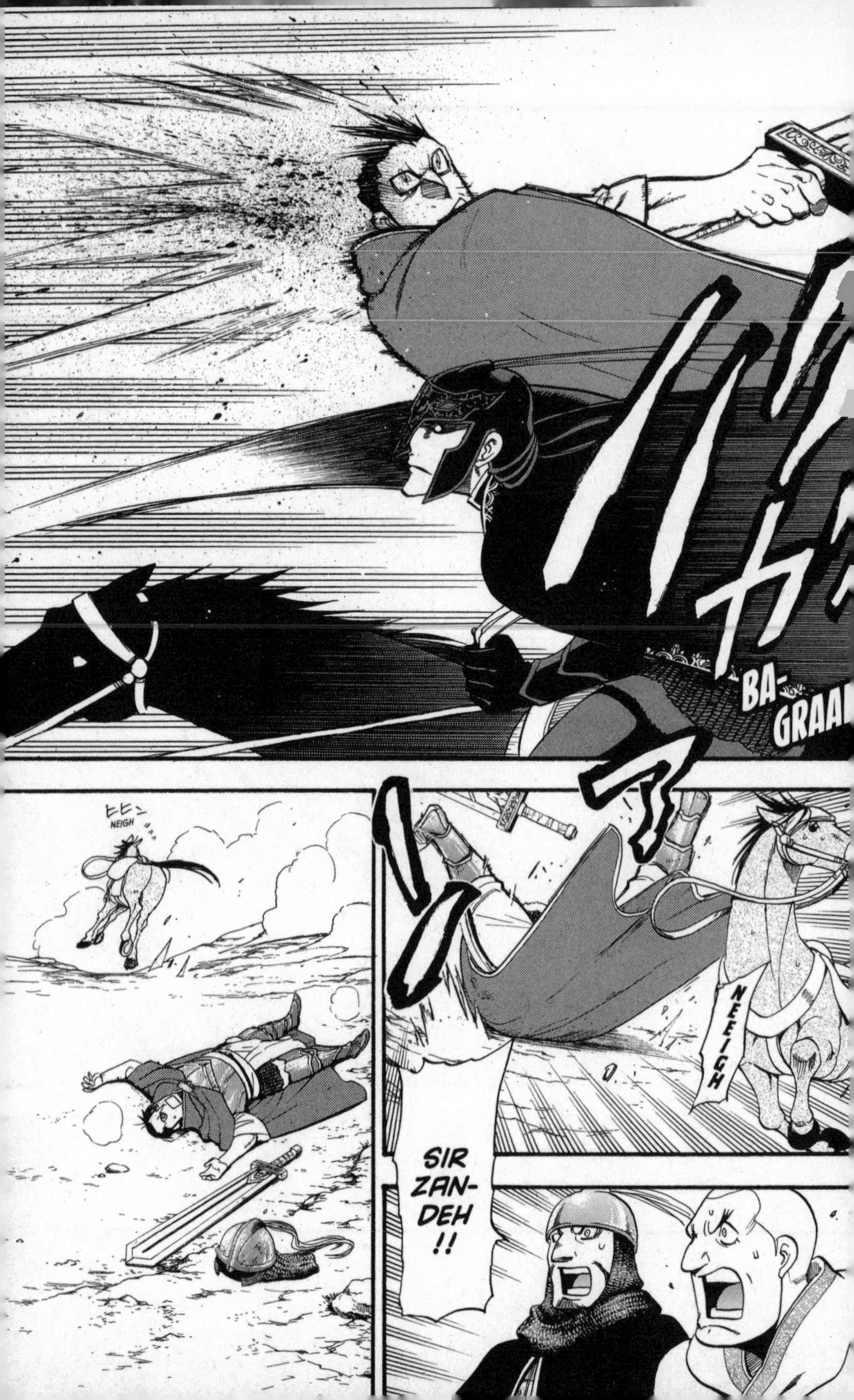
BA-
GRAA
NEEEIGH
SIR ZAN-DEH!!
ヒヒン
NEIGH

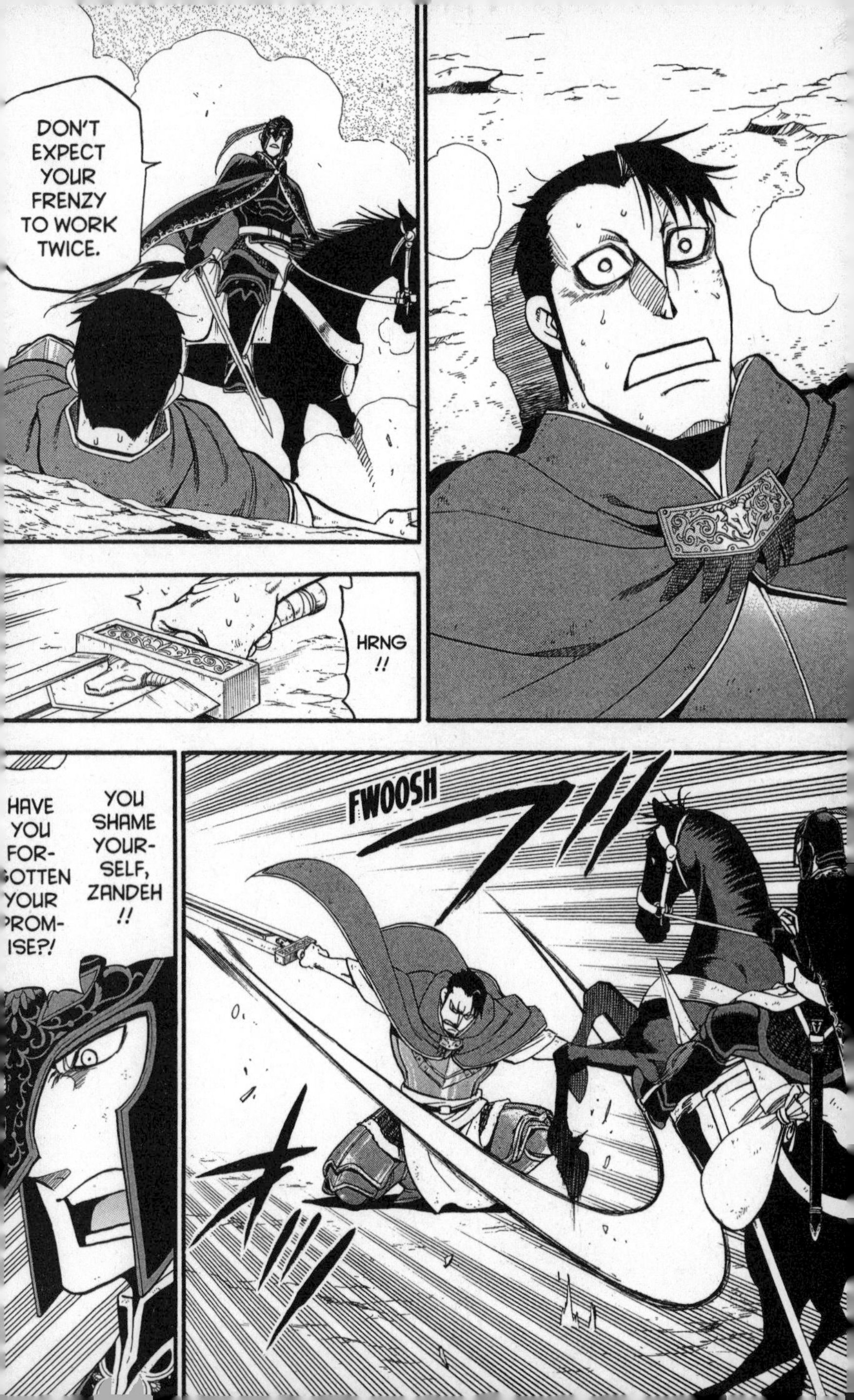
DON'T EXPECT YOUR FRENZY TO WORK TWICE.
HRNG !!
FWOOSH
YOU SHAME YOUR-SELF, ZANDEH !!
HAVE YOU FOR-GOTTEN YOUR PROM-ISE?!

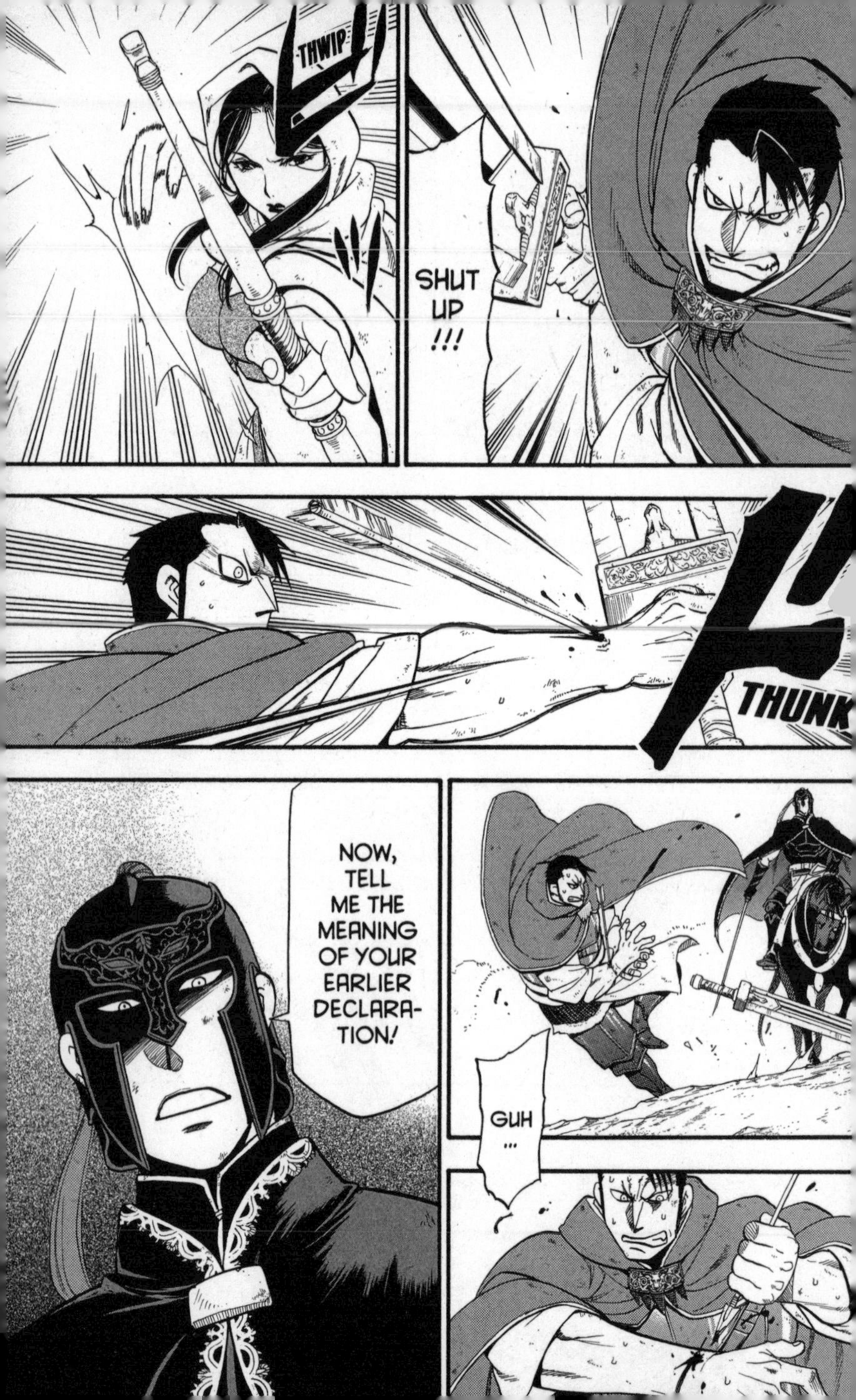
SHUT UP !!!
THWIP
THUNK
GUH ...
NOW, TELL ME THE MEANING OF YOUR EARLIER DECLARA-TION!

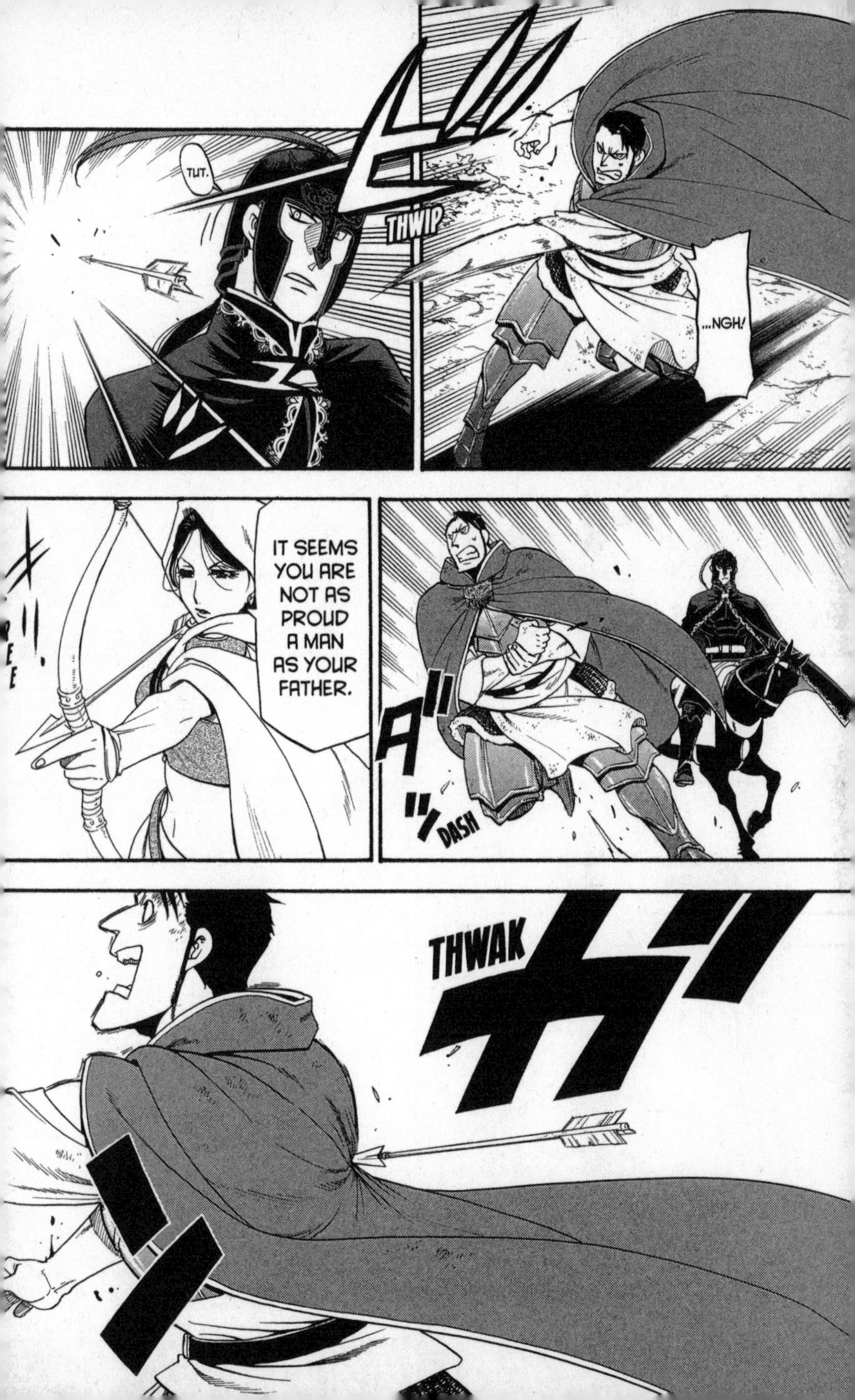
THWIP
...NGH!
TUT.
DASH
IT SEEMS YOU ARE NOT AS PROUD A MAN AS YOUR FATHER.
THWAK

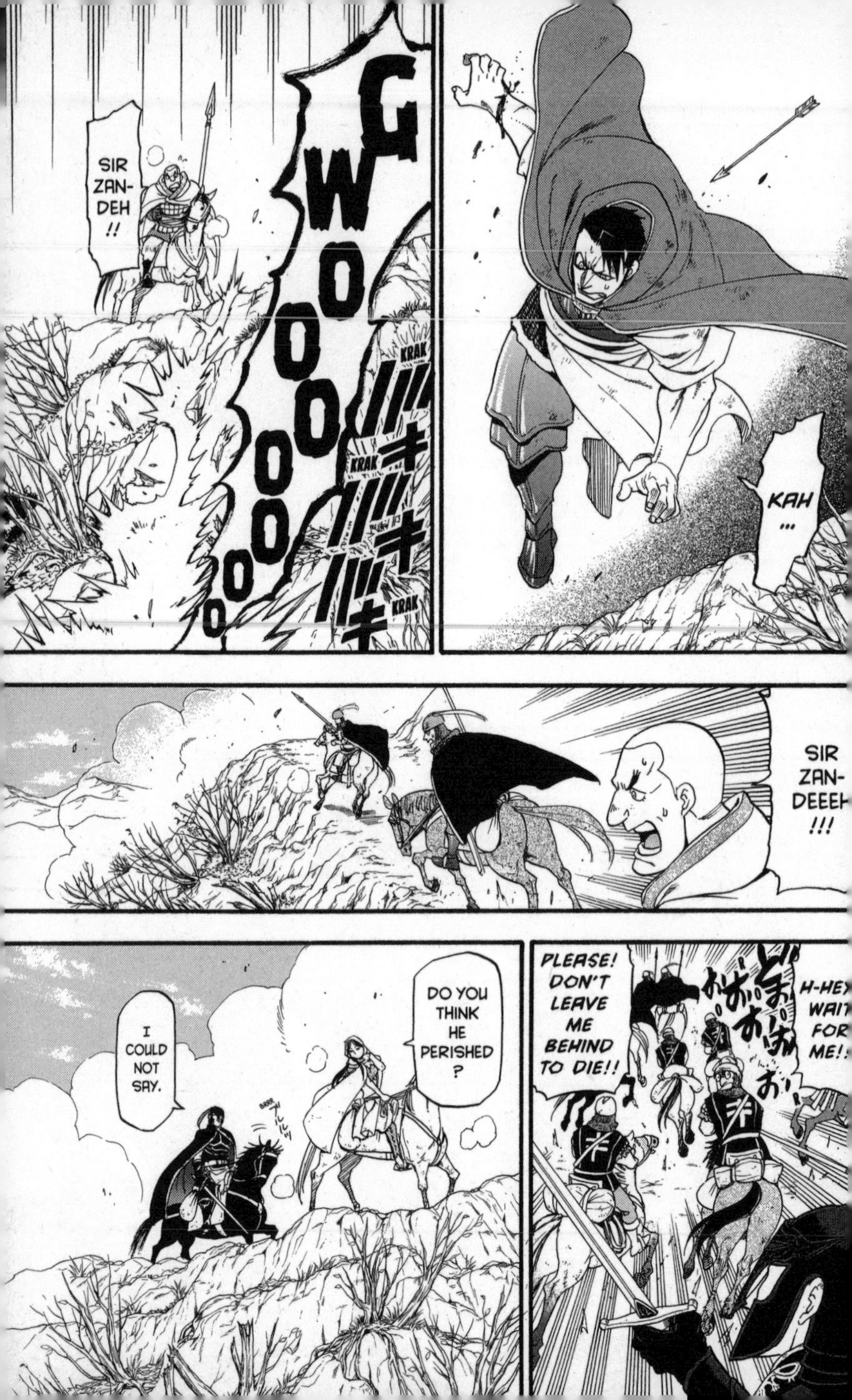
KAH ...
GWOOOOOOO
SIR ZANDEH !!
KRAK
KRAK
KRAK
SIR ZANDEEEH !!!
H-HEY WAIT FOR ME!!
PLEASE! DON'T LEAVE ME BEHIND TO DIE!!
DO YOU THINK HE PERISHED ?
BRRR
I COULD NOT SAY.

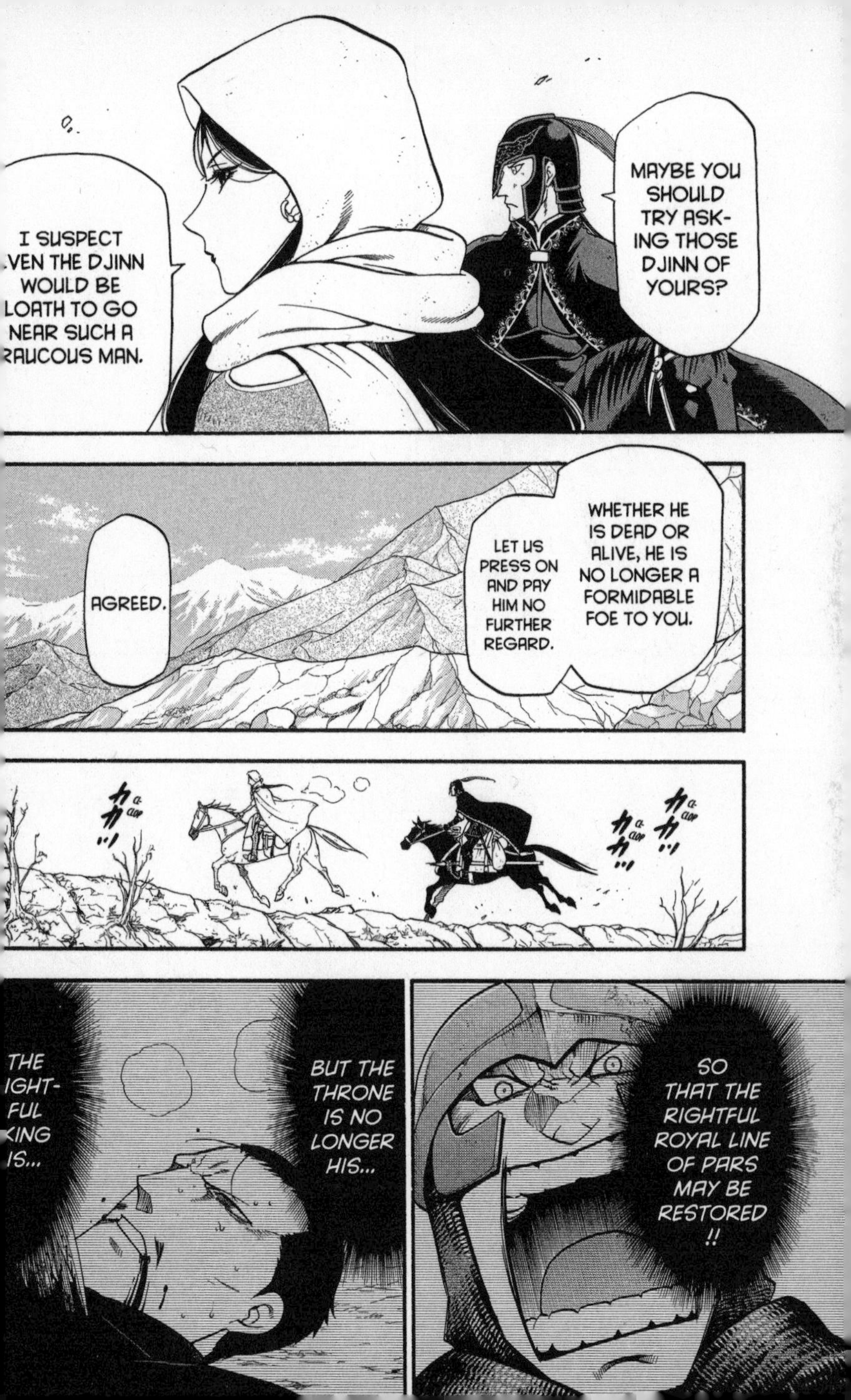

MAYBE YOU SHOULD TRY ASK-ING THOSE DJINN OF YOURS?
I SUSPECT EVEN THE DJINN WOULD BE LOATH TO GO NEAR SUCH A RAUCOUS MAN.
WHETHER HE IS DEAD OR ALIVE, HE IS NO LONGER A FORMIDABLE FOE TO YOU.
LET US PRESS ON AND PAY HIM NO FURTHER REGARD.
AGREED.
CA-CLOP
CA-CLOP
CA-CLOP
SO THAT THE RIGHTFUL ROYAL LINE OF PARS MAY BE RESTORED!!
BUT THE THRONE IS NO LONGER HIS...
THE IGHT-FUL KING IS...

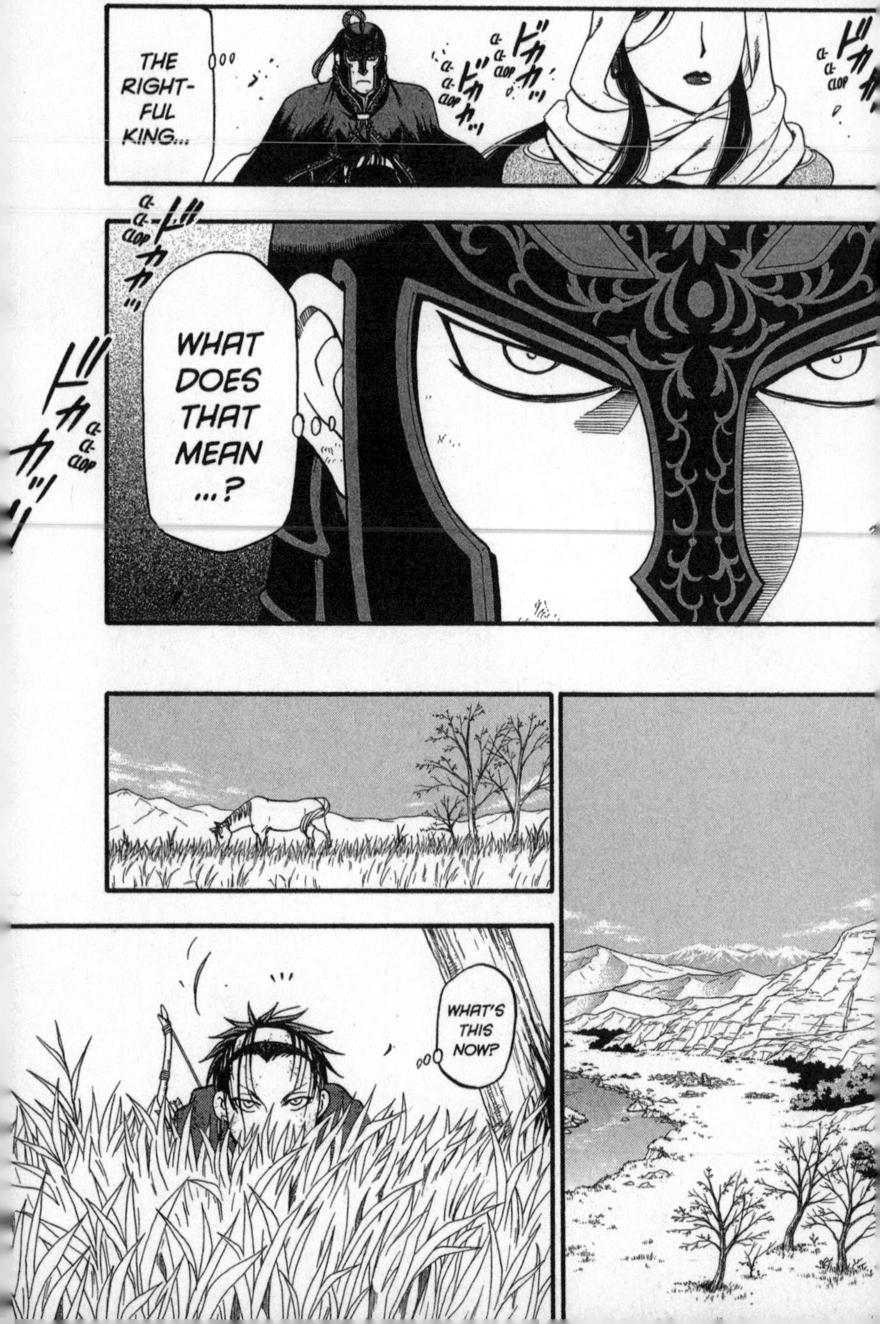
CL-CL-CLOP
CL-CL-CLOP
CL-CL-CLOP
THE RIGHT-FUL KING...
CL-CL-CLOP
WHAT DOES THAT MEAN ...?
CL-CL-CLOP
WHAT'S THIS NOW?

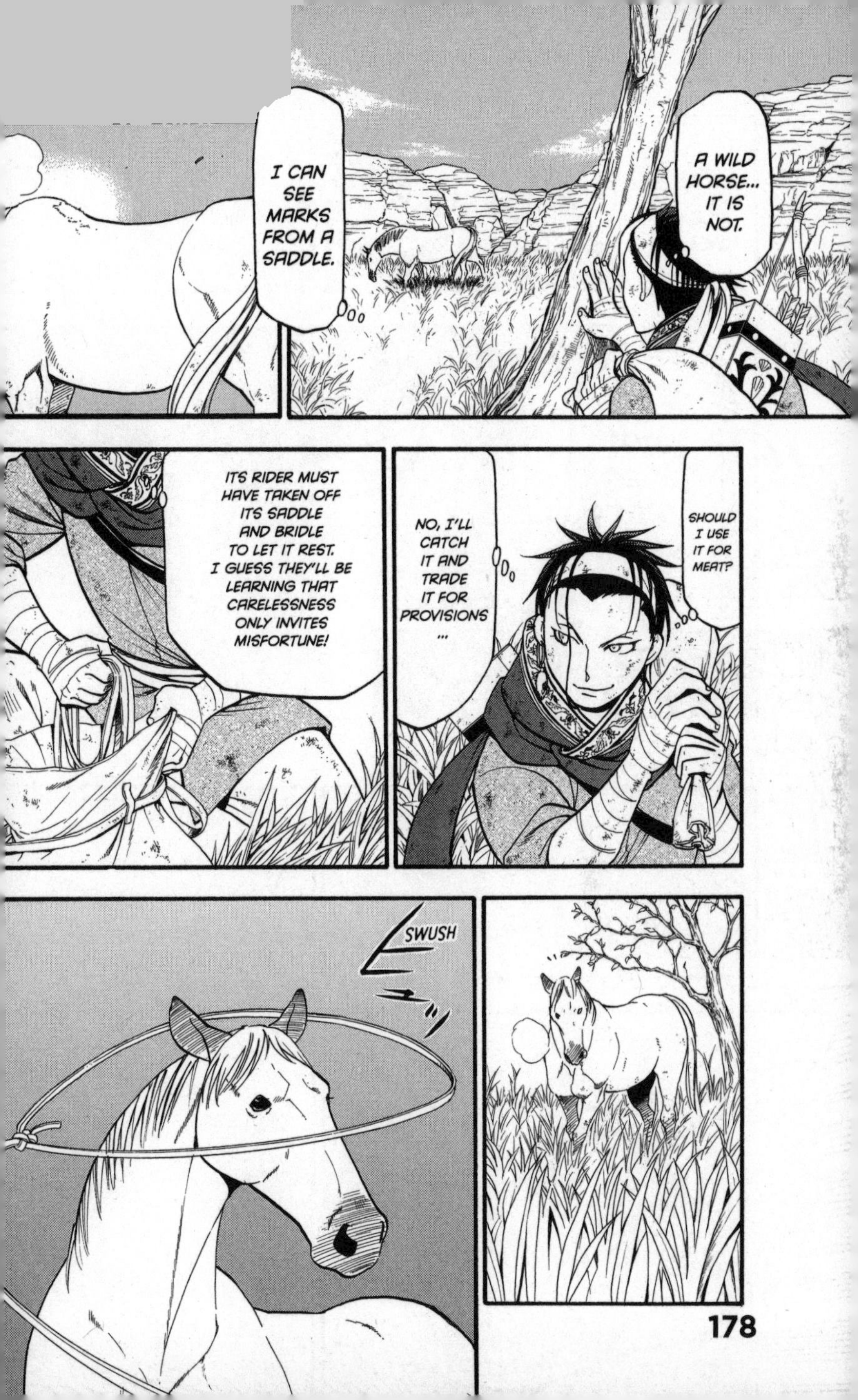
A WILD HORSE... IT IS NOT.
I CAN SEE MARKS FROM A SADDLE.
SHOULD I USE IT FOR MEAT?
NO, I'LL CATCH IT AND TRADE IT FOR PROVISIONS ...
ITS RIDER MUST HAVE TAKEN OFF ITS SADDLE AND BRIDLE TO LET IT REST. I GUESS THEY'LL BE LEARNING THAT CARELESSNESS ONLY INVITES MISFORTUNE!
SWUSH

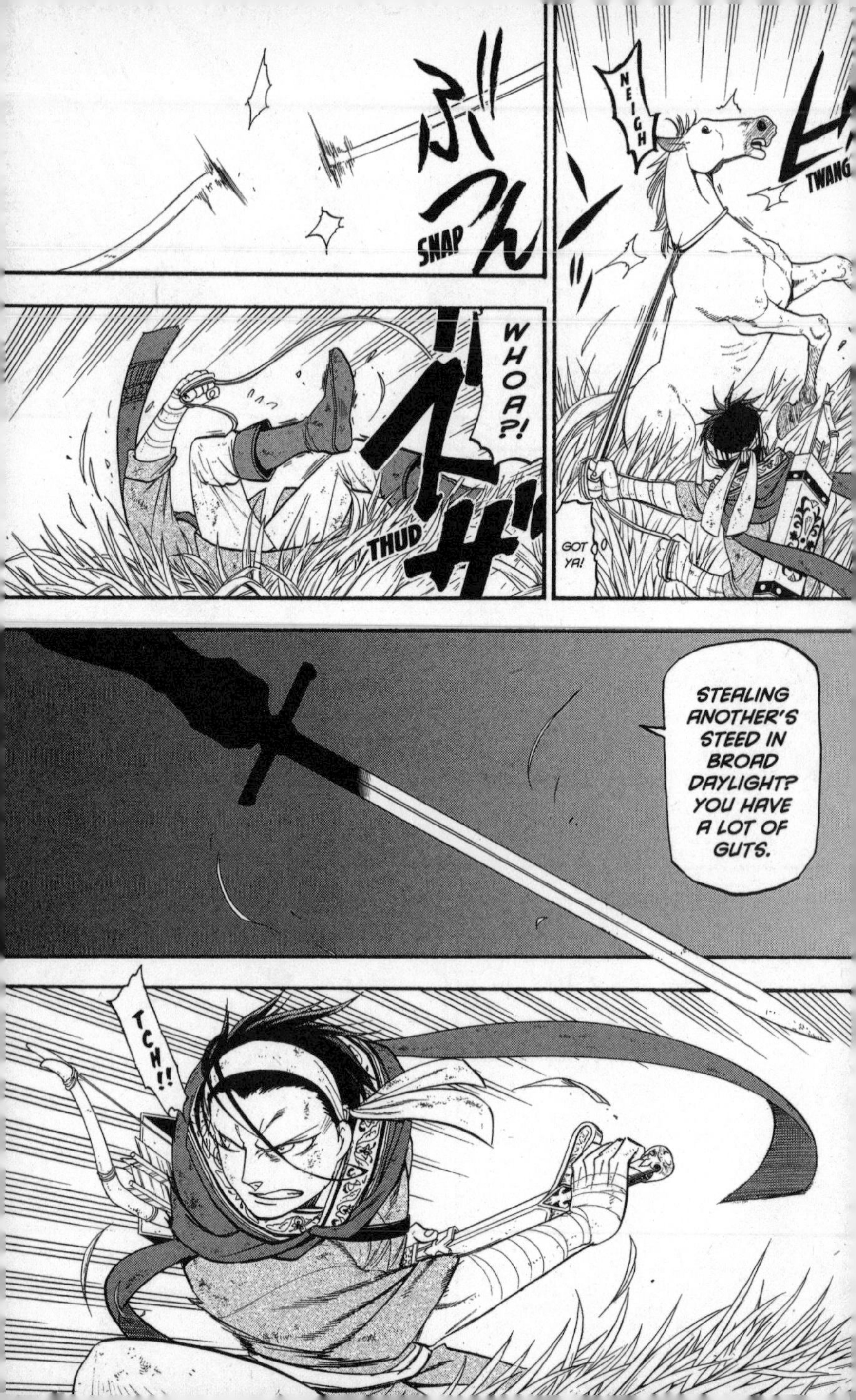
NEIGH
TWANG
GOT YA!
ぶつん
SNAP
THUD
WHOA?!
STEALING ANOTHER'S STEED IN BROAD DAYLIGHT? YOU HAVE A LOT OF GUTS.
TCH!!

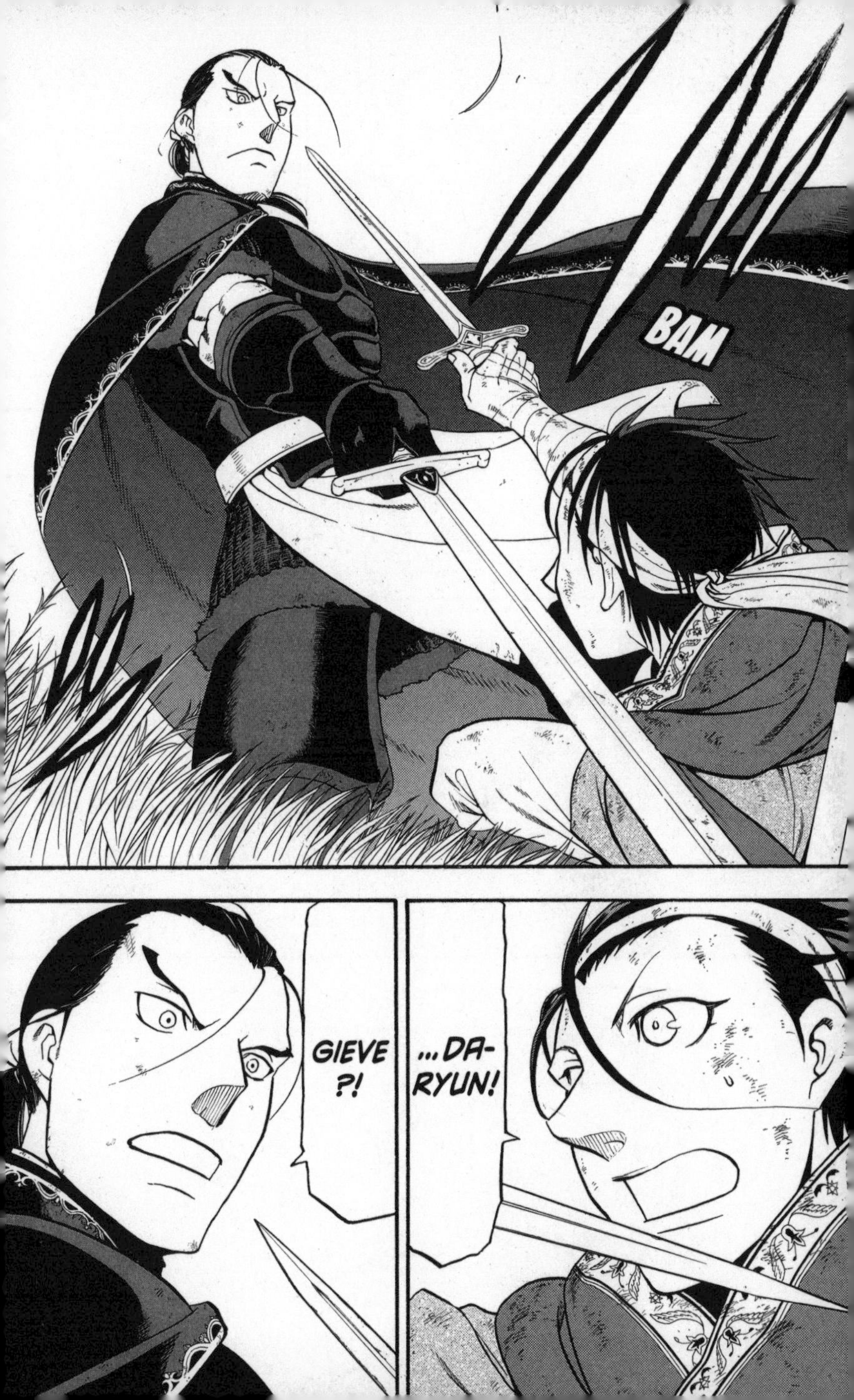
BAM
...DA-RYUN!
GIEVE?!

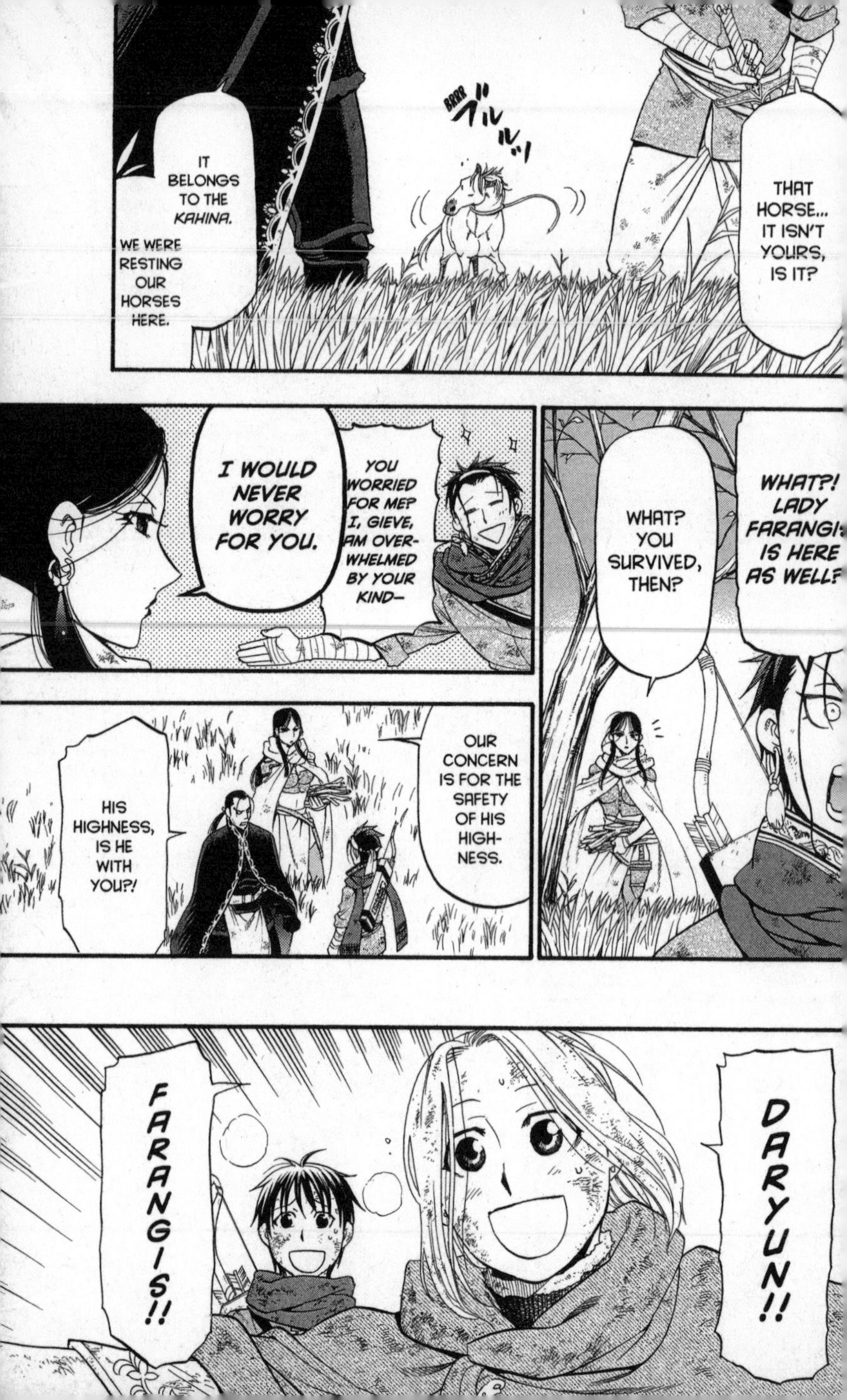
THAT HORSE... IT ISN'T YOURS, IS IT?
BRRR ブルルッ
IT BELONGS TO THE KAHINA.
WE WERE RESTING OUR HORSES HERE.
WHAT?! LADY FARANGIS IS HERE AS WELL?
WHAT? YOU SURVIVED, THEN?
YOU WORRIED FOR ME? I, GIEVE, AM OVER-WHELMED BY YOUR KIND—
I WOULD NEVER WORRY FOR YOU.
OUR CONCERN IS FOR THE SAFETY OF HIS HIGH-NESS.
HIS HIGHNESS, IS HE WITH YOU?!
DARYUN!!
FARANGIS!!

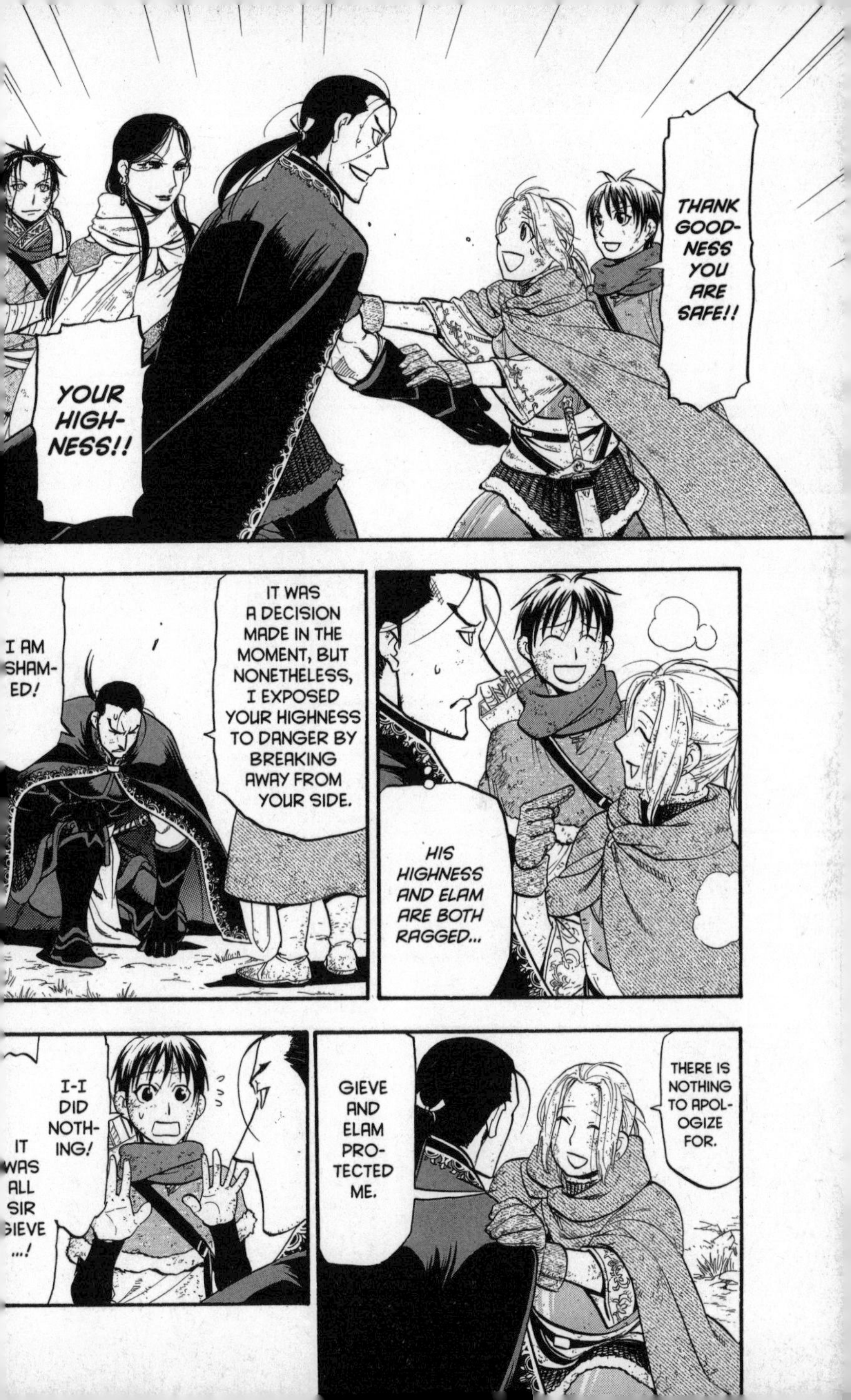
THANK GOODNESS YOU ARE SAFE!!
YOUR HIGHNESS!!
HIS HIGHNESS AND ELAM ARE BOTH RAGGED...
IT WAS A DECISION MADE IN THE MOMENT, BUT NONETHELESS, I EXPOSED YOUR HIGHNESS TO DANGER BY BREAKING AWAY FROM YOUR SIDE.
I AM SHAMED!
THERE IS NOTHING TO APOLOGIZE FOR.
GIEVE AND ELAM PROTECTED ME.
I-I DID NOTHING!
IT WAS ALL SIR GIEVE ...!

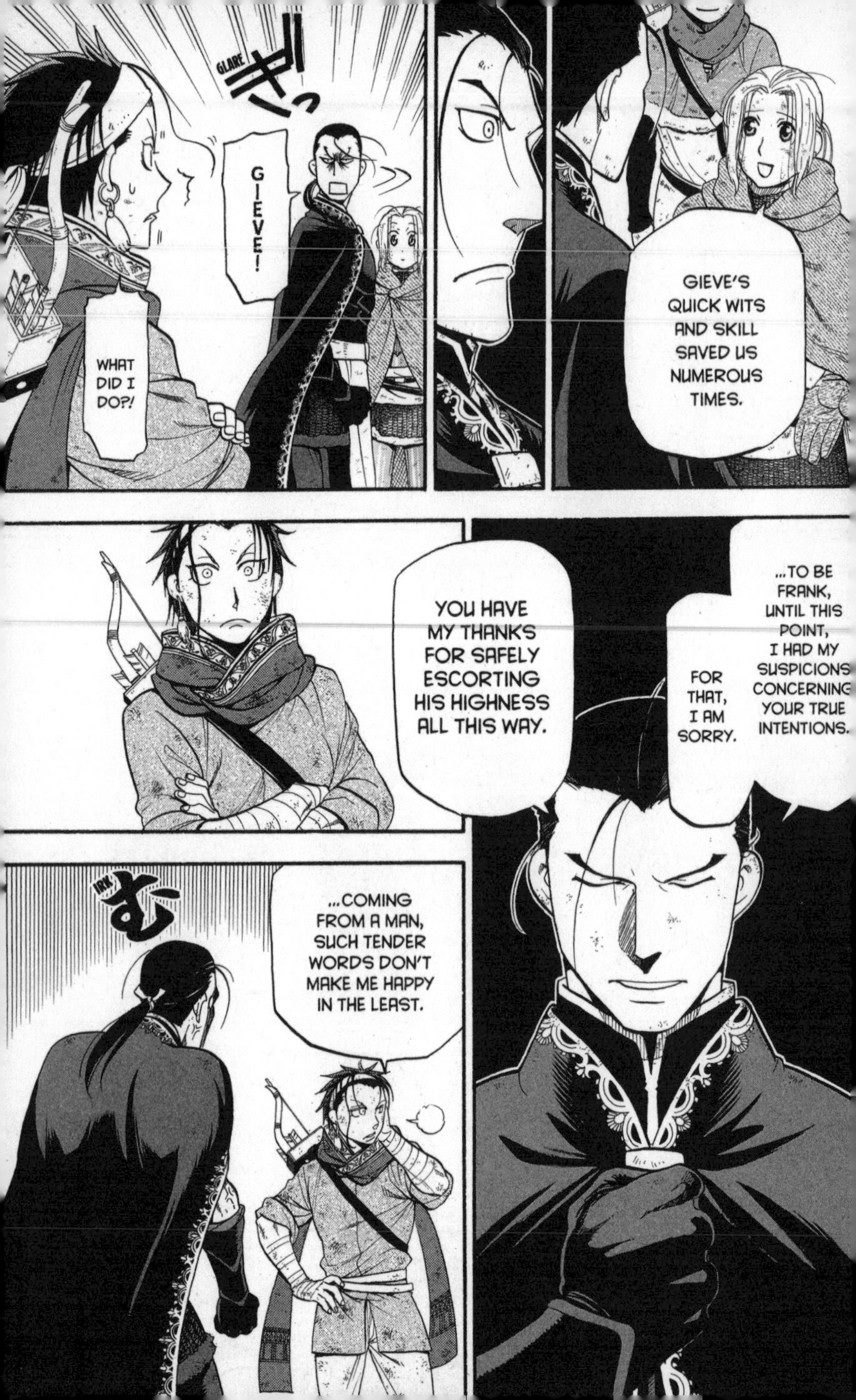
GIEVE'S QUICK WITS AND SKILL SAVED US NUMEROUS TIMES.
GLARE
ぎっ
GIEVE!
WHAT DID I DO?!
...TO BE FRANK, UNTIL THIS POINT, I HAD MY SUSPICIONS CONCERNING YOUR TRUE INTENTIONS.
FOR THAT, I AM SORRY.
YOU HAVE MY THANKS FOR SAFELY ESCORTING HIS HIGHNESS ALL THIS WAY.
IRK
む
...COMING FROM A MAN, SUCH TENDER WORDS DON'T MAKE ME HAPPY IN THE LEAST.

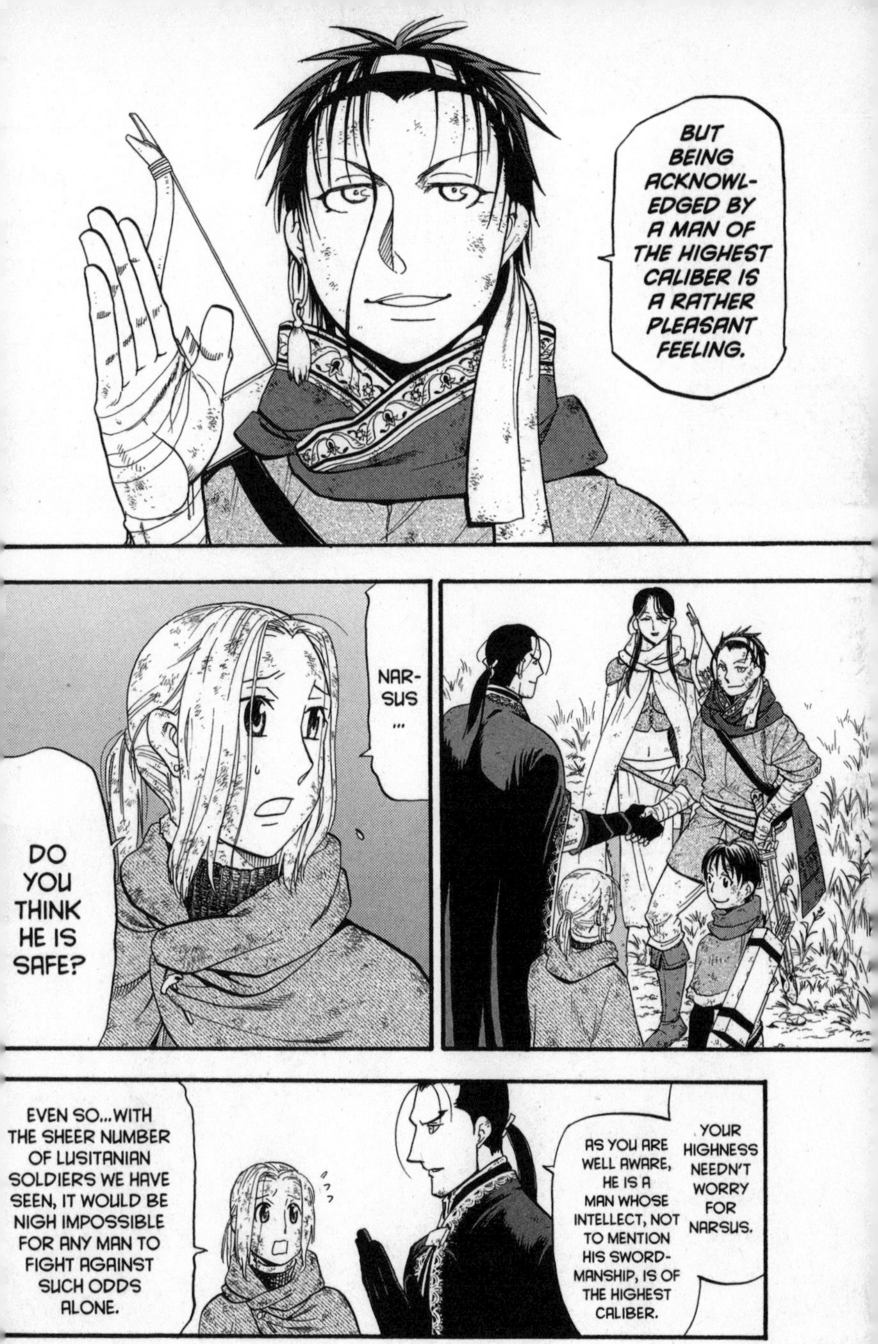
BUT BEING ACKNOWLEDGED BY A MAN OF THE HIGHEST CALIBER IS A RATHER PLEASANT FEELING.
NARSUS...
DO YOU THINK HE IS SAFE?
YOUR HIGHNESS NEEDN'T WORRY FOR NARSUS.
AS YOU ARE WELL AWARE, HE IS A MAN WHOSE INTELLECT, NOT TO MENTION HIS SWORDMANSHIP, IS OF THE HIGHEST CALIBER.
EVEN SO...WITH THE SHEER NUMBER OF LUSITANIAN SOLDIERS WE HAVE SEEN, IT WOULD BE NIGH IMPOSSIBLE FOR ANY MAN TO FIGHT AGAINST SUCH ODDS ALONE.

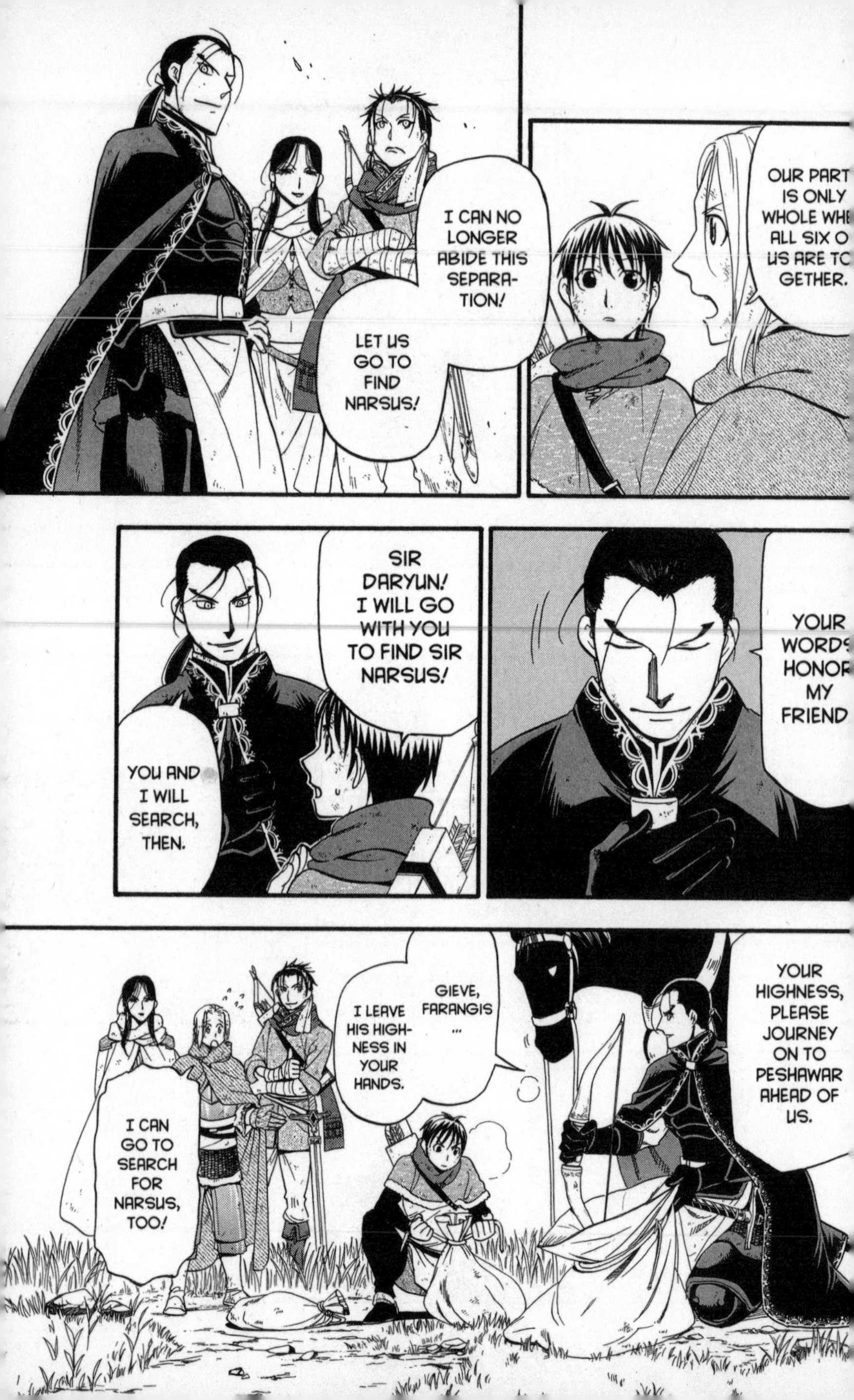
OUR PART IS ONLY WHOLE WHE ALL SIX O US ARE TO GETHER.
I CAN NO LONGER ABIDE THIS SEPARATION!
LET US GO TO FIND NARSUS!
YOUR WORDS HONOR MY FRIEND
SIR DARYUN! I WILL GO WITH YOU TO FIND SIR NARSUS!
YOU AND I WILL SEARCH, THEN.
YOUR HIGHNESS, PLEASE JOURNEY ON TO PESHAWAR AHEAD OF US.
GIEVE, FARANGIS ...
I LEAVE HIS HIGHNESS IN YOUR HANDS.
I CAN GO TO SEARCH FOR NARSUS, TOO!

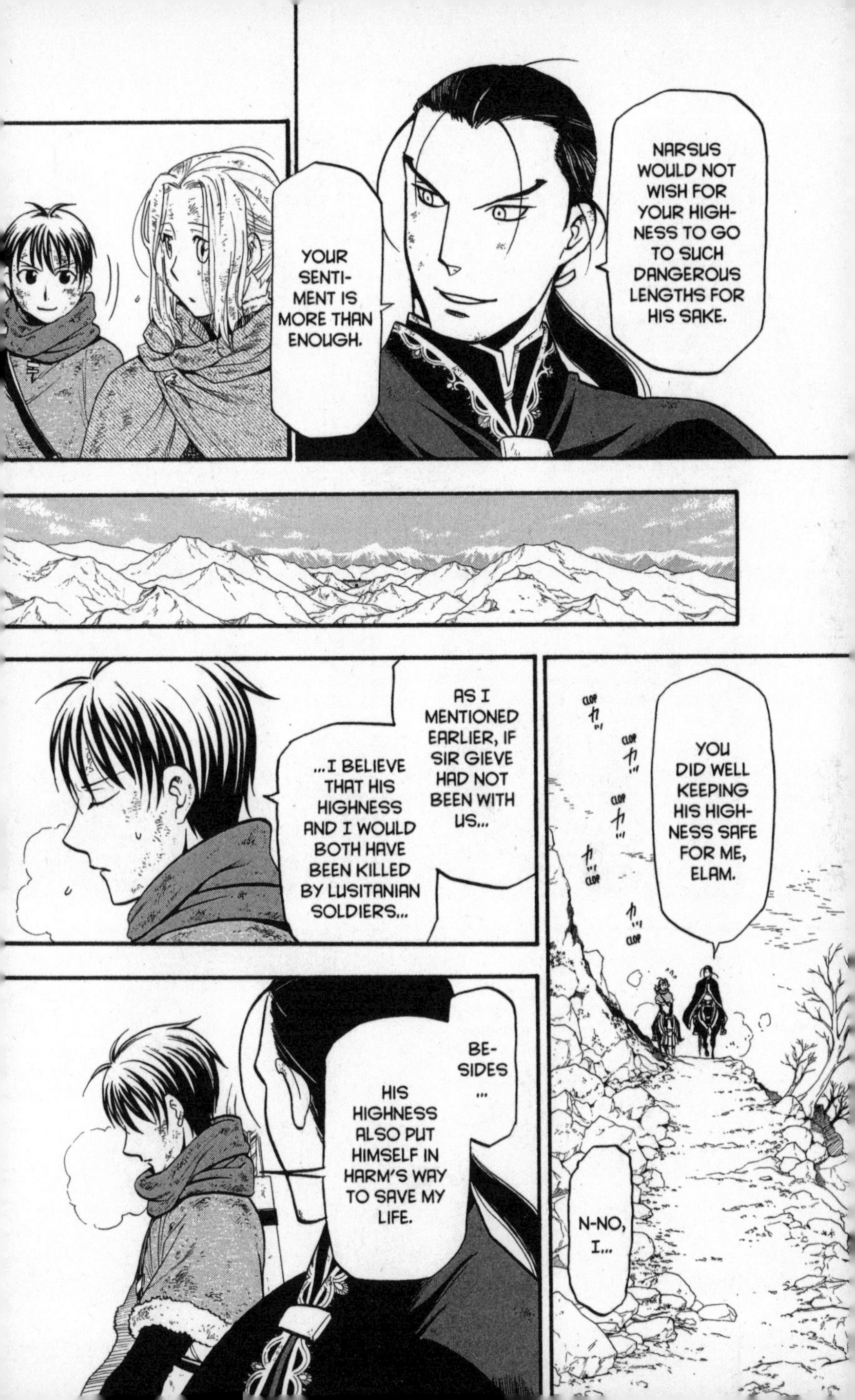
NARSUS WOULD NOT WISH FOR YOUR HIGHNESS TO GO TO SUCH DANGEROUS LENGTHS FOR HIS SAKE.
YOUR SENTIMENT IS MORE THAN ENOUGH.
CLOP
CLOP
CLOP
CLOP
CLOP
YOU DID WELL KEEPING HIS HIGHNESS SAFE FOR ME, ELAM.
N-NO, I...
AS I MENTIONED EARLIER, IF SIR GIEVE HAD NOT BEEN WITH US...
...I BELIEVE THAT HIS HIGHNESS AND I WOULD BOTH HAVE BEEN KILLED BY LUSITANIAN SOLDIERS...
BESIDES...
HIS HIGHNESS ALSO PUT HIMSELF IN HARM'S WAY TO SAVE MY LIFE.

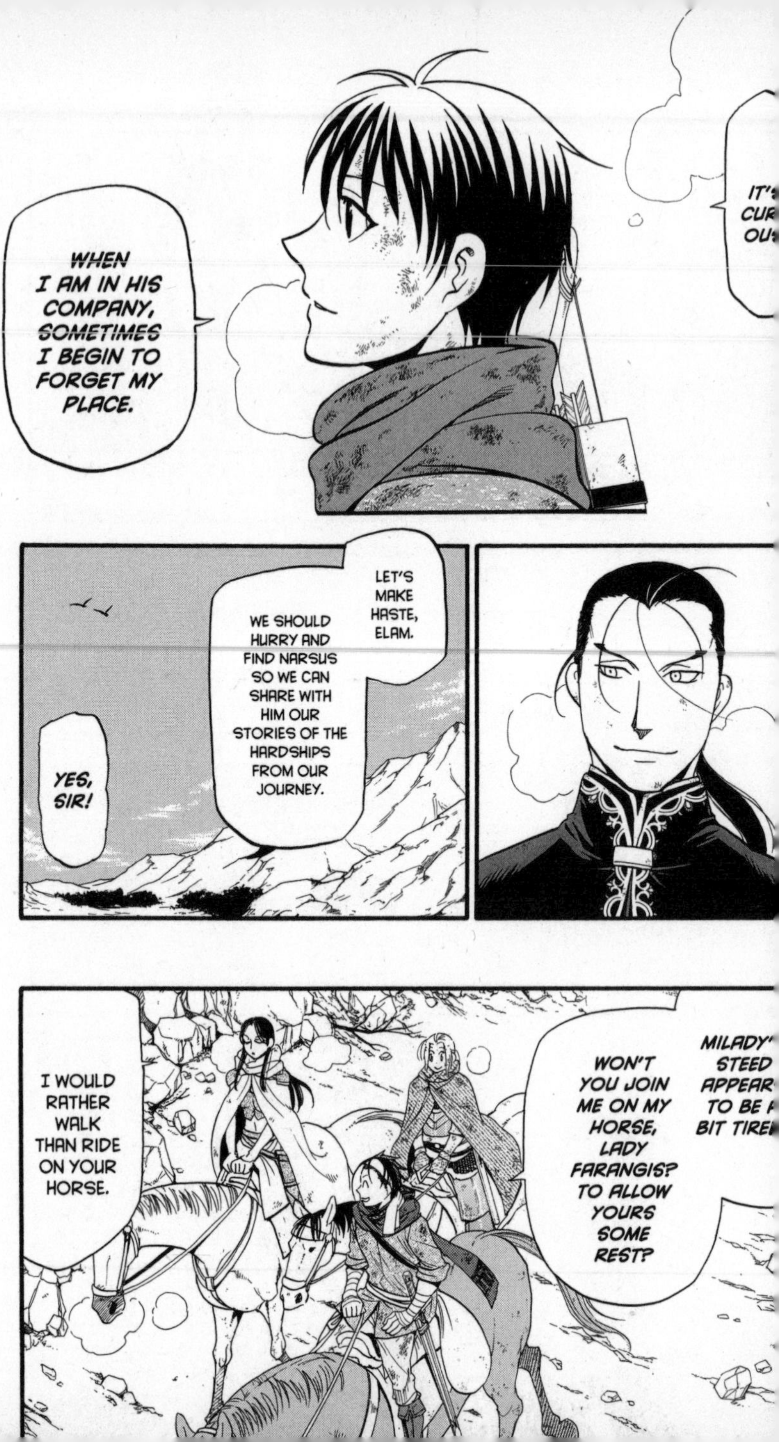

IT'S CUR OU
WHEN I AM IN HIS COMPANY, SOMETIMES I BEGIN TO FORGET MY PLACE.
LET'S MAKE HASTE, ELAM.
WE SHOULD HURRY AND FIND NARSUS SO WE CAN SHARE WITH HIM OUR STORIES OF THE HARDSHIPS FROM OUR JOURNEY.
YES, SIR!
MILADY' STEED APPEAR TO BE BIT TIRE
WON'T YOU JOIN ME ON MY HORSE, LADY FARANGIS? TO ALLOW YOURS SOME REST?
I WOULD RATHER WALK THAN RIDE ON YOUR HORSE.

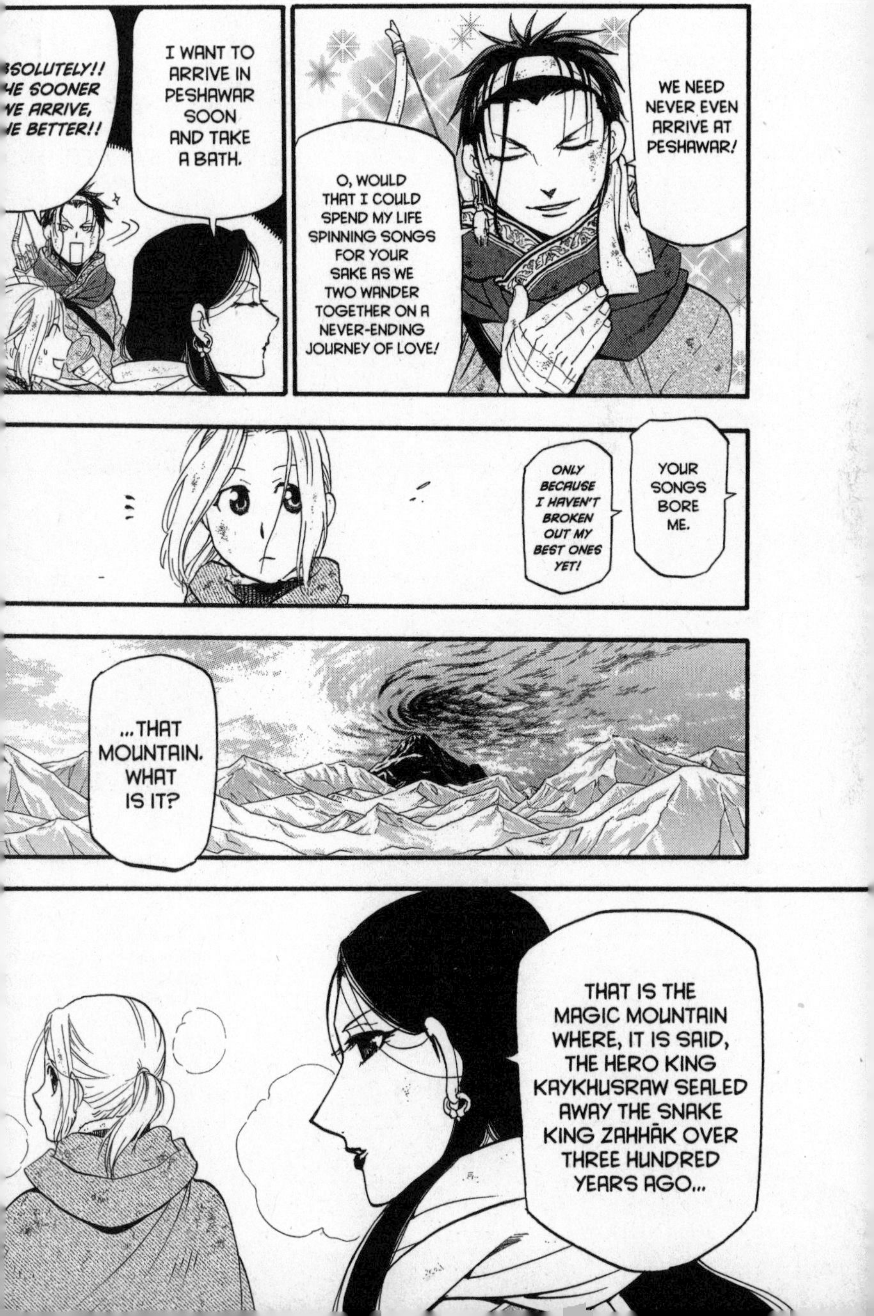
WE NEED NEVER EVEN ARRIVE AT PESHAWAR!
O, WOULD THAT I COULD SPEND MY LIFE SPINNING SONGS FOR YOUR SAKE AS WE TWO WANDER TOGETHER ON A NEVER-ENDING JOURNEY OF LOVE!
I WANT TO ARRIVE IN PESHAWAR SOON AND TAKE A BATH.
BSOLUTELY!! HE SOONER VE ARRIVE, IE BETTER!!
YOUR SONGS BORE ME.
ONLY BECAUSE I HAVEN'T BROKEN OUT MY BEST ONES YET!
...THAT MOUNTAIN. WHAT IS IT?
THAT IS THE MAGIC MOUNTAIN WHERE, IT IS SAID, THE HERO KING KAYKHUSRAW SEALED AWAY THE SNAKE KING ZAHHĀK OVER THREE HUNDRED YEARS AGO...

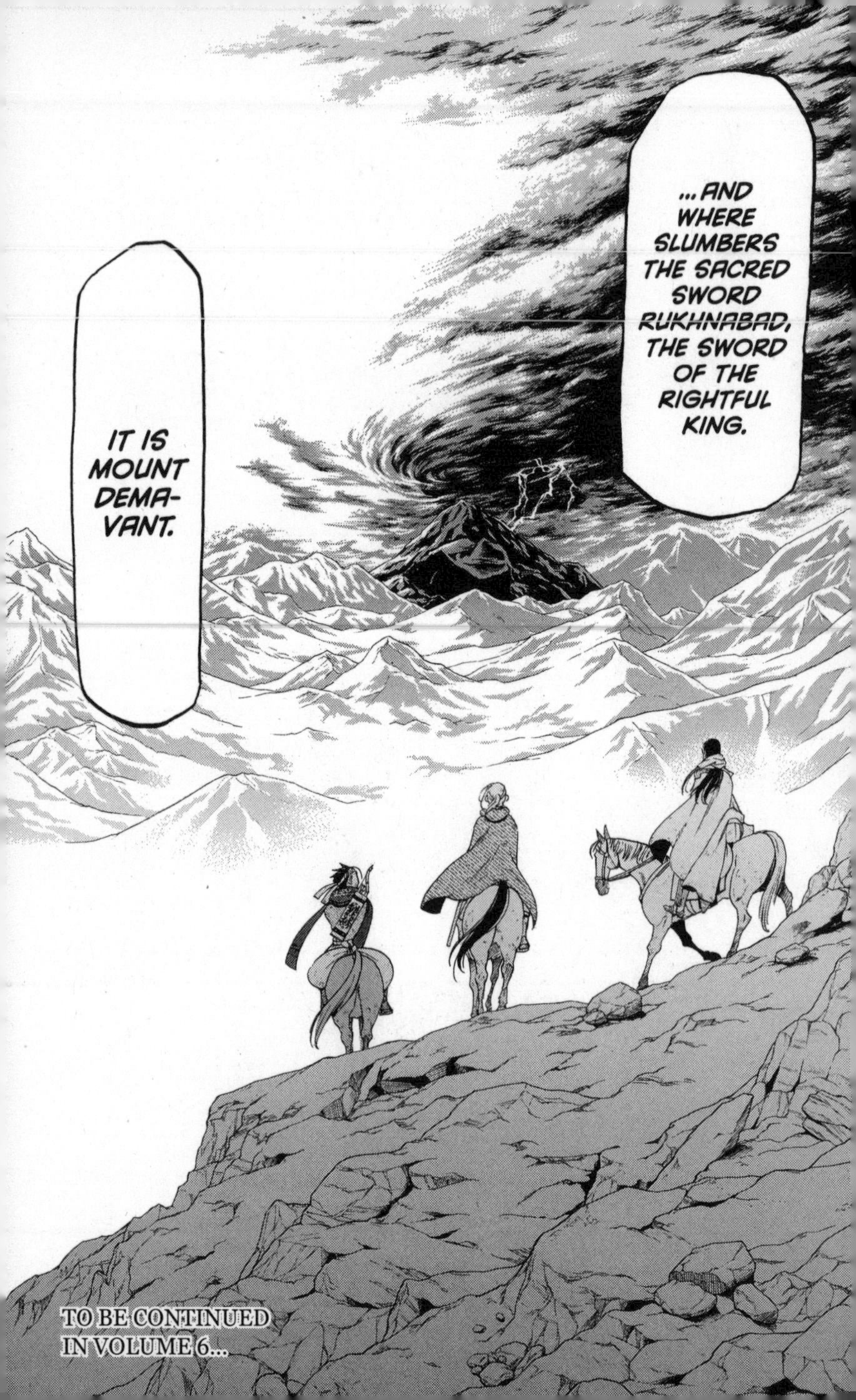
...AND WHERE SLUMBERS THE SACRED SWORD RUKHNABAD, THE SWORD OF THE RIGHTFUL KING.
IT IS MOUNT DEMA-VANT.
TO BE CONTINUED IN VOLUME 6...

- BONUS SKETCHES -

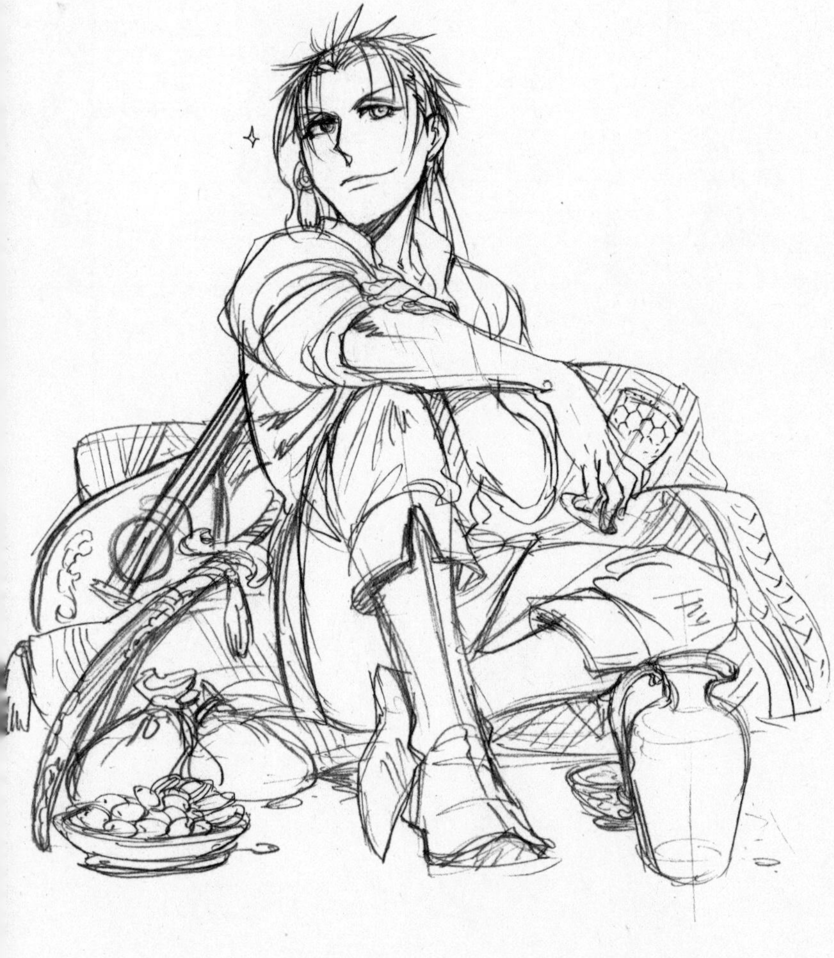

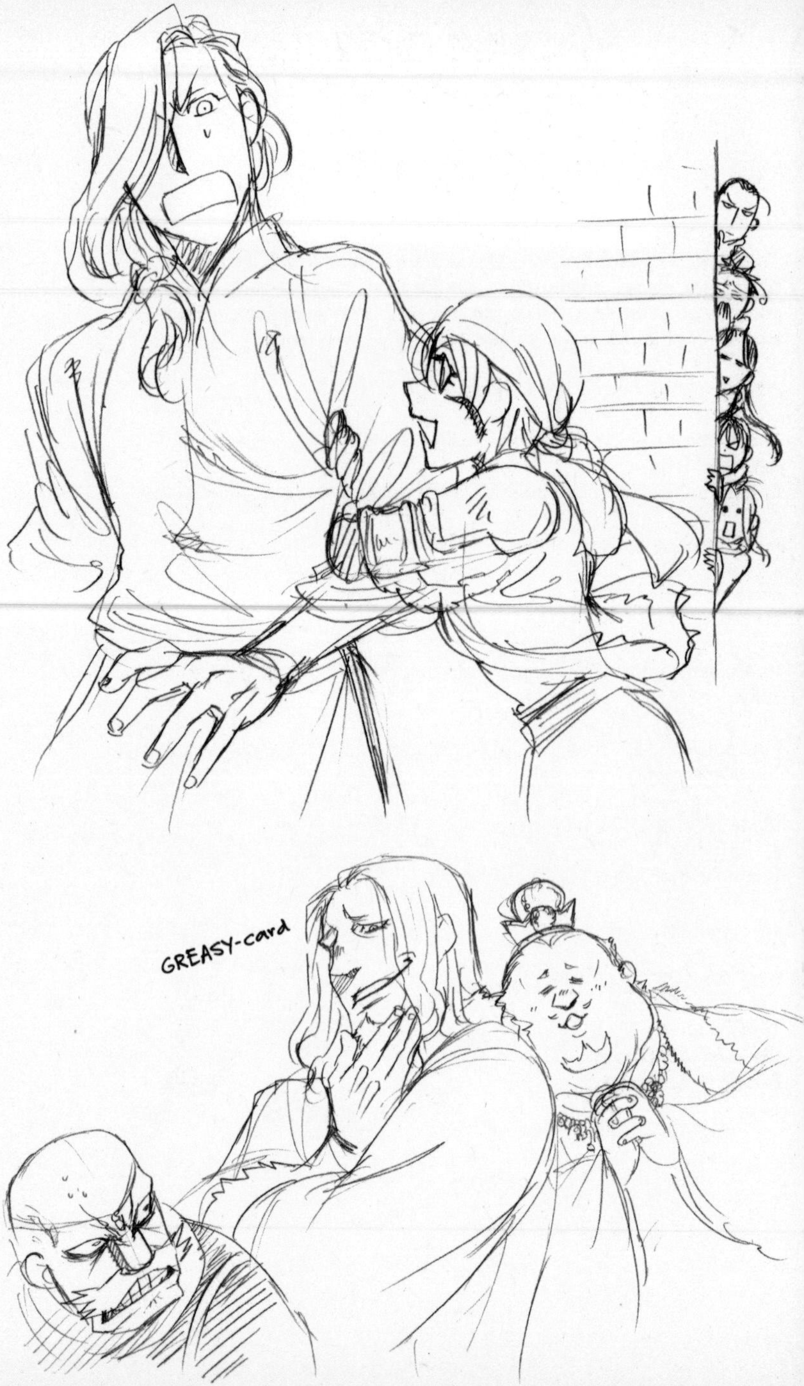
GREASY-card

The Heroic Legend of Arslan volume 5 is a work of fiction. Names, characters, places, and incidents are the products of the author's imagination or are used fictitiously. Any resemblance to actual events, locales, or persons, living or dead, is entirely coincidental.

A Kodansha Comics Trade Paperback Original.

Published in the United States by Kodansha Comics, an imprint of Kodansha USA Publishing, LLC, New York.

Publication rights for this English edition arranged through Kodansha Ltd., Tokyo.

First published in Japan in 2016 by Kodansha Ltd., Tokyo, as *Arslan Senki* volume 5.

ISBN 978-1-63236-218-6

Printed in the United States of America.

www.kodanshacomics.com

9 8 7 6 5 4 3 2 1

Translation: Amanda Haley
Lettering: April Brown
Editing: Ajani Oloye